Animation – Process, Cognition and Actuality

Animation – Process, Cognition and Actuality

Dan Torre

BLOOMSBURY
NEW DELHI • LONDON • OXFORD • NEW YORK • SYDNEY

BLOOMSBURY INDIA
Bloomsbury Publishing India Pvt. Ltd
Second Floor, LSC Building No. 4, DDA Complex, Pocket C–6&7,
Vasant Kunj, New Delhi 110070

BLOOMSBURY, BLOOMSBURY ACADEMIC INDIA and the Diana logo are
trademarks of Bloomsbury Publishing Plc

First published in India 2024
First published 2017

This edition published with permission from Bloomsbury Publishing Plc,
50 Bedford Square, London, WC1B3DP, UK

Library of Congress Cataloging-in-Publication Data
A catalog record for this book is available from the Library of Congress

ISBN: 978-93-61319-53-2

Cover design: Eleanor Rose

Cover image © Fox Searchlight / Courtesy Everett Collection / Mary Evans

Typeset by Integra Software Services Pvt. Ltd.
Printed and bound in India by Replika Press Pvt. Ltd.

To find out more about our authors and books
visit www.bloomsbury.com and sign up for our newsletters

CONTENTS

FIGURES

ACKNOWLEDGEMENTS

I would like to especially thank Angela Ndalianis for her very constructive feedback and strong encouragement throughout this project. I would also like to thank Susan Buchan for her extensive feedback and support. Thanks also to Paul Wells, Thomas Lamarre, Richard Leskosky, Lienors Torre, Chris Pallant, Scott McQuire and members of the Society for Animation Studies for their many helpful comments. Thanks also to Katie Gallof and the rest of the team at Bloomsbury. I would also like to express my gratitude to Richard Allen and to Phung Allen. Finally, a big thanks to my family for their constant support.

NOTE ON TEXT

Chapters 1 and 3 contain some elements that were previously published in the journal article: 'Cognitive Animation Theory: A Process-Based Reading of Animation and Human Cognition' in *Animation: An Interdisciplinary Journal*, 9(1) 2014. Chapters 1 and 2 contain some brief elements that were previously published in the journal article: 'Boiling Lines and Lightning Sketches: Process and the Animated Drawing' in *Animation: An Interdisciplinary Journal*, 10(2) 2015. A section of Chapter 7 includes some material from the previously published chapter, 'The Metamorphosis of Place: Projection Mapped Animation' in *Animated Landscapes – History, Form and Function*, ed. Chris Pallant (Bloomsbury 2015).

Introduction

The focus of this book is on the *process of animation* – not just how animation is made (although that is very important), but also a broader more theoretical consideration of what it means for animation to *become* animation and to *be* animation. In doing so, this book will also consider how we might think *about* animation, and how we might think *through* animation, and the different ways in which animation might interact with the real world.

Animation has become a rather elusive creature, particularly when considered against the many forms that it may take: stop-motion, pixilation, drawn animation, cel animation, the many different forms of digital animation, visual effects, video games; as well as a number of non-screen-based forms such as flipbooks, zoetropes and even modern-day robots. This diversity is further complicated by technological advances that have, to some degree, resulted in a unification of aesthetic between live action and animation – aspects that, traditionally, have been distinct. This potential for the loss both of an unequivocal aesthetic, of the broad range of styles and genres, and even its real-world manifestations encourages an analysis of animation not only in terms of the end product but also comprehensively in terms of process and the theorizing of this process.

Over the years, there has been a diverse array of definitions of animation, ranging from the all-embracing conceptual (everything is animation)[1] to the most narrow, involving exclusively the traditional frame-by-frame animation technique. So often the 'definitions' and descriptive paradigms of animation have been bound to one particular production process of animation, such as the cel animation tradition. Even philosopher Gilles Deleuze's very brief mention of animation in his *Cinema 1* text takes a very narrow view that assumes animation to be primarily restricted to drawn animation.

> Any other system which reproduces movement through an order of exposures [*poses*] projected in such a way that they pass into one another,

> or are 'transformed', is foreign to the cinema. This is clear when one attempts to define the cartoon film; if it belongs fully to the cinema, this is because the drawing no longer constitutes a pose or a completed figure, but the description of a figure which is always in the process of being formed or dissolving through the movement of lines and pointes taken at any-instant-whatever of their course. The cartoon film is related not to a Euclidean, but to a Cartesian geometry. It does not give us a figure described in a unique moment, but the continuity of the movement which describes the figure.[2]

In all of Deleuze's writings on cinema, this appears to be the only direct mention of animation, and his reference to 'drawings' and to 'lines and points' essentially limits his discussion to 'classical' or 'drawn animation'.

Further to this, a majority of analyses of animation have ultimately centred on the end product of content, the contrasts with traditional live action aesthetics, and narrative effects. Such comparative discussions can run into complexities, particularly when we begin to consider the many types of abstract experimental film, or the ever-advancing photo-realistic possibilities of computer animation. We can generally think of animation as being a medium of highly mediated visuals, often wholly constructed (either in terms of form or motion, or indeed both), making it quite distinct from live action. Whereas live action may necessitate an incredibly complex, collaborative and expensive production process, in its most elementary form it can simply involve someone's 'turning on a camera'. Disregarding content and aesthetics, live action cinema can be almost devoid of a deliberate, image/movement construction process. Animation, on the other hand, cannot normally be paired down to such a minimalist production process. For animation to become extant, it must comprise a much greater totalization of process regardless of content and final aesthetic.

Norman McLaren demonstrated in the 1940s that the animation process did not require an image at all when he, *in effect*, animated sound. A prime example was his animated film, *Neighbours* (1952), in which he drew, frame by frame, a synthetic sound track; he then photographed these drawn images to the optical strip, running them parallel to the visual frames. Norman McLaren's approach to animation allows us to see it in a much broader scope. Perhaps it does not, in fact, require overt visuals at all. It is the process of animating that is quintessential: what transpires becomes secondary. This in turn encourages the exploration of more conceptual interpretations of animation. Furthermore, when animation is considered essentially in terms of process, the world of animation becomes much more encompassing.

In her invitation to the animation studies community, Suzanne Buchan urged the 'developing [of] approaches that pose essential queries specific to the form [of animation] that can, in some cases, rework theory that has been successfully developed from live action cinema'; and, more importantly, 'to develop a language for animation studies that clarifies ongoing and increasingly detailed discourse around the form'.[3] Crucially, we have witnessed a decided shift in the manner in which recent studies of animation have set about redefining its form and processes. No longer does the traditional 'frame-by-frame' manner of description predominate – if for no other reason than that majority of animation is now created digitally (or at least augmented or edited through digital processes), demanding a shift in production processes. How then does one define animation?

It does seem that more contemporary animation studies texts have approached animation in more encompassing ways and have sought to recognize its many affiliations. In this light, Paul Wells and Johnny Hardstaff strived to make sense of the ever-changing world of animation and its increased prevalence by setting out to define animation as being simply: 'a form destined to be defined ultimately not by formal conditions – frame-by-frame manipulation of materials in the creation of phases of representational motion – but by the artist, context and condition of expression'.[4] Though they concede 'it is clear that animation can still signal difference in nominally traditional ways…',[5] the essence of their argument relates to animation's *animus*, the motivating force that ostensibly brings things to life. Undoubtedly, many recent discussions have sought to reposition animation within the realm of creative process and to develop a more phenomenological reading of the form. Such approaches effectively seek to elevate animation beyond both the technical (how it is made) and the textual (considerations solely of the narrative of the final product).

Kenny Chow considers animation in terms of what he calls its 'liveliness' and sets up a continuum wherein varying degrees of such 'liveliness' can reside. On one end of the scale are 'vigorous and lively' expressions of animation, 'which stands for something in reality, [and] becomes the means of animation'. At the reverse end of the scale, animation can be applied merely as a functional process – such as the programmed application on a mobile device.[6] Animation can be thought of in terms of a living *presence* that seemingly occupies our everyday existence – some manifestations more vibrant than others. According to Jenkins,

> Animation creates movement where there was none before, from a never-has-been. Animation produces the artistic imitation of motion, creating any-instant-whatevers that can be projected into movement from a raw material that was never any-instant. Where cinema's content is movement-in-time, animation's content is drawings (or clay, and so on) that create movement.[7]

Lamarre has pointed out that animation should not be thought of as merely 'an illusion-of-life', because what it provides us is something much more real: 'Movement in animation is not a matter of illusion or representation.

[...] It affords a real experience of movement, of actual movement'.[8] Echoing this, Donald Crafton asserts, 'It's important to realize that cartoons are not records of performances, the way non-animated film may in part be, but rather they are performances themselves.'[9]

Ultimately animation is a very diverse form, and there are equally as many diverse approaches to its analysis. This text will seek to appraise animation in rather broader terms. Importantly, it seeks to acknowledge a number of constructive commonalities that exist between the numerous forms of animation. Rather than focus on the aesthetics of animation, the phenomenal, or even the animator's creative spirit, the aim of this text is to consider animation primarily in terms of process. It will also seek to consider the process of animation, where appropriate, in philosophical terms, and to elevate animation above the narrow technical or aesthetic definition while still allowing for an intense interrogation of both the form and the process. It is with these approaches to the contemplation of animation that this text will describe a fresh set of parameters that will seek to outline its form and process, while still allowing provision for requisite expansion.

Describing animation

As stated above, animation is a very extensive medium (with a very long history) which can be produced using innumerable production techniques. Additionally, animation can be made to look like almost anything – from the most abstract graphical image to the most photo-realistic. It can look exactly like live action; alternately, it can also move so slowly (or in such a limited manner) that at first glance it appears to be motionless. And, it can be presented to us – that is we can experience the animation – through innumerable devices (film projectors, zoetropes, DVD players, computers, video game consoles, billboards, building facades, mobile devices and virtual reality systems). Furthermore, the process of animation, its appearance and its range of uses have evolved and expanded considerably in recent decades – and are likely to continue to do so. In fact, a colleague once suggested (half joking, half serious) that perhaps it would be better to start with defining what animation *is not* in order to get a better grip on its seemingly elusive nature.[10] However, there are several key components or conditions that can help to provide us with a fuller understanding of what animation is.

Over the decades there have been many attempts by practitioners and theorists to provide a comprehensive definition of animation, and it may seem curious that so many such attempts have been made – and continue to be made. Some of these definitions have been successful in establishing what is unique about animation; however, in doing so, some have become extremely precise and end up excluding a number of techniques or examples that most would indeed consider to be animation (such as pixilation or flipbooks); or their definition becomes so broad that they could easily include, for example, wind chimes or autumn leaves wafting in the breeze.

In its simplest definition, animation is 'the process of making something move or change through the application of external movement'. But what makes 'animation' more than merely 'making something move' and different from the act, say, of flying a kite, or of tossing a rock into a pond, is that 'animation' generally encompasses three important phases.

The first phase can be referred to as the Construction Phase, in which movement is added to a form. It is essentially the *animating* process whereby

a) an object or image is imbued with intended movement in order to become animation;

b) crucially, this 'animating' involves a separate consideration of image and of motion.

We can refer to the second phase as the Animative-State, where the form and its separately assigned movement sit 'in waiting'. It is essentially an intermediate phase where all of the animation elements have been prepared and readied, and manifested as a strip of film, a flipbook or a string of computer code. In this state, the animation is normally not visible – but it is *ready* to be made visible.

The final phase, the Presentation Phase, is where the animated motion is made percept to the viewer through the use of a separate (that is, independent of the original animator) mediating device to 're-animate' the images, in effect uniting the image and motion and binding them together as a visible movement-image.

Some theorists (such as Alan Cholodenko) have, and rightly so, identified aspects of animation, including the essential middle phase (what is referred to here as the animative-state) as being almost indistinguishable from all forms of cinema.[11] This is, undeniably, an essential reading of animation, however, from the perspective of this text, and what can uniquely define animation, and what can set it apart from many other mediums (including traditional live-action film) is its process of becoming – the processes by which it first enters into the animative-state.

What makes the *construction phase* of animation fundamentally unique from traditional live action is that there needs always to be a separate consideration of its image and of its motion. Not only is the separate consideration of movement and form an essential aspect of animation – allowing for its existence (things can move in remarkable ways) – but it also allows for remarkable flexibility during its *presentation phase*.

Because of changing technologies, the final two phases might necessarily be compressed or expanded – for example in some cases of real-time animation, where an 'animator' might perform live and in effect control some interactive element. In these cases, the role of the presentation phase and to some degree the intermediate 'animative-state' might be expanded not only to include the holding and projecting of the animation information but also to contribute to its becoming through the generating of different and unique iterations of the originally constructed animation. For example in many computer games: animated characters, walk cycles, libraries of actions and assets, might all be reconfigured and transformed in 'real time' during each occasion that the game is played. These, according to Gaut, essentially 'take an initial state, combine it with user input and produce some new state…'.[12] The animator animates the forms in the first phase; the game player then performs the animation within the guidelines set by the animators and game designers during the presentation phase (which arguably constitutes an auxiliary role to the first phase). Fundamentally, it is this that makes interactive animation (such as video games) possible. Being composed of separate streams of movement and image, it can continue to be handled in this manner, even at its presentation. Quite simply, recorded live action cannot be dealt with in this way. In animation, they are conceived as distinct entities, and they can persist as distinct entities throughout all of animation's different phases.

Considering animation to be essentially a three-stage process, in which movement and form are necessarily distinct conceptions, permits a very inclusive understanding. Virtually all forms of animation can be included and, importantly, it also serves to distinguish itself from live action and helps to outline what is *not* animation. It can include all approaches: drawn animation, stop-motion, computer animation, animatronics, robotics and computer games. While these parameters specifically exclude traditional live-action cinema, they do, however, include many aspects of digital cinema practices – particularly when we consider the seamless inclusion of many forms of animation (from animated characters to generated visual effect elements).

The initial point of this description of the *construction phase* also suggests the predestined nature of animation – that it comprises 'an object or image that is imbued with *intended* movement in order to become animation'. Essentially every form of animation can effortlessly fit this description: drawn animation, stop-motion, pixilation, flipbooks, zoetropes and most computer animations. Even in *algorithmic animation*, which is generated by a computer program, it is still generally the result of a computer programmer's coding by which a number of parameters have been installed for the animation to 'follow'. Perhaps here, the animator could be seen as providing *guidance* or *direction*, rather than directly animating. But this point also emphasizes that the animator will be engaged in a deliberate act of making 'animation' – rather than say, merely (but intentionally) turning on an electric fan.

Positively, the most important consideration of the process of animating is that it 'involves a separate consideration of image and of motion'. Drawn animation clearly requires an animator to create images; then to 'make them appear to move' as he or she creates subsequent images, each with differences. In stop-motion, whether the object was created specifically for the production or it is a 'found-object', its creation was distinct, and its frame-by-frame manipulation imbued it with movement that it would have been unable to achieve in isolation. Similarly, in 3D computer animation the model is first built, then moved about, sometimes by setting key frames, sometimes by inputting motion-capture data and assigning this to the model, usually involving a combination of the two. Again, this point clearly excludes live action cinema in which the image and motion are inextricably linked in the recording process.

A number of scholars have suggested that animation should involve two simultaneous expressions: movement and liveliness.[13] Though, generally the most engaging animation will tend to express a convincing sense of life; it is not an absolutely essential aspect. For example, one could (through whatever animation technique they wish to use) animate a drop of water trailing down a windowpane, or simply a blob of the colour red slowly and mechanically passing across the screen. Neither of these examples would particularly express much 'animated liveliness' (and would arguably be pretty boring to experience), yet they would certainly constitute valid examples of animation. It is the act of animating and the resulting animative-state and then its ability to be presented to an audience that is animation's most fundamental descriptive quality – although it is certainly the liveliness of the form that engages us.

Philosophical concepts in this book

This book encompasses a wide spectrum of animation and related media. Ultimately, however, the focus of the text revolves around the practice of animation and, through the use of an original proposed model (in Chapters 1 and 2), it will seek to redirect our consideration of animation more towards the theoretical and the philosophical. Though this book will freely draw upon several different philosophical perspectives, it will primarily consider animation in terms of *process-based philosophies*. Process philosophy is a philosophical discourse that envisions *process* as a fundamental aspect of everything that exists, that places emphasis on the concepts of time and flux, diminishing the importance of material objects.[14] Such a process-based approach has been overlooked in animation's scholarship and is, it will be argued, indispensable to a fuller understanding of the form, and how animation's incredible diversity might be considered in a more unified manner.

To consider the world in terms of process does not necessarily imply a disregard for the object or the outcome; rather it encourages the concept that behind every *thing* there are processes at work. Process, therefore, represents no more than a shifted perception of actuality: another means by which to perceive and comprehend the things in our world more accurately. An alternative interpretation of process is to reflect that processual philosophy normally requires an interpretation of the world in terms of *verbs*, rather than nouns. A river, for example, is conceived, not as an object, but as an 'endless and uninterrupted *flow*'.[15] Things are merely the consequence of process, and processes are what constitute things; in another words, 'processes are basic and things derivative'.[16] Process philosophy is often associated with Alfred North Whitehead, with the ideas that were articulated in his 1929 text *Process and Reality*. However, as Nicholas Rescher argues, process philosophy is much broader and more encompassing than any one person's particular concepts: it encompasses the ideas of Henri Bergson, Gilles Deleuze, John Dewey, Samuel Alexander, Charles Sanders Peirce and William James, as well as a number of more contemporary philosophers.

When we consider animation in terms of its *process*, we tend to focus less on the character of, for example, Bugs Bunny, and more upon the layering process and general construction of the animation. When we are able to recognize things as having been constructed from many constituent processes, we can find that distinctly different things are often constructed of similar and repeatable processes.[17] Thus, even though, for example, there is great diversity in the world of animation, there are also wide arrays of repeatable and shared tendencies that can be usefully identified.

A process is, in fact, a *procedure* that is enacted. It is 'a sequentially structured sequence of successive stages or phases'.[18] Processes are always forward moving; even those that might appear to be going backwards (an eroding hillside, a rusting nail, the crumbling of ruins) are all, in reality, progressing forwards. Similarly, this applies to memories: even though we may be remembering something from our childhood, we do not think *backwards* from the present, we always remember forward[19] and, as will be discussed later, each time we remember something (even if repeating the same memory) it is a new, unique and forward-progressing process. Processes are temporal, and are therefore always *progressive* and *developmental*.

Processes, like time, are ceaseless and they 'successively [actualise] possibilities that are subsequently left behind as the process unfolds'.[20] That is, processes *transform* abstract potentialities into actualities.[21] Accordingly, that actuality is replaced by *another* abstraction, newly concretized. Inherent within this assiduous successivity reside change and flux. The notion of processual change is perhaps best encapsulated by Whitehead who claimed that, 'the very essence of real actuality ... is process ... this process involves a physical side which is the perishing of the past as it transforms itself into a new creation'.[22] This idea is echoed in Deleuze's frequent discussions of the process of *becoming*. For Deleuze, *becoming* is an ongoing process that does not have a demarcated beginning and ending; 'a line of becoming has only a middle'.[23] It is quite impossible to specify a point of commencement or of completion within a process of ceaseless flux. Thus all things are continuously becoming *other*, and within this concept it becomes difficult to recognize any one *thing*.

If something is engaged in a continuous process of becoming, then we must consider this becoming as *integral* to the thing, and it is essential to recognize this position in any definition or exposition of the thing. If we know how something came about (its becoming), then we will have a greater understanding of it. John Dewey, in his discussion of process noted, '... events turn into objects, things with meaning'.[24] If we invert Dewey's claim, then *things have meaning because of the events that made them*. Rescher states emphatically that the world is 'ongoingly and inexorably *characterized*' by processes which are 'fundamental for its understanding'.[25] Ultimately, if we know how something *became* then we are able to understand it better. It is this argument that facilitates much of the discussions in this text, particularly in regard to the chapters on cognition and on the animated documentary film's investigation of the actual.

This text will also partly draw upon Deleuze's somewhat poststructuralist discussions of *difference and repetition*, and although it is outside of the scope of this book to endeavour to intensely or comprehensively engage with these rather complex philosophical theories, we can draw great inspiration from his monograph *Difference and Repetition*, and we can find convincing parallels that can be applied to the process of animation. 'Process thought writes the connections. Poststructuralism traces the differences.'[26] With this summation, Catherine Keller identifies the distinct difference between process philosophy, and the more poststructuralist approach that Deleuze takes in his text *Difference and Repetition*.[27] However, as Keller later notes, there is common ground in that both approaches de-emphasize the actual object, and look at the areas that surround it. In the analysis of the animated form it can be argued that *both* perspectives are useful. On one hand, the animator seeks to make things move, but on the other hand, the animator will often have to conform to the framic condition of the cinema,[28] which is devoid of all direct representation of movement. The condition of movement is only implied and made visible by the difference between the frames. By looking at animation both from the perspective of process and from poststructuralism, arguably, a fuller understanding will emerge.

Process philosophy is very focused on 'change' and 'becoming', but within this continual flux we can envisage there resides the alternating concepts of difference *and* repetition. While these two terms may seem, initially, to be mutually exclusive, Deleuze argues in his text *Difference and Repetition* that they are interrelated; there is manifestation of repetition in difference, and there is expression of difference in repetition. We soon discover differences within the seemingly repetitive as 'repetition interiorizes and therefore reverses itself'.[29] For Deleuze, repetition does not necessarily require a direct contrast with difference: one may isolate the notion of repetition, and in so doing will ultimately find within it conceptions of difference. Similarly we can find that the apparently distinct becomes 'swallowed up in difference' and thereby loses its individual identity to a more general state of *pure* difference.[30] When we strip objects of their identity and, for example, no longer refer to the walking stick as a 'walking stick', or the chair as a 'chair', we can see that they are both made of wood and that they inherently share commonalities. We can further strip these objects of their material identity (wood) and understand that they are made up of atoms, and so on down the chain until they become pure conceptions. Contrastingly, we can consider a repetitive sequence of chairs and, once we strip them of their 'chair' identity, can concentrate upon their differences in terms of their variations of colour, lumpiness and scratch marks.

The process of animation can at once exemplify the spirit of both poststructuralism and process philosophy. We can apply Keller's above summation of the differing approaches of *process* (that which 'writes the connections') and poststructuralism (that which 'traces the differences') to the conflicting concepts which may be simultaneously at work in the animation process. On one hand, the animator seeks to make something move from 'here to over there'; yet at the same time, the animator must also consider the multitude of incremental step movements that are required for the illusion of movement to be achieved. Take, for example, a stop-motion animator who desires to make a puppet dance across a stage. In order to do so, he or she must first break down this movement into perhaps hundreds of incremental movements. The animator must in a sense deconstruct the broader movements into much smaller components, essentially 'tracing the differences' from one frame to the next. And it is through the process of transformation and of forward motion (both of which exemplify the notion of process) that allows for the 'writing the connections' (thus creating the animation effect) between all the incremental frame-by-frame movements. In this text, it is the idea of a *temporal* difference and repetition from one successive state to the next that becomes most important in relation to the *temporal structure* of animation.

Because all things are in flux, all things exhibit a temporal difference. Yet, at the same time, there are also repetitions within such differences. Consider a musical score that is being played. It could be said that the music is a continuous flow, an evolution of acoustics. At the same time there are many instances of repetitive notes; an *a-sharp* may be repeated hundreds of times within the flow of difference. 'One simply cannot identify a process that is not a process of a processual type and which, in consequence, is not at that level of abstraction capable of repetition.'[31] On the other hand, the appearance of repetition or stability can be found in some things in which, as Dewey notes, 'the rate of change ... is so slow, or is so rhythmic, that these changes have all the advantages of stability'.[32] Thus even within the apparently static, change does occur because processes are ceaselessly at work.

A key element in Deleuze's discussion of difference and repetition is the idea that they are *not* mutually exclusive: that they are, in fact, mutually *inclusive*. Through careful analysis, one finds that such disjunction embodies overlapping conjunctive concerns, and from this may emerge new forms of understanding. This concept is, for Whitehead, the 'ultimate' principle and trajectory of process: it exemplifies 'the advance from disjunction to conjunction, creating a novel entity other than the entities given in disjunction'.[33]

Such an idea can be illustrated within the traditional form of animation. The traditional process of animation involves the creation of an entirely new image for each successive frame. Though each frame is unique, when combined together, we no longer *see* a series of distinctive images, but a wholly new phenomenon – animation. In many cases the difference of each successive animation image may be quite subtle; however, in the animated short film *Sisyphus* (1974), each frame exhibits a radical difference. In addition to the varying poses of the character, the actual form and shape of the figure dramatically changes as well (see Figure I.1). Yet the final animation effect is one of relative consistency of appearance because the

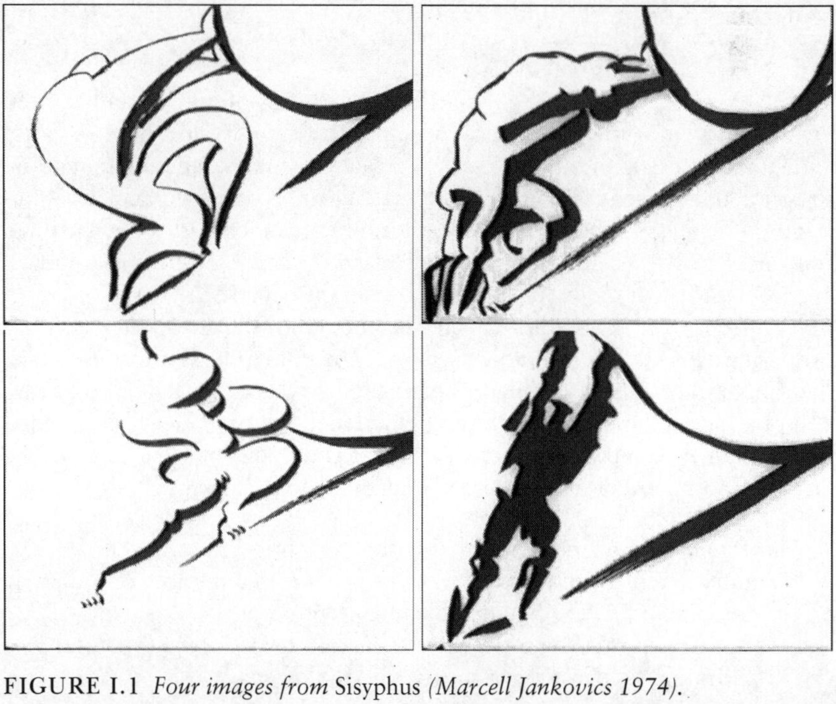

FIGURE I.1 *Four images from* Sisyphus *(Marcell Jankovics 1974).*

form of animation is effectively able to conflate dramatic differences in time and space into a temporal capsule of cohesion. When we consider animation in the above manner, it could be said to be the very embodiment of process. Furthermore, when we start to think about how animation can actually interact with and collaborate with the real world (as will be discussed in Chapters 6 and 7), then the broader conceptions of cosmological processes can become even more significant.

Structure of this book

Because of animation's incredibly diverse character, it makes sense to approach the form of animation both in terms of practice and in terms of theory, and from a diverse set of perspectives and disciplines. Therefore, this book champions a very interdisciplinary approach to the topic of animation, and as a result a much fuller understanding of the form will be possible. This book is divided into three distinct sections. Chapters 1 and 2 comprise *Process and Animation* (which focuses on the theorizing of the animation process). Chapters 3 and 4 consider the topic of *Cognition and Animation* (which looks at links between the process of animation and the process of human cognition as well as some of the ways in which we might interpret or 'read' animation). Finally, Chapters 5, 6 and 7 form *Animation and Actuality* (which looks at how the process of animation can interrogate, and be applied to, the real world).

In Chapter 1, 'Processing Animation', the process of animation has been divided into nine different themes, which together can contribute to a fairly wide understanding of the process of a great many approaches to animation. In doing so, a revised reading of the animated form is proposed, which locates it within the perspective of process philosophy, advancing it further through references to Deleuzian poststructuralism and other relevant philosophical approaches. It will therefore position animation beyond the scope of genre, of aesthetics, and of traditional approaches of production technique by proposing a *process-philosophy*-based model of animation. Within this model, the chapter delineates a number of important aspects of the animation form, and provides a number of supporting examples. The chapter will be divided into a number of subsections which will look at important key aspects of the animated form and process. These will include the following:

Movement: Movement is arguably the most important aspect of the animated form, and this section considers it in a number of unique ways, including the philosophical concept of 'pure movement' and the fact that the process of animation nearly always dictates a separate consideration of movement and of image.

Metamorphosis: Animation's *other* type of movement is metamorphosis. This section examines the unique manner in which the animated image can be made to evolve and transform over time. It considers a number of key examples, as well as some of the broader philosophical conceptions of metamorphosis.

Frames and Forms: This section considers the differing concepts of the single image-frame and the successive temporal frame. It also pays close attention to the discreet and recognizable forms found in animation, from characters to abstract shapes, and considers both their physical and metaphysical make up.

Layers: The importance of layers and the general constructive nature of animation (both in terms of movement and image) is discussed in this section.

Sound: This section explores the unique connection that animation can have with the auditory, particularly since sound is quite often imposed upon the animated form and the imagery is therefore animated in deference to the audio track.

Time: This section looks at the unique relationship that animation has with time and how it invariably represents both an asymmetrical documentation, as well as a 'compression' of time. It also considers animation's innate ability to simultaneously display differing representations of time.

Abstraction: Here it is argued that all animation (either in terms of image or motion) is predicated upon the concept of abstraction. Animation tends towards the generalized – and rather than providing a true representation of reality, it gives us the irreal, which is always decontextualized, and quite often this imagery and/or motion is noticeably simplified, exaggerated or distorted.

Process-Document: Self-reflexivity is quite commonly found in animation, something that can be referred to as animation's 'process-document'. Ultimately, this can be a very important aspect of the animated form, as it can present the viewer with a revelatory record of the animation's very becoming.

Each of these sections will form an important foundation upon which the analysis of the animated form will continue throughout the rest of the book.

Chapter 2, 'Cycled and Recycled Animation', continues to look at animation in terms of process through a discussion of one of its most important arrangements. The cycle is one of the most significant structures within the animated form, yet there has been virtually no scholarly publication devoted specifically to this topic. The chapter delivers a detailed account of the use of the very important (but quite underrated) cyclical structure often found in the animated form as well as a consideration of the pervasive recycling of elements that occur in most animation productions.

This analysis of the animated cycle builds upon the various aspects of animation process outlined in the previous chapter.

Chapter 3, 'Cognitive Animation Theory', looks at relationships between animation and human cognition in terms of process and articulates some common ground between the *processes* of animation and the *processes* of human cognitive imagery. In doing so it suggests a new *cognitive theory of animation* – one that differs dramatically from the bulk of the literature surrounding cognitive film theories, which tend to focus only on the viewer's cognitive response to the completed film. By contrast, this theory addresses a number of process philosophy-based ideas that, together with a discussion of the use of cognitive imagery, can position animation quite apart from other media. This chapter builds upon the original animation model proposed in Chapter 1, 'Processing Animation', by applying it to our cognitive system, specifically to our visuospatial working memory. It also follows a structure similar to Chapter 1, relating the various core concepts of animation to that of human cognition. Through this linking of animation to human cognition, the discussion journeys beyond mere comparative analogy and provides quite an original perspective to the animated form.

Chapter 4, 'Reading Animation', builds upon the previous chapter in its discussion of cognition and animation. However, the discussion here focuses more on how the viewer might cognitively *receive* animation. It sheds some light on how the human brain might cogitate the animated image, including the double cognitive coding that can occur when viewing animation. This chapter also explores particular manifestations of anthropomorphism and animated performances that are often quite significant both within the production and the reading of the animated form. Further sections consider states of hybrid animation, animated video games and stop-motion animation.

Chapter 5, 'Non-Fictional Animation and the Transformation of Actuality', looks at animated documentary and the representation of actuality from a perspective of process. It argues that issues of indexicality are quite complex and can therefore be divided into numerous subsets of representation, including image, movement and sound. It also argues that an essential consideration of the animated documentary lies within the process of the real world *becoming* animation – and not just standard matters of representation. This is an important distinction because the 'animated object' of most fictional animations does not derive from any prior existence, whereas animated representation of actuality must personify a prior condition: they begin as actuality, and through a transformative process *become* animation. Ultimately, it is through this process of 'becoming animation' that one can utilize it to gain a better understanding of the actual world.

Chapter 6, 'Investigative Animation', considers how animation can be used to directly investigate the real world through the use of digital simulations and virtual reality. This chapter also introduces a *forensics approach to animation*; that is, rather than merely representing actuality, animation can be thought of as a tool to effectively interrogate actuality. For example, it can be used to methodically expose the potential energy of motion within stationary things, and can be used to discover the essential sequential states of difference which can then be expressed through the process of animation. It is also, more broadly, an effective reading of how we sometimes go about animating – carefully deducing how a form should move and how it might have previously moved.

Chapter 7, 'Animating the Real World', considers how animation can also be used directly to animate the real world. It will consider such methods as the growing trend to large-scale animations of urban spaces and landscapes (referred to as landscape animation); architectural projection mapping (in which animation is projected onto site-specific structures); and finally a consideration of how robotics and other real-world apparatuses might be examined in terms of animation.

Throughout this text, a wide variety of animated films will be referenced which have been selected to showcase the extensive diversity of animation techniques, and to represent distinct genres, locations and eras of animation production. Some of the chosen animations will be regarded as relatively mainstream and will be familiar to most readers, while others might be deemed relatively more obscure (but are easily accessible online). This broad corpus of animated examples is intended to both illustrate particular points and showcase how the many different ideas and forms that will be discussed might fundamentally inform each other. Ultimately, the aim of this book is to delineate these connections and to find common ground between the many disparate forms and expressions of animation and to broaden the conventional discourse of animation.

PART ONE

Process and Animation

1

Processing Animation

This chapter will look closely at the numerous processes of animation. To facilitate this study, it has been divided into nine different thematic sections which together contribute to a fairly wide understanding of most approaches to animation. These sections will consider animation in terms of movement, metamorphosis, frames, forms, layers, sound, time, abstraction and the *process-document*.

Movement and animation

'Cinema', declares philosopher Gilles Delueze at the beginning of *Cinema 1*, 'does not give us an image to which movement is added, it immediately gives us a movement-image'.[1] For Deleuze, movement and its related image are inextricable in the cinematic image; they are recorded simultaneously and subsequently presented simultaneously to the viewer. In fact, from the perspective of the spectator it is quite difficult to consider anything independent of motion – whether it is on screen or in the actual world. A person walks along a path: that movement appears as an all-encompassing permutation of that person; a rock rolls down a cliff and its movement and form are undeniably simultaneous. Yet, when we consider the world in more processual terms we can appreciate that movement is a force that is enacted upon all things. A chair will not move unless pushed. Gravity forces the rain to fall downwards. We exert energy, and we stand up. Even when things do not move, we understand that at one time or another movement forces have affected them. Len Lye suggests,

> the history of any definite form is the movement of which the form is the result. When we look at something and see the particular shape of it we are only looking at its after-life. Its real life is the movement by which it got to be that shape.[2]

Further to this, in *Animate Form*, Greg Lynn suggests, 'force is an initial condition, the cause of both motion and the particular inflections of a form'.[3] When we consider the world in more processual terms, we understand that movement is a force that is *enacted upon* all things. Henri Bergson hints at this conception when he observes that 'In reality, life is a movement, materiality is the inverse movement.'[4]

Live-action cinema, however, cannot record motion independently; it can only provide us with a *movement-image* in which movement and image are bound together. In order to consider pure motion, we need to disentangle it from form. There have been a number of processes emerging over the years that have attempted to record isolated motion from images. In the 1880s, Etienne-Jules Marey developed a 'geometric chronophotographic' system that allowed him to isolate graphic representations of movement that were discreet from the original subject. In one example he attached an apparatus (essentially just a multiple cross section of white sticks) to the subject's back and sequentially photographed the subject walking. The white lines from the apparatus were then isolated in the resulting photographic images, then composited on a single plate detailing the 'oscillations of the vertebral column, shoulder and hip'.[5] In another version he attached white joint-marker points (connected by white lines) to a human subject. The subject was dressed completely in black and placed before a black background (see Figure 1.1). In the resulting images the person would 'disappear' leaving only the denoting white lines.[6] These provided a simplified representation of human motion that effectively disentangled the human movement from the human form.

Current motion-capture technologies do essentially the same thing. Motion-capture systems can be generally either magnetic or optical based;

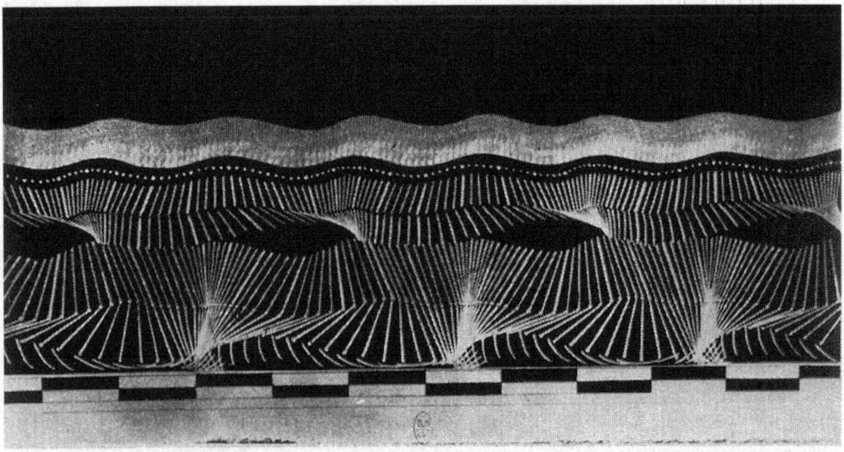

FIGURE 1.1 *Composite image by Etienne-Jules Marey denoting abstracted movement.*

both normally rely upon the placing of points on an actor, which are then read by a series of sensors or cameras. A third type of motion capture, referred to as mechanical mocap systems, 'directly measure joint angles of a capture subject who wears an articulated device that consists of straight rods and potentiometers'.[7] These in turn provide a recording of essentially 'pure' movement, abstracted from the original form. A similar process, referred to as *video-based motion capture,* allows one to extract pure movement information from already existing film or video footage. Once the footage is digitized, one can use computer software to place tracking points upon specific parts of the image, which then allow for the motion tracking of the figure or object on screen. This also provides a recording of 'pure' movement, abstracted from the original form (in this case existing film or video footage). More recently, motion-capturing abilities are finding their way into everyday appliances such as video games systems and mobile devices. Each of these motion-capture systems represents a significant shift in the recording of pure motion and an effective method by which to consider movement abstracted from form.

Importantly, the process of animation construction does normally require that we consider motion and image as very distinct entities. This motion does not originally emanate from the characters or objects themselves. It is imposed from outside through the process of animation. Animation, in fact, directly contradicts Deleuze's avowal that cinema 'gives us a section, but a section which is mobile, not an immobile section + abstract movement'[8] for, in contrast to live action, this is *exactly* the process of animation's construction. Although motion capture expresses the most obvious amalgamation of abstract movement and image, nearly all forms of animation involve this process to some degree. In stop-motion, the puppet is physically built; the animator then physically moves it. In 3D computer animation, the object or character is virtually built, and then virtually moved. Even in the case of cel animation, the act of moving the cels or backgrounds in front of the rostrum camera, or the lowering or raising of the camera, creates some of the movement.[9] But even in the case of exclusively drawn animation, in which the animator must encode each new drawing with motion rather than overtly add to it, one could argue that the animator must at least have an awareness of the pure motion, distinct from the form that they are engaged with, in order to create a convincing movement of that form.

One might consider the uncanny and utterly eccentric movement found in a Tex Avery short animation, such as *Red Hot Riding Hood* (1943), to be an epitome of classical animated films. But from a process perspective there is no concept of motion that does not exist both in the physical world and in animation. Removed from the animated context, every possible movement found in an animated film comprises exactly the same types of motion that we witness in the actual world (up, down, forward, back, left, right, accumulation and dispersion). The dancing of a bonfire flame, the splashing of water, the vibration of quantum particles: all represent a potentially greater eccentricity of motion – if it were to be applied to an animated form – than a Tex Avery cartoon has ever achieved. With regard to process, Nicholas Rescher asserts that all processes when removed from their concrete context become 'inherently universal and repeatable'.[10] Movement, when it is removed from its bodily context, *also* becomes 'inherently universal and repeatable'. For example, in the feature film *The Hulk* (Ang Lee 2003), the director, himself, delivered the motion-capture performance of the animated Hulk character: his movements were then abstracted and applied to the Hulk 3D model. For Rescher, once a process is applied to an event, then it is 'at once concrete and universal'.[11] Similarly, the movement of the Hulk is not only the Hulk's, but also that of Ang Lee; at the same time it is a pure movement (movements of up, down, forward and back) that can be applied to any other 3D model. The unique ability to separate the processes of motion and image allows for a new context and a greater complexity for both. A snail can move like a tornado, a triangle like an old man. As one stream of information plays off against the other, the combined meaning of such a disjoint may be superior to a synchronous narrative.

Animated methods

Traditionally, there have been two primary methods in the creation of animated movement. The first method, which can be referred to as *manipulated animation*, involves the manipulation of a single image or object. Most stop-motion puppet animations are produced this way – the animator will incrementally, but directly, move the forms. Cut-out animation, paint-on-glass animation and a lot of 3D computer animation are other clear examples of this manipulated animation process. Because this approach always involves the application of movement to a form (either directly by the animator or added via the motion-capture process), it represents a rather direct expression of how image and movement can be considered as distinct concepts. The second method is a form of animation that is best described as *replacement animation*. Replacement animation is arguably the oldest approach to animation, particularly if we consider its pre-cinematic (and pre-photographic) roots. It normally involves the creation of multiple completed images that are then *sequentially replaced*, one at a time, in order to create the illusion of a unique and persistent form that *can move*. Most instances of traditional cel animation would fall into this category. For example, 10,000 individual drawings of Felix the Cat and friends (each slightly different in pose) might have been necessary to produce a seven-minute animated film of the characters running about.

Additionally, most of the animation that would have been produced for such pre-cinema devices as the zoetrope, phenakistiscope or flipbook would have also been produced in this manner. Each drawing was in a sense encoded with difference which when played through an animation apparatus would produce the effect of movement. Nobody directly *moved* Felix (in the puppetry or stop-motion sense), but he was made to move by secreting bits of movement within the difference of each successive frame. Later in the 1940s, stop-motion animator George Pal applied this term when he developed his 'replacement animation system'. Though he also animated his figures in the traditional stop-motion (manipulated) method, he also created a lot of the movement (particularly the more fluid effects of squash and stretch) through the replacement system. Thus, in order to make a figure's arm stretch out to pick up an object, he would replace it frame-by-frame with a slightly longer arm (see *Jasper and the Haunted House*, George Pal 1942). Though replacement animation does not follow the literal and direct process of applying movement to form, the animator is certainly aware of this conception and the idea of 'making the drawing-form move' is more than likely the impetus of their efforts. And since this process does not allow for the direct puppetry-like movement of forms, the animator must encode each still image with movement. The result is that there is differential movement encoded within the interstices of the frames – in a sense a moment of encoded pure movement. On the other hand, it is important to acknowledge that even in the most direct puppetry-like animation technique, the animator will also need to consider, to some degree, individual moments and layers of constructive processes. Quite often these two traditional approaches will overlap both in technique and in theory.

However, even though most cel animation can be categorized as replacement animation, much of it (especially in limited animation) is also partially achieved through the use of manipulated stop-motion. For example, most background pans or zooms and even some simple character movements (such as flying through the air, or skidding along the ground) were achieved by the camera operator. Thus, not only would he or she take a photograph of each painted cel, but he or she would also be responsible for manipulating the plates and cels in a frame-by-frame manner, one increment at a time.

One animation process that often involves an important overlapping of manipulated and replacement animation processes is the technique of rotoscoping. The rotoscoping process was invented by Dave and Max Fleischer in 1917. Rotoscoping is the process by which live-action footage is traced from 'single-frame projections'.[12] Similar to motion capture, the process of rotoscoping involves the extraction of movement from one form, and its application, to another. Depending upon how carefully the original images are traced, the resulting motion information will either be comprehensive and faithful to the original or dramatically altered. In many cases, the animator will only trace (rotoscope) every other frame (or even every third frame) of live-action footage. In this case, the result will be a more jittery, *anime-ic* motion (a term coined by Thomas Lamarre). In addition to live-action footage, rotoscoping can also 'capture' the movement of existing animation. For example, this process was used extensively in the production of Disney's *Robin Hood* (1973), in which animation from the studio's previous features, the *Jungle Book* (1967) and *Snow White and the Seven Dwarfs* (1937), were heavily reused through a rotoscoping process.

In a slight variation of the traditional rotoscoping process, Australian animator David Barker patented an animation process in 1921 in a number of the Commonwealth countries (Australia, England, Canada), which was essentially a facsimile of Fleisher's earlier (1917) US patent. It too involved the tracing of live-action actors directly onto cels, and then the 'opaquing in of the figures'. But what made his approach somewhat different is that he would frequently create large photographic prints of the original live-action film and use these as the background on which the 'rotoscoped' cel animation would be placed. These would then be photographed on an animation stand in the normal cel animation production process. The result was a hand-drawn form that was imbued with captured movement but then reconstituted back into its original filmic space.

Using a rather unique approach to rotoscoping, the animation team known as Rymdreglage has created a number of stop-motion animations, including *Insert Coin* (2010), *Zombie Pace* (2014) and *Terminator 2* (2011), which appear to subvert the traditional rotoscoping process. While most traditional approaches to rotoscoping involve the tracing of actuality in order to transform it into an animated context, these films involve the tracing of digital animation in order to bring it into a real-world context. Each of these films began first as a simple digital animation. The animators would then project these digital animations, one frame at a time, into a real-world space. Each projected frame would then be overlaid and filled in with such items as coins, plastic beads or Lego blocks. Once the projected image had been accurately overlaid, the projector would be turned off, and the visible image (made entirely of beads or coins) would then be photographed. The next frame in the digital animation would then be projected and the real-world objects (beads, blocks or coins) would be moved so as to overlay accurately the next successive image. The process would be repeated until the entire digital animation had been rotoscoped and transformed into a material-based stop-motion animation. Despite its radical transformation, the resulting animation will continue to express the movement of the original projected footage.

A further variation of the rotoscoping process can be found in the pre-digital use of *video prints*, whereby the live-action film image was printed out as a series of black and white still images on paper. The animator would then draw and colour on top of each print, and finally, photograph these (one after the other) to create the final animation. Wendy Tilby and Amanda Forbis' animated short, *When the Day Breaks* (1999), is a good example of this process. Because each image is drawn *on top of* the video print, the result is an embellishment to the original image. Rather than having to be extremely careful in the tracing of the original image (as with most approaches to rotoscoping), here the animator's approach can be a much looser one, as the defining image is still always present. So rather than movement being abstracted (removed) and appended to an image, the image is altered and obscured, yet remains bound to its diegetic movement. Nevertheless, if the image becomes obscured enough, then the end result is the same – a dislocation of movement from its original image (see Figure 1.2).

Similar digital expressions of rotoscoping are now quite common and can be achieved by a number of software packages. Digital rotoscoping processes were used on two of director Richard Linklater's feature films, *Waking Life* (2001) and *A Scanner Darkly* (2006). In these instances, Linklater employed a propriety digital rotoscoping process called Rotoshop that allowed for digital tracing and drawing on top of the video footage, essentially creating vectorized images.[13] The process of converting a bitmap image into a vector image, aesthetically, smooths out the edges and simplifies the lines of original image. Much has been made of Rotoshop's 'interpolated rotoscoping' feature, which speeds up the process by not requiring the animator to trace over every frame, thus saving a lot of production time.[14]

FIGURE 1.2 *Image from* When the Day Breaks *(Wendy Tilby, Amanda Forbis 1999).*

However, what is perhaps most remarkable is how this process results not only in the interpolation of image but also in the interpolation *of movement*, often creating a remarkably fluid motion aesthetic.

This interpolation of movement is a form of automatic in-betweening (also known as parametric animation) and signals a growing trend of many automated forms of animation – that is animation that is produced without the traditional frame-by-frame construction process. In these cases the animator will normally define starting and ending points, and the computer will fill in the movements (or essentially move the object from a specified 'here' to a specified 'there'). Sometimes this involves setting key frames within software packages that carefully mimic traditional animation production exposure sheets and filmic timelines and, increasingly, it might involve simply touching a figure on a screen and dragging the object from one side to the other. In more algorithmic digital animation, the animator's role is often to simply devise guidelines, perhaps cycles of movement and directional cues, which the computer then produces (potentially with quite varied results upon each iteration).

Regardless of the methodology used, it is possible to consider that all animation involves the important distinction of applying or considering movement independent of form. Undoubtedly, this view is becoming more noticeable as digital animation processes advance and become less dependent on a conventional frame-by-frame construction process.

Metamorphosis and animation

Metamorphosis is in many regard a unique manifestation of animative processes, one that has helped to differentiate animation from the traditional film image, and a number of scholars suggest that it is a fundamental aspect of the animated form (Wells, Furniss, Klein, Sobchack). Metamorphosis provides 'the ability for an image literally to change into another completely different image'.[15] We could refer to metamorphosis as animation's *other* movement – whereas the previous section primarily referred to directional movement that corresponds to such manoeuvrings as up, down, left, right, forward, back and so on. Though the idea of metamorphosis may contain all of these, it also contains the essential concepts of growth and evolution. In fact, some animated films have derived nearly all of their movement from the display of metamorphosis. For example, the process of making the 1974 animated short, *Hunger* (Peter Foldes 1974) (regarded as one of the earliest *character* animated films made entirely through digital computer animation), first involved the creation of digital line drawings, which represented the key drawings of each scene. From these, the computer was directed to computationally morph the first image into the second. Since at the time it wasn't technologically possible to digitally create and animate a character in the traditional manner, *Hunger* derives nearly all of its movement from what *was* computationally possible – metamorphosis. A more recent animated short, *Love & Theft* by Andreas Hykade (2010), also derives nearly all of its movement from the exclusive use of animated metamorphosis (see Figure 1.3). Therefore, instead of featuring stable and persistent characters and forms that move around and spatially interact with a defined landscape in customary ways, the characters are seen to continually transform from one design into another. Thus instead of having a figure 'walk' across the screen, it instead 'transforms' across the screen. For example, a figure may

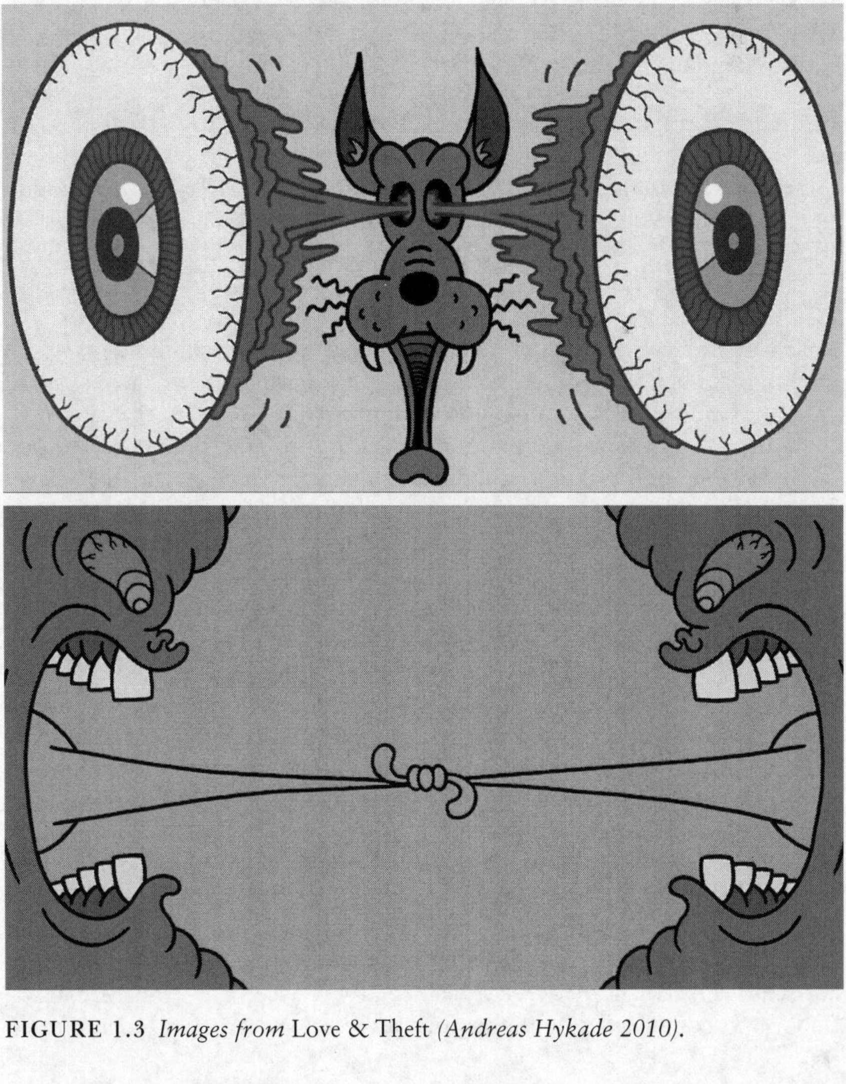

FIGURE 1.3 *Images from* Love & Theft *(Andreas Hykade 2010).*

begin on the right-hand side of the frame, inflate out and split into three very different figures that fill up the whole screen, and then contract back down into a different smaller form on the left of the screen. The result is on one hand a continually evolving amorphous sequence, and on the other a very dynamic presentation of figures who interact with each other (and the greater screen space) in novel ways.

One of the fundamental tenets of process philosophy suggests that everything is in a state of flux, everything is becoming other: therefore, continually metamorphosing. However, much of the metamorphosis of the real world occurs at a much slower pace than is humanly perceptible. Therefore, we can see the effects of it, but not the occasion. We can see the butterfly, but not the caterpillar changing into it; we can see the canyon, but not the erosion that hollowed it out. Vivian Sobchack suggests that we are 'intellectually familiar' 'yet experientially' unfamiliar with these ongoing processes. For example, even 'our bodies at the cellular level [are] ceaselessly forming and reforming', making ourselves, 'not "ourselves" at all'.[16] Thus, although we know that dramatic change is occurring, we just cannot witness it. We can, however, witness a similar (albeit limited) conception of the process of metamorphosis in such naturally *amorphous* substances as water and clouds; the cascading waterfall continually changes shape, and billowing clouds visibly change form, even into *recognizable* structures (like dogs, cats and ships).

The actual conception of metamorphosis can be made visible with animation. Even so, while time-lapse photography can show us the transformation of a caterpillar into a butterfly by imbuing the continual flow of space and time with temporal gaps, it is limited to the acceleration of the visible process of change. Yet animation can go further, either through its process of replacement animation or through manipulated animation. For example, by conflating multiple unique *images* (in addition to providing gaps in time), it can showcase extraordinary permutations, such as those found in Bill Plympton's *Your Face* (1987), in which the character's 'head' transforms from one outlandish form into another (see Figure 1.4). Such animations, as discussed earlier, normally involve the process of replacement animation – the conflation of numerous unique images that are constructed in an extemporal manner. As a result, the conflating of both time and objects can produce astonishing paradigms of animated metamorphosis. Some materials and processes do not *require* the amalgamating potential afforded by the replacement animation process, and instead can rely upon a single, but inherently non-stable object. As Michael Frierson notes, for example, clay, because of its malleable properties, lends itself to the structure of metamorphosis.[17] In such cases, a single lump of clay can achieve both the beginning and ending states of stasis, as well as the in-between transformative phase of the transformation. One of Aardman's early animation successes was actually predicated

FIGURE 1.4 *Images from Bill Plympton's* Your Face *(1987).*

on the idea of metamorphosis, and on the inherent ability of clay to accomplish this. The 1976 British television series of 'VisionOn' featured a character, appropriately named, Morph. The character 'had a propensity for "morphing" into animals, objects or sometimes just a ball of the raw material of which he was made'.[18]

Dissecting animated metamorphosis: Stasis

For Phillip Brophy, animation conveys flux and transformation of actuality, not in the depiction of things, 'but as the markings and recordings of energy fields, transmissions and events'.[19] Paul Wells observes that metamorphosis suggests a 'dominant characteristic in animation where all the events depicted in the graphic space are literally "acts of becoming", transitory and formative'.[20] Deleuze also seemingly takes this perspective in his brief description of animation:

> The drawing no longer constitutes a pose or a completed figure, but the description of a figure which is always in the process of being formed or dissolving through the movement of lines and points.[21]

These views suggest that animation, through its continuous process of evolutionary change, exemplifies the conception of metamorphosis. Such perspectives would seem, therefore, to indicate that *all* animation is to some degree metamorphic. Yet when we think of metamorphosis in animation, we normally think of a particular effect: one in which *one thing* changes into a *different thing*. So, what differentiates this from the more conceptual and metamorphic description of animation? The answer is *stasis*.

Vivian Sobchack portrays the oppositional form of metamorphosis as 'meta-stasis', which she defines as essentially the still point in our ever-evolving (morphing) universe.[22] From a process perspective, stasis is what allows us to live apparently stable lives in the undulating flow of the processual. To exist, we need to be able to pick up a rock or climb a hill, and not to have it continually eroding beneath our feet. Similarly, for us to recognize the metamorphic structure in animation, we need to be able to see the *from-to* of its flux. There needs to be at least a moment of stasis, a pause, at either end of the transformation so that we are able to recognize the 'complete and marked change of form',[23] for example, the transformation *from* Popeye *to* a steam engine. As Bynum notes, we need to be able to identify the form through the process of transformation:

> The question of change is, of course, the other side of the question of identity. If change is the replacement of one entity by another or the growth of an entity out of another entity in which it is implicit, we must be able to say how we know we have an entity in the first place.[24]

Otherwise metamorphosis, despite its exemplifying process philosophy's conception of continual flux, will result only in the purely abstract. The work of Oskar Fishinger, for example, can only be described in generalities of metamorphosis, of shape and colour, rhythm and pattern or as Brophy might suggest, 'energy fields and transmissions'.[25] In contrast, asserts Rescher, 'What concretizes processes is…their spatiotemporal emplacement, their positioning in the framework of reality'.[26] And, furthers Anne Daniell, 'creative transformation […] is dependent for its actualisation upon the concrete, upon that which is already established or given'.[27] Moments of stasis serve to provide such a context to the transformative, so that we can recognize the 'caterpillar' as a stable entity before it transforms into another stable state, the 'butterfly'.

Dissecting animated metamorphosis: The in-between

The in-between flow of change, which makes the animated metamorphosis possible, can be considered through both the Deleuzian/Bergsonian conception of *multiplicity* and process' idea of *becoming*. That is, we can think of metamorphosis as the change that is occurring, *and* in terms of the constituent parts that make up this change. Clearly, metamorphosis is defined as one thing becoming something other and, by the process by which it changes, affects (and composes) this new *thing*. As with all animated movements, metamorphosis involves a *separate* application process of motion to image. As previously affirmed, virtually every conception of animated movement occurs in the actual world (growth, changes in form, erosion).[28] By means of the separation of process, the animator is simply applying the transformation motion of one thing to a different thing: thus we can apply the growing motion of a flower to a brick, or the melting-motion of an ice cube to a house.

Metamorphosis is about becoming *other*, changing and leaving the old form behind. It is during this fluid phase, in the middle, that the animated form becomes amorphous, in anticipation of its being reformed into something other. The image is neither this nor that; it is a liminal space which Norman Klein refers to as the 'animorph', which suggests for him the constructive nature of the form and, because of it amorphic ambiguity, presents us with a 'lapse or a hesitation'.[29] For Deleuze the in-between space of becoming 'does not designate a localizable relation going from one thing to the other and back again, but a perpendicular direction, a transversal movement that sweeps on *and* the other away'.[30] The in-between cannot truly be identified, therefore its progression is not of a quantifiable known. It is at once both, but also an amorphous state that can be anything. For, not only does metamorphosis transform from one thing to another: it simultaneously 'destabilizes the image'.[31] Thus, for example, if a cat is transforming into a dog, the cat may first turn into a soupy substance, before it stabilizes as a dog.

Metamorphosis is composed simultaneously of an assemblage of elements and processes: in a sense, a *multiplicity* – which can be thought of as an assemblage of many separate elements. Metamorphosis can be conceived as an *embodiment* of multiplicity because it is the amalgamation of many things over time and space (conflated time, conflated objects). In *Bergsonism*, Deleuze points out that Bergson considers there to be *two* types of multiplicity; one can be thought of as that which makes up a concrete object (in space). He notes that if such a spatial multiplicity were to be cut up, the resulting elements would still be similar to that *of* the original multiplicity (if you cut up a watermelon, the *slices* are still watermelon). Deleuze, while further referencing Bergson, notes that when this multiplicity is in *duration* it must be considered to be a 'continuous multiplicity'. If a continuous multiplicity were to be cut up, the resulting elements would be 'changed in kind'.[32] Time at once changes things, but also unifies them in a multiplicity. This raises the important idea that animated metamorphosis is composed of many elements which are not necessarily of the same thing; therefore a metamorphosis is not any singular 'thing'. Sobchack, in fact, refers to metamorphosis as a 'metaphysical object'.[33] The assemblages of these different elements, collectively, happen to create the changes (the metamorphosis) throughout time. For Deleuze and Guattari, a multiplicity is *composed* of many things and is therefore, 'a phenomenon of bordering'.[34] It has many states, and many associations. However, these are

> defined not by the elements that compose it in extension, not by the characteristics that compose it in comprehension, but by the lines and dimensions it encompasses in 'intension'.[35]

When we think of metamorphosis, we should not necessarily analyse it as to how the constituent elements relate to each other externally or by 'extension', that is how they might relate to each other outside of metamorphosis ('that image is very similar to one we saw earlier'). Nor is it essentially relevant how the images relate cognitively to each other (this image does not look like a dog, but this does look like a cat). But what is essential to metamorphosis is how the images associate with each other *internally* by 'intension' *within* the metamorphic form. In the morphing process of, for example, a cat into a dog, the transformation does not necessarily conform to the structure of each of the objects (the cat or the dog). As Paul Wells notes, it resists 'logical developments and determines unpredictable linearities'.[36] Thus, the animator will determine how the objects (that make up the metamorphosis) transform by the manner in which he or she cuts up the transformation phase. And in turn, it is how these slices relate to the one after it and the one before it, and to every other one *within* the transformation, that dictates the final path of the metamorphosis.

Metamorphic beginnings

As with a number of animation's essential elemental features, metamorphosis can be found widely in pre-cinematic animations that would have been displayed in such devices as phenakisticopes, magic lanterns and flipbooks. In the depicted example of a Phenakisticope disc from c.1833 (see Figure 1.5), we can see a young woman gradually transforming into a hideous monster in a never-ending spiral of metamorphosis.

Another early manifestation of visual metamorphosis can be found in the live (and later film animated) performances of lightning sketch artists. As part of their act, the lightning sketch artist would often begin with one recognizable drawing and then, through further development, 'transform' it into a different recognizable drawing. The lightning sketch artists exploited the concept of the drawing process as they drew their large images in front of the audience. Spectators would delight in witnessing a talented artist draw something very quickly and with great efficiency and precision. But

FIGURE 1.5 *Phenakisticope disc (c. 1833) depicting a metamorphic transformation.*

in order to add additional layers of conceptual information, the artist would often provide an oral description of the drawing's progress through humorous 'patter' and, most importantly, the drawing would often appear suddenly and dramatically to transform before the audience's eyes. Thus a fly might suddenly become an angry housekeeper, or a cat might transform into a giant mouse. This was the most popular genre of the lightning sketch and came to be referred to as the *evolution sketch*. Writing in 1926 (towards the very end of the lightning sketch trend), Tarbell describes:

> Evolution pictures are produced by drawing a picture and then with a few strokes of the crayon changing it into something radically different from the original conception. Such a picture never fails to hold the interest of an audience, because it always keeps them on tiptoe with curiosity until the drawing is finished.[37]

These drawing performances presented a combined fictionalized spectacle and factual demonstration of the drawing process. The audience were able to witness the actual drawing process of an image, mark by mark, but at the same time be entertained through the overlays of fictional narrative and, as a climax, by a dramatic metamorphic twist. Once cinema came into more widespread use, the lightning sketch artists came to recognize that animation could give them a performative edge. Not only could cinematic animation seemingly speed up the drawing process but it could also facilitate the transformative effect that they so desired.

Animation and frames

Historically, the production of animation has been regarded as a frame-by-frame process; and most earlier texts have described animation in this way. And although animation can still be described like this (at least in part), many now recognize that this is not necessarily the most comprehensive, or even most important, point of discussion. For example, Paul Wells and Johnny Hardstaff have set out to define animation in much more expansive terms: '[Animation] is a form destined to be defined ultimately not by formal conditions – frame-by-frame manipulation of materials in the creation of phases of representational motion – but by the artist, context and condition of expression.'[38] In actuality, the understanding of animation in terms of the frame-by-frame process has never been as straightforward as one might think. Even in relation to the earliest historical productions, this conception of animation has varied dramatically depending upon which technique was used. For example, more limited animation has meant that rather than a frame-by-frame process, it was more accurately an every-fourth-frame process. Replacement animation has required completely distinct 'objects' for each new instance of movement, while manipulated animation has required altered states of the same image or object. More recently, digital animation has in some cases nearly obliterated the concept of the frame, and in other cases it has striven to emulate the traditional filmic frame. And as will be discussed later, the very common process of layering and compositing that has been an essential part of many forms of animation has also complicated the idea of the discrete frame. However, the constituent image (frame) is still relatively pertinent to a great deal of contemporary animation practices and certainly critical to the analysis of a bulk of the more historical animated productions.

Quite often the animator is compelled to add movement to a form, but in order to achieve this, they must encode the movement both within and in-between a series of still images so that from that sequence an animated effect will arise. There are obvious differing methodologies in the creation of the still image and the moving image, and the animator has often had to balance these; the animator might need to be continually aware both of the micro-process of each image's construction and of the macro-process which determines how the various images collaborate. The still image exhibits properties that become absorbed into the moving image; yet at the same time, the moving image is dependent upon the distinctive properties of the individual image. This reading of the animation process is also evident in the frequent discussions of how animation is composed of 'a combination of movement and stillness in space and time that produces shifting, time-tied activity within a constant context'.[39] That is, how the devices of animation conflate movement and stillness through their successive display of still images. Yet what is overlooked in these discussions is that the animator is nevertheless conscious of the act of adding movement to the form. In fact, in working in this manner, the animator is essentially encoding the individual frame with abstract concerns of pure movement. In this way, the idea of pure movement still exists; it is just encoded by the animator into the drawings. And this pure movement can still be conceptually isolated, as being that force that resides between the frames. Of course movement is not actually visible without an image. Each image is what concretizes the pure movement into the 'event' of animation.

Although animation requires a multiplicity of images to convey motion, the single image can also provide a degree of non-temporally *implied* motion, and this to varying degrees must be taken into account in the animation process. Cholodenko pronounces that the photographic image is by no means still because it has captured a *section* of time; it resides somewhere 'between the still of nonmotion and the still of motion'.[40] One could suggest that photographically implied motion stems from this ambiguity; furthermore, based on particular visual clues, the viewer may cognitively imbue the 'still' photograph with movement. In the first instance, a photograph containing *motion-blurred* or *streaked* elements will visually suggest that movement was occurring at the *time* of the photograph, and as a result will readily articulate the motion paths of the elements. The early-twentieth-century photographer Anton Giulio Bragaglia, in an effort to extend the work of Etienne-Jules Marey, explored what he termed 'photodynamism' (a technique which utilized a very slow shutter speed) in order to capture the 'visible wake' of movement.[41] Such blurred photographs (for example of a person rising up or bending over) contained no visibly discrete images (as did most of Marey's); yet clearly demarcated an uninterrupted path of motion. It was quite simple for the viewer to envision this movement within the still image.

Another representation of implied movement relies upon our understanding that the photographic still frame is an image that has been snatched *from* time and, subsequently, that the image has been *disentangled* from its *motion context*. Thus, we instinctively attempt to *cognitively* reconnect it with motion. Imagine a photograph of a car that has driven off of a cliff and can be seen to be suspended in mid-air. Such an image would accurately depict a car merely suspended in the sky, but what the viewer would percieve is that the car was in *mid-motion* (that it had previously been driving on the road, and that it is currently flying off the cliff, and that it will soon crash to the ground). Such an example is what Tony Schirato and Jen Webb refer to as the 'arrested image', in which the viewer might see *apparent* movement but, in actuality, it is the viewer who fills in the missing motion.[42] This also conforms to what Brian Massumi would describe as a *perceptual feeling*, which involves 'not-seeing something – yet directly experiencing it in vision all the same'.[43] We understand that movement put the car there, and we envision that movement will continue to affect it until it reaches the ground again. This concept of arrested motion is not limited to photography, and can be simulated in the crafted image as well. For example, in the depicted still frame from the animated short *Presto* (Doug Sweetland 2008), we see a rabbit character 'frozen' mid-step. Because of its asymmetrical balance, and our general knowledge of the laws of gravity and physics, we can surmise that it is not a figure at rest, but indeed an 'arrested image' (see Figure 1.6).

Nevertheless, true cinematic movement is 'a function of equidistant instants, selected so as to create an impression of continuity',[44] and even though each single image may contain *implied* motion, when combined and presented in succession, this implied motion (though very important) effectively vanishes and a new variety of motion is presented, one derived from the *differences* inferred from one image to the next. This new cinematic

FIGURE 1.6 *An example of what Schirato and Webb would refer to as an 'arrested image' from the animated short* Presto *(Doug Sweetland 2008).*

motion could not exist if the single image were allowed undue recognition; at the same time, it could not exist without this fundamental base of differing images. For Tom Gunning: The single image contains only 'the possibility of motion' and 'the wonder triggered by animation comes from its pivot from stillness to motion'.[45] And yet as will be discussed further, in some cases, animation might not be as effective without the implied movement found within its constituent single images.

Philosopher Dorothy Emmet describes how a colleague once misread process philosophy as being about 'just one damn event after another'; instead, she clarifies, the concern is with the 'difference between processes, facts and events or just things changing'.[46] Similarly for animator Norman McLaren, animation is not about 'one damn image after another' but is concerned with what 'lie[s] between frames' ..., it is the interstices between the frames which generate the animation effect.[47] These interstices are never actually imaged by the animator, yet one must be aware of them. One must comprehend the implied movement of each frame, and consider *how* and to *what degree* it will become absorbed into the greater sequence of images. In a sense, one must envisage the Bragaglian 'visible wake' of implied movement within each frame, even though it always remains virtual and, ultimately, is always changed when combined with the other images.

It is pertinent to reflect upon Deleuze's ideas of difference and repetition as a way of considering how a single animated frame-image relates to a greater sequence of images. In *Difference and Repetition,* Deleuze considers how the general ideas of these two contrasting concepts ('difference' and 'repetition') actually reveal a substantial degree of overlapping commonality. Quite simply, we look for differences in repetitive patterns of images, and we look for repetitions and commonalities in unique images. But within each concrete example of difference or of repetition, there are larger enveloping concerns. Deleuze reflects upon this expanded concept of difference, one that thinks beyond that which might exist between two objects: 'Every object, every thing, must see its own identity swallowed up in difference, each being no more than a difference between differences.'[48] *Difference* and 'repetition' are essentially opposing terms, yet by linking them together in his discussion with the conjunction 'and', Deleuze is reiterating his worldview of an *inclusive disjunction* – an overlapping concept containing the many opposing, yet similar, qualities of opposing perceptions. Mullarkey, in fact, sums up Deleuze's overall philosophical approach as an *inclusive disjunction* 'between and/or'.[49] Although Deleuze does not apply these perceptions directly to animation, his discussions are relevant to a dialogue pertaining to the imagery of animation, particularly in regard to the contrasting notions of 'full' and 'limited' animation. As Furniss explains, 'In true full animation, every drawing in a production is used only once.' Additionally, full animation requires that the animation be shot on 'ones'; that is, each frame contains a unique drawing, different from the last frame. Limited animation, on the other hand may be constructed of anything less than this, with varying degrees of repeated drawings.[50] To put it in more Deleuzian terms, full animation tends towards *difference,* and limited animation tends towards *repetition.*

Movement is normally made apparent as the consequence of the difference *between* successive frames. The still image requires subsequent images to enable motion to become ostensive. On this level, animation and live action *can* describe movement in equivalency, but even here there can be remarkable variances between the construction of a strip of traditional film and a strip of filmed animation. It is in terms of the economy by which animation can achieve this effect of movement that is remarkable. In fact, animation requires only *two* uniquely fabricated images for movement to become visible. In traditional live action, each and every frame normally displays a difference to the next frame. There is rarely any demarcation from this succession of differences. However, it is quite common for many types of traditional animation to be shot on 'twos' (or more), thereby only every third frame displaying a difference, the previous two being a repetition of frames. Such an irregular patterning of differences and repetitions of image can affect the viewer's reception of the image and time. For example, three frames of the same image are then replaced by a new image followed by another repeat of that image, and then a change of image followed by two more repeats and so on. The result is a sequence of images which express an irregular patterning of difference and repetition.

A strip of traditional live-action film displays the normally minute differences from one frame to the next. In considering their uniqueness, these can be thought of as this image 'or' that image. When run together as a filmstrip, they become this image 'and' this image. Their *individual* differences are no longer apparent: they flow as a singular entity. It is this consideration of difference that, in the cinematic experience, is so important in understanding the nature of the frame as part of the whole. One image plus another image creates time and motion. A series of 'any-instant-whatevers' (the term that Deleuze uses to express each film frame's image) creates Deleuze's *movement-image*. For Deleuze, image and movement are one.[51] There is no 'or' in the resulting cinematic motion, either in its construction or in its playback for, as Deleuze notes, they are correlated. He comments on similarities of time in the filming and projection processes: 'the apparatus for shooting was combined with the apparatus for projection, endowed with a uniform abstract time'.[52]

In animation, however, this proposition becomes more complex since the form lacks the direct correlation between production and presentation. When making animation at the single frame level, there is an image 'or' another image. The difference is visible, intact in the production process – in fact, it is absolutely imperative that it be considered. These images are then placed together in succession and they become like all other cinema:

Deleuze's *movement-image*. The differences *appear* to be subsumed; the unique image becomes absorbed into the greater concept of difference. But in animation, the 'or' (the *difference*) always remains, and will often be observable (to varying degrees) at different moments. The more 'limited' the animation, the more we can see the difference (the 'or') between the images. With fuller animation, the 'or' tends to vanish. Generally, if there are more than three or four frames of repetition, the result will be a consciously perceptible individual image. However, this perception will also be heavily influenced by variance in the *animated movement* – that is how far an object appears to move from one image to the next. The more disparate the two sequential images (the 'or'), the more dramatic (full of perceived motion) becomes the 'and'. From this ensues either a more vigorous, more dramatic movement, or else greater lapses and condensations of time. However, as with the repetition of images, the process of animation places limitations on this exponential effect of motion. In Figure 1.7a, for example, the resulting animation is cinematic ('and') because the distance (difference) that the object appears to move from frame to frame is not greater than the size of the object. 'And' successfully subsumes 'or' as each image is 'swallowed up in difference'. In Figure 1.7b, however, the resulting animation is no longer cinematically smooth.[53] The distance (difference) is greater than the size of the object: thus, the object will appear to 'pop' from one place to another, causing the 'or' to display its prominence. In Figure 1.7c the animation is again made convincing by the addition of 'speed-lines'. Despite the distances (difference) being greater than the size of the object, the 'speed-lines' provide a visual bridge that maintains the illusion of a distance less than the size of the object. These symbolic representations of speed are similar to the coding of the graphic still image, particularly common in comics.[54] Yet in animation they also serve the utilitarian purpose of *smoothing out* the motion of limited animation by visually bridging vastly different images.[55] Thus, these examples suggest how the filmic 'and' is able to subsume the framic 'or'. And this uneasy compromise between 'and'/'or' helps to preserve a record of the animation process that is kept either just visible or just concealed from observation. It is a process that must simultaneously acknowledge the properties of both the still image and the moving image.

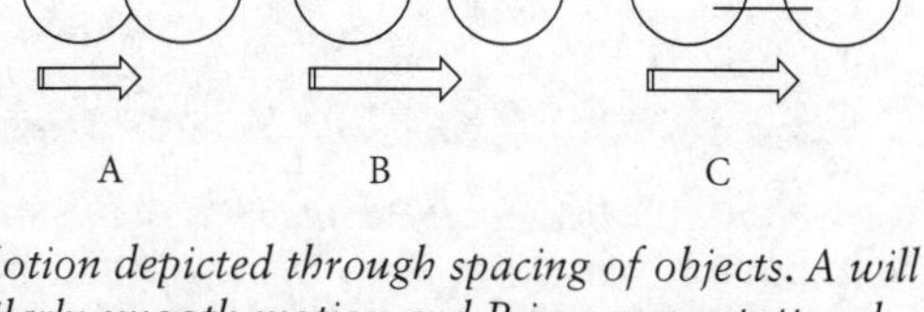

FIGURE 1.7 *Motion depicted through spacing of objects. A will result in smooth motion, C in similarly smooth motion and B in a more stuttered movement.*

There are a number of other methods by which the individual images of limited animation can be modified so that the overall movement of the sequence will appear to be more fluid – more fully animated. An exaggerated use of stretching or smearing is one potential strategy. For example, a figure that is shown leaping through the air can be stretched and elongated – serving not only to clarify the direction of the form, and define its velocity, but also to help associate the 'distances' between each drawing. This way, any noticeable spatial gaps between the positioning of the image-frames will be effectively smoothed out, and will help to obliterate the stuttering effect of limited animation. In some cases the figure can be made to stretch and distort into a noticeably smeared image as can be seen, for example, in many of the early episodes of the original *Astro Boy* television series (Tezuka Osamu 1963–1966). In Figure 1.8 Astro Boy can be seen flying through the air, and in some of the images his body (that is normally quite solid) literally oozes and smudges out behind him. Yet this technique is not limited to cel or drawn animation – it can also be found in many other approaches to animation, even in the very constructed and tangible form of puppet stop-motion animation. An interesting example of the smearing effect can be found in the stop-motion animated feature, *ParaNorman* (Chris

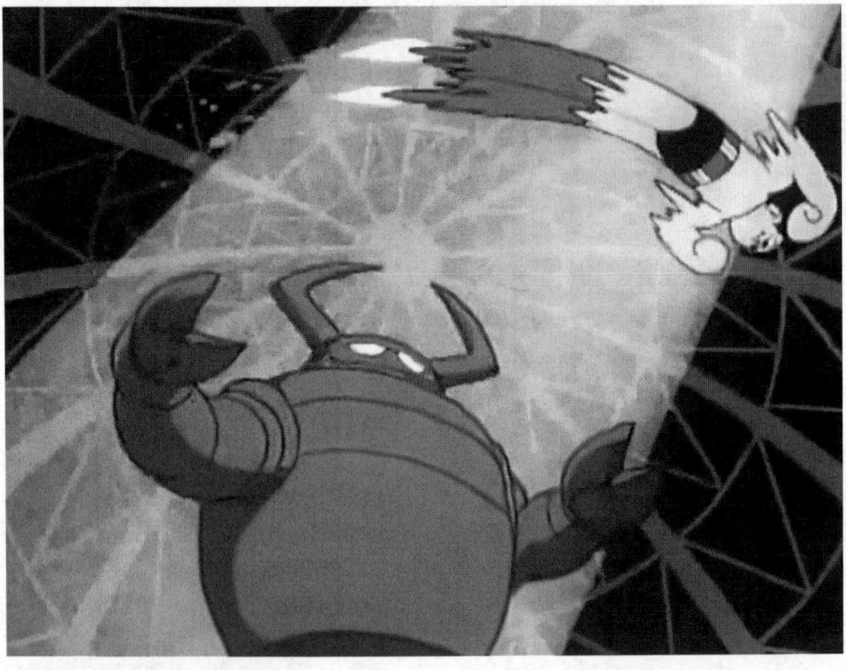

FIGURE 1.8 *Note the smeared lines on the flying character,* Astro Boy *(Tezuka Osamu 1963), which allowed for it to appear to zip across the screen in a very fluid manner.*

Butler, Sam Fell 2012). In this feature, the animators strove to create a very fluid and smooth animated effect – an aesthetic that is often lacking in stop-motion animation. In order to help achieve this, they employed frequent use of the replacement animation technique, so that rather than having to rely on manipulating the form to create squash and stretch or smear lines (as one could conceivably do with a clay model), they successively replaced parts of each puppet with modified elements as needed. For example, a series of increasingly smeared replacement heads were created and when used in succession allowed for the character to appear to zip across the screen in a very fluid manner. By using this technique as a method in stop-motion animation, the animators are essentially taking purely conceptual ideas (such as motion blur) that do not physically exist in the actual world and concretizing them through the process of animation. However, some optical motion blurring can be achieved within the traditional practice of stop-motion by slightly moving the puppet during the camera exposure. Ladislas Starewicz effectively pioneered this method in the production of some of his early stop-motion films in the 1920s. But it was brought to more popular attention when Industrial Light & Magic began using a similar process (which they dubbed, 'Go-Motion') for several of the stop-motion effect sequences in *Star Wars: The Empire Strikes Back* (George Lucas 1980) as well as in several other blockbuster feature films.

Animation and forms

Manipulated forms

The traditional stop-motion puppet is perhaps the most obvious example of the practice of *manipulated animation*. It normally involves a recognizable and stable form that is then made to move by incrementally repositioning it. Quite often these puppets will be constructed with internal armatures, which further define their stable form, yet allow for them to be 'moved'. Two-dimensional cut-out figures and even people (such as the pixilated animations of Norman McLaren or PES) are further familiar examples. Many instances of 3D digital animation, such as the features *Frozen* (Chris Buck and Jennifer Lee 2013) or *How to Train Your Dragon* (Dean DeBlois, Chris Sanders 2010), would also normally fall into this categorization. Even some examples of modern-day robotics can effortlessly be conceived as a physical expression of manipulated animation. Whereas in the past the conception of robots as animation might have seemed somewhat incongruous (imagine a stiff robot plodding along, powered by gears and pneumatic devices) yet, increasingly, the process of making robots move is merging with a very overt process of animation. For example, the Japanese roboticist, Tomotaka Takahashi, uses 3D animation software first to animate a virtual version of his robot; he then directly transfers this pure movement data into the robot itself. The result is a physical form that moves identically to the original animated form.

However, the manipulated animation image does not always require a stable object (such as a puppet, the arms and legs of which are easily moved around). Instead, it may be of an object which is in persistent flux. Lee Whitmore's film *Safe House* (2006) and Caroline Leaf's *The Street* (1976) are known as paint-on-glass films. In these, each scene is essentially a single oil painting created on a pane of glass; by smearing the existing paint, or by progressively applying additional paint to the image, the animator will gradually work and transform the image. The evolving image is then photographed at various moments in its progression. From the working perspective of the animator, it remains a single object, yet one of ceaseless transformation (see Figure 1.9). South African animator William Kentridge, who works primarily with charcoal on paper to create his animated works, often approaches animation in much the same way as the paint on glass animator. His works normally stem from a single image, usually charcoal on paper, which is progressively worked and photographed. At the end of the animation process, all that he is left with is a single charcoal drawing. There are no other replacement drawings, only replacement *stages* of the evolution of a drawing. Thus the animations will emanate from a single non-stable image, one that is ceaselessly in flux, whose becoming is captured at various important moments to produce the manifestation of this change. His animated works, such as *Felix in Exile* (1994) or *Automatic Writing* (2003), are primarily focused on the evolution of a single drawing.

> My technique begins with a sheet of paper stuck up on the studio wall. Halfway across the room is my camera, usually an old Bolex. A drawing is begun on the paper. I walk across to the camera, shoot one or two frames, walk back to the paper, continue and change the drawing (marginally), walk back to the camera, walk back to the paper, to the camera, and so on. So each sequence, as opposed to each frame of the film, is a single drawing.[56]

In one sequence of *Automatic Writing*, a procession of words and letters appear to write themselves, only to be overdrawn by an image of a rather banal domestic scene. Once this image is complete, ongoing transformative movements, sometimes isolated in small areas, remain visible. The entire image then becomes smeared and smudged as it is transformed into yet another scene.

For the process philosopher, this act of transformation of becoming something else is of primary importance. Whitehead claimed that 'the very essence of real actuality … is process … this process involves a physical

FIGURE 1.9 *Image from Lee Whitmore's* Safe House *(2006).*

side which is the perishing of the past as it transforms itself into a new creation'.[57] Manipulated stop-motion animation is a manifestation of this progression of ceaseless flux; as the image changes before our eyes it sheds its prior form, adopting a new one with each manipulated adjustment. For Deleuze, the process of *becoming* is an ongoing one that does not have a demarcated beginning and ending; 'a line of becoming has only a middle'.[58] It is quite impossible to specify a point of commencement or of completion within a process of ceaseless flux. Thus all things are continuously becoming *other,* and within this concept it becomes difficult to recognize any one *state*. The manipulated animation approach celebrates this fluidity, at once isolating and concretizing the processual nature of the image creation.

Replacement forms

Replacement animation is the method by which the animator substitutes each preceding image with an entirely new one. From this process of the amalgamation of disjointed imagery arises what could be regarded as an entirely new metaphysical form. In these cases, animation engages not only in a time-lapse process (where gaps of time are procured between each image) but also in a process of *object-lapse*. The image or object represented on screen is not a *single* entity, but the amalgamation of *many*, which together simulate a singular and enduring *animated form*. Although composed of many different images, they coalesce in the guise of the unified.

Animation, because of its discrete images and further manipulation of layers, can exploit the phenomenon of an unstable and space-shifting *metaphysical object*. In many occurrences of replacement animation the difference of each successive animation image may be quite subtle and the viewer will not normally recognize that it is, in fact, made of many different images. However, in the animated short film *Sisyphus* (Marcell Jankovics 1974), each new drawn image exhibits a radical difference. In addition to the varying poses of the character, the actual form and shape of the figure dramatically changes as well. Yet the final animated effect is one of relative consistency of appearance because the form of animation is able effectively to conflate dramatic differences in time and space into a temporal capsule of cohesion. Based on the myth of Sisyphus, the animation portrays a figure continuously pushing a large boulder up a very steep hill. His struggle is immense, but he perseveres, pushing and heaving the boulder throughout the duration of the film. The animation is rendered in a very loosely hand-drawn style. Each new drawing is only moderately based on the *form* of the previous drawing, revealing an obvious evidence of the disjointed construction of the images. And even though the character alters radically, it is read as being consistent because of the direct and progressive motion. Throughout the extreme struggle that he must endure in attempting to push the boulder up the hill, it is always the same Sisyphus (see Figure 1.10). *Sisyphus* demonstrates animation's remarkable propensity to exhibit motion's dominance over the replacement image. Thus, we can surmise that more dynamic motion will tend to absorb the animated replacement image – and contrastingly, more limited motion will tend to amplify the individual forms of the replacement animation process.

The replacement technique is also increasingly being used in 3D digital animation productions. For example, in *The Peanuts Movie* (Steve Martino 2015), replacement forms were used to create a more faithful interpretation of Charles M. Schulz's drawing style. As character development supervisor, Sabine Heller described:

> In the real world, the shape of a human's face doesn't change as they move from side to side, but that's not the way [Schulz] drew the characters, so in the world of Peanuts, when a character turns, the shape and positioning of their features change.[59]

Thus to create a head-turn (and the required head shape change) the animators would simply replace, for example, Charlie Brown's 'front-view' head with a 'side-view' head. The character of Snoopy required that there be six different model variations – depending on whether he was to be seen in profile, head-on or in more exaggerated poses.[60] Furthermore, each of the human figures shared the same body torso, and the directors would simply swap the limbs and heads around to create the various different

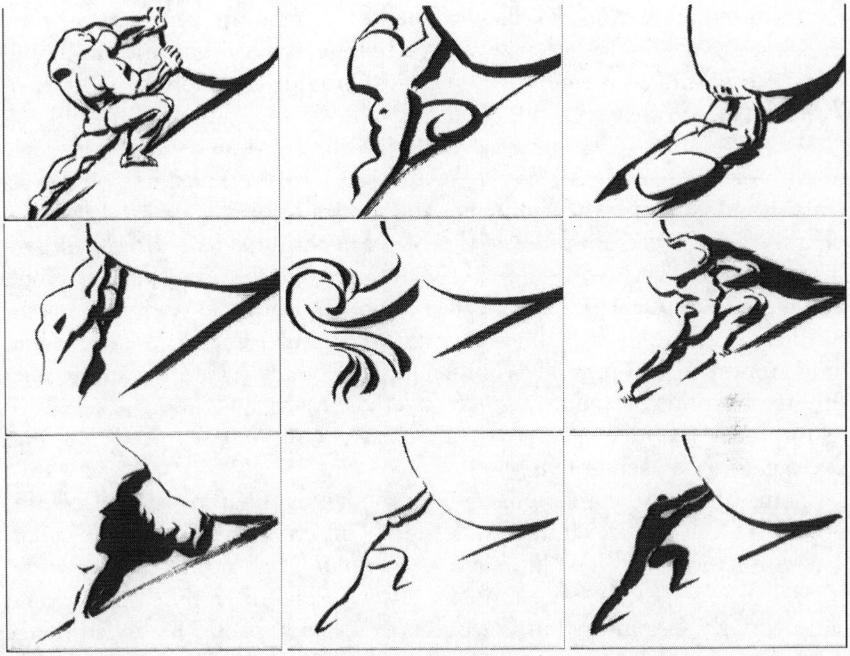

FIGURE 1.10 *Nine still frames (though not entirely sequential) from the animated short film* Sisyphus *by Marcell Jankovics (1974).*

characters and extreme poses. Because the producers aimed for a stop-motion aesthetic, the use of replacement animation actually facilitated a more traditional 'jittery' style. Furthermore, *The Peanuts Movie* was animated on 'twos' or 'doubles' (12-frames per second), which both helped to make the replacement technique work better (the moments where each replacement took place was less jarring) and at the same time added to the film's decidedly stop-motion aesthetic.

Boiling

'Boiling' is a term used to describe an animated effect in which the outlines or surfaces of an otherwise still character or object are made to frenetically wiggle or 'boil'. It is essentially a modification of the traditional method of *replacement* animation, but instead of creating multiple unique drawings, it is achieved by making several tracings from a single original drawing. In order to create the boiling effect, an original drawing is made and then a number of slightly inexact tracings (normally somewhere between three and eight) are prepared. These are then played back cyclically for as long as necessary and, depending upon how carefully the images are traced, the resulting animation will have either less or more quivering movement. There are two primary motivations for boiling, either to merely sustain an image (or part of an image) over time or to provide the impression of life or liveliness to an otherwise still image.

Winsor McCay's 1914 film, *Gertie the Dinosaur*, shows an early example of the boiling effect. As this was made prior to the invention of the cel animation technique, the characters and the backgrounds had to be drawn on the same layer. This meant that the background had to be redrawn (traced) onto every new drawing that depicted the dinosaur character moving. The result was a consistent background of rocks and trees on the one hand, and quivering lines on the other. More recently, independent animators such as Raimund Krumme, Kathy Rose, Bob Godfrey and Joanna Priestly have also produced single-layered drawn animation. These also feature background imagery that appears to boil as it is traced over and over again onto each drawing.

Quite often the contemporary independent animators have used this process as an economical means of adding 'life' to their drawn animations. Therefore, instead of having to actually *animate* the character into moving (that is to redraw it in a substantially different pose each time), they would simply make an almost (but not quite) exact copy of it. The boiled image materializes a unique dichotomy of movement *and* stillness. It can also subtly convey a sense of liveliness, in effect vivifying the immobile form. For example, it can simulate the act of breathing, imitating a very visible inhaling and exhaling cyclical action that can seem to encompass the entire form. Bill Plympton is one standout animator who has extensively used this strategy, particularly in some of his earlier pencil-drawn animations such as *25 Ways to Quit Smoking* (1989), *One of Those Days* (1988), *How to Kiss* (1989) and his feature film, *I Married a Strange Person* (1998). For example, in *25 Ways to Quit Smoking*, we see numerous instances in which a character is made to boil as it stands (otherwise still) in the frame. This character is at once motionless and full of effervescent life. In this case, the boiling effect serves to draw attention to and compound the humorous effect of the rather lengthy pause as the character is seen to be waiting and waiting in anticipation of some over-the-top animated antic to occur.

The American television series *Dr Katz: Professional Therapist* (1995–2000) also used the boiling technique quite effectively, essentially to create an animated series composed of almost nothing more than traced-over still images (thus with quivering 'animated' lines). The producers of the show developed a digital drawing process which they trademarked as Squigglevision™. The following is a summary of the original process:

> An artist creates a still image and it is manually traced four times, resulting in a total of five very similar versions of the same image. While these five versions are quite similar, there are, in fact, slight random

> differences between each of the five images as a result of the manual tracing process. Each of the five images is then pasted on to identical copies of a background image. Then, these five images are displayed sequentially in successive video frames in a repeating sequence.[61]

Later they patented an automated version of this process in which computer software would automatically 'boil' the edge lines (see Figure 1.11).

Of course, the reason that an image appears to boil is because each tracing is slightly different. However, if one were to compare the original image and its tracings side-by-side, they would all look virtually identical, but when they are subjected to the animation process, their minute differences become fundamentally apparent. This type of animation can be very successful in revealing the differences that are inherent within the seemingly repetitive image (an idea that will be discussed further in Chapter 6). Deleuze states that 'Difference lies between two repetitions.'[62] When this concept is applied to the animated boil, it too can reveal that each repetitive tracing is actually a unique event that can overtly foreground the construction process in animation.

FIGURE 1.11 *Image from* Dr Katz: Professional Therapist *(1995–2000), an animated television series that extensively and almost exclusively uses the boiling technique.*

When and where animation 'first began' has been the subject of many discussions within animation studies. And since animation comprises a great many different production methods, one of the difficulties of this debate is that its origins might arguably stem from varying sources depending upon which animation technique is being considered. However, many have traced the roots of drawn animation back to the ancient cave paintings of Lascaux.[63] These paintings, in particular, seem to imply movement within the depicted figures. Some of these figures, for example, are shown with extra limbs in various positions of locomotion, which can imply an accurate sense of movement. However, in terms of the *process* of creating the animated boil, perhaps a more direct linkage can be found in the ancient, and still practised, rock art of the Australian Aborigines. What is most remarkable about these is that some of the images (particularly those in central Australia) have been repeatedly traced over with the same image during a period of hundreds (or thousands) of years as a means of revitalizing the image.[64] They do not simply present a single image or archaeological artefact but are, by contrast, *enduring* images which have been continuously updated. A single image would of course fade and degrade over time – but a continually redrawn figure will endure from year to year and from generation to generation. Intriguingly, each redrawing will at the very least exhibit subtle differences that indicate the current drawing event (the particular qualities of the current artist, the materials used and the general environmental conditions at the time), placing it unquestionably within a particular moment in time. This continual updating serves to contemporarily recontextualize and reify the drawings of the rock art, enabling them not only to last *over* time but also to persist *through* time. In drawn animation, one artist would normally perform the tracing process over a relatively short term (a few minutes, perhaps an hour). In the case of the indigenous Australians, there would perhaps be many different artists tracing over the images across a span of countless years. Yet, similar to the animated boiling process, there would inevitably be significant differentiation between the drawings so that, if they were to be treated as animation (being photographed and projected as a time-based sequence), they too would appear to incorporate significant motion and undulating line work.

A boiling image is a sustained form that is comprised of competing, yet unified notions of difference and repetition. Boiling not only provides a visible and concrete application of Deleuze's idea that difference can be found within repetition but also presents us with a vibrant construct of the dynamic *being-state* of the form. In this amalgamation the individual images, though present, become nullified and then transformed as components of a persistent and dynamic animated image. Furthermore, boiling presents an animated form, expressing mobility, yet always tethered to its place of origin – it does not normally appear to move or translate from one place to another, yet it is full of movement. It is a unique dialectical form, alive

FIGURE 1.12 *Images from* Furniture Poetry and Other Rhymes for the Camera *(Paul Bush 1999).*

yet sedentary, moving yet immobile: a form or character on one hand but, more importantly, it is always a grouping of nearly identical images. Boiling is not entirely limited to the use of replacement drawings – a variation of it can also be achieved through the replacement of stop-motion objects. For example, Paul Bush's *Furniture Poetry* was created by sequentially replacing similar items of furniture, tableware and everyday objects (see Figure 1.12). For example, in one scene he replaces a succession of similar, but differently styled, armchairs; the result is an undulating real-world form. Though the rest of the scene is completely devoid of movement, the 'one chair' expresses a surging and flickering degree of liveliness.

Animated layers

Nicholas Rescher notes in *Process Metaphysics* that 'The idea of discrete [things] dissolves into a manifold of processes which themselves dissolve into further processes.'[65] This particular view of process is in some ways a re-assessment of the Whiteheadian idea of process 'atomism' in which every object or event could be broken down to a smallest unit (an atom equivalent).[66] Whitehead was a product of his time (1861–1947): today it is conceivable that matter can exist in units smaller than the atom.[67] If we can consider everything to be an assemblage of smaller and smaller processes, correspondingly it would appear to be erroneous to consider the frame as the smallest unit in the animated movie, just as it is overly simplistic to suggest that the view through one's window is a singular entity. Obviously the view is composed of many elements: trees (made up of leaves, branches), houses (made up of roofs, chimneys, walls), cars (made up of engines, wheels, doors).

The frame as the smallest unit is perhaps the result of the predominantly textual reading of traditional film. Films are dissected into scenes and shots, and (in some rare cases) frames. The smallest unit the viewer can 'see' in the final cinematic product (the reel of film) is the frame. Certainly elements within the frame are considered, for example composition, cinematography and mise en scene[68]; but it could be argued that these are essentially 'supra-frame' elements, that is elements that make up the larger shot, not necessarily the single frame or image. Deleuze, also considered the frame, the *any-instant-whatever*, as the 'atomic' unit of cinema, and all of his other conceptions (for example the *perception-image,* the *action-image* and the *affection-image*)[69] can be thought of as supra-frame elements, for they are more concerned with broader considerations of the viewer's experience rather than with a processual consideration of the single frame.

Live-action production has, of course, engaged traditionally with animation processes (for example, travelling matts and optical printing processes) in which the frame then becomes an amalgamation of layers or sub-frame elements. Importantly, contemporary digital movie-making has, in many instances, become very much akin to animation-making through the seamless use of digital visual effects and the inclusion of various constituent animated elements. The construction of many forms of animation dictates an assemblage process. Each animated image can be (and usually is) an amalgamation of many sub-frame elements that, at the very least, separate character from background. In his discussion of editing, Sergai Eisenstein spoke of a 'polyphonic montage' and a 'vertical montage' in which,

> the simultaneous movement of a number of motifs advances through a succession of sequences, each motif having its own rate of compositional progression, while being at the same time inseparable from the overall compositional progression as a whole.[70]

Here, Eisenstein is referring principally to the coordination of multiple visual elements that exist within the live-action scene, all of which would have been captured at the same moment with the same camera. His discussion of any degree of postproduction vertical layering is quite limited – for example two superimposed layers of film in an optical printer. Of course, writing in 1938, Eisenstein would have been aware of the layering process inherent in cel animation; however, his writings seem to reflect the division between the production processes of animation and of traditional live-action film-making. At that time, live action did not lend itself to the literal layering process of animation; therefore, Eisenstein considered the layering of cinema in more conceptual terms. In later writings he does refer to the work of Disney,[71] but still does not fully equate his discussion of the polyphonic montage to the essentially limitless possibilities of a literal vertical montage and layering of distinctive elements that is afforded to animation.

The animation process readily encourages the separation of the animation frame into multiple independent layers (or sub-frames), a process that was exploited with the advent of the cel animation process, but that in actuality can be traced back to some of the pre-cinematic animation devices.

The thaumatrope, for example, utilized two distinct images that, when manipulated, appeared to composite into one.[72] When correctly operated, the thaumatrope would provide a convincing single image; but more often than not it emphasized one or other of the images, which not only kept the viewer continually aware of its conflictive construction but also allowed for new readings of each of the images. Another early example was the magic lantern. Some lanterns had two or more inbuilt slide projectors that allowed for the layered projection of multiple images, referred to as the biunial (two in one) lantern or the triunial (three in one).[73] Additionally, some of the slides contained multiple glass layers that could be manipulated independently, either by 'slipping' a glass slide over another (slipper slides) or by turning a mechanical crank that would move the elements independent of each other as they were projected onto the screen.

Later, the cel animation process facilitated a very complex layering of images. 'The crucial aspect', writes Thompson, 'of cel animation is its separation of the different foreground and background layers'.[74] The process of layered cel animation was invented by Earl Hurd and John Bray in 1915; its use reached a new milestone in 1937 with the debut of Disney's multiplane camera system used in the production of the animated short, *The Old Mill* (Wilfred Jackson 1937). As production processes advanced, the characters themselves were often further 'slashed' into many distinctive parts; thus, only the essential portions of a character would require movement. This mechanism was fully exploited in more 'limited animation', as prominently expressed in Hanna-Barbera's television series, *The Flintstones* (1960–66), which can be considered in terms of its proficient use of this technique as a means of cutting costs, while at the same time forging a distinctive and dynamic aesthetic that worked well with the studio's designs.[75]

For Thomas Lamarre, these multiple layers of the cel animation image are one of its most significant aspects. He extends Norman MacLaren's conception of the significance of 'the interstices between frames' and instead suggests that 'the invisible interstices between layers'[76] is of even greater importance. For not only does this allow for a complexity of image, but more importantly, it also allows for a complexity (and potentially singularity) of movement.

> Compositing is what makes for a sense of the coherence of the image under conditions of movement in animation. It is a question of what kind of 'body' will emerge or, more precisely, what sort of sensorimotor schema will serve to harness and channel the force of the moving image.[77]

However, the idea of layering in animation can go deeper than the easily demarcated layers of the animation cel (or even the individual elements used in the digitally composited image). For example, the cel animation process required separate production tasks that effectively split the form (the character mass) from its outline, and from its colour and texture. The drawings would be outlined onto the cel (either by ink or photocopying); paint would then be applied to the reverse side providing the form with mass and colour. Occasionally, painted highlights or textures would be painted on top of the cel (creating an overlay on top of the primary paint).

An equivalent separation process also occurs frequently in 3D digital animation. For example, a character is modelled – which defines its form – and is then rigged with a skeletal support structure. This form is given a surface, then a colour, finally a texture. Atmospheric conditions may be added, such as lights, which can further dramatically alter the appearance of the previous layers. Compositing is then used to further layer the images.[78] The more cinematic stop-motion animation, that which involves dimensional objects and is shot in real spaces (*Wallace and Gromit*, *Gumby*), does not traditionally involve the clearly segmented sub-frame element (as does the cel layering system); yet by analogy it, too, involves layered elements. The animator will still need to manipulate various elements independently within each frame; for example each character (and even each appendage) that is visible in the frame will require isolated consideration by the animators.

It is significant to note that this process of layering is not limited to conceptions of the image per se; it can also be considered in terms of motion. As noted previously, movement should be considered as a 'layer' within the animated form, and furthermore, this layer of movement can be thought of as a composite of many sub-layers of movement. Particularly in the 3D animation process, it is very easy, not only to add layers of imagery, but also layers of action/animation. Thus, one can animate someone drinking a cup of tea, and then very easily add in another layer of motion – wiggling their ears – while engaged in the action of drinking the tea, with no affect on their primary actions.

Animation and time

Production time

According to some discussions of narrative theory, time may be considered in terms of both narrative time (the amount of time that is spanned in a story) and discourse time (the amount of time it takes to experience the story through reading or watching it unfold).[79] To this, and particularly when considering animation, we could add 'production time'. An important and often recurring characteristic of the animation process is that it can take an unbalanced amount of time to create an image as compared to the length of time it would normally take to view it. By contrast, film in its most pure, unedited state can exhibit an equivalence of viewing time to production time.

In traditional live-action cinema each frame is an instant, snatched from time, in real sequential time.[80] However, animation's construction process can often involve the creation and the detailed appraisal of each image component, yet the average viewing time might be as brief as a twenty-fourth of a second. Even in the most extreme examples of limited animation, where a ten-second sequence might be composed of only two unique images, it would quite likely have taken the animator in excess of five seconds of production time to create each of the distinct images.[81] Of course there are many different approaches to animation, but in terms of purely drawn animation, Birgitta Hosea remarks:

> A sequence of drawings played back consecutively in the form of an animation has duration, yet single drawings, taken on their own out of sequence, also record the time that was taken in their creation. The making of a drawing is a time-based activity and a complex drawing may take hours to complete.[82]

If we were to further consider traditional cel animation, not only the drawing, but also the transfer to cel, the painting process, the layering and photographic process on the animation stand, all might account for an even greater amount of production time. If we consider a 3D-animated production such as *Rattatouille* (Brad Bird and Jan Pinkava 2007), the figures and forms would have first been modelled and rigged, then textured and lit – and later, of course, animated, which was for the most part done in a key-framed manner. And, because of its complexity, there is a very good chance that each 'frame' will actually include multiple key positions (one for the left eye lid, one for the mouth, one for the right arm, etc.). And to top it off, the studios have publicized that it took on average nineteen hours to simply render each frame, not including additional time spent on compositing additional layers to further enhance each sequence. In another example (and using a totally different technique), Darcy Prendergast's films *Lucky* (2009) and *Rippled* (2011) both utilize long-exposure photographs to create streaks of stop-motion animated light which take the form of characters.[83] In these productions, the photographed image took much longer to 'create' than it takes to play it back. In fact, the exposure of the photograph will normally last for several seconds while it would take approximately a twelfth of a second to view it in an animated sequence (see Figure 1.13). In these cases, and echoing Hosea's above assertion, each photograph clearly describes a profound 'compression' of time.

This consideration is quite different, however, to the more basic time-lapse photography. Pure time-lapse photography embodies a very marginal process of animation since, although it produces a manipulated

FIGURE 1.13 *Images from* Rippled *(Darcy Prendergast 2011).*

representation of time, its approach involves the selective snatching of instances from time, generally as evenly spaced photographed instances. Thus the accelerated view of the opening of a flower would normally represent a proportional relation to narrative time (one second = one hour). Additionally, each instance is not *constructed or manipulated* but is *selected* in a time-bound manner. Each frame is an instant taken out of time, *in real time.* It may take a twenty-fourth of a second to 'make' a frame, and a twenty-fourth of a second to play it back.[84] The only distinction time lapse may have from traditional live action is that of containing much larger gaps of time *between* each recorded instance. What most approaches to time-lapse photography also avoid is a direct manipulation of forms or spaces to create movement. Therefore, not only does animation often contain gaps in time from one image to the next; it also involves lapses in space (if it is manipulated animation) and lapses in objects or images (if it is replacement animation).

Similarly, animation can present a complex heterogeneity of time. Time cannot only be sped up or slowed down: it can be manipulated in an asymmetrical manner. And, because animation is not normally bound to a linearity of time from image to image, complex anachronistic qualities can be made perceptible. When Deleuze asserts that 'Time is necessarily an indirect representation, because it flows from the montage which links one movement-image to another',[85] he neglects to take into account some of the processes of animation. Animation does not necessarily depend upon the full cut of montage to divide one movement-image from another. This can occur *within* the movement-image. Time, in animation, is additionally signified by each occasion upon which the image changes – which may be every frame, every three frames or every thirty-seven. Thus, this disjunction of time and image permits a far more egalitarian collaboration: it does not unquestionably permit itself to be subsumed by time.

In *Cinema 2*, Deleuze argues that when the motion that is presented is 'normal' or coherent, then the resulting *motion-image* will be bound to time. But when the motion becomes distorted, then the image will dominate and manipulate time. 'If normal movement subordinates the time of which it gives us an indirect representation, aberrant movement speaks up for an anteriority of time that it presents on the basis of the disproportion of scales, the dissipation of centres and the false continuity of the images themselves.'[86] Because animation does not necessarily attempt to depict 'normal' movement – its motion, in fact, is often deliberately distorted – and frequently makes us very conscious of time. But when shot on 'fours' or more, we actually *see* the segmentation of imagery and in a sense the representation of time, an effect that is normally only visible as a jump-cut in traditional recorded footage. However, it is an important aesthetic in a lot of anime, seen even in the somewhat 'westernised' *Spirited Away* feature where, particularly in 'long-shots', the characters visibly 'stutter' as they walk across the screen. Quite a different effect is often achieved when producing 3D digital animation. In productions in which very few key frames are used, the software will automatically formulate the time to motion ratio into either a linear or a bell-shaped curve, and *then* evenly segment this into divisions of time. This will often result in a most noticeable distortion of movement and likely a skewed perception of time.

Additionally, animation normally represents an anachronistic process – that is it can be made from many disjointed bits of time, a condition that George Griffin refers to as 'synthetic time':

> synthetic time is meant to suggest the artifice of animation in contrast to the essential documentative process of cinema, which records and plays back real time events. Using myriad techniques animators piece together sequences of discrete images or objects to build either an imitation of continuous motion or an indifference to continuous motion based on strategies of discontinuity. In either case, the result is not a record of an actual performance.[87]

When the animator takes a series of independently constructed replacement images or objects and strings them together to make an animation, he or she is creating a new sequence of time composed of images from a separate time context. These individual images contain a particular time context; when amalgamated with others, this contextual time is absorbed and a new time emerges. Thus an animated film may, within one scene, contain drawings or images that were made last week, as well as some that were made last year; or it may contain motion-capture data that was recorded several years ago and applied to a digital model made last week.

The temporal interstice of change

Norman McLaren asserted, 'What happens between each frame is much more important than what exists on each frame.'[88] That is, it is the difference between the frames that generates *movement*. But for this effect to occur, it has to be acknowledged that the space between the frames also embodies time. For, as Whitehead suggests, process (or change) *requires* time. Dorothy Emmet in her text, *The Passage of Nature,* provides two illustrative figures (which are transcribed here, see Figure 1.14) which help to elucidate this concept. With the aid of these diagrams she argues that oppositional states do not just 'happen' but must embody time for the change or transformation to occur. Figure 1.14 (the grouping on the left) shows that a division can be made between two different states (A and B), and such a cut 'would have to be made where some change was occurring' (A'B'). 'This change A'B' could then', she continues, 'be seen as another event, having duration'.[89] Thus to visualize this, one would need to allow for a space between A' and B' (see Figure 1.14, right).

If it could be said that all embodiments of flux must also have duration, then we could apply this concept to the moving image: the interstices between the filmic frames must also have a screening duration. First, there must always be a temporal gap (however small in comparison) between the two images. Second, it could be said that the combination of the two images, along with their common liminal space, is able to generate a further suggestion of time. As Tom Gunning notes in 'The Cinema of Attractions', 'The difference between two things is, at the same time, the sum total of the two.'[90] When consciously working in a frame-by-frame methodology, the animator is also creating gaps of time – it is within those gaps of time that the pure movement data is in effect sequestered. Further to this, and to borrow the terminology of Deleuze, if every film frame is an 'any-instant-whatever', then between every 'any-instant-whatever' there is an *any-interstice-whatever.*

Most would argue that time is generally syncategoremic: that is it only makes sense in conjunction with the form/event that it is bound to. To remove such an affiliation and to reconnect time to a different form/event would conceivably alter the meaning of the duration entirely. Yet, like movement, time, at least to some degree, can be independently considered. According to Bergson, time ('duree') is a discreet aspect in and of itself; it is 'succession without distinction'.[91] In *Creative Evolution,* he claims that duration is 'immanent to the universe'; it is by extension the essence of everything.[92] And, it is from this *pure duration* that events ultimately transpire.[93] Whitehead takes a different approach to time to Bergson, instead claiming that it stems from *processes.*[94] Thus, without the initial process (or change),

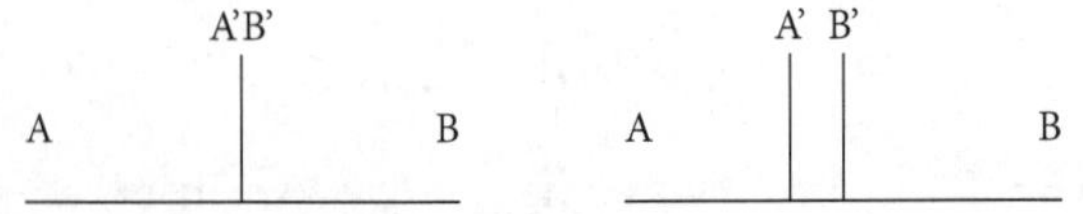

FIGURE 1.14 *Diagrams depicting the interstices of time derived from Dorothy Emmet (1992).*

in a sense time would cease. In *Cinema 2*, Deleuze echoes this sentiment when he asserts: 'Time is necessarily an indirect representation, because it flows from the montage which links one movement-image to another.'[95] When considered in relation to the animation process, the animator can certainly affect the representation of time in much the same manner that he or she can affect the imagery with movement.

Layers of time

Traditional live action and traditional frame-centric readings of animation suggest that the imagery is composed of one discreet frame following another. In this regard, the frame holds a fixed relation to time and motion: it is synchronously contained in the Deleuze's *motion-image* and *time-image*. In their essay 'The Illusion of Illusion', Keith Broadfoot and Rex Butler echo this notion that the frame both composes and binds time:

> if time is defined as a kind of succession or succession as a kind of time, for a moment to appear, the moment prior to it must disappear; there can never be two moments at once. But that first moment must wait for the second to appear before it can disappear. It can disappear, in other words, only in time. But precisely time itself, the succession of time, is only possible because of this disappearance.[96]

And although this is a sound reading of how the cinematic presentation of moving images can describe time, it could also be argued that, in terms of process, the sub-frame (or layer) defines another succession of time. Actual events take a specific time to unfold. Bergson argued that time is 'what prevents everything from being present all at once'.[97] However, because animation is an additive process, many subsequent layers can be added – each possessing its own duration and speed, each providing us different conceptions of each particular event. Thus the assemblage process of animation dictates that, not only is there the ability to construct the frame at the equivalent of the sub-frame level, but also that each sub-frame element can interact with time and with motion in a distinctive and carefully controlled manner. In this manner, time can be regarded independently, and animation also allows for the representation of multiple layers of time. As noted previously, many early animated television series exploited the layering of animation as a cost/time saving approach. For example, a scene may feature the main character from *Speed Racer* moving and talking in front of a motionless crowd of people; after he has finished speaking he may 'freeze', while two or three arms from members of the crowd might wave about (accompanied by an audible cheer). Not only does this increase the efficiency of animation production but an enormous amount of freedom is also afforded with the ability to individually manipulate certain elements, allowing for independent timing structures within the overall time structure of the animation.

Even when an animation does not overtly require layering, a divergent layering of time can occur. For example, in stop-motion animated films that are made in open outdoor spaces (what can be referred to as landscape animation), they not only contain the animated movements which are created by the animator but often they also depict the incidental processes and movements of the natural world. Therefore landscape animation often presents us with a unique documentation of *time*. In fact, the amount of time that it actually took to create a scene can sometimes be revealed in the final animated film. We might for example see clouds racing across the sky, or shadows of buildings traversing quickly across the ground – authenticating that it indeed took several hours to create a particular shot. Remarkably, in *Big Bang Big Boom* (Blu 2010) there is a fifteen-second sequence where we can actually tell, if we look at the oscillating shadows, that it took him a full five days to complete the sequence. This conception of production time is often lost in the timelessness of many forms of animation, yet here we can on one hand see the very carefully animated stop-motion animation appearing to move in at a 'normal time and speed' while the rest of the world moves in a form of hyper-temporality.

From the viewer's perspective, however, such representations of time actually give us a notable duality of time. We see simultaneous representations of what could be referred to as *environment time* and *animation time*. Because of this distinction, landscape animation (see Chapter 7) actually subverts time by presenting animation as being part of the natural flow of time, and the natural world as adhering to an unnatural syncopation of time. This unique presentation of time is quite evident in Kirsten Lepore' animation, *Bottle* (2011). The stop-motion animation of *Bottle* takes place in two distinct environments – snow and sand. Through this manipulation of the existing environment two 'characters' are introduced, a snowman (made of snow) that resides in a frozen winter world of snow and ice, and a sandman (made of sand) that inhabits a more temperate sunlit beach. It is a tale of unrequited love, as the two characters, not only from, but also actually composed of very different environments, endeavour to meet each other. The sand and snow creatures and other animated elements appear to move in a very smooth and natural manner (animation time), while in contrast the real-world elements, such as the ripples and waves of the lake, appear frenetic and disconnected (environmental time). Similarly, Frank Budgen directed an animated commercial for Sony Bravia televisions (2009) which was shot in the middle of New York city involving hundreds of large clay rabbit figures as well as a massive eighty-foot stop-motion puppet. The advertisement was shot in an 'open set' and was witnessed and experienced by thousands

FIGURE 1.15 *Image from Frank Budgen's animated advertisement for Sony Bravia televisions.*

of people. In this advert as well, the 'animated' rabbits move and hop in a very fluid manner, while all the other naturally occurring elements (cars, people, clouds) appear to move in a very jittery manner and seem to be in contrast – very poorly animated (see Figure 1.15).

Animated sound

It should be noted that animation is traditionally a *silent cinema*. But for a few exceptions and the promise of future advances, the process of constructing animation is exclusively a visual endeavour. Deleuze distinguishes that silent cinema was both seen *and* read because of its use of the intertitle. While the image was direct and natural, the intertitled speech was indirect and stylized. With the advent of the talkies *directness* was brought to the speech-act.[98] The intertitle was a graphic (and sometimes animated) element, which was largely discarded with the advent of sound. It could be said that live action abandoned some of its animated processes upon the introduction of sound. Animation also employed the intertitle, and in many cases it actually integrated the written dialogue directly into the animated image, utilizing the speech balloon (and graphic onomatopoeia), which it borrowed from the newspaper-comic image (see Figure 1.16). With the advent of sound, the alien *non-animated* soundtrack was imposed upon animation. At this point, animation, for the most part, transformed into an intertextual hybrid of recorded sound and crafted image.

FIGURE 1.16 *Images from* Mr. Nobody Holme – He Buys a Jitney *(1916), depicting imbedded text.*

As discussed earlier in relation to animation and movement, animation normally must consider image and movement asynchronously: as separate processes. By contrast, the processes of live-action film-making are able to consider image and motion contiguously. Similarly, animation has also to deal separately with auditory and visual elements, while live action has the option to record sound either synchronously or asynchronously. Normally it is only in the final animated form that the sound and image will become reconciled. This dictates the standardized process by which the majority of dialogue-focused animation is produced. First the dialogue is recorded: this in turn dictates the animated visuals.[99] As Maureen Furniss notes, the advantage of such an approach provides 'the ability to achieve greater synchronization of lip movements to dialogue and the ability to use voice tracks for inspiration in character design and movement'.[100] Thus, it is the audio track that, in effect, drives the animation of the animated character – a succession that dramatically inverts the natural sound and motion process of the natural world. If we, as humans, wish to make a sound, we have to first use our body to generate that sound. The sound is subservient to the movements of our bodies. We might clap our hands together: a sound emanates as a result of this action. When we speak, we have to first move our muscles, generating airflow against our vocal cords; again the actions generate sound. The way in which we move the rest of our body while making those sounds also has an effect on the ultimate aggregate of sound. If you are jumping up and down while speaking the voice will have, at the very least, a noticeable quiver.

Such natural phenomena have comprised the impetus for the many sound-producing machines – for example the music box, where the process of motion is required to generate sound. Early music boxes 'consisted of a barrel [or later a disc] arranged with projections conforming to the notes to be sounded'. As the barrel or disc spun around it would 'pluck the teeth of a tuned steel comb and so play a tune'.[101] Although such constructed objects have emulated a natural process of sound generation, the constructed object of animation requires a decidedly divergent approach. Having been grounded in the animation process, it was a logical progression by which Walt Disney developed the concept of 'audio animatronics'. In their production, first the audio was recorded (the standard animation production process); the movements of the characters were then directed and conducted by the audio recording. The audio-animatronics device goes a step further in that it also used audio impulses (which were not audible to the viewer) quite literally to trigger and drive the physical machinery of the characters.[102] These were automatons which had inverted the natural ordering of sound and motion, instead embracing a physical manifestation of the filmic animation process.

Michel Chion describes the traditional live-action relationship between audio and visual as a 'simultaneous vertical relationship with narrative elements contained in the image (characters, actions) and visual elements of texture and setting'.[103] For Chion, sound and image are normally bound in an equilibrant relationship. However, in animation, sound (specifically dialogue) normally finds itself in a very non-egalitarian coupling with animation; the audio clearly commands the visual. Such a conception is perhaps an apt expression of how animation might echo process philosophy's claim that 'what exists in nature is not just originated and sustained by processes, but is in fact ongoingly and inexorably *characterized* by them'.[104] In many cases, it is the soundtrack's guiding processes which define every nuance of the visual artefact. This is exemplified by Disney's early use of sound, in which the visuals were so carefully choreographed to the musical scores that they inspired the (somewhat derogatory) term 'Mickey-Mousing' to describe this close link between image and audio.[105] The widespread use of lip-synching in animation is, of course, a prime example of this relationship, where every syllable of dialogue can directly affect the movement of a character's mouth (and further influence the character's bodily actions).

Further examples of intensive speech to image relationships can be found in the animated documentary *I Met the Walrus* (Raskin 2007), where every word of the interviewee, John Lennon, is taken to extraordinarily literal levels. In one scene, John Lennon's voice recording, though spoken in gentle conversational tones, takes total command of the visuals as he says, 'I'm anti-war, so they try to keep me out.' This vocal direction conveys such visualized force that an enormous wall is instantaneously erected, which subsequently knocks back his animated form (see Figure 1.17a). Moments later his voice asserts, 'But I'll get in', and immediately a previously invisible door opens in the wall and his character is propelled through the hole with immense force (see Figure 1.17b). The visible differences between Figures 1.17a and 1.17b are entirely the result of the kinetic force that is thrust upon the imagery by the audio track. With these examples in mind, it could be claimed that from the epicentre of the aural radiates a *processual structuring* of the animated image. In effect, sound can animate the animation.

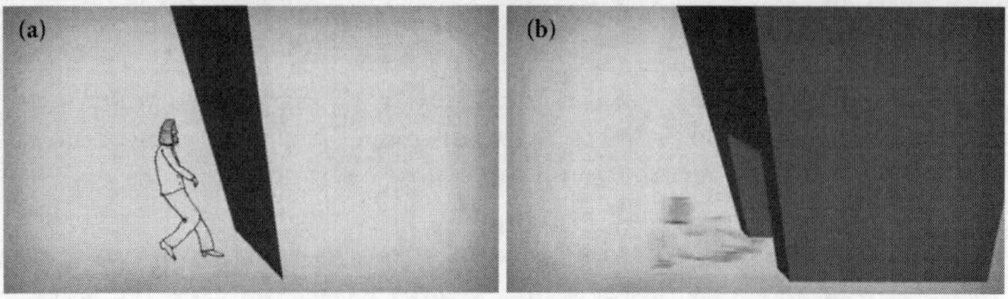

FIGURE 1.17 *Images from the animated short* I Met the Walrus *(Josh Raskin 2007). (a) John Lennon's character is blocked from entering by a protruding wall; (b) he is then propelled through a newly formed opening. All of these actions appear to be entirely driven by the audio track of the animated film.*

Abstraction and animation

Animation, in particular because of its construction process, encourages an abstraction; and it invariably provides a decontextualization of time, image and motion, making it quite removed from actuality. A great deal has been written about the aesthetics of animation, how its imagery tends towards the non-realistic.[106] Maureen Furniss claims that, in general, animation rejects the notion of *mimesis* in favour of *aesthesis*. She also proposes an animation continuum which extends from the 'abstract' to the 'mimetic', suggesting the placement of a number of key animated films within this scale.[107] Paul Wells iterates the abstract aspect of animation: in an attempt to differentiate between what he calls 'orthodox animation' and 'experimental animation', he advocates that more 'configured' animation belongs to the orthodox realm while more abstract animation belongs to the experimental realm.[108]

Such a spectrum becomes increasingly expansive when we consider the addition of *movement* in the animated film. Because of this, we can think of not only the imagery being abstract, but we can separately consider *movement* to be abstract and non-representational as well. For example, a human figure could be depicted very abstractly (made from simple shapes or dots), but still be made to walk and move in a very realistic and human-like manner. Or on the other hand, a human figure could be depicted photo-realistically, but made to move in a very non-representational or abstract manner – it could spin like a top, quiver like a bowl full of jelly or simply float across the screen. Animators who work with abstraction have the opportunity to consider and to manipulate both movement and imagery in unique and collaborative ways. In locating animation *away* from the aesthetic and towards the processive, the vital concept is that *all* animation tends towards the abstract – that is, in the *process of its construction*, all elements invariably become (1) simplified, (2) distorted and (3) decontextualized in form and/or movement.

The process of assembling animation often facilitates the *generalization* of the image and the motion. Walter Ruttmann (1887–1941) believed that the strength of abstract animation was that it could translate the real world into generalized arcs of movement and transformations, rather than getting tethered down with the depiction of intricate details.[109] This ultimately allows for a much broader (albeit less specified) consideration of the world. From a practical standpoint, even if the aspiration is there, it is nearly impossible to fabricate and emulate *every* realistic detail of image and motion in an animated form. Even in the case of the most advanced 3D image simulations *some* details of form must be omitted. In animation it is normally too onerous to render every nuance; and since such detail is unnecessary, therefore it is often avoidable; it is often the case that only the essentials *require* visualization in order to convey the desired essence. It can certainly be argued that by utilizing simplified lines, shapes and fewer blocks of colour, the animated image (particularly in the earlier cel animation process) saved enormous amounts in time and resources. The American UPA studio (*Gerald McBoing Boing*, 1951; *The Tell-Tale Heart*, 1953; *Mr. Magoo*, 1949–1959) and Tezuka Osamu's original *Astro Boy* (1963–1966) are prime examples of this. These productions also benefited from the simplification of motion. For example, the use of limited animation: the abundant use of cycles, and the fact that virtually all character movements take advantage of the omission of vast quantities of kinetic detail. Similarly, due to purely technological limitations, *some* motion data will not be recorded even in cases of the most sophisticated motion-capture facilities, and therefore will not be transcribed to what is the already simplified animation form.

There are, of course, motivating factors other than economy and technological limitations for the creation of simplified imagery and simplified motion in animation. These include issues of graphical design, clarity of communication and condensation of information, to name just a few. For example, UPA studios utilized an extreme simplification of imagery and motion for both reasons of economy *and* in seeking to bring to life the contemporary print graphics of the 1940s and 1950s.[110] It can be argued that animation does not necessitate the depiction of mimesis and, furthermore, that its narrative (and, as will be argued later) epistemic strength lies in its ability to reject the mimetic. William Moritz asserts that the only 'true animation' is abstract animation because it is within this realm that the genuine potential of animation can be realized.[111] Charles Solomon clarifies that this potential stems from the fact that the animator 'must imagine every aspect of the images and motion' and is therefore free from dependence upon real-life observations.[112]

Furthermore, animation also makes use of *distortion* in its process of abstraction. Distortion is a condition closely related to *simplification*: the act of whittling away detail ultimately creates a *distortion* of form and motion. For example, a 'smiley' face image is an obvious simplification of form (it is a highly generalized representation of a human face). Viewed from a different perspective, one could consider it to be a dramatic *distortion* of an actual human form (rather than merely a generalization). Yet *distortion* diverges from pure *simplification* when, for example, a highly realistic image of a human face is endowed with extraordinarily large eyes. Such an image would clearly be considered a *distortion* and furthermore, we may label it to be an *exaggeration* or *caricature* (two modes in which animation delights in). Similarly, a highly detailed naturalistic character would be considered to distort physical laws and movement if it were made to fly through the air or transform into other objects.

Even when animation does achieve a certain level of realistic effect, behind it often lies a vast amount of distortive processes: the traditional Disney ethos is testament to this fact. Veteran Disney animators Frank Thomas and Ollie Johnston, in their seminal text, *The Illusion of Life*, outline a number of Disney's strategies for the creation of convincing motion. By employing such procedures as 'squash-and-stretch' and 'overlapping action' one will invariably produce a more fluid motion, and therefore a more credible outcome.[113] It is paradoxical, however, that these processes dramatically distort the form of the character. It would appear that Disney recognized that radical distortion of the image was essential in order to edge it closer to his desire for the mimetic, for the animated image cannot avoid but *become* a form of abstraction even if its purpose appears otherwise.

In addition to *simplification* and *distortion*, another important transformative state, which can lead to the abstract, is *decontextualization*. When something is removed from its native context, abstraction ensues. From a process perspective, abstraction is inevitable in even the most mimetic examples of animation. Even in pixilation (the animating of actual persons and life-sized objects) the animation process inherently abstracts the *motion* of the figures that become 'animated'. Similarly with stop-motion, even though the final animation may provide all the details of the physically extant object of the puppet, the motion applied to it serves to challenge and therefore abstract the final product. Rescher argues that all processes removed from their context become abstractions, thus becoming freely transferable and repeatable.[114] Whitehead concurs that the abstract is that which is decontextualized, thus omitting the sensual experiences, which are 'an essential element in the life of nature'.[115] The general progression of animation is the removal from the concrete and the transformation to the virtual. In the process of animation, motion, objects and images are constructed out-of-context in a time-independent and, often, non-chronological manner, *and* are frequently amalgamations of many disparate elements which combine to create a wholly new construct. Thus in traditional cel animation numerous layers may make up the form of a character (for example, Astro Boy) which has been subsequently placed upon an independently constructed background. The result is, therefore, an *instinctive* abstraction composed of transferable processes (and elements) that have been stripped of their original circumstances. For Deleuze the recontextualized assemblage (an abstraction) is a vital aspect of becoming 'other'.[116] More conceptually, anthropomorphism (which will be discussed further in Chapter 4) is one commonly observable conclusion of the recontextualization process of animation, for the anthropomorphic character represents an assemblage of human and animal characteristics (both in image and motion).

Structuring abstract animation

Thus far it has been argued that all animation, whether intentional or not, possess certain characteristics that are aligned with the concept of abstraction. There are, of course, an enormous number of abstract animated films that are intentionally designed to be abstract. Certainly, for example, Oskar Fischinger did not just happen to make abstract films because the medium compelled him to. Len Lye also, without a doubt, aimed 'to create a sensual experience of pleasure generated through colour whose abstract and direct appeal avoided narrative forms and the kinds of associations that [he] believed plagued realistic imagery'.[117] In fact there are countless examples of abstract animation, and just a few of the more historically celebrated ones include *Rhythmus 21* (Hans Richter 1921), *Allegretto* (Oskar Fischinger 1936), *Dots* (Norman McLaren 1940), *Gumbasia* (Art Clokey 1955), *Two Space* (Larry Cuba 1977), *The Meadow* (Jules Engel 1994) and *The Dowager's Idyll* (Joan Gratz 2001).

Animation scholar Paul Wells has effectively outlined a number of narrative strategies that are unique to (or at least very applicable to) *non-abstract* animation. These strategies detail the many ways in which animation can effectively communicate its narrative information. However, it can be rather difficult to interpret the purely abstract animated film in terms of narrative, representation and other more tangible discussions. Wells has suggested that a consideration of the basic abstract imagery can be enough on its own to convey meaning:

> Primal forms may be read as an expression of their progress towards rational and associative forms, and may be understood by the narration which may be given to the division of space, the kinds of movement occurring within a particular context, and in relation to what may be termed the energy or suggestiveness of the line or shape itself.[118]

Taking inspiration from this, we can identify three key *movement strategies* that can be found in nearly all intentionally abstract animations, and represent an effective practical approach (in terms of motion) to creating and structuring abstract animation. These strategies are movement-centric in their approach; they do not, therefore, focus on the design of the image, but instead on the movement of the imagery. Furthermore, since these strategies are not concerned with the imagery of the animation per se, they can also be applied to abstract animations that none the less contain very identifiable imagery, as in a number of contemporary abstract stop-motion animated films. These three movement strategies can be identified as: *evolution*, *deconstruction* and *patterned movement*. What all three of these strategies have in common is that they encourage what Rescher suggests is the very essence of the abstract – a lack of 'specificity and concreteness' and an inherent resistance to 'individualization'.[119] Thus, these three approaches can be found in virtually every abstract animation and they all encourage a destabilization of identity and an emphasis on the indeterminate.

The strategy of *evolutionary* movement comprises all types of growth, change and metamorphosis. Thus when such movement is applied to forms, they may become bigger or smaller, they might change shape or perhaps completely transmute in shape, colour, texture and overall quality. This approach can create a very dynamic presentation that can effectively substitute traditional considerations of narrative: it is a staple of nearly every abstract animation. Such developmental movement can also shift the emphasis away from particular forms or recognizable characters and instead highlight the process of change itself. In many ways, the aforementioned animated short *Love & Theft* (Andreas Hykade 2010), though made up primarily of identifiable figures, has many of the hallmarks of an abstract film. In this movie, the forms continually morph and change at such an intense rate that the viewer is not permitted the opportunity to become accustomed to any one of them and must simply absorb the instability.

The strategy of *deconstructive* movement is partially related to evolutionary movement as it involves forms changing; however, rather than the more organic movement that the term 'evolution' suggests, this aspect tends to exemplify the breaking apart and the process of elemental construction. It might involve larger structures that visibly break apart or crumble to reveal their constituent parts. Alternatively, smaller elements might cluster together to build larger forms. In this manner, the larger forms are revealed to be rather unstable both in form and in identity – further edging it towards the abstract. Optical flickering can also be used as a means by which to destabilize the form – this can be achieved, for example, by removing the image (or object) from view during every odd numbered frame, and then replacing it back into view during every even numbered frame. Though the form does not actually break apart, it does over time, create the appearance of particulate instability.

Patterned movement involves a choreographed manipulation of repetitions of similar forms. Together, these repetitive forms no longer represent their singular identity, but a larger collective – an amorphous mass. Patterned movement is essential in transforming recognizable forms (be they triangles or rabbits) into abstract animations. Thus we can have a movie such as *Rabbit Rabbit* (Greaves 1995) that begins with a focus on two similar rabbits that are engaged in a typical cartoonish character feud; however, as they subsequently are duplicated, they lose their individual identity and become merely patterns of repetitive imagery and movement – which far overshadows their original sense of character (see Figure 1.18).

Currently there seems to be a growing trend towards what could be classified as abstract stop-motion animation. This, of course, represents a slight contradiction, since stop-motion animation requires the photography of real, normally identifiable, objects. However, as stated earlier, the process of adding incongruous motion to these forms represents at least a partial abstraction. And furthermore, through the calculated use of patterned movement, deconstruction and evolution, these recognizable forms can effectively devolve into the irreality of the purely abstract.

One early example of abstract stop-motion can be found in Gumby creator, Art Clokey's *Gumbasia* (1953). This short abstract clay animation, created in 1953, was set to music, and playfully alludes to Walt Disney's animated feature, *Fantasia* (1940). Though it is very evident that it was constructed from blobs of clay (usually spheres, rectangles and other non-descript amorphous forms), it effectively employs a wide array of movement strategies: metamorphosis, patterned movement, shattering and amalgamating of forms to ensure that it primarily showcases the spectacle of abstract transformation. More recently, Jonathan Chong's *Against the Grain* (2012), which is a stop-motion film made almost entirely from actual

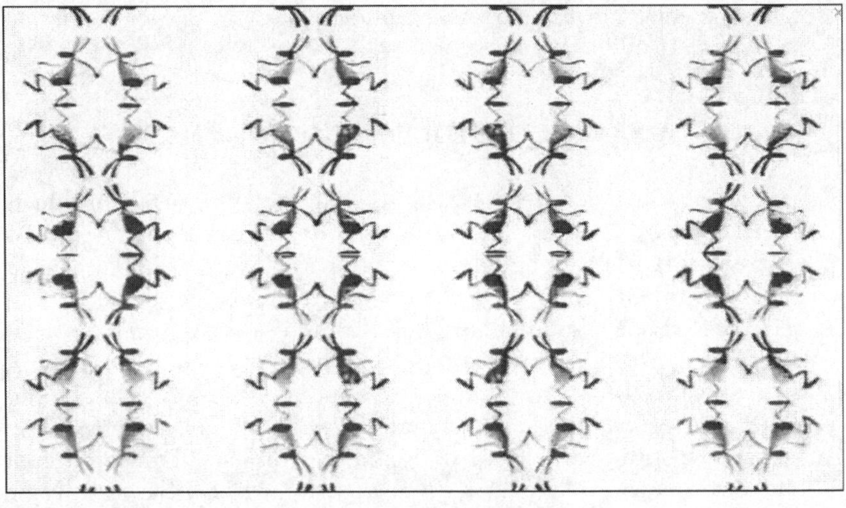

FIGURE 1.18 *A patterned array of rabbits from* Rabbit Rabbit *(Daniel Greaves 1995).*

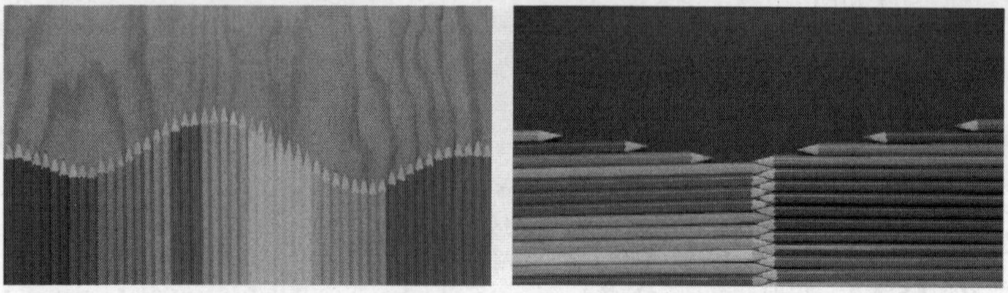

FIGURE 1.19 *Images from* Against the Grain *(Jonathan Chong 2012).*

coloured pencils, becomes not about the pencil objects, but about the shape's colours and motion-patterns of the moving imagery. As these pencil forms are subsequently duplicated, they lose their individual identity and become complex patterns of repetitive imagery and movement – no longer representing their singular identity, but a much larger collective, effectively stripping the individual form of meaning and significance and thereby transforming it into the realm of abstraction (see Figure 1.19). Similarly, animator Max Hattler has produced several abstract stop-motion films, such as *AANAATT* (2008), *Shift* (2012) and *Model Starship* (2012). He too employs various strategies that not only create visually interesting sequences but also ultimately shift the viewer's attention away from the original context and identity of a single form and towards a purely abstract viewing experience. For example, in his stop-motion piece *Shift* (2012), the images (even though identifiable as real stop-motion objects) continually change appearance and shape. This kind of developmental movement shifts the emphasis away from particular forms or recognizable characters and instead highlights the dynamic and visually compelling movement of abstract imagery.

Animated process-document

'A process ontology', declares Rescher, 'sees things not just as the products of processes (since one cannot avoid doing) but also as the manifestations of processes – as complex bundles of coordinated processes'.[120] When we take the opportunity to analyse these 'manifestations of processes' it is conceivable that one might find, residing within, a *process-document*. That is, if we look at a 'thing', not only should we recognize that it is a result of multiple processes becoming all at once;[121] but often we should be able to interpret some of the inherent metadata of the 'thing'. For example, if we find a window with a large crack in it, and there is a small indentation at one end of the crack, we are likely to be able to infer how the crack came to be. More than likely, a small stone or other projectile was 'thrown' at the window.

This section will continue to present a processually biased view of animation. It will consider how the final animated film, the document itself, can serve as a revelatory record of its very becoming. Mitchell describes instances in which a photograph can represent a 'metapicture', that is one that is 'used to show what a picture is'.[122] Animation can also hold the secret as to how it was made, the processes behind, and of, its construction. In *Difference and Repetition*, Deleuze seems to argue that (what is referred to here as) the *process-document* is normally obscured by the final effect, '[The artist] introduce[s] a disequilibrium into the dynamic process of construction, an instability, dissymmetry or gap of some kind which disappears only in the overall effect.'[123] However, this is not necessarily the case with animation as the disequilibrium of the animator's hand (or the animation production in general) may, in fact, become further noticeable when presented through the cumulative effect of animation. Such disequilibrium may highlight both the animator and the specific production processes used in the construction of the animation. There will normally be *two phases* of the animation process that we can investigate in terms of the process-document. We can, of course, watch the animation as it was intended to be presented, and from this reading, there is a very good chance that we will be able to infer some of how the animation was made. Additionally, we will most likely be able to carefully step through the object or file that embodies the animative-state (the strip of film, the digital file) and analyse it very closely – perhaps one frame at a time. From this we will be likely to be able to determine even more details on how the animation was fabricated. Quite often it is the comparative analysis between these two phases of the animation that will give us the best understanding of the first phase – the making of the animation. In sum, we can often see a manifestation of process in the animated form and this makes a process-based study of animation all the more pertinent.

The visible animator

Animation is generally a hidden and an anonymous art. Unlike the possibilities allowed in performances and traditional film productions, the individual is not normally spotlighted. However, particularly in regard to independent or materials-based animation, there may be ample opportunity for the animator to exhibit what Buchan refers to as the medium's 'self-reflexive tradition'.[124] Many early animation productions did make a point of featuring the animator. As a number of animators began their careers as lightning sketch artists (Winsor McCay, Harry Julius, J. Stuart Blackton and others), it is understandable that they would wish to continue their performative tradition. Much of the success of the lightning sketch artist relied upon an ability to speak to and interact with the drawings that they were creating before an audience.[125] Yet at the same time, the trickery and magic that film afforded could also greatly amplify the performative effect; drawings could be completed at truly lightning speed, hats could 'suddenly' appear on a drawing's head and, most spectacularly, the still drawing could literally and suddenly come to life, which for Gunning signalled an emphasis on the spectacle and showmanship and a de-emphasis on the narrative.[126]

Most of the early American animators, such as J. Stuart Blackton, featured the artist in front of the camera for at least part of the film, as did the films of Australian animator, Harry Julius. Winsor McCay, in particular, would centre much of the narrative of his animations on himself and his animation process (albeit often from an exaggerated perspective) as in the films *The Sinking of the Lusitania* (1918) and *Gertie the Dinosaur* (1914). In each of these, McCay is featured bragging (and sometimes making a wager) with his colleagues about how many drawings he will make and how fast he will produce them to make his animated films. As Donald Crafton notes in *Before Mickey*, 'To interject oneself into one's film is a fairly audacious thing to do', but it occurred quite frequently in early cinema animation. Over time, there was a noticeable shift in this tendency from the earliest days of cinema in which it was 'obvious and literal' to a more subtle and metaphoric approach decades later. But in general the appearance of the animator was 'very flattering, for he was pictured as (or implied to be) a demigod, a purveyor of life itself'.[127] McCay was an extremely skilled animator, but for Scott Bukatman, some of the brilliance of the McCay animation 'derives from the contrast with everything that we have seen leading to it [the actual animation]'.[128] This is due, in part, to McCay's ability to 'build up the audience' (clearly a skill derived from his showmanship background), but also to the striking contrast between the aesthetics of the black and white live-action footage that precedes the animation and the often hand-coloured brilliance of the stylized graphics of his animation. Another factor at play is that audiences are invariably impressed by the sheer number of drawings that he purports to make for the animation, and the apparent ease at which he produces them (he doesn't even seem to need to register his drawings to the previous ones).[129] This knowledge of the sheer labour force (of one man) behind the production makes it all the more impressive.

The visible production process

In other cases the animator may not be visible in the frame, but still leave traces of his or her actions. In clay animation, for example, we may see the artist's fingerprints still visible in the malleable clay. This is quite noticeable in the early Aardman films such as *Wallace and Gromit: A Grand Day Out* (1989), and particularly *Ident* (1989). In the Aardman film *Chicken Run*

(Nick Park, Peter Lord 2000), the studio devoted considerable resources to the digital (frame-by-frame) removal of surface marks.[130] The resulting image lacks some of the handmade qualities of the earlier Aardman productions. It might seem that an animated film is appreciated more if the viewer *understands* the production process. If, for example, they can see the fingerprints in the character, they can get a sense of the model's scale, and of the material construction (soft clay). Additionally, fingerprints suggest both the human-hand and the reality of the object. Film-maker Wes Anderson recognizes that some of the most creative elements can emerge from the unscripted moments where control is lost; and this was no exception when he directed the stop-motion feature *Fantastic Mr. Fox* (Wes Anderson 2009).

> You have to have room for the accidents, and with [*Fantastic Mr. Fox*] I was kind of wondering where's the room for the accidents going to come in? And part of recording the voices outside of a controlled environment was just so we'd have the opportunity for some things to go wrong, or some things to surprise us. And also, every animator brings their own perspective, and the same accidents happen on a stop-motion set. They just happen very slowly [laughs].[131]

The material object and the hand of the animator became quite evident and constituted an important part of the viewer's experience. For Suzanne Buchan, there is nearly always a twofold impact on the spectator, for which 'identification is both with the objects and figures and with the animator who has made the film'.[132] Furthermore, such traces may also indicate the extensive 'production time' of the film. It can be quite an important marketing perspective to consider the length of production time, and studios tend to highlight this fact (for example, that a seventy-five-minute feature took four years and 300 people to produce).

Until well into the 1990s virtually every 2D-animated television show utilized a hand-painted cel animation process; for example the *Dilbert* television series' first season in 1999 was still entirely hand painted on cel. Its second (and final) season in 2000 was digitally painted. Such a production process necessitated a huge labour force comprising hundreds of cel painters. This assembly line-type process sought to keep the individuality of each human cel painter virtually undetectable, and each cel object invisible. Although each resulting image would be unique, there were certain properties that were required to remain consistent. Flat unmodulated colour, carefully applied up to the line edges was required, without variance between the cel images.[133] Even though there were meticulous quality controls in place, and each image would be thoroughly scrutinized throughout the production process, numerous errors would survive. Sometimes these inconsistencies were the result of oversights: sometimes they were the result of insider pranks. For example, in Walt Disney's original animated feature *The Rescuers* (Wolfgang Reitherman, John Lounsbury 1977), a photographic representation of a nude woman was placed in the window of a building in the background (most likely by the camera operator). It exists in the background for only two frames as the two mouse characters (Miss Bianca and Bernard) fly through the air on the back of the bird-taxi. This inclusion illustrates an example of an intentionally subversive inconsistency within the animated image, which was not 'discovered' until it was released on home video, which enabled the viewer to freeze-frame, or slowly scroll through the scene.[134]

One fairly common visible production error that can be found in cel animation productions is known as the 'paint-pop' – where one or more frames might not be properly painted, and thus appear to chromatically 'pop' when viewed as animation. For example, rather than painting the flesh colour of an arm that protrudes out of a blue short-sleeve shirt, the painter might accidently paint the whole arm blue on one of the cels. A rather conspicuous example can be found in the Warner Brothers Studios-animated short film *Herr Meets Hare* (Freleng 1945), which featured Bugs Bunny. In one sequence, and on a single cel, the clothing on the upper body of a character was mistakenly painted flesh-tone rather than the darker colours of his clothing, making him appear partly nude. However, because it happened to be a 'held cel' that remained motionless and in camera for sixteen frames (while Bugs Bunny and the camera continue to move), the semi-nude figure became quite detectable, even during normal viewing (see Figure 1.20).

Less noticeable, but much more pervasive was the misuse of colour tone. Because the transparent cel sheets used in cel animation were not entirely transparent, the thicker the stack of cels used in a particular set-up, the more they would block out the light from passing through. Therefore, even

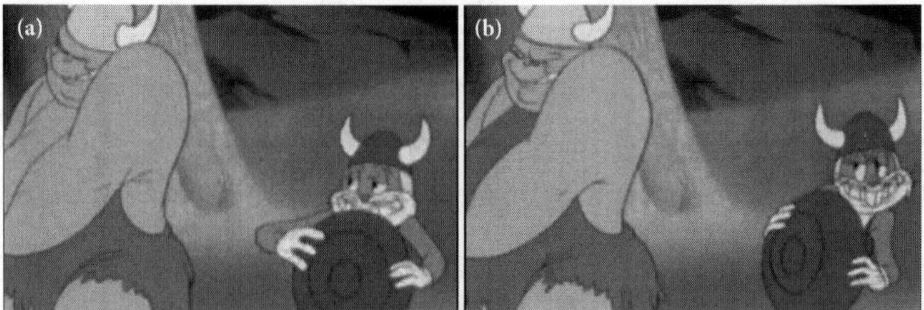

FIGURE 1.20 *Images depicting a 'paint-pop' production error from* Herr Meets Hare *(Fritz Freleng 1945). Because of a production painting error, the character in image (a) appears to be topless and he appears to be clothed in image (b).*

if a figure were painted with the exact colour tone, an image on a bottom cel layer will appear slightly darker than one on top. To combat this, cel painters would paint the bottom layer with a slightly brighter tone (of for example yellow) to match the mid-tone yellow on the top layer. As Shamus Culhane notes:

> The most common error is to use a set of colors designated for another cel level. This will cause a flash on the screen because the character will suddenly become lighter or darker. It is difficult mistake to catch in the checking department. Even the expert checkers at Disney's have allowed color flashes to appear in many of the studio's short subjects.[135]

Most inconsistencies in cel painting are fleeting and noticeable only in a held cel lasting at (the very) least four consecutive frames. Laura Mulvey, in *Death at 24x,* notes how the increased proliferation of DVD players and other more recent digital image devices has raised our awareness of the individual frame which 'can be easily revealed at the simple touch of a button'.[136] As a result, many of these anomalies, unintentional or deliberate, are coming to light as animation enthusiasts seek the secrets of how a scene was animated, and suspicious parents search for inappropriate content.

In addition to traces left by the 'hand of the animator', there are a number of other elements that compose the animated process-document. On the most basic level, one is normally able to look at the animation one frame at a time and discover if (in terms of more traditional animation) it was animated on singles, doubles or if a new image was used only every fourth frame. Furthermore, the use of specific materials in the creation of the animation might be evident. In traditional animation the material used to animate, be it sand or paper cut-outs, is normally quite discernable. And, in addition to the resulting aesthetics, these material techniques may also have an impact on the content of the film. Michael Frierson suggests in *Clay Animation* that the process and materiality of clay animation, for one, facilitates the use of metamorphosis.[137] For Norman Klein (as discussed earlier) an essential aspect of metamorphosis is what he terms the 'ani-morph', the point at which the morphing process – the transformation between two discreet things – becomes discernible.[138] Interestingly, Klein also describes this point between the extremes as appearing to be 'a *lapse* or *hesitation*', for it is at this moment that the viewer also becomes aware of the 'craftsmanship' of the animation.[139] Further to this, it could be suggested that any moment of noticeable change within the animated form is the moment that we are witness to the process of the form. Limited animation does this each time; after a sequence of stasis there is movement, followed again by a still image. It is this dramatic oscillation between movement and stasis that reveals animation's fabricated structure. Such inconsistencies make manifest the balance between the micro-processes and macro-processes of which the animator must be continually aware of during the animation production.

Perhaps the most observable examples of the process-document can be found within the growing trend of large-scale outdoor animated productions that can be referred to as 'landscape animations'. With landscape animation various production artefacts may be particularly evident, one immediate reason being that the set is generally much larger and outside the controlled environment of a traditional studio. Therefore, instead of simply seeing the stray hand of the animator or a bit of lint pop into the frame, we may actually see stray dogs, people and cars pop into (and out of) the frame. Therefore we see, in Prendergast's *Rippled*, the found bricks that served as support rigs to enable creatures to jump through the ruinous spaces – the animator never bothering to remove them. And from time to time the animator, Blu, pops into frame visibly painting a huge wall with a telescopic paint roller – perhaps in an intentional effort to highlight the Herculean nature of this animation process. Furthermore, the process of this variety of animation often necessitates the inclusion of extraneous elements. For example, in Prendergast's *Rippled*, there are a number of sequences that involve the animation of 'light drawings', which are made by taking photographs with a very slow shutter speed in order to achieve streaks of light (see Figure 1.21b). Though this process minimizes the visibility of the animator, a ghostly residue of the animator's form nevertheless remains. Another aspect of the process-document of landscape animation is that the viewer will be likely to have a good idea of the scale and, often, the material nature of any elements that have been used. Unlike many stop-motion films that involve an ambiguity of scale, we can be assured that the imagery in landscape animation is pretty much all life-sized, and this also gives us clues as to how the animation was executed. For example, we know how big the shark image must have been that was painted on the fence in Blu's animation, and we know roughly how much aluminium foil must have been used to create the ripple effects in *Rippled* (see Figure 1.21a).

With the advent of computer animation, many of the human- and material-induced production traces are absent in the final product. In this era of digital simulation, much of the material technique of earlier productions (which had left many tell-tale clues about the film's production) are now simulated by the computer (digital 3D is made to look like stop-motion, or sand or paper cut-outs). However, the computer itself often reveals its process. This may be evident through its reliance on 'spliney' movement, or its limitations in visual detail, or even through visible artefacts of compression or rendering errors. Those that are well versed in particular softwares can often correctly identify the type of software or even renderer that was used as they tend to leave tell-tale artefacts (particularly if the default settings are utilized). Additionally, the resulting computer animation file will be

FIGURE 1.21 *(a) Still frame from Rippled (Prendergast 2011), featuring a large animated ripple effect, which was made from concentric rings of rolled aluminium foil and set in an abandoned building site. (b) The animator can be seen behind the animated light image, drawing it with a glowing light stick.*

likely to contain enormous amounts of 'metadata'. This may include such information as when it was made, which software and which version of that software produced it and, in some cases, even detailed information on the specific computer that was used to produce it. And as technology advances, it is normally quite easy to determine the decade in which a particular digital animation was made in, simply based on the lighting and texturing that was used in the animation. Thus the first *Toy Story* (John Lasseter 1995) feature has a very different technological aesthetic than does the more recent Disney feature, *Frozen* (Chris Buck, Jennifer Lee 2013).

More interactive digital animations, such as the animated video game *Grand Theft Auto V* (RockStar Games 2013), might make it rather difficult to 'step-through' the animation one frame at a time, yet the game can be manipulated in such a way that it can be forced to display the underlining physics, animation and structuring of the game architecture. That is, one can, by manipulating the characters, find 'errors' in which a figure can be made to partially walk through walls in some sections of the game-space. One can also find glaring inconsistencies such as the fact that a car can smash right through a towering traffic light pole at very slow speeds, but be completely obstructed (and likely destroyed) by trying to drive through a low-lying hedge. The repetitive use of cycles (such as walk and run-cycles) can also be very evident and reveal a further portrayal of how the animation is constructed. Furthermore, for those that have the desire, 'glitches' can be found or the game-code can actually be modified so that, for example, in *Grand Theft Auto V* all the water might be drained from the lakes and oceans surrounding the city of Los Santos. The characters can then be made to drive their cars through these suddenly emptied spaces, where previously only boats and submarines could venture. Such exploitations of a video game can be referred to as a form of 'counterplay'. 'Counterplay is in contrast to the norm' it breaks with the conventional expectations of a game's 'etiquette, rules, its spirit, and discourses of legitimacy, ideology, and/or law'.[140] Ultimately, such modifications or 'counterplay' also help to reveal how the animated game was constructed.

Regardless of what form the final animation may take, the process of animation is indeed an essential aspect of this investigation of the animated form, and some of this processual information can actually be gleaned through a poststructuralist analysis of the animated text. By revealing this process-document we can gain a further understanding of the animated form, which can be argued, is fundamentally about process.

2

Cycled and Recycled Animation

It could be argued that the cycle is one of the most significant and perhaps one of the oldest structures within the animated form. The animated cycle originated long before the advent of cinema and constitutes the structural basis of many pre-cinematic devices (such as the zoetrope and the phenakistiscope) (see Figure 2.1). It quickly made the transition into cinematic animation and became one of the defining (but rather underappreciated) distinctions between animation and traditional live action. The cycle flourished in the cel animation era and has continued to thrive and evolve in the digital era.

The animated cycle is a configuration, a formal structure, of sequential images that are repeated, at least once, in a consistent order. A cycle may involve the repetition of an entire scene, or simply the repetition of a single

FIGURE 2.1 *A phenakistiscope disc.*

element, such as the footsteps of a character as it walks across the screen. Perhaps the most prevalent reasons behind the use of the cycle in cinematic animation has been for reasons of economy – the fewer new drawings or movements the animator needed to complete in a sequence, the lesser time and money would be required. However, there are many other motivations for its use, including narrative structuring, informational emphasis, humorous effect, rhythm, clarification of complex systems and even as an expression of specific emotional states.

Origins of the animated cycle

The animation cycle was first developed with the advent of a number of pre-cinematic animation machines and can be readily seen in such devices as the zoetrope, phenakistiscope and praxinoscope – making it one of the pioneering structures of the moving image. In these devices the animation is physically constructed in a circular manner (either upon a clock-face-like disc or on the interior of a cylindrical drum). To view the animation, these devices would be spun around, presenting an animated effect from start to finish and then seamlessly beginning again in an endless succession of movement. Because of their circular structure, these devices required a continuous repetition of action. They also severely limited the length of the animation. The zoetrope, phenakistiscope and praxinoscope were generally limited to about sixteen images per 'movie'.

> The very nature of the apparatus thus condemned it to an inalterable demonstration of a series of figures forming a loop. In a sense, the fundamental forms of attraction are reflected in the inherent characteristics of how the device functions: the absence of any temporal configuration (that is, the impossibility of identifying the beginning or the end of the action), the brevity of the series of images and its ad nauseam repetition, its purely monstrative value, etc.[1]

In addition to its limitation of length, for an illusion of motion to succeed, a *uniform* speed of rotation had to be maintained. An attempt to commence, then stop at the logical beginning and end of the animation would not only create an extremely short animation but it would also cause an undesirable ramping up and ramping down effect on the motion. The movement *and* the narrative, therefore, had to be cyclical. Dulac and Gaudreault describe:

> The phenakisticope's format and the way it functioned suggest a 'world' in which everything was governed by circularity and repetition, a world

> which annihilated any hint of temporal progression. The subjects are like Sisyphus, condemned ad infinitum to turn about, jump, and dance. In another sense, the figures are machine-like: untiring and unalterable, they are 'acted-upon subjects' rather than 'acting-out subjects'. The lack of interruption in the sequence of images was essential to the creation of this effect of uninterrupted and perpetual movement, this a-historical temporality within which beings and things could turn about for ever, without any threshold marking the beginning or end of their wild journey.[2]

Although only one person could view the phenakistiscope comfortably at a time, other devices, such as the zoetrope or the praxeniscope, could have a larger audience of perhaps three or four simultaneous viewers. Each could take their place around the device, gaining a different perspective, and therefore a different entry point into the animation's narrative. Because of the cyclical nature, one could come or go at any point in time, and still make sense of the actions. In around 1885 Etienne-Jules Marey created a three-dimensional zoetrope that depicted a bird in flight.

> Instead of a strip of paper covered with figures, we introduced into the zoetrope a series of wax models painted in oils, and representing the bird in all the successive phases of its wing movement. The illusion was complete, and a flying bird could be seen flying round and round the apparatus; sometimes flying away from the observer, sometimes across, and sometimes towards him.[3]

This approach has in recent years been greatly expanded with dimensional zoetropes which, instead of requiring the viewer to peer through small slots, utilize stroboscopic lights to create an animated effect. What is remarkable about the 3D zoetrope (and especially in the more contemporary efforts) is that one can see the animation from any position around the device, and because it is dimensional it can be seen from a variety of vertical perspectives as well. The viewer becomes like a 3D camera able to move about and witness the cycle from nearly any point of view. So, even though the cycle is a pure reiteration, the viewer's experience of each repetition can be quite novel (see Figure 2.2).

At this pre-cinematic stage in animation history, the cycle was never used as a means of speeding up production – it was simply the structural basis of most animation. Usually the cycles would be humorous in nature, but often the viewer would simply delight in seeing something continuously move whether the intent was humorous or not and frequently this delight could sustain itself for multiple repetitions.[4] In some cases, the cycle could be quite complex, and would *require* numerous viewings (revolutions of the disc) to unpack all of its visual and narrative condensation. Once traditional cinema was invented, there was little need for the cycle in the live-action film. No

FIGURE 2.2 *An example of a modern-day 3D zoetrope.* Ty the Tasmanian Tiger *by John Aitchison. On display at ACMI, Melbourne, Australia (photo by author).*

longer was the playback apparatus bound to a brief circular object; the new film projector apparatus transformed the circular structure into the linear and at this point a new era of animation commenced.

Structures of the cycle

An animated cycle can actually exhibit a few different structural archetypes. We normally think of a cycle as a loop, like a wheel turning round and round or the hands of a clock rotating. However, at least in the production of animation, we can also consider a few other forms of the cycle. The four basic structures can be described as

1) Looping cycle
2) Oscillating cycle
3) Random cycle
4) Stationary cycle.

The *looping cycle* (originating in such devices as the zoetrope) is what also constitutes the classic walk cycle and most recognizable forms of the cycle. Its beginning is identical to its conclusion. And technically, one could start viewing it from any point in the loop. The *oscillating cycle* is a sort of back and forth repetition – a ping-ponging of action. A swinging pendulum is perhaps the most basic example. In the animation process one would need only to animate it swinging in a single direction (to the left), and then reverse play it the other way. The *random cycle* is feasible in only the most rudimentary of movements, such as in 'boiling'. For example, the six or seven tracings (trace-backs) that one might make of a drawing boil could be played back in any random order and it would not really affect the outcome – it would still appear as a boiling line. In fact, veteran animator Tony White suggests that trace-backs should be shot: 'in random order to keep the held line convincingly alive, while avoiding a cyclic action that would show up as repetitive and predictable if shot in their logical order'.[5] In this way, the random cycle uses the components of a traditional cycle, yet abandons the precise structure of that cycle. And finally the *stationary cycle* is perhaps the most simplistic conception of a cycle. It is merely a repetitive single image (a held image) that is played back over and over again in order to create a stable and immobile form. As with all cycles, either the entire frame could be considered as a stationary cycle or merely a component of it. The background in most traditional cel animation would be one obvious embodiment of a partial stationary cycle, as would the 'unmoving' portion of a lip-synched character in which only the mouth was made to move.

The economic cycle

Unlike the pre-cinema devices that had an imposed structure and an upper limit of possible images, thus necessitating the use of the cycle, film animation offered virtually a limitless array of available frames. Instead the limitation of cinematic animation became one of economy and production speed. Writing in 1920 in his highly influential book *Animated Cartoons: How They are Made, Their Origin and Development,* Lutz declared,

> Of all the talents required by anyone going into this branch of art, none is so important as that of the skill to plan the work so that the lowest possible number of drawings need be made for any particular scenario.[6]

The cycle was just one of those 'plans'; more than likely the experiences of the zoetrope and other pre-cinema devices still resonated with the early animator and its narrative and aesthetic potential was redirected into their own use of the cycle. In his book, Lutz devotes a number of pages to the cycle, describing how to create the walk and run cycles for both human and animal characters as well as how to create a five-drawing cycle for a flapping flag, a three-drawing cycle for 'an effect of falling water', a cycle for the 'puffing exhaust from an automobile' and a cycle to create 'a constellation of stars encircling a dazed man's head'.[7] He sums up his discussion with:

'The animator would make very little progress if he were to refuse to take advantage of any proper expedients or tricks to accelerate his work.'[8]

Without a doubt, the cycle had very quickly become an essential aspect of early cinematic animation. Winsor McCay famously made the claim that his *Gertie the Dinosaur* film (1914) contained 10,000 drawings. But as Donald Crafton and David L. Nathan have pointed out, because of his heavy use of cycles, the actual number of original drawings was far fewer.[9] In fact, the cycle became a very common part of animation practice during the first half of the twentieth century, significantly facilitating the speed of animation production. The layering of cel animation and other forms of compositing greatly expanded the potential of the cycle (and also served to subdivide it into many parts, which could be interchanged). Thus a cycle did not have to be all-encompassing and could represent just a segment of the action – even just a minor background element such as a flapping flag or billowing of a plume of smoke.

Not only was each drawing of strong economic value, each cel image was exponentially more expensive and time consuming to produce. Each new image that could be avoided would amount to a substantial savings.

> The concept of the held cel and cycled movement is a time- and money-saver which has been used to the maximum on television programs. It is standard practice to put an entire figure on a held cel and then to animate the mouth and eyes or arms and legs with a cycle of cels. This very small number of cels is then used in conjunction with cuts, camera zooms and pans, and background pans to fill the greatest possible length of screen time with a minimum of artwork. Often a figure can be made to walk and talk for 60 seconds with no more than a dozen cels. Considering that full animation photographed on ones requires 1,440 cels for this single minute of screen time, cycling represents a considerable economy.[10]

The most common form of the cycle is the walk cycle, in which one complete stride is animated, and is then repeated over and over as needed. In (particularly 2D) animation, the background image may be cycled as well, there thus being two independent cycles working in partnership. Traditionally the looping background would consist of two independent background paintings in which each end would have similar traits to the ends of the other. In this way, they could seamlessly and repeatedly loop. This seam is referred to as the 'hook-up'[11] and is still a guiding principle for some digital animation.

The cycle dialectic

According to Whitehead, what is essential about the concept of any cyclical structure is that 'its own completion provides the conditions for its own mere repetition'. Thus in the animated cycle, the last frame of a cycle is always the antecedent to the first frame. However, 'No actual occasion can happen twice', clarifies process philosopher, William Christian in his discussions of actuality. And though nothing may be entirely repeated, he nevertheless concedes that there can be some common elements that are shared between occasions (such as the colour red).[12] Consider for example: when we walk, each step that we take is different; the next step is not a repetition of the past, even though it may have numerous elements in common with the previous steps (of the past).

In this way, a cycle can be thought of as a type of dialectic, for even though it repeats, it also pushes forward. It is a linear progression that folds back upon itself, having the potential to be eternally repetitive but at the same time to develop into an infinite progression. Every cycle can therefore be considered to be both *repetitive* and *appetitive*. They simultaneously convey both cyclical and progressive properties. One reason for this is that time is always experienced in a linear manner – actions may be repeated (or more precisely re-enacted), but not *time*. Richard Hanley, in his philosophical discussion of time travel, considers a major theoretical problem with time travel is that it requires time and events to be *repeated*, a condition known as 'causal loops'. Such a looping would, in fact, require an amazing array of coincidences (far beyond a repeated use of the colour red) to ensure that *every thing* is in place (and in its original condition) and able to occur in exactly the same manner as it did before. Many of the examples that he explores rely upon the concept of travelling back in time in order to 'repeat' the said occurrence.[13] Yet with animation all of the 'elements' required of a cycle can be repeatedly reused; it is simply a matter of realigning them – although it is important to emphasize again that the cycle is not a repetition of *time*: it is a repetition of *actions* through *linear* time. Time cannot be repeated; nevertheless, a cycle repeats actions, and thus can *apparently* repeat time. The swinging pendulum of a clock is bound in a repetitive action loop, yet time forever continues forward. We use the cyclical face of a clock to keep track of our linear time.[14] Similarly, the earth spins around in a cycle and we experience another day *passing*. The earth cycles around the sun and we have progressed forward another year. We make repeated footsteps to reach to the top of a flight of stairs and our car's wheels spin repeatedly in order to transport us *across* town. Many of our progressive actions are either supported by or characterized by cyclical repetitions.

We do seem continually to experience cyclical structures in our daily lives; they can be found residing everywhere from the microscopic level to the colossal, from the organic to the inorganic and from the concrete to the conceptual. The earth rotates; our heart beats rhythmically; we wake up in the morning, go to bed at night and wake up the next morning; chickens lay eggs which hatch into new chickens which again lay eggs; we might have the same work routine over and over again each day. On the other hand, no two days are alike, no two breaths or footsteps are identical, but by *thinking* of them as a rhythm or cycle we are able, in a way, cognitively to 'contain' them. Even in the very repetitive rotation of a windmill there can be found difference – there might be slight variations in speed, or the blades might tremor slightly more or less from one rotation to the next. But if we were to highlight these inconsistencies in an animated representation of a windmill, it would become unnecessarily distracting – particularly if it were intended to be merely a background element in a scene.

An animated cycle can be thought of as a distillation of our real-world perceptions. Though no two footsteps are alike in the real world, the animated walk cycle presents us with a generalized shorthand of how people walk. Similarly, for Bergson, the world seemingly 'present[s] to us repetitions that make generalization possible', even though the world is actually comprised of 'an unceasing transformation'.[15] If we see a few similar occurrences, then we can make cognitive sense of those – that is we read them as repetitive cycles – even though they are actually forward progressions.

Although there are very specific pragmatic reasons for employing the cycle in animation, it can also be thought of as an expression of something much deeper and much more complex. In speaking about cycles in general, Tyler Volk declares that rather than being ineffectual repeaters, 'Cycles define and make things.' For example, 'one of the cosmic consequences of any spinning in space is the confining of matter in motion to a finite region'.[16] Furthermore, enormous amounts of force and energy are involved in these cyclical events. Consider the driving and containing forces that pervade the planets as they encircle the sun, or even the infinitesimal electrons encircling an atom. In actuality, the force generated from these high-speed rotations should burst these groupings apart and subsequently throw the objects far away from their epicentre, but other forces press with even greater strength to keep them in cyclical containment. In a sense, 'cycles preserve the entity'.[17] It is also from cyclical repetition that even our brain structures are defined: 'neuronal pathways need a certain frequency of firings to maintain their structure; we thus invigorate memories by remembering them'.[18] The more often we repeat the same action, view the same action or think the same thought, the more our brain physically changes to accommodate these repeating cycles.

And though the world is made up of cycles, Volk suggests that it might be better to think of these not as merely round cycles, but instead as helix shaped.

> Sameness and difference are united through the archetype of the helix. Helixes embody cycles as parts of arrows. The cycles repeat; but at a larger time scale the process, the system, is going somewhere. Each year I celebrate or, more often, ignore my birthday; it comes like clockwork, but I am getting older. Of more cosmic import is the helical path of evolution.

> Disparate atoms coalesce into molecules, molecules into cells, cells into more complicated cells and organisms. Meanwhile, in each level at each coalescence, new relations radiate, pulling the stream of life outward into all the nooks and crannies of a level and, fatefully, up into an altogether new level.[19]

Even when, for example, an animated cycle appears to be an absolute repetition, as a *viewing experience,* we can garner new things with each successive screening – we might derive increasing humour or disgust or, in the case of the illustrative, we can gain (bit by bit) a greater understanding of how a mechanical process might work.

Amplified meaning

Animation simplifies; the cycle simplifies even more. A walking action with all its varying steps can become simplified into a repetition of just a few image positions. The cycle can serve as a tool for us to attempt to make sense of the world and to assist in finding connections between various events. If we are able to perceive some of the world's randomness and novelty as similarities (repetitions), then we might have a better comprehension of it. Animation simplifies and generalizes, and the cycle can compound this further. For example, we may not need to know all the details of a mechanical system to understand its primary functions – otherwise we may become distracted by inconsequential variances. Think of a steam engine: if you want to understand how it works, what is important is how the valves and pistons move – not the ever-varying clouds of steam that are expelled. The cycle can simplify and focus the viewer's attention onto the essential aspects. Such simplification can make sense of a repetitive but complex process – yet out of it can come a more complex understanding of a many-staged process.

However, the bulk of animated cycles are quite simple in nature. They do not illustrate complex processes, but instead signify the simple and the mundane. Thus, it does not take numerous repeated viewings to comprehend it – everything that the viewer needs to 'grasp' may be absorbed on the first revolution. Yet, the inculcating effect of repeatedly viewing something will invariably begin to imbue it with supplementary meaning. Humour is a common intentional narrative application of the cycle. We may see a cycle featuring Daffy Duck being thumped on the head, and imbue it with more and more humour at each viewing. Such a sequence viewed once is pretty absurd, but to witness it happen over and over, and the fact that the characters would perpetrate and subject themselves to such senseless actions more than once – let alone seven times – raises the level of absurdity to epic proportions, compounding the meaning well beyond the action itself.

On a more temperate scale, we can see the use of cycles in Winsor McCay's *Gertie the Dinosaur* as a means by which to imbue the character with gentle and endearing qualities. On several occasions we witness the dinosaur repeatedly stepping in place and nodding her head (clearly made from cyclically repeated drawings). This repeated action helped to convey the dinosaur's amiable and gentle personality, suggesting that she was eager to perform for the audience (although perhaps slightly bashful). Furthermore, these iterations also demonstrated her obedience to her master McCay, who (as if using a harness) was able to keep her (for the most part) in cyclical check.

Lutz mused about this cumulative effect of humour that can be derived from the animated cycle.

> A windmill effect, a twirling, a spinning, and a merry-go-round movement are of striking import in animated cartoons. They never fail to cause laughter when depicted in some such fashion or other. [...] Sometimes in a pursuit in a comic picture there is an introduction of a chase around the house or around a tree. The gyration about the house is particularly productive of laughter. The slight interruption while the figure passes back of the house gives occasion for the necessary pause in this comic business.[20]

But here Lutz brings up another important concept that can underpin the whole notion of the cycle, and that is the alternating uncertainty and anticipation of its recurrence.

> A pause is a necessary element in any continued comic situation. It is, in fact, proper to any series intended to arouse the emotion of laughter. And in some respects a pause corresponds to the negative moment of flexion – adverting our thoughts for a moment to physical activity – while the outburst of laughter corresponds to the positivity of extension.[21]

During the repeated anticipation of animated repetition, we can wait and wonder, 'will he bump his head again? Yes he did! – Wait, he couldn't possibly do it again, could he? Yes! He did!' It is similar to the 'peek a boo' game played with babies – after a few iterations, it becomes more about the anticipation of the 'boo' rather than any surprise of experiencing the 'boo'. We naturally respond to such rhythms and anticipate the next beat or 'for the other shoe to drop' – if it is delayed we wait even more expectantly. When it arrives, we might give a sigh of relief, or perhaps a bit of nervous laughter.

Interestingly, the cycle can also suggest that something is broken. A broken record is one that skips and thus plays only one revolution, then

FIGURE 2.3 *Images from* Dumbland *(David Lynch 2000).*

skips back and plays the same groove cycle again and again. In David Lynch's animated series *Dumbland* (2000), he often used the cycle to represent the breakdown of social structures and emotional stability. For example, in one cyclical sequence (Episode 6), Lynch depicted a very dysfunctional family scene. The scene, set in a lounge room, showed an absurdly hyperactive cycle; a screaming mother waved her arms, while a child bounced incessantly on a trampoline. The television also exhibited a relentless cycle, and a complimentary cycle of roaring cars and trucks hurtled past the bay window. This particular cycle lasted for nearly two minutes, with only a few close-up shots of the various cyclical elements in the scene, and the occasional reaction shot of the 'father' character. The reaction shots consisted of a quivering open mouthed, and clearly agitated, cyclical view of the character's expression. Lynch's lengthy portrayal of such outrageous and incessant cyclical behaviours conveys to us that, without a doubt, something is terribly broken within this animated domestic scene (see Figure 2.3).

Hiding and highlighting the cycle

The animated cycle usually seeks to do one of two things: either to disguise itself as linearity or else deliberately to announce its phasic properties. Normally, in the interest of economy of production, it seeks concealment. One means of achieving this is for the animated cycle to be repeated only a few times, being thus likely to escape the viewers' notice. Most viewers expect linear films to be just that – linear: they are not, therefore, 'looking' for cyclical attributes. An alternative is to create a very *elongated* cycle, one that because of its length will not easily be recognized as a loop.

In his philosophical consideration of our experience of life, Whitehead suggested that the perceived tedium and repetition of our existence sometimes overwhelms us. In his analysis, Whitehead outlined several different conditions which have an affect on our perception of, what he regarded as, 'Life-tedium'. He labelled these conditions as: 'the Way of Blindness, the Way of Transience, the Way of Rhythm'. The first two conditions, 'blindness' and 'transience', work together and essentially prevent us from seeing the 'flashes of novel appetition' and instead draw our attention to the seemingly mundane and repetitive.[22]

In animation, we can take this concept and intentionally highlight little 'flashes of novel appetition' to alter the otherwise repetitious cycle. One approach is to occasionally bring in moments of difference. Tony White suggests varying a walk cycle occasionally in order to avoid it looking too repetitive:

> If the scene in which the walk cycle is going to be seen for a long while, then it might be advisable to mix in an occasional alternative walk cycle with a slightly different action, to give a sporadic break in the predictable action that the single cycle movement will eventually reveal. Moving the arms differently, or having the head look up or around, or doing a slight little jump in the step from time to time, serves this purpose adequately. If the walking cycle sequence is especially long, then perhaps more than one alternative cycle action would be advised. The secret of good animation is that if you're using cycles, only you should know![23]

Sometimes, if the above described action is required to continue for a substantial duration, then the described 'slightly different actions' might also be repeated several times, effectively creating a nested cycle (a shorter cycle interspersed within a much larger cycle).

Often, in 2D animation, a repeating background (a repeat pan) will be utilized. This involves the cycling of a panning background, where two backgrounds with perfectly matching end and start points will be repeatedly panned across the frame. Usually a character will be seen walking (in place) in the foreground, giving the illusion that they are travelling over a long distance. In such cases, both the animator and the compositor will be required to make certain that the cycles work together. The animator will need to ensure that if the character's foot comes into contact with the ground, it will need to slide backwards in line with the previous image (so that it appears to be walking in place) and, at the same time, the camera operator (or digital compositor) will need to ensure that the background cycle moves at the same rate as the walking character.[24] However, if the pan lasts more than a few seconds, the repeating backgrounds can become painfully obvious, making the character appear to be going nowhere fast.

There are a few means by which this repeating pan can be disguised; one method is to create a very long background (however, this would essentially negate the time-saving process of a repeating background). Another strategy is 'not to put in too much detail – when the same very recognizable house goes past four or five times, the illusion is broken'.[25] Another important strategy is to make the background connection points as seamless as possible so that the viewer does not see the repeating joining line, which would provide an obvious detail (the disjoint) to fixate on. White advises:

> It actually doesn't matter how long the background art is on a repeat pan, as long as the first field and the last field are identical in shape, content, and color. Note that for the repeat action to work, everything in the front and end fields must be 100 percent identical to each other, in design, coloring, texture, etc. If this doesn't happen, there will be a noticeable jump in the action.[26]

The cameraman played a very important role in the use of the cycle. The animator would create a cycle, but it was up to the camera operator to implement it and to make sure that it worked within the scene. He could also add variances to it, for example, by zooming in or out on a cycle. This would technically make every frame different, but the animation contained within may have consisted of only a ten-frame cycle. And in contemporary 3D animation it becomes much easier to hide a cycle – one can simply move the camera around in any manner or position and further obscure the repetition of one element's motion.

Jules Engel's animated short film *Accident* (1973) is a cyclical-structured animation that also has a great deal of additional novel elements that were added while it was being shot under the camera. It is a three-minute, short animation of a dog running; but it meets with an 'accident', at which point the dog begins to be smudged and erased away. The film is made up of a series of pencil drawings inspired from a Muybridge photographic series of a dog's run cycle. Though working from an Eadweard Muybridge book, Engel exaggerated the movement and modified the cycle so that it would result in 'a very beautiful, rhythmic movement'. Engel began with a repeating cycle of the animal running and then sought to 'disturb' the cycle 'so completely that you almost end up with something else'.[27] During the first portion of the film we see the dog gracefully running in place. After a short time the dog begins to be rubbed out, one small portion at a time; progressively the sprinting dog disappears, and in the end only the very faint remnants of the dog figure remain – but even so, a faint running motion is still visible. It is a cyclical film that is continually evolving as it is eroded away over time.

There might be some occasions on which the animator would *want* to express an essence of Whitehead's 'Life-tedium' in an animated cycle. If made simply enough, the cycle can become an overt distillation of tedium. It is the representation of the banal in the American television series *King of the Hill* (1997–2010) that, for Furniss, provides both a self-reflexive analysis of the form of the animated cycle and a social commentary on suburban life. She describes one scene, in which the principal character, Hank Hill, is seen repeatedly circling around the same path on his tractor-lawnmower. The absurdity of this overly repetitive cycle becomes very evident and thus provides a comedic effect.[28] The repetitive nature of this action is also an overt expression of the banality of American suburban life.

Another animated film that does *not* attempt to conceal its use of the animated cycle image is Zbigniew Rybczynski's Academy Award-winning short animated film, *Tango* (1980).[29] Even its title, *Tango* (a stylized and repetitive series of dance movements), suggests the cyclical form. The animation comprises eighteen brief cycles (each lasts only 10–20 seconds before repeating). Yet, because of their temporal spacing and nested placement with the other cycles in the scene, the result is a compellingly complex eight-minute film which, although very repetitive in structure, results in a chaotic maelstrom of activity. It is an incredibly dense film, and requires repeated viewing to unpack all of its information. As with other examples, this incongruous use of the cycle raises a strong awareness of its form, while making a sharp critique of contemporary life. In this instance, rather than absurd banality, the escalating repetitions might convey a sense of claustrophobia or repression.

Similarly, the animated short film *Revolver* (Jonas Odell 1993) is composed of approximately twenty different scenes, which are in turn composed of repeating cycles (each duration of the cycle lasts for approximately five seconds before it repeats). The entire film lasts for nearly eight minutes, but there is less than two minutes of original animation – the rest being comprised of repeating cycles. However, economy is only part of the impetus behind the heavy use of cycles in this film: the cycle actually becomes its structural device. And to a certain extent, we also perceive a feeling of being trapped, particularly in scenes where the theme of repetition seems particularly overt – such as a monkey trapped in an underwater laboratory, or a character gasping for breath, struggling to stay afloat in a rough sea. The soundtrack, primarily composed of repetitive heavy breathing, further amplifies the sense of repetition and constraint (see Figure 2.4).

The other condition that Whitehead describes that is relevant to our discussion of the cycle is what he refers to as 'the Way of Rhythm'. This is an essential condition that permeates our world – it 'pervades all life, and indeed all physical existence' and it works to 'eliminate the fatigue attendant upon the repetition'. Though a rhythm might at first seem repetitive, it succeeds in doing just the opposite. Rhythm helps to obviate the seemingly repetitious by combining and highlighting all of the 'variation of the concrete details of succeeding cycles'.[30] This is a quality inherent in music, and an aural phenomenon that we constantly experience. That a popular song may repeatedly sing the choruses is not for reasons of economy, nor because the writer could not imagine a new line of text: such repetition occurs as an

FIGURE 2.4 *Image from* Revolver *(Jonas Odell 1993).*

expedient by which to quickly engage the listener and provide a constant and pleasurable experience. We respond to repetition: the beating of a heart, the ticking of a clock. The spinning of the earth and its rotation around the sun provide us with the important cycles that direct our lives. Through rhythm the apparently repetitious is actually 'capable of an enormous elaboration of complexity of detail'.[31]

In Disney's 1934 short *Funny Little Bunnies* (Wilfred Jackson), the cycle is used heavily to depict the hard working bunnies engaged in their repetitive tasks; it shows with visual rhythm the eager bunnies hard at work on their chocolate egg assembly line. The bunnies display joyousness in their embracement of repetitive labour – but instead of banality they find danceable rhythms. Cycles are also used heavily in Disney's 1929 short *The Skeleton Dance* (Walt Disney) to help accentuate the rhythmical and musical qualities of this early example of synchronous sound animation. Similarly, Erica Russell's animated films *Feet of Song* (1988) and *Triangle* (1994) are replete with cycles, yet at the same time are infused with an infectious rhythm of vision and sound that quickly overturns any sense of tedium. Importantly, cyclical rhythms become the primary organizing structure in Russell's films, where repetitions and cycles help the viewer to 'make sense' of the predominantly abstract and non-narrative imagery (see Figure 2.5).

FIGURE 2.5 *Image from* Feet of Song *(Erica Russell 1988).*

In a similarly playful manner, video games are also perfectly suited for the use of cyclical arrangements, and it is repetition that often constitutes the very basis of their organization. As Miguel Sicart has argued, games

> appropriate players' need for leisure and ability to recognize patterns and turn them into experiences that players want to traverse again and again because they find joy in repetition and learning. Games systematize the pleasures of play and make them repeatable.[32]

Although a player may occasionally complain about the excessively repetitive tasks that one might need to complete in order to attain the next 'bonus' or next 'level', there is generally pleasure to be found in adhering to, and then eventually mastering, the game system.

Animated GIFs

There are many movie file formats that proliferate on the internet, but there are a few that readily present the observer with a never-ending cyclical viewing experience. One of the most pervasive of these is the animated GIF format. An animated GIF (Graphics Interchange Format) is a computer file that is composed of a series of images (anywhere from two to several hundred) that are automatically played back as a looping sequence. Though a relatively dated file format (it was invented in 1987), it still persists today. It is because of its small file size and ease of use that in recent years it has enjoyed a huge increase in online use. A GIF can be composed of photographic-based video frames or any form of animated imagery. Generally limited to a few seconds, the loop can be seamlessly constructed (that is with no visible start or end point); however, this is not always the case. The animated GIF generally conveys the same concepts of any animated cycle except that, theoretically, the presentation of these self-repeating image sequences is endless. It is normally the viewer who moves away from it and on to some other link or content when they have 'had enough'. Interestingly, these looping images are often used to comment playfully on social media postings – and represent a rather intriguing visual shorthand of one's 'reaction' to a particular online comment or news item.

> 'Actual' reaction GIFs occur in comment threads, message boards, and email chains when someone posts or sends a GIF to directly respond to what someone else wrote. 'Hypothetical' reaction GIFs are when a writer proposes a hypothetical situation then posts a GIF to perform a reaction […] The role of these GIFs is not primarily aesthetic; they are gestures, performed reactions that are not fully realized until they meet their catalysts. While the users of these reaction GIFs do not typically create the files they post, their use constitutes its own form of authorship.[33]

There has developed a sort of currency in these animated cycles, which express one's thoughts entertainingly in little encapsulated moments of endlessly repeating visual commentary.

Another somewhat recent trend in the online use of the animated cycle has been with the proliferation of 'living photographs' or 'cinemagraphs' (the term coined and trademarked by designers Jamie Beck and Kevin Burg in 2011). Cinemagraphs are normally seamless animated GIFs that originate either from a still photograph or from brief video clips. If originating from a video, the creator will employ masking, animation and other digital visual effects to convert the originally fully moving live-action sequence into a mostly still image. Or, if originating from a still photograph, the creator will insert small focused elements of animation into the image. As a result, only a small portion of the image will actually 'move', while the rest of the image will simulate a still photograph. These particular GIFs seek to highlight the striking contrast between the still and the moving; presenting an image that is predominantly locked into an immobile trance, while the rest of it pushes on in an endless loop of seamless cyclical movement. Though many people were creating similar effects by digitally animating photographs since, at least, the 1990s, it is the seamless looping for online consumption (or digital billboards) that has made this format of particular widespread interest.

A further intriguing manifestation of the animated GIF cycle can be found in the recent practice of animating vintage stereograph cards, sometimes referred to as 'stereogranimation'. The stereograph, a nineteenth-century invention, was a device by which two slightly differently angled photographs of the same scene would be printed side by side onto a card and, when viewed through a special viewing device, a 3D effect could be seen. The differences between the side-by-side images are normally too minute for the average person to notice when merely comparing them. However, *because* of the differences between the images, when they are viewed together (as one) they produce a remarkable 3D view. Recently, the New York Public Library began offering an online application known as the 'Stereogranimator', which allows one to upload a scanned image of a stereograph card to their website. The application will then automatically extract the two different images and then loop these two images into an endless oscillating cycle (known as a 'wobble GIF'). The end result articulates the surprising difference that is inherent in the two (seemingly identical) images of a stereograph card. Additionally, it exposes the fact that the apparently concrete form of the 3D image is actually composed of constituent images that can elicit a type of movement and cyclical duration.

When cycles are not used

As has been previously outlined, there are basically two approaches to traditional frame-by-frame animation; the first may be referred to as *replacement animation* and the second as *manipulated animation*. For the precise implementation of an animated cycle in traditional animation, the *replacement animation* technique is normally the most suitable. In this way, the animator can carefully plan and ensure that the last frame of the cycle is truly the *antecedent to the first frame*. However, the technique of rotoscoping (although involving replacement animation) is somewhat unique in that it involves the *tracing of live action* – a form that normally resists the cyclical structure. In constructing the cyclical form, the animator will often search for similarities and connections over the span of a movement in order to ensure its connectivity. Yet, with rotoscoping, the animator tends to focus on copying the action and the precise outline of each reference frame, imbuing it with all of its progressive and appetitive differences. In the animated feature *Hoppity Goes to Town* (Fleischer 1941), we see a curious mix of traditional animated insect creatures (replete with cycles) and rotoscoped human characters that are almost completely devoid of repetition. In this movie, the cycle was used primarily for reasons of efficiency; however, there are a number of scenes where the cycle is also used to signify the insects' diligent dedication to hard work and productivity. In general, the humans look very fluid and almost otherworldly with their unpredictable line work and non-repeating actions, compared to the much more stable line work and forms of the insect characters. Their stability is further accentuated by the heavy use of cycles in their movement, which in effect helps to concretize the insects' presence.

Some forms and approaches to animation, such as straight-ahead drawn animation and most examples of traditional stop-motion, do seem to actively discourage the use of the cycle. And though the lack of the cycle can make their creation process more labour intensive, it can also lead to a much more fluid expression of animation – one that has not been subjected to the intensive pre-planning that the cycle generally requires. For example, the delightfully free-flowing stop-motion animation of clay animator Bruce Bickford (for example, *Prometheus's Garden*, 1988) undoubtedly would have suffered from the inclusion of cycles; for it is the surprise of *not* knowing what will come next that makes such animations so compelling.

Occasionally, stop-motion animation has been able effectively to incorporate the cycle through the use of replacement elements – as were used extensively in George Pal's stop-motion films. In these instances, the sequences utilized carefully pre-planned and pre-fabricated elements to allow for very controlled cyclical actions. In some other rare cases, the cycle structure has merely been imitated in order to convey a mechanical type of movement. Buchan outlines below how the Quay Brothers chose this approach:

> In *Street of Crocodiles*, the Quays [...] recycled and reiterated gestures, the empty movements that emphasize the nonhuman condition of automata: screws rotate aimlessly and the Tailor's Assistants' arms rotate in their arm sockets. A rubber band machine is either just that or it is a metaphor for the vitalist, soulless urge of the Street of Crocodiles, transformed into a repetitive-compulsive gesture by the camera movement, framing, and sound.[34]

In the case of *Street of Crocodiles* (1986), the Quays animated their repetitive movements in a linear straight-ahead manner – effectively creating forced cycles. However, in other cases animators might separately shoot a stop-motion element against a green screen and then digitally composite and endlessly loop that element into the greater scene.

Live action rarely uses the cycle; however, some examples of digital cinema have incorporated a type of forced cycle aesthetic, effectively creating seamless loops out of live-action elements. Occasionally we can see examples of this in music videos or television advertising, which are achieved by digital animation-like manipulations of the images. One intriguing example can be found in the live-action film *Speed Racer* (Andy Wachowski, Lana Wachowski, 2008), which took on many of the stylistic affectations of animation. Not only did the film employ large amounts of photo realistic 3D animation, it also incorporated some cyclical structures. For example, in several scenes stadium crowds were looped into recognizably repetitive actions of cheering and clapping. This was a deliberate aesthetic, achieved by digitally duplicating live-action actors into seamless action loops, which was meant to pay homage to the limited animation style of the original television series.[35]

Recycled animation

One important aspect of a process philosophical perspective is that everything is novel and progressive, but at the same time composed of comparable components; 'one simply cannot identify a process that is not a process of a processual type and which, in consequence, is not at that level of abstraction capable of repetition'.[36] A musical score, for example, can be thought of as a continuous flow, an evolution of acoustics. However, there are many instances of repetitive notes; an *a-sharp* or even a whole melody may be repeated dozens of times within the flow of difference. Likewise, animation can be composed of many repetitive elements to express its continual flow of difference.

Therefore, closely related to the animated cycle, but lacking in its formal organization, is what can be referred to as the *recycling* of animation. Recycling does not constitute a direct repetition, but instead the reusing of essential elements in another form or context. Recycled animation might involve the reuse of characters, drawings or perhaps portions of a complete scene. In some cases, the animators might translate only the movements found in a previous sequence, and then apply these to different characters or objects. Again, although economic reasons provided the primary incentive, other motivations such as narrative continuity and referential homage do arise.

In addition to the standard cycle, Frank Thomas and Ollie Johnston outline two other significant varieties of repetition. One is known as the *cross-over,* in which the action of one element is repeated in other elements (in a chorus line of dancers, for example, or a crowd of people). The use of the 'cross-over' was greatly amplified with the advent of Xeroxography, and used heavily in *One Hundred and One Dalmations* (Wolfgang Reitherman, Hamilton Luske, Clyde Geronomi, 1961). And, with the advent of digital animation, the cross-over (and variations of it) has become increasingly commonplace. The second technique that Thomas and Johnston highlight is known as *repeat action,* where only a portion of the animated action is repeated.

> In these cases, the animator could repeat part of the action by borrowing drawings from the earlier scene. In other cases, there would be an action that could be repeated intact in the same scenes – a character climbing a slippery pole, or sliding down an incline, or being knocked down by a mechanical device. Between times, the character would do something different in his attempts to avoid or to conquer, but when he came again to the same spot on the paper, the action of the climb, slide, or hit could be repeated.[37]

In these instances, the recycling of action is not limited to the duplicating of fully rendered or filmed scenes. Because of the possibilities afforded through the *layering process of animation,* the same drawings or the same *elements* (or any combination of these) may be reused in different scenarios. In these cases, movement becomes an abstract and recyclable element. This concept has become increasingly relevant in the use of 3D animation where the key-framed (or motion captured) movement can be easily transferred, dissected and layered.

As mentioned earlier, the Walt Disney studios often reused animated *movement* through the rotoscoping (tracing) of its previous animations. It was perhaps most noticeable in *Robin Hood* (1973), which utilized rotoscoped imagery from both the *Jungle Book* (1967) and *Snow White and the Seven Dwarfs* (1937). But rather lengthy sequences can also be found in a number of other Disney features. For example, animated footage from the *Jungle Book* (1967) was rotoscoped and reused in *The Many Adventures of Winnie the Pooh* (Wolfgang Reitherman, John Lounsbery 1977); footage from *The Sword in the Stone* (Wolfgang Reitherman 1963) was rotoscoped for use in *The Jungle Book* (1967); and footage from *The Adventures of Ichabod and Mr. Toad* (Jack Kinney, Clyde Geronimi, James Algar 1949) was also rotoscoped for use in *The Jungle Book* (1967). It seems that much of this appropriation happened during the time when the animation studio was in both a creative and economic depression. Disney had recently died, many of the older animators had retired and, instead of looking forward or outward for inspiration, instead it began revisiting previously successful productions for guidance (see Figure 2.6). However, Disney was not the only studio to do this, and examples can be found from a number of other studios, including Warner Brothers. In Australia, an interesting example of 'recycling' occurred with the production of animated television advertisements. For many decades Australia imposed strict rules which dictated that virtually all advertisements should be produced in Australia and in some cases, in order to circumvent these rules, production houses would import already produced animated advertisements from America. These would then be rotoscoped, frame-by-frame, resulting in a (nearly) duplicate copy of the original ad, but at the same time effectively conforming to the letter of the law.

FIGURE 2.6 *(a) From Walt Disney's* The Sword in the Stone *(1963); (b) from* The Jungle Book *(1967); (c) from* Snow White and the Seven Dwarfs *(1937); (d) from Walt Disney's* Robin Hood *(1973).*

In his article on *Astroboy*, Steinberg has described the established process of reusing elements in cel animation, particularly with regard to animated television series. In these productions, elements would not only be reused from scene to scene, but also from episode to episode:

> *Dual-use or cel bank:* a 'bank' of images or movements is created to eliminate the need to draw every image of every episode; particular movements and backgrounds are archived and then re-used across episodes, further reducing the production time.[38]

Perhaps the most common reuse would involve the recycling of mouth shapes, which a character will use to 'form' various sounds and words in synched dialogue.

Though recycling in animation has always played an important role, the practice has reached even greater proportions with digital productions. Studios will routinely create libraries within their 3D software of basic poses for each character (such as a standing pose or a seated pose) and animation clips (such as walk cycles, or various actions such as the shooting of a bow and arrow).

This practice can be found to an even greater extent within the production of video games. In games, as with any other 3D animation production, there has been a strong emphasis historically on economy and labour costs; but with games there is also the underlying issue of computing power limitations that has also been a facilitating factor in the use of cycles and reused assets. These productions will frequently utilize repetitive walk cycles and actions, recycled characters and poses as well as repetitive background assets. However, because games normally reconstruct all of their prearranged animated elements into new configurations during game-play, they have become perhaps the most efficient recyclers of the animated form. Thus, not only can an element be reused, but it can also be retextured and rescaled (in real-time) to disguise its recycled nature.

PART TWO

Cognition and Animation

3

Cognitive Animation Theory

This chapter will look at relationships between animation and human cognition in terms of process; it will articulate some common ground between the *processes* of animation and the *processes* of human cognitive imagery. In doing so it will detail an original *cognitive theory of animation* – one that differs noticeably from the bulk of the literature surrounding cognitive film theories, which tend to focus only on the viewer's cognitive response to the completed film. By contrast, this theory will address a number of process-based ideas that, together with a discussion of the use of cognitive imagery, can further position animation quite apart from other media. This chapter will build upon the original animation model offered in Chapter 1 by applying each of the various core concepts of animation to our cognitive system, specifically to what is known as our 'visuo-spatial working memory'. Through this linking of animation to human cognition, the discussions will endeavour to go beyond mere comparative analogy and to also provide a unique perspective of the animated form. Ultimately, it will be suggested that many of the processes of animation and, in fact, the very concept of animation is a basic and natural extension of our real-world experiences.

Cognition as process

Human cognition is a vast area of study; as mentioned, this chapter will focus specifically on our visuo-spatial working memory, the part responsible for creating mental imagery (and for cognitively processing recent visual perceptions). In past decades there has been a shift in the terminology used to describe memory in the literature of cognitive psychology; there has been a decided emphasis placed on the role of our 'working memory' and less on the function of 'short-term memory'. Working memory 'is assumed to be a temporary storage system under attentional control that underpins our capacity for complex thought'.[1] This, according to Andrade, makes it a 'cornerstone of cognitive psychology'.[2] The original *working memory* model developed by Baddeley and Hitcham in 1974 is, with only some minor modifications, a current widely accepted model. It describes a multicomponent system, dividing our working memory into two distinct sections, the visuo-spatial sketchpad (responsible for imagery) and the phonological loop (responsible for language). A *central executive* controls and coordinates both of these. In 2000, Baddeley proposed an additional component, the *episodic buffer,* essentially an interface, which solved the problem of how our working memory is able to work in such close collaboration with our long-term memory (LTM).[3] As the name implies, our *working* memory system is 'a dynamic system that plays a critical role in a wide range of complex cognitive activities'.[4] We can think of it as being continuously active, and in a constant state of flux. This is, of course, appropriate since we live in a world that is in continual flux – to which, quite simply, our cognition has to be able to adjust.

The act of painting a picture from the landscape provides a good example of the utilization of our working memory.[5] As a painter, not only does one have to remember what one sees as one glances away from the real landscape to the canvas, but one is also continually accessing other information: how to paint, one's past perceptions, one's own biases as to what a landscape is. Similarly, the act of picking up a pencil may invoke a 'memory' of a childhood drawing experience; but this is just one of many complex amalgamations of stored knowledge and contemporary perceptions that work together. In short, our working memory is concurrently an immediate processor of both sensory perceptions and recent experiences that work hand-in-hand with our long-term memory, via the *episodic buffer*. It is a very fluid system, which interacts with the more crystallized system of long-term memory. Nicholas Rescher calls for a 'processual view of cognition'; what our cognitive processes can deliver to us is 'putative knowledge' and it is never 'irreversible [or] categorically certain'.[6] Because the world is in flux, our comprehension of it necessitates its continuous re-evaluation; our inquiry processes should also, therefore, be considered as a process in flux.

It is believed that humans are quite limited as to the amount of information they can perceive or cognitively process at any one time. These restrictions were first identified by G. A. Miller as our 'cognitive load' – the maximum amount of information that can be processed at once.[7] For example, we cannot see and process everything that is in our environment. Our mind, therefore, requires a simplification of the world; we do not 'photograph' the world, but select bits of it as needed. Additionally, we do not necessarily store those fragments of information for any length of time, but instead continually re-reference the world, using the world as our storehouse of information rather than our brain.[8] But there is another reason for this process of continual re-referencing and simplification of the world. Because the world is in continual flux, we cannot afford to rely upon outdated photographs. We need to know *now* if a fly has just flown into our space, so that we can blink to discourage it from landing on our eye. Additionally, we do not need to see every detail of that fly; just realizing that a small object is there is enough to stimulate us to react.

Towards a cognitive theory of animation

This particular study of cognition and animation is located at a substantial distance from the traditional approaches of cognitive film theory. These have tended to focus almost entirely on live action (thereby excluding most studies of animation), and have also focused almost exclusively on the viewers' *experience* of the film. Such theorists as Noel Carroll, David Bordwell, Gregory Currie, Torben Grodal and Joseph Anderson have employed this approach, which is invariably concerned with the audience's emotive responses and intellectual interactions with the film. Grodal, for example, details how a cognitive film theory seeks to 'describe the experience of viewing visual fiction and the way in which this experience is created by the interaction between fiction and viewer'.[9] In other instances, these studies strive to sketch associations between the film viewing experience and the experience of actuality.[10] More recently, there have been great advances in the field of neuroscience, particularly in our ability to observe how the brain is actually working, and these technologies are being applied to film studies, though to date most of these studies have also focused on the viewer's reaction to particular films or sequences. To this end, Arthur Shimamura cautions that

> Merely recording brain activity while watching movies is not enough, it is important to consider the psychological processes that are defined by such neural activity. That is, we cannot fall into a modern-day version of phrenology where bumps on the head are replaced by bright spots in the brain. We need to go further and develop neuropsychological theories that describe the functional dynamics of brain activity and how they operate in the service of cognition.[11]

As will be considered later in Chapter 4, 'Reading Animation', there have been a growing number of studies that have looked at animation in terms of viewer perception and cognition. However, these studies have only begun to scratch the surface of how we might jointly consider the ideas of animation and cognition.

Though animation can be considered in similar ways to other forms of cinema, it can be argued that animation should be situated on a different level than traditional film based primarily upon its production processes. It is for this reason that we will bypass much of the discussions on traditional cognitive film theory in this investigation of animation and cognition. This approach will help to clarify both the processes of animation and (to some extent) of cognition (specifically the processes of our visuo-spatial working memory). Therefore, this *cognitive theory of animation* will focus to a lesser degree on how the viewer cogitates animation (although this will be considered somewhat in the following chapter), centring instead on how one can cogitate the world *through* animation. This chapter will consider two concepts: firstly, the manner in which our cognitive processes are analogous to the process of animation; secondly, the fundamental manner in which animation can seemingly embody cognition.

Movement and cognition

Fundamentally, we require the element of motion in order to understand our environment more fully; and if something is lacking in motion, we will attempt to *imbue* it with action. Even the still image or photograph may be 'the basis for constructing dynamic mental models' which can facilitate a better *understanding* of the image's content.[12] There is a rather basic expression about the physical laws of matter, which asserts that 'nature abhors a vacuum', implying that when there is a vacuum, matter seeks to fill it. Similarly, we can consider that our mental processing abhors a *motion-vacuum*, and that we cognitively seek to fill it with movement. The still image (such as the photograph) may contain implied motion, but it is completely lacking in *visible* motion. We can, however, fill such a *motion-vacuum* by the use our 'animate vision'[13] and through the use of what Mary Hegarty refers to as 'mental-animation'.[14]

As was argued in Chapter 1, the process of animation construction requires that we regard motion and image as very *distinct* entities. Movement in animation is always extra-diegetic in process – an imposed element that can be added *to* the image in a number of ways, and even *copied* from other moving forms. Likewise, in cognition, movement and image often require separate considerations. This section will investigate how we cogitate motion and image separately, and how this animation-like process can be used to *animate* our world, thus allowing us to better understand it. It will continue to draw upon relevant ideas from cognitive psychology and process philosophy.

Animate vision

Animate vision, a theory first proposed by Dana Ballard, calls for a consideration and linking of how we *look* at things, with our *cognition* of those things. We do not simply look at a room, take a mental 'photograph' of it and work from that stored image. Our vision is much more akin to our cognitive processes; it is continually *in* process. Animate vision involves the movement of, not just our eyes, but also our head – in fact, our whole body is in constant motion as we visually perceive our environment. (And often we are not particularly aware that we are so active in our vision-related bodily movements.)[15] Andy Clark refers to one primary reason for our engagement in the animate vision process as the '007 principle': we only know what we need to know about things.[16] Not only does such an approach lighten our cognitive loading: it is much more practical to continually reference the present state of our environment than to rely on outdated images of it. That way we can reflexively blink if something flies towards our eye, or quickly reach out to catch a falling flower vase. So rather than being static, our vision is acutely active. We make 'use of rapid and repeated saccades to survey a visual scene', selecting the important details at a high resolution, and gleaning some less important aspects at lower detail, such as broad forms or colours.[17]

Another key factor is that our animate vision allows us to *better* understand our environment, providing increased capabilities of understanding and creativity. It is the act of looking around at a scene and our shifting perspective (our animate vision) that allow us better to understand the space that we are in. Furthermore, our fragmentary saccades of the scene are amalgamated in our working memory, and it is through this amalgamation that a deeper understanding occurs. Not only do we take countless 'mini-detailed-snapshots' of our surroundings that are continuously overlaying previous ones, but we are actively moving around the objects, moving our head slightly or at least physically moving our eyes around to give ourselves a *moving* view. Although not using the term 'animate vision', in an explanation as to why shot-to-shot transitions 'make sense' to the viewer of a film, Anderson notes: 'We explore, we search with our eyes. We move our eyes, we turn our heads, we rotate our whole bodies and we walk around and among objects in our environment.'[18] Therefore the 'leaping' from one view to another in film editing is cognitively plausible. Clark makes comparison to the act of touching (based on the research of MacKay)[19] in which he points out that, if we try to discover something by touch alone, we do not simply place our hand or our finger tips on it; instead we *move* the hand around. This act of movement and exploration allows us a more comprehensive understanding of the object.[20] By using an *active* sense of touch, we can rub our hands upon and over things in order to better understand their form, shape and texture. We do the same with our animate vision: we *hapticly* look over and around things to better understand them. Laura Marks furthers this concept in her discussion of the tactile qualities found in some experimental video works, where she suggests that such a way of looking is a form of 'haptic visuality' in which 'the eyes themselves function like organs of touch'.[21] Most surprisingly, we also engage in a form of 'animate vision' when we dream.

Recent research has shown that our REMs (Rapid Eye Movements) are 'highly similar to saccades during wakefulness in terms of their kinematic properties'.[22] Effectively, our eyes (while we sleep) will physically move about in the same way and engage in the same sort of 'animate vision' actions, as we 'look' at our dream images, that they do when we are awake and actually looking at and experiencing a real-world scene.

The still image can tell us a little about something, but the moving image can tell us something else. Think of a camouflaged 'leaf insect'. When it is motionless on the tree, it is nearly impossible to see. But if, as we look at it, we move around, our shifted perspective may begin to reveal its inconsistencies in comparison to the 'real' leaves on the tree. And when *it* moves, then we are able to discern very clearly that it is something 'other' than a leaf. We see the difference from our movement, from which further cognitive information results. An applicable concept from Deleuze, 'The role of the imagination, or the mind which contemplates in its multiple and fragmented states, is to draw something new from repetition, to draw difference from it'[23] helps to underscore one of the key cognitive roles of motion – that it expresses differences that would otherwise be indistinguishable. The idea that movement can add to our cognitive understanding was established early on with the experimental work of Marey. A person dressed wholly in black, but having white lines painted on his or her costume, when stood in front of a black background will seemingly disappear except for the white lines. These visible white lines will look nothing like a human – except when they move, then they become undeniably human[24] (see Figure 3.1).

By contrast to the still image, movement in the image can provide us with supplementary information – which, however, needs to provide us a significant amount of difference. For example, if the included movement portrays merely that of a swinging pendulum, not much new information is available; but if it provides a great deal of difference, for example a person moving about, then we can infer a great deal more. Schnotz and Lowe give an example of a person walking in a normal and repetitive walk cycle as opposed to a person with a slight limp. The difference inherent in the limp 'deviates from the expected pattern in a specific way' and will provide us with the further suggestion that they have injured their leg.[25] Conversely, cognitive scientist Robert Logie suggests that there is a visual similarity effect: the more similar a series of images, the less likely they are to be remembered. Greatly dissimilar things, because of their noticeable difference, are more easily remembered.[26] When things are not very different, they may blend more into repetition (and sameness). When things are very different, they are better perceived because of their difference.

In animation the more different the images, the more dynamic and noticeable the 'animation' will be and, in turn, the greater the information the image might offer to the viewer. Schnotz and Lowe also stipulate that, for increased cognition, the movement may be *more important* to our

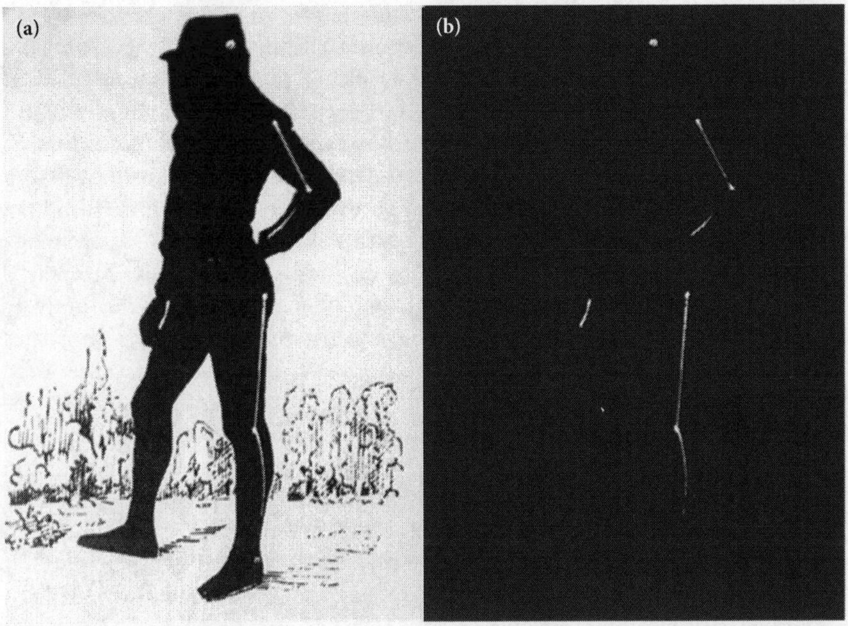

FIGURE 3.1 *Image (a) illustrates Marey's process of painting white lines and points on a figure clad only in black. The altered image (b) demonstrates how the human form virtually vanishes when placed in front of a black background. The human form emerges again when movement is introduced.*

understanding than the image, citing a trend in scientific instructional animation which operates with a very graphic, simplified image but very realistic (complex) movement. This provides a significant 'external analog representation of the temporal changes that occur in the referent situation'.[27] Morrison clarifies that when it comes to learning, the addition of animation has the ability to aid in our understanding of processes, but not necessarily in our *retention of fact*[28]; this implies that in some cases animation will enable a greater level of cognition, but not necessarily provide a greater level of epistemic value. This is one reason why many educational animations are first presented as still images; and then, either automatically or by the users' control, will 'become animated'.[29] It allows the viewer to first 'memorize' the image content and then, when the animation kicks in, to build upon the stored knowledge to better understand *how* it works.

Motion and image as distinct cognitive processes

As has been discussed in the above section, movement has a cognitive power that can extend beyond the still image. In effect, an image without movement only takes advantage of *half* of our visuo-spatial cognitive capacity, while an image *with* movement takes advantage of both halves (the visuo and the spatial) because our visuo-spatial working memory has two distinct processes for accommodating motion and accommodating image.[30] Often, if the still image does not provide us with movement, then we may through the use of our animate vision, or our animate *envision*, attempt to imbue it with some. This addition of movement can further aid our understanding, as both cognitive processes will be activated.

One of the most significant considerations in this analysis of the animated form is that the process of image and that of movement are distinctively asynchronous. This condition also occurs in the process of perception and cognition, which process allows for a complex multiplicity of outcomes. Chapter 1 outlined a number of processes by which movement may be applied to an image. It was argued that the animator must *always* consider the application of motion *to* an image, even if the particular animation technique requires a specific working practice that ostensibly binds it to the filmic image-frame (such as scratch on film animation, or some drawn animation in which movement is derived solely from the difference inherent in each successive image). Even in these cases, the animator must be able to cognitively disentangle movement from form in order to create animation. Nonetheless, there are a number of approaches in which the application of movement to the image is quite a literal and a highly discernible process. Nowhere is the separation of motion and image in the animation process more evident than in the use of motion-capture systems. It is interesting how clearly one can discern the raw data that results from this process. Visual representations of simply a few 'moving dots' can be distinguished as a human, a dog or whatever else was used for capture. Only the thinnest, most rudimentary information is needed to contextualize the visual representations of such 'pure motion' data.

As discussed earlier, a number of philosophers have suggested that the concepts of image and motion should be regarded as separate processes. Henri Bergson claimed that 'in reality, life is a movement, materiality is the inverse movement'.[31] In *Matter and Memory* (1988), he examined how the mind takes sequences of still images and stores them independent of mobility.[32] Furthermore, Samuel Alexander considered motion to be a separate layer and a pure continuum, independent of everything else.[33] Theorist Semir Zeki has observed not only a measurable difference in perception time of colour to form but also a measurable difference in the time that it takes to perceive *motion* distinct from form. He noted that 'colour is perceived before form, which is perceived before motion, the lead time of colour over motion being about 60–80 milliseconds'.[34] A difference in time perception would suggest that there is a separate process involved in the perception and cognition of these aspects. And even though Zeki's studies show that movement is *perceived* last, there are a number of instances in which motion is *cogitated* first. We might, for example, recognize someone from a distance based on his or her motion, long before we distinguish his or her unique visual features. Each has his or her own signature motion; we define a person by that motion. The surveillance/security industry is exploiting this phenomenon, developing various forms of motion identification systems based strictly upon movement.

Just as motion is perhaps the most essential aspect of animation, so it is also perhaps the most significant aspect of our visuo-spatial working memory. According to Robert Logie, our

> visual and spatial working memory are best thought of as separate cognitive functions. In this two-component model, spatial working memory retains dynamic information about movement and movement sequences, and is linked with the control of physical action. [Whereas] visual working memory is passive and contains information about static visual patterns.[35]

This animation-like process can in turn be used to animate our world, thus allowing us to better understand it. The expression of motion will help us to understand our environment more fully; and if something is lacking in motion, we will attempt to imbue it with action. Some researchers have conceded that there may be some limited instances in which image and motion may be considered simultaneously. Stephen Kosslyn offers the example of the viewing of a running horse, in which one might later be able to mentally image it running exactly as it was perceived. This would qualify as 'motion-encoded transformation'. However, Kosslyn continues that this is quite rare; most of the time we experience what he refers to as 'a *motion-added* transformation' in which we add motion to static imagery, or alter the movement of moving images.[36] Motion-added transformations allow us to 'transform the orientation, size, or location of an imaged object'. And, more than likely, motion-encoded transformations are actually augmented with motion-added transformations.[37]

Recent research into 'mirror neurons' also suggests our distinctive comprehension of motion. Mirror neurons are portions of the brain that are activated when we perform a particular physical activity. Significantly, the same neurons are activated in an identical manner when we simply see the same physical activity being performed by another. For example, if we see someone stand up from a seated position, our brain simulates the same 'pre-process' required for us also to stand up. That part of our brain actually carries out the same series of processes and work that it would if we were actually *performing* the action that was witnessed, albeit that they do not culminate in the final action of 'standing up'.[38] Patrick Power, in his discussion of the process of mirror neurons in human perception, suggests that not only does this give us the ability to perceive the 'intentionality' of movement of animated forms, but also that these scientific theories provide confirmation of the 'usefulness of embodied approaches to character animation'.[39] That is, if the animator has experienced a particular movement, then he or she is more likely to be able to transfer it effectively into animation.[40] This not only assists us in our capacity to become better animators, but it also adds further perspective that we are able to consider movement separately from form. Mirror neurons allow us to capture, in a sense motion capture, pure motion independent of form. And if mirror neurons can be compared to motion capture, it is relevant to note that we are able to recognize movement when it is incongruously applied to an alien form. For example, the bouncing of the animated Tigger character adopts the recognizable movement of a spring, and the movement of the Road Runner often exemplifies the movement of a speeding car. Additionally, as noted in earlier chapters, there have been many instances in which Disney (and other studios) has reused animation. Observant viewers (especially animators, who are trained to consider movement independent of form) have been able to detect and identify the reused animated movements of one character when it has been applied (through the use of rotoscoping) to another.

This phenomenon further illustrates how humans are capable of independently considering, and indeed independently 'experiencing', motion disconnected from image (or form). And although Deleuze's assertion that 'Everything, that is to say every image, is indistinguishable from its actions and reactions'[41] is quite accurate, there are two exceptions: our cognitive ability, and the ability (in fact the requirement) of the animation process. Whitehead declares that even though our perception of motion and rest are only observable when *bound to events*,[42] it is axiomatic that we require a conception of pure motion and pure rest, extricated from forms, in order to understand these phenomena. That is, we are often able to better understand the movement of things, when we *segregate* the movement from the thing.

Movement, of course, can add important epistemological layers to animation – it can give life to the character, giving viewers the capacity to identify with the rat in *Ratatouille* (Brad Bird and Jan Pinkava 2007), or the fish in *Finding Nemo* (Andrew Stanton and Lee Unkrich 2003). Movement can also add supplementary meaning to even the most abstract forms, a concept that is clearly expressed in Oskar Fischinger's short, *Allegretto* (1936). This film is composed almost entirely of line, colour and geometric forms; beyond these it contains no clearly identifiable imagery. Yet, because of the manner in which these elements move, they do begin to express an identity. In a number of scenes, movement can be seen to transform these purely abstract forms quite plausibly into easily definable representations: schools of swimming fish. Thus movement can add to, and even completely alter, our reading of an image.

The real strength of animation derives from its capacity to amalgamate motion and image in new ways. Thus the movement of a feather floating in the air is not that extraordinary; but when this movement is applied to a rock, something new and amazing is manifested. Our cognitive strength also derives from our ability to conflate image and motion. We too are able to cognitively conceive the animation process. For example, we may notice only briefly a person sitting on a train, yet subsequently we dream about them that night; and even though we have never *seen* them walk or even move much, we may imagine them walking around and gesticulating wildly. When this occurs it is most likely that we are assimilating various diverse memories. Perhaps we have taken the walk cycle of our cousin and the lip-synced mouth movements of our neighbour, applying them to the person whom we only briefly noticed sitting across from us on the train. Clearly, in doing so, we are considering movement and image as separate cognitive processes. That is not to say that we may still associate particular movements with particular things or events, but as will be discussed further, we are certainly capable of such cognitive separation, and this is explicitly concretized in the process of animation. We could refer to this as a form of *animate envisioning*. In doing this, we are in a sense *making sense* of the images that we have accumulated in our waking hours. Thus, our animate vision provides explication to our perceptions, and our animate envision provides explication to our mental images.

Animated photographs

This section will explore further the practice and theory of animated photographs. In doing so, it will also consider how we might use movement through both our *animate vision* and our *animate envision* to gain a better understanding of the still image. Furthermore, it will be argued that the still image can be considered to contain a scaffolding of motion – in a sense a storehouse of motion that is 'released' when it is viewed. A photograph is an image that is captured from actuality in a rather peculiar manner. It may *look* like a representation of human vision, but it encompasses some very non-human characteristics. One of these is that it normally has a square/rectangular frame around it; another, that it is a whole, complete and unmoving image. The human eye scans and selects bits of visual material that are collaged together, and furthermore, the human eye is continually moving. When we look at a photo, we go through these same processes, but because it is 2D representation, we are severely limited in what can be achieved through our animate vision process. With a moving (cinematic) image we are less 'frustrated' by this dilemma as either the camera moves (thus moving the frame) or the elements within the frame move (thus minimizing the need to activate our animate vision process, at least in terms of comprehension of a still image).

To borrow Martha Langford's description, the photograph may be thought of as a 'subjunctive' medium in that it is not fully realized until the viewer 'looks' at it, requiring the viewer to use their imagination. Much of the photograph's inherent information 'will never materialize without the viewer's active participation', as the photograph requires a shifting back and forth between the 'image and the imagination'.[43] For Alan Cholodenko, a photograph is a *section* of time and not a *frozen moment*. Because the photograph represents the *exposure time* of the capturing of the image (be it at a 1/50th or a one-second exposure setting), the photograph depicts that section of time.[44] If the photograph can be conceived as capturing a section of time, then it could also be considered as an encapsulation of a sequence of movement. This movement is not, of course, immediately apparent. But it is a stored implication of motion which can be released to the viewer, for at that point the viewer activates his or her animate vision and animate envision, spurred on by the inherent visual clues of the image. Schnotz and Lowe have argued that still pictures 'can also be the basis for constructing dynamic mental models'; essentially becoming images that move.[45] In many instances, adds Farrell and Shepard, the mental processing of these images 'can have a perceptual force comparable to that produced by real motion'.[46]

As mentioned in Chapter 2, the stereographic card represents a unique historical example of a dimensional photograph that, because of its unique construct, arguably contains further indications of time and movement.

> The experience of stereoscopy, in particular that which uses viewing devices, makes us aware of the very act of viewing *while we are viewing*. This awareness happens because we feel the tridimensional effect occurring before our eyes, the moment the two images merge. Also, there is a certain tendency of the viewer to spend more time on each 'image inspection' (although the viewing time is completely personal). We peer into the image and into those figures turned into statues for a miraculous 'medusa effect', with an intensity that is not comparable to that of monocular viewing.[47]

This sustained deliberation of the image and its 3D effect can cause us to further extend our animate vision beyond what is normally feasible within the flat image. In this case we may actually shift our eyes and head back and forth as we attempt (and almost succeed) in seeing around the 3D 'frozen' forms. What makes the stereograph furthermore intriguing is that it is essentially a composite of two different images – captured at the same moment, but at different points in space.

> We have no actual movement, no 'movement-image': but the two images of the pair, mentally fused one with each other, and their effects upon the

consciousness of time, space and the gaze enable us to think of a kind of 'time-image'.[48]

And as was explained earlier, when we actually subject the images to the process of animation, we indeed see its movement difference and thereby a very ostensible suggestion of time (see Figure 3.2).

If we look at a still photograph of, for example, a person frozen mid-step, our natural tendency will be to cognitively imbue the still image with movement. Perhaps, we will imagine the person completing the step and we may even see them continuing further on their way. At the same time, we likely marvel at the sight of time suspended – at the 'arrested image'.[49] Thus, the still photograph often presents us with two conflicting expectations: the enchantment of frozen time, and the anticipation or illusion of movement.

In the now common practice of digitally animating photographs (such as those found in the 'cinemagraph'), these conflicting dispositions are often expressed as well. Usually, the movement within an animated photograph will be limited to selected elements of the image. Thus, much of the image will remain frozen in a moment of time while other elements push on in time or, quite often, are looped in an endless segment of time. And as will be discussed more in Chapter 5, there is also the long-standing process of subtly animating photographs for use in documentary film (often as a replacement for the lack of any live-action footage). Viewing such an animated photograph (with limited movement) can be a strange experience. We will normally witness only portions of it moving, the other elements remaining frozen. Our eye immediately travels to the moving elements; but it then travels back to the still portions and these, by contrast, seem

FIGURE 3.2 *An example of a 3D stereograph card (c. 1900).*

even 'stiller' than before. This seems to express an amplified version of the Deleuzian idea of 'abnormal movement' and its affect on the image, 'aberrant movement speaks up for an anteriority of time that it presents on the basis of the disproportion of scales, the dissipation of centres and the false continuity of the images themselves'.[50] Animated photographs, even though animated, simultaneously privilege the single moment, yet in turn extend this moment beyond the normal temporal confines of the still photograph.

Metamorphosis and cognition

This section will detail the process of cognitive metamorphosis, linking this process to animated metamorphosis. Metamorphosis is an essential component of the actual world, but one that we rarely encounter. This is because it often requires an extended period of time to eventuate. But the animated morph through its process of manipulations and replacements provides us with an opportunity to perceive all manner of metamorphosis taking place. It allows us to see change quickly and seamlessly, without traditional conventions of the 'reflexive temporal "gap" or "ellipsis" [of] the cut or dissolve'.[51] Chapter 1 detailed a number of important aspects of metamorphosis in animation. Although metamorphosis can be described as an ongoing process of flux and transformation, to be recognized as such it is generally located within a specific animated structure. One essential aspect of this structure is that it be bookended by two points of recognizable forms, a beginning state and a concluding state, with a sequence of in-betweened transformation. Another important note is that it can be achieved either by an amalgamation of many different objects or through the manipulation of a single malleable object into progressively visible states. Our cognitive processes can also employ a similar metamorphic effect, allowing us to cogitate in a far more fluid manner than if we were bound to, for example, the cinematic conventions of cut and dissolve. Remarkably, cognitive metamorphosis employs a number of analogous strategies that can be found in the use of animated metamorphosis.

In our cognitive processing most 'visual' thoughts appear to be linear and, importantly, to follow and simulate the temporal, spatial and physical laws of the real world. However, these 'laws' appear to be ignored in the *in-betweening* transitional phase which characterizes the progression from one thought to the next. Kosslyn in his discussions of mental imagery does not specifically use the term 'metamorphosis', but instead refers to the 'shape shift subsystem' which is responsible for our ability mentally to transform one object into another. It achieves this both by manipulating objects that we have envisioned and by augmenting them with other image materials which are stored in our memory.[52] Metamorphosis can be an important concept in discussions about the transitioning of thought. When we 'change' from one thought to the next, we do not cogitate in traditional filmic cuts. Particularly in dreams, we may find ourselves in one particular place, only to transition seamlessly to another; or, speaking with one person, to be seamlessly speaking to someone else in the same location. Similarly, in animation, metamorphosis allows us 'to create a fluid linkage of images through the process of animation itself rather than through editing'.[53] Importantly, as with animation, in order to recognize and make sense of metamorphosis, we need to have a starting and concluding object – or, at the minimum, 'a *pause* at a recognizable object' in the animation to allow us the 'unconscious comparison of the present object and the memory of what it was'.[54] Kosslyn also hints at this structure when he asserts that 'one actively anticipates what one will see' next when the 'shape shift subsystem' is employed.[55] In a sense, we 'know' already what the end state will be before we go through the mental morphing process; we are therefore able to comprehend the transformation phase from one thing to another.

Our metamorphosis of thought is aptly illustrated in Caroline Leaf's biographical animation, *The Street* (1976). In this film the animator depicts the childhood memories of Mordecai Richler; scenes morph from one to the next in a strange yet convincing manner. In fact, the film is essentially one continuous morph. Figure 3.3 depicts a sequence where the grandmother is seen mixing a cake, which morphs into her combing a child's hair, and then to her scrubbing the floor. It is very relevant in the context of this animated example, that the thought patterns of the human brain do not normally follow the rigid and decisive cutting language of live action editing, and we can draw comparison to our own visual memory processes.

In the previously mentioned animated documentary *I Met the Walrus* (Raskin 2007), we can see a prime example of how metamorphosis can be used to trace visually our mental variability (although in this example

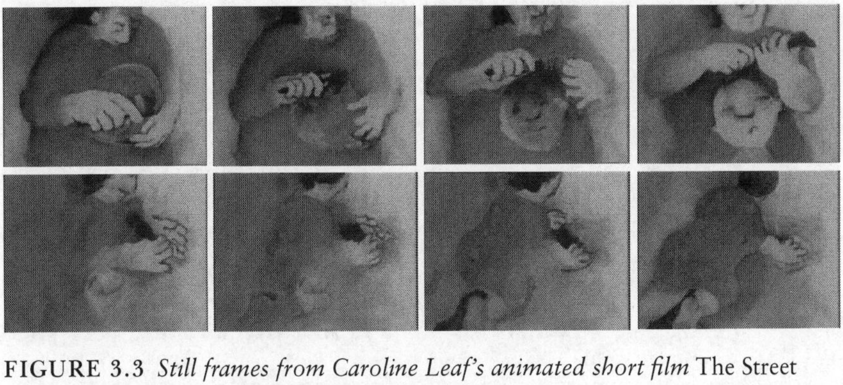

FIGURE 3.3 *Still frames from Caroline Leaf's animated short film* The Street *(1976) depicting a very fluid metamorphosis.*

the animation follows, instead of a dream or a memory, the meanderings of conversational speech). The imagery perpetually changes and transforms as the speaker, John Lennon and the interviewer, Jerry Levitan, discuss a variety of subjects. The animation carefully emulates the progression of subject matter (often down to the individual word), semi-concretizing the flow into an ever-malleable visual display at the same time as a building transforms into a telephone, and a strand of hair into John Lennon. Such visible metamorphic change 'asks that we perceptually accept as real illusions we know cannot be true'.[56] Surprisingly, when our fluid thoughts and conversations are made actual through the convincing illusion of the metamorphosis, the transformations themselves, though appearing conceptually impossible, achieve a physical feasibility. This feasibility, in turn, can provide another layer of understanding.

The use of metamorphosis can allow us to understand very complex processes. By *transforming* our thoughts from one thing to another, we are able to make important associations that allow us to solve complex problems. We can easily imagine things moving up and down (we see this happen all the time in the real world), but we also need to be able to comprehend *how* things change during their various stages of existence. Mathematical and chemical equations, for example, require such a conceptual process of metamorphosis. Additionally, we can imagine a seedling growing into a tree, and thus consider its impact in our garden twenty years into the future. Ultimately, the metaphysical nature of animated metamorphoses allows us to *see* the process of change. Just as we are able to follow a 'train of thought', so metamorphosis can lay down visible processual tracks for evolutionary change. Metamorphosis literally illustrates how the caterpillar transforms into a butterfly: becoming a morphing changing flux-object that can also overtly express its underlying processes of change. Whitehead suggests that when we analyse the world,

> there emerges a process with a form of transition. This unit of process is the 'specious present' of the actuality in question. It is a process of composition, of gradation, and of elimination. Every detail in the process of being actual involves its own gradation in reference to the other details.[57]

Because the world is constantly changing, it can be very beneficial to be able to trace and follow some of these changes. Through animated metamorphoses, not only are we able to see change happen, but we are also able (because of its accelerated change) to compare its beginning and ending states. Referring to clay animation, Frierson notes that 'Metamorphoses are visually stimulating and occupy the mind in an active, extended perceptual game of discovery as the viewer engages the transforming object and finally understands the transmutation in the resulting object.'[58] By our being able to see a real-time morphing process, we are able to see not only the time-space continuum accelerated (which is admittedly an amazing spectacle) but also a compression of information: the forty-volume encyclopaedia, that is the universe is abridged into an easy-to-digest paragraph. However, animated metamorphoses can only readily show us transformation in terms of generalities. We may be shown the overall transformation of the caterpillar into a butterfly, but we are not simultaneously able to see all of the granular inherent processes. Though animated metamorphosis could show us a single set of cells within the morphing caterpillar→butterfly, even this would be merely a single facet of the much greater caterpillar→butterfly transformation, and a generalization of many smaller constituent transformations – for example transformations occurring within the nucleotides and the endoplasmic reticulum. Whitehead suggests that we actively simplify conceptions in order to observe their transformation. For example, we are able to see a moving object because we are able to abstract it out from the individual molecules within the object.[59] Therefore, animated (and cognitively animated) metamorphoses both simplify and generalize the inherent complexity of our world's transformation into readily understood impressions.

Frames and cognition

The process of animation often involves a calculated balance between the individual frame and the larger image sequence. Chapter 1 considered a number of significant issues regarding this relationship. These included issues of detail, movement and the external and internal spaces of the animation frame. Deleuze's concept of *difference and repetition* has also been discussed, particularly in relation to limited animation and fuller animation. This section will focus on the importance of the image in cognition, and of a continuous, linear consideration of these images and the potentially animation-like fabrication of the images in our visuo-spatial working memory.

Cognitive images

For a number of decades prior to 1970, there seemed to have been a certain amount of scepticism surrounding the study of mental imagery. There was substantial debate as to what extent our cognitive processes actually engaged with the creation and manipulation of images. For the majority of those researching cognitive psychology, their focus was on the brain's *non-imagery* functioning. Some from the linguistics disciplines (Noam Chomsky, for example) argued that linguistic structures are hardwired into the brain and that this is the basis of cognition.[60] In the 1970s a greater interest in the study of mental imagery emerged. John Richardson claims that a facilitating reason for this shift in interest was 'the experimental demonstration of the effectiveness of instructions to subjects to use mental imagery in their learning'.[61] As perhaps a direct opposition to the established linguistic model, one alternative theory emerged known as the 'radical image theory' which posited that all sensory perceptions (sight, sound, touch, taste or smell) and experiences are converted and stored in our memory as a series of images. In turn, these images are reconverted back to their original perceptive form when recalled.[62] Later studies in the 1970s and 1980s attempted to bridge these extremes, suggesting a 'dual-coding' approach in which language and imagery are dealt with simultaneously, but within two different processes. According to the 1974 model proposed by Alan Baddeley and G. Hitcham, language is dealt with in an area referred to as the 'phonological loop', images are dealt with in the 'visuo-spatial sketchpad'; each is controlled by what is known as the 'central executive'.[63] Although this model is widely accepted, there is still some debate as to *which* area plays the more significant role. As would be expected, those researching visuo-spatial working memory tend to place a much stronger emphasis on the role that visuals play in cognitive functions.

Traditionally there have been two main areas of cognitive imagery research. The first has been an investigation into how much detail one's cognitive image may contain; the other has focused on the degree to which a cognitive image can be manipulated.[64] The latter has tended to focus on the mental rotation of objects. Stephen M. Kosslyn suggests that this was due to a surprising series of results from the initial experiments in this area, in which subjects were asked to mentally rotate an object: the further they were asked to rotate it, the *longer* it took, suggesting a real-life temporality.[65] More recently, however, there has been a growing interest in the study of creating and manipulating many different kinds of mental images.[66] Kosslyn has explored, perhaps more than others, the creation, movement and transformation of mental objects and has outlined a number of systems and theories to accommodate both the mental generation of still images and of moving images. He has outlined three types of cognitive images: *single-part images*, *multipart images* and *novel images*. *Single-part images* are those that are perhaps closest to the idea of photography being images based on actual perceptions; but quite often they are the result of multiple 'exposures' aimed to encode the full object (for example if something is being partly obscured by a car for a brief moment, a second exposure of the obscured portion will be required when it re-emerges). 'If so, then one subsequently must amalgamate several distinct representations to form a complete image of the object.'[67] *Multipart images* are composites from a number of different sources; they allow us, for example, to visualize Charlie Chaplin sitting on a zebra, on the surface of the moon.[68] Finally, *novel images* are completely new constructs, based on nothing that exists: they are pure abstractions, effectively fabricated from scratch. These may include patterns and abstract forms.[69] These studies effectively illustrate that, as with animation, our cognitive images are normally fabricated and thus represent *highly creative* and *highly controlled* mediations of actuality.

Sequential images in cognition

Although it is not exactly accurate to think of our visuo-spatial working memory as a movie projector in which a sequence of still images are 'played back', every mental image that we create does seem to exist *in* time and *through* time. And, in a comparable process to animation, these images are often fabricated *out-of-time* from a series of time-disjointed elements. Some of these may perhaps even be retrieved from as far back as our childhood, while others may derive from immediate perceptions or from newly devised 'novel images', all of which may be incorporated into one image sequence.[70] In fact, each time we image something, even if it is an apparent 'repeat' of a mental image we 'viewed' yesterday, it is a newly constructed sequence, stemming from a unique act of fabrication. Deleuze, in channelling Bergson, sums up this idea of working memory best by contending 'each present is only the entire past in its most contracted state'.[71]

The idea of a *continuous* mental image is important to the study of cognitive imagery. As mentioned earlier, beginning in the 1970s there were a number of experiments conducted on what are known as *mental rotations*, in which the subject was shown a series of images of rotated 3D shapes in different stages of transformation.[72] Significantly, the subjects were not only able to mentally fill in the gaps of movement but were also able to mentally rotate them around. Interestingly, the subjects always rotated them *in progressive sequence*, that is they rotated them around fully to get to the desired spatial placement, rather than just *flipping* them.[73] These types of experiments exhibit how we are able, when presented with 'key frames' (to use an animation term), to cognitively in-between them (to use another animation term). Clearly this is part of the working process of the animator, one which appears to be echoed in the working process of our mental imagery.

One notorious experiment (that expressed how we perceive the world) involved subjects who were stopped on the street and questioned; but before they could answer the question, two people would walk between them carrying a large door. During this momentary interruption another person would replace the questioner. Surprisingly, even if the new questioner looked completely different, the subject would rarely notice the change, instead perceiving a constant continuum. For Baddeley, 'the fact that the world appears continuous implies that we are storing information about it somewhere, albeit in transformed and reduced form'.[74] Kosslyn suggests that such an effect occurs because we may record a number of partial images: our cognitive processes, working from memory, will then fill in or add to in order to create a continuous sequence.[75] What is perhaps most significant about this experiment is that it conveys how the inconsistencies which are inherent in the varying images of our visuo-spatial working memory can be absorbed into an apparently continuous form. In a sense, we are able to find repetition in difference. There is a parallel to be found in the previously mentioned short animated film *Sisyphus* (1974), which demonstrates the amazing ability by which we are able to merge (with the help of the animated structure) dramatically different imagery into a continuous progression. Even though each new drawing portrays a radically distinctive form, we absorb it and accept the countless different Sisyphuses to be the *same* Sisyphus.

Chapter 1 discussed the detail in the single image and its relation to *accumulative detail* in the successive image. There may be variations, with either a net gain or a net loss of successive detail. For example, each single image may be low in detail, but a greater *accumulation* of detail may result when the single image is put into succession; or there may be a great deal of detail in the single image which becomes obscured in the successive image. Our cognitive imagery also must balance 'a scope-resolution trade-off' when imaging an object or scene. Kosslyn contends that when we create a mental image, we will generally form a simplified 'global image' first, 'which can then be elaborated if need be'. For example, when subjects were asked to imagine a bear and then asked a specific question about its claws, most reported that they had begun with a rather vague image lacking in detail, and then added in more details as necessary.[76] From a cognitive load perspective, this is logical. Why waste all that brainpower making a perfect image if it is not going to be used? Likewise, for the traditional animator, it does not make sense to waste all that effort creating a highly detailed single frame if it is going to be lost on the viewer when watching it in succession. As with animation, simplification of image is a very important concept in cognition.

The spatial frame

Further to the lack of detail *within* the cognitive image, the lack of detail *around* the image also invites consideration – the ambiguity of the cognitive image spatial 'frame'. Although the mental image usually has what could be described as 'outer limits', it normally does not exhibit the unambiguous containment of a film frame, the rectangular frame, full of imagery up to its edges and cut off like a photograph. As we tend only to visualize those objects or people that are important or essential, there may be a void or semi-void around the object of interest. An interesting visualization of this 'effect' is evident in Caroline Leaf's short animated film *Two Sisters* (1990), where we see images that do not 'fill up the frame'. Paul Wells labels such a phenomenon with the literary term 'synecdoche' in which 'a device by which the depiction of part of a figure or object represents the whole of the figure or object'.[77] In *Two Sisters*, we see many free-floating elements. We see a dislocated hand, holding a teapot. The hand pours from this pot of tea. We see the stream of tea beginning to descend into a black void, but as the stream reaches the lower region of the frame, a teacup materializes to 'catch' it. As the teacup begins to fill up, the hand, and then even the teapot, vanishes.

This visual form and aesthetic is employed not only as a visual strategy: it represents also an economic strategy. In animation, particularly in the case of non-layered animation such as the direct animation technique of 'scratch on film' used to create *Two Sisters*, economy of image is essential. In such an instance, the animator is required to draw and repeat every visible element on each and every film frame (see Figure 3.4). By rendering only the essential elements, a lot of production time will be saved. This approach also mirrors our cognitive economic strategy, whereby we might only visualize what is essential in order to adhere to our cognitive load limitations. However, as with the above mentioned animation it also allows for a concerted focusing of attention upon the most essential aspect of the visual image.

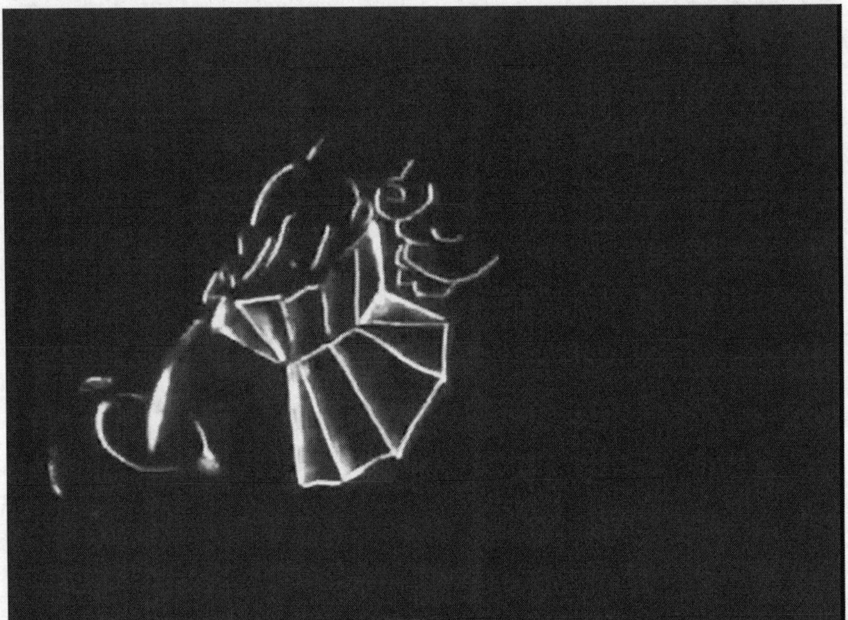

FIGURE 3.4 *Image from the animated short film* Two Sisters *(Caroline Leaf 1990).*

Forms and cognition

Chapter 1 also considered how there are two primary approaches to animation: one involving the manipulation of a single object or image, the other involving the sequential replacement of many different objects or images (although in many cases both approaches will be used in tandem). Similarly, our analogous system of cognitive animation will normally take one or both of these approaches. Kosslyn outlines two types of mental imagery that follows this pattern, the first being the manner in which we progressively construct and augment a mental object. In one experiment (as mentioned earlier) participants were asked to imagine a bear; they were then asked specific questions about the animal, such as 'does it have curved front claws?' In most cases the participants reported that the mental image did not initially display this information; 'they started with a rather vague image of the overall shape, and added the parts as necessary'.[78] The second type of mental imagery demonstrates our ability to create 'novel images' in that we are able to 'mentally draw' patterns and 'squiggly forms' which are 'not simply new combinations of familiar components'.[79] We can progressively draw and alter these forms in much the same way that an animator might progressively alter an oil painting, a blob of clay or a pin-screen.

However, many animated images, and most cognitive images, are better thought of as a form of replacement animation where amalgamations of *many* objects pose as a single object. This is, of course, a common practice in replacement stop-motion animation in which similar (but progressively differing) objects are replaced one after the other in order to create movement out of the differences in their shape, and traditionally drawn animation also normally relies upon this technique as each new drawing replaces the previous drawing. Generally the desired effect is to create the illusion that the animation was generated by one object which has *moved*. We undertake a similar process of cognition when we amalgamate previous images, memories and perceptions. As we look at a car, for example, we select from (in a sense 'see') other cars that we have known, permeating the car at which we are looking with visions of these previously experienced cars. This process of cognitive object-lapse allows us to perform many cognitive manipulations: to close our eyes, for example, and mentally rotate the car or turn it upside down. We could even imagine that we were lifting the bonnet and 'seeing' the engine inside – perhaps even taking it for a drive. If we did not engage in such a mental object-lapse, then every time we saw a new car we would need first to walk around that specific car, looking at it from every angle (inside and out) before we could engage in such mental manipulations.

Because of this amalgamation process, animation 'objects' and mental 'objects' can also be thought of as metaphysical objects: they represent specific objects and at the same time encompass many objects. The reason why an animator might use this process is because it allows one to create the illusion that something very rigid (like a rock) can appear to be a fluidly moveable formation. Similarly, the reason that we engage in a comparable cognitive process is to allow us to fluidly transform and move objects in a manner that may not be possible in the real physical world, but that allows us better to cogitate about them.

One of the reasons why we are able to perceive the many constituent objects used in replacement animation as if they were a single object is that we do this sort of thing all the time in our perception of actuality. The actual world is a very busy place, and when faced with a barrage of multiple images, we often will amalgamate them into a single conception, which allows us to reduce our cognitive loading. We naturally try to find likenesses in similar things so that we do not need to waste energy looking for differences. If there are no significant differences, then we can just write off all of THAT as being the same. When numerous items of difference are presented we will often try to minimize the need for individual scrutiny: we assimilate the differences as repetitions. Thus, rather than having to think about all twenty unique ducks swimming on the pond, we can simply think 'duck' because they all look essentially the same. This idea has been supported by a number of experiments that have shown that when given a series of distinctly different objects or words, participants were able to recall them; but when given a series of quite similar objects or words, they had great difficulty in remembering them, as they would in effect merge together.[80] When we see a series of things in a single view, we have to scan back and forth over them, foveate each one *and* hold a mental image of it in our working memory. When we look at a series of objects, we may look closely at the first few and then, because they all seem to possess the same colour, same size, we may ignore all other features of the subsequent objects. Invariably we skip over details when looking at a series of things and thus simply fill in those gaps from our working memory: by doing so we delude ourselves, and the difference is absorbed into repetition. This is why, for example, it is often difficult for us to perceive the differences between the individual traced drawings that make up an animated boil, yet when played successively through the animation process, we are able to immediately see their differences.

Layers and cognition

The frame is not normally the smallest unit of the animated form; often it is a composite of many other elements, thus making the layer or sub-frame element the fundamental base of animation. The processes of image perception and of image generation also involve a compositing of visual material in our visuo-spatial working memory. Rather than imaging as the camera does, we *see* by amalgamating saccadic fragments of visual information to create a 'visual trace' image, and we generate cognitive images by a multifaceted compositing of stored imagery elements.

Animation clearly benefits, both economically and creatively, from a construction methodology that is comprised of layers. From a perspective of efficacy, by the reuse and reconfiguration of some elements from one frame to the next, only some portions of the image need to be newly created rather than the whole image. In addition, the assembled image offers a greater visual and narrative flexibility as to how it might be animated, transformed or integrated into other images. Similarly, our visual trace images (visual perceptions) and our cognitive imagery (generated images) benefit in much the same way. It is due to issues of cognitive loading that amalgamated images of partial elements are more efficient than the rendering of every detail and nuance. Also, the associative relationship of amalgamated images allows for a greater creative and more complex thought.

These applications embody the process philosophies declaration that everything is made up of processes. All processes (even cognitive processes) can be subdivided into increasingly simpler processes, and their resulting complexity stems not from the individual processes, but from their cumulative effect.[81] This idea of a layered approach to process allows for a complexity beyond the capacity of one single internally complex process. Also, because of this segmentation, each micro-process can be duplicated and applied to some new event without infusing it with old event biases. Similarly, fragments of visual images from other times and places (a camping trip when you were a child) may be incorporated into more contemporary imagery without those fragments necessarily signifying a partial collage of your childhood camping trip.

Perceptive layers

In *Cinema 2*, Deleuze notes:

> We do not perceive the thing or the image in its entirety, we always perceive less of it, we perceive only what we are interested in perceiving, or rather what it is in our interest to perceive, by virtue of our economic interests, ideological beliefs, and psychological demands.[82]

Because of the limited area that our eye's fovea is able to 'see in detail', we need continually to move our eyes around to perceive our environment. What we experience is not a persistent absorption of detail, but a series of small minute saccades that select snippets of visual material.[83] These snippets of vision are then amalgamated into a 'visual trace' image.[84] The 'visual trace' is imagery generated directly by the act of seeing. At the same time it is, to some degree, a collaged image of what we have just seen. This information is interacting simultaneously with information stored, not only in our visuo-spatial working memory, but also in our long-term memory.[85] Kosslyn refers to this as 'high-level' vision as it 'relies on previously stored information about the properties of objects and events', which is similar to our process of constructing cognitive images.[86] By accessing stored information, we do not have to see an entire object each time in order to recognize it.[87] If only a corner of a book is visible, we can still identify it as a book.

We perceive our surroundings in many little saccades which we then use to construct a picture. We do not visually scan everything, but select what seem to be the most important bits; our working memory (in cooperation with our long-term memory) fills in the gaps. These gaps may be filled in from other saccades from just a few seconds earlier, or even from visual information from many years ago, perhaps even from entirely different locations.[88] For example, if we quickly view a room we will visually select items of information, perhaps seeing only one leg of the table, in which case our memory will then fill in the remaining legs, giving the table four legs. Where did the other three legs come from? They may be modelled on legs that we have observed in the past, or they may be replications of the one leg that we actually just foveated, or they may be from composite sources.

For efficacy, we may visually scan a room and use 'rapid and repeated saccades to … extract detailed information only at selected foveated locations', while the rest of the room may be recorded by the 'exploitation of coarser cues (such as colour) that can be detected at the low-resolution peripheries'.[89] We do not need to see everything in full detail. In some instances we may only see the colour of a thing, not the object itself. As described earlier, in his investigation of visual perception, Semir Zeki observed a measurable difference in the time that it takes to perceive colour distinct from form. Noting that, 'colour is perceived before form, which is perceived before motion, the lead time of colour over motion being about 60–80 milliseconds'.[90] Additionally, because of this visual differentiation process, we can take advantage of these 'coarser' colour-based clues in other situations. For example, if we are looking for a bright yellow shoe in a room, we do not have to concentrate on looking for the object – 'shoe': we can simply scan for masses of yellow, which will be more efficient and still likely do the job.[91]

Cognitive layers

One of the most dramatic and frequently used layering processes in animation is the application of a character on a separate layer to the background – a process pioneered in the cel animation technique and continued in many forms of digital animation. By placing characters on separate layers from the background one not only saves expense, but can also explore more freely the transcendence of space and time. Not only does the background not have to be redrawn (or re-rendered) each frame, but also characters and objects can freely move from one space to another without being bound to a particular backdrop. By being able freely to associate various elements in the animation process we can create very complex relationships between objects, characters and spaces that we could not achieve by other means.

In cognition, we can also consider individual objects and their backgrounds as being distinctive. 'The "object-properties-processing" and the "spatial-properties-processing" systems are able to deal with objects and spaces separately.'[92] Not only does this allow us to recognize objects out of context and away from their background (a rose on a garden rose bush, and a rose in a vase at the florist), but it also allows us to imagine an object moving or transcending space and time. We can imagine ourselves travelling from one place to the next. In his description of multipart images, Kosslyn states that

> One of the reasons [cognitive] imagery is useful is that we can visualize objects with novel parts or characteristics or we can visualize scenes we have never actually witnessed. For example, we can form an image of what furniture would look like in different parts of the room.[93]

And, more creatively, it allows us to, for example, envision a clown sitting on an elephant in the Antarctic.[94] By recombining elements we can create new ideas. Finke in 1990 demonstrated how one could, through re-combining elements, invent new and completely unexpected hybrid forms. In his study, subjects were asked to look at two different forms, then mentally to shift and rotate them. After a few minutes they were asked to detail their resulting mental images. Many of the resulting forms were completely unexpected, and would not have been likely to come to fruition if it were not for this amalgamating process.[95] By our being able to 'imagine' an object in a different context, we can gain a different and perhaps a better understanding of it.[96]

Additionally, in many types of animation (especially in traditional cel, and 3D digital) one needs also to consider *colour* as a separate layer to that of the form of the character or object. The cel animation process necessitates the separate application of paint to the reverse side of the inked or drawn cel. And 3D computer imagery begins as a smooth-skinned form that then requires the application of colour, light and texture as separate processes. The benefit of this layering process allows one to independently change one aspect of the image, without having to change the entire image. Similarly in mental imagery there is also evidence that we consider colour as a separate element of form. This is the case in both our visual perception and our working memory systems. In our visual perception, Zeki has demonstrated that colour is actually the first layer that we perceive (ahead of form and motion).[97] Watkins and Schiano (1982) devised a test where subjects were successfully asked to imagine a car (of a particular colour) parked in front of a house, and then to imagine the *same* car changed into a different colour.[98] Such a test clearly demonstrates a capability to manipulate colour and form independently of each other. This study 'not only provided good evidence that people can mentally "paint" a form with colour but also that the coloured shape is then encoded into memory'.[99] Furthermore, Cornoldi et al. differentiate between colour representation in perception images and memory images. They conducted a series of tests comparing colour representation in 'visual traces' (mental images that are formed directly from looking at an object), and 'generated images' (images that are constructed either from recollections or from given instructions). In all cases, the representation of colour was found to be distinctly different in each of the two types of mental images.[100] It could thus be inferred from these studies that, because we cognitively process colour as a separate layer, we can easily affect that particular layer of information without having an effect on the object itself.

There are two primary reasons why both animation and cognition engage in such layering processes: for economy, and for increased flexibility. Because we do have a significant visual and cognitive load limit (we can only see or process so much at once), any reduction that we can achieve is advantageous. Therefore, we only 'see' what we need to, and we only cogitate what we need to. Separating elements to 'different layers' is one beneficial approach. The animator, by splitting things into layers, is only required to move or affect the portion of the image that needs to be moved, which allows for a much speedier and efficient result. This approach was heavily exploited in cel animation, and has continued in much the same way in many applications of digital 2D animation. Perhaps most importantly, the ability to recontextualize layers of mental imagery allows us to develop a more complex understanding of what it is that we are considering – which is also an enormous creative advantage to the animator.

Time and cognition

This section considers the idea that cognitive imagery is time based, and that it can also profit from (as presented in previous chapters) the separation of the conception of time into narrative time, discourse time and production time. Both animation and cognitive imagery are temporal experiences, each constructed from extra-temporal components. Because of this, the raw elements which make up the temporal mental image possess their own unique temporal context, which is absorbed to varying degrees into the larger cognitive animated image. These elements belong both to their native temporal succession (stored memories) and to the current cognitive animation (manipulated mental images).

Our cognitive animation may present us with scenarios and narratives that span varying lengths of narrative time. They might encompass events lasting a fraction of a second, or spanning our lifetime. As with the previous discussions of animation, what is significant here is how this narrative time may contrast with the other readings of time. We imagine or recall scenarios that take place in time and through time. Time progresses always forward, as do our thoughts which are bound *in* time. Even though we may remember something that occurred in the past, we always go back to the beginning of that event, and then 'play it forward'. 'Memory can admittedly take you backwards and forwards in time, but when reproducing events you can only reconstruct the sequence of your experiences the way that they happened.'[101] Live action cinema can afford us the unique experience of viewing events backwards (someone falling *up* off the ground). Obviously, when we watch a film recording played backwards, we are watching it in a forward progression of time; but it depicts an actual event that, we, the viewers are subsequently able to experience 'backwards'. Animation is less effective in its perceived ability to provide us with this experience. We may view the animation of a character that was animated to appear to fall *up* from the ground; or we may watch the animation of a character falling *to* the ground, that is *played* backwards. Yet each of these scenarios becomes irrelevant when we consider that the animation was *made* disjointed of its narrative time (and space) through a complex production-time process. Yet with all of these (live action, animation and cognition), although they may represent a reversal of narrative time, we still 'watch' in a progressive discourse time.

In most instances our working memory is bound in time. Thus when we imagine an action, we think it through in 'real time', just as we would if acting it out in real life. As has been indicated earlier in the discussion on the *continuity* of mental imagery, there have been a number of studies involving the mental rotation of objects; one such study asked participants to look at a picture of a cube and then to mentally rotate it in three-dimensional space. The studies found that not only did the participants rotate the cubes as if orientated in actual space but also that the *further* a participant was asked to rotate the cube, the proportionately *longer* it would take to do so.[102] We mentally move our cognitive images in the same real-time manner in which we move real-world objects. Another study asked its participants to imagine the act of carrying a small, round air-filled balloon across a room, and then to imagine carrying a similar sized cannonball across the room. Each of the participants took longer to imagine the time to carry the cannonball the same distance as it took to carry the balloon.[103] In another series of studies, Mary Hegarty demonstrated that when subjects engage in 'mental animation' as a means of solving a visual problem, solution time was proportional to the number of spatial manipulations that were needed to be performed, suggesting an 'isomorphism between the physical processes and their mental analogs'.[104] So, even though mental imageries of events are constructed *out of time*, they are still presented to us in an apparently normal progression of time.

Like most animation processes, our mental images are not at all linear in their construction. The previous chapter referred to the amount of time that it takes to construct and amalgamate the animated image as *production time*. Although it may appear that we are able to construct a *mental* animation instantaneously, every image that we construct is potentially made up of elements from the full span of our lifetime. Henri Bergson in *Matter and Memory* noted that we are continually referencing childhood and various other points in our life where we learned or experienced something new. Because of this continual recalling of memory, we exist in a sort of non-chronological time. Memory defines us; we are a flow of memory. Every perception is related to a memory that allows us to move and to act.[105] Logie asserts that when we perceive something, the information first travels to our long-term memory to access our stored knowledge of the world (which could date back to our childhood), and then moves to our working memory for cognitive processing.[106] As demonstrated in the 'Layers and Cognition' section, we store many fragments of information, and we can combine these to make a single mental image. This mental image is continually updated, continually retrieved and re-amalgamated. This collage process is invariably a time-disjointing process. Thus, although we remember in a linear fashion, the elements of the memory are not necessarily of cohesive time. In a sense the production time of a mental animation is as protracted as our age.

Memories are at once composed from the past; but at the same time, and more importantly according to Bergson, they combine something original with something in the present.

> Memory remains attached to the past by its deep roots and, if once realized it did not feel the after-effects of its original virtuality, if it were not, at the same time as it is a present state, also something contrasting with the present, then we would never recognize it as memory.[107]

Memories (and therefore virtually all mental imageries) are not past events; they are present- and, more importantly, future-looking creations. Despite the memory processes often being associated with things past, all processes (including memory) are forward-looking. Rescher notes, 'processes develop over time: any particular natural process combines existence in the present with tentacles that reach into the past and the future'.[108] Memories are contemporaneous constructions that progress forward through future-time. Additionally, they do not draw all of their constructive elements from the time that is concurrent to the recollection event, but draw upon a complex amalgamation of time-disjointed events. In our cognitive imagery, we are continually amalgamating memory-specific elements into new constructs. Bergson notes that the mental image is 'no longer successive, but simultaneous, of a *before* and *after*, and that it would be a contradiction to suppose a succession which was only a succession, and which nevertheless was contained in one and the same instant'.[109]

As discussed earlier, animation essentially pervades through a disjunction in time. To begin with, the amount of time it takes to create animation is usually far greater than the amount of time it takes to view it (although film in its most pure, un-edited state could exhibit an equivalence of viewing time to production time). When the animator takes a series of independently constructed images or objects and strings them together to make an animation, he or she is creating a new sequence of time composed of images from a separate time context. These individual images contain a particular time context; when amalgamated with others, this contextual time is absorbed and a new time emerges. Again, we can consider the manner in which studios such as Disney have reused animation from previous productions. In such cases the animator is at once creating a new construct, but also reusing past elements. Thus the animated feature *Robin Hood* is at once *Robin Hood* of 1973 but also *Snow White* of 1937.

Sound and cognition

In animation and in cognition, sound and imagery are controlled by at least two distinctive processes. As outlined at the start of this chapter, sound and language information is handled within our working memory by what is known as the 'phonological loop', while visual and spatial information are dealt with in the 'visuo-spatial sketchpad'. There is evidence that these two sections work closely with each other and, most notably, that we are able to build up visual images based upon verbal descriptions.[110] Also as discussed previously, the production of animation often requires that the auditory precede the ocular (particularly in instances of lip-synched dialogue animation). Consequently, the animator will create and animate the visual imagery in *response* to the audio-soundtrack. There is, of course, the quite literal physical effect that sound can have on us; 'for example, loud noises – either recorded effects or musical sounds – can elicit instinctual reactions from spectators'.[111] Sounds can make us jump, and we may even follow complex orders from someone whom we perceive to be in authority (for example, 'please sit down in the *green* chair'). But sounds can also illicit cognitive imagery.

There have been a number of recent studies that have looked at the 'language-to-representation interface' in human cognition; humans have a unique ability to 'construct and inspect visual images of spatial configurations that have come to their knowledge through some indirect experience mediated by language, rather than through direct perceptual (visual) experience'.[112] We engage continuously in this activity. Someone tells us a story: we visualize the scene in our minds. Much of our cognitive visual imagery is 'driven' by acoustic language. This process, in which audio triggers cognitive 'imagery' and 'animation', is in many respects identical to the process of animation (specifically, the application of motion to form in response to a pre-recorded soundtrack) – which (as argued earlier) is contradictory to many of the processes of the physical world. In the latter case, the body must first move in order for sound to be physically generated. In fact, our *vocal* communications require an *intimate* manipulation of the body, which is quite different from the act of knocking on a door. According to Whitehead, 'voice-produced sound is a natural symbol for the deep experiences of organic existence' because it involves the excitation of such 'vague intimacies' as the essential organs of the 'lungs and throat'.[113] There is something quite deep and unique about the creation of vocal sound; but there is an equal complexity in the creation of vocally induced mental imagery.

In a series of studies on visuo-spatial working memory a number of participants were asked to imagine that, looking through the window, they could see the Statue of Liberty and that a daffodil was hidden inside the torch held by the statue.

> In the majority of cases, the subjects reported making the concealed object visible directly, imagining being able to 'see through' the concealing surface, or imagining some movement or change of position which brought the object into view.[114]

This study demonstrates a number of important animation-style concepts. For example, it demonstrates the complex aptitude of our cognitive imagery and cognitive animation. It also demonstrates what is, for Paul Wells, one of the most significant strategies of animation's narrative form, which he terms 'penetration'. Wells describes this unique-to-animation effect as 'the ability to evoke the internal space and portray the invisible'.[115] The act of creating mental animations that travelled from the exterior space of the Statue of Liberty, penetrating the walls to reveal the inside space, shows an important comparative strategy between animation and our visuo-spatial imagery.

Audio contexts

But perhaps one of the most vivid examples of the audio to cognitive imaging process is experienced when one listens to an audio-only medium, such as a radio broadcast, and experiences a sound-driven 'animate envision' – a sound-driven cognitive experience. We hear the words, sounds and intonations: we create mental pictures, then we animate those mental pictures. It is not surprising that some of the liveliest discussions of how audio can affect mental imagery derive from the area of radio studies.

It is also significant that in radio dramatizations where narratives are presented purely through sound, scenes and characters can seem very ephemeral. According to Andrew Crisell, as we listen to a broadcast 'Anyone present in a scene has to be identified – given speech, addressed or referred to fairly regularly so that the listener remains aware of her.'[116] If, for example, there is a scene in which a group of people are sitting at a dinner table, eating and having conversation, our 'mind's eye' will normally visualize only those characters that are speaking or have very recently spoken. If an element or character remains silent for too long, 'if not regularly heard or referred to, she "disappears"'.[117] If sufficient time is allowed to pass, we may even envisage the conversation as taking place in a bland featureless space, devoid of table and food, until we are 'told' to focus on particular elements again. Such a scenario has led Crisell to assert, 'Radio is positively besieged by silence – a silence which portends non-existence, annihilation.'[118] But rather than finding this to be a deficiency, Crisell notes that since the radio drama is a constructed space which must be continually renewed, it is well suited to 'the presentation of fluid, indeterminate worlds'.[119] Similarly one could claim that because animation is a *visually* constructed space, it is similarly well suited to the presentation of the instable.

Perhaps the most unique aspect of the audio-to-cognitive imagery process is the complexity of the imagery that can result. For example, while listening to an audio-only presentation, we will often envision multiple spaces. We might visualize the speaker inside the radio studio as he speaks into a microphone; and if the speaker is describing a particular place (the beach), we might suddenly visualize him as being there while he describes it to us; later we might visualize a described event (a shipwreck) that occurred 150 years ago. This complexity is illustratively made available to us in two examples of 'animated radio' broadcasts: Dennis Tupicoff's animated short *His Mother's Voice* (1996) and *The Ricky Gervais Show* animated series (2010–2012).

The Ricky Gervais Show was an animated series derived from the original audio recordings of the Ricky Gervais radio show that were produced between 2001 and 2005 (and some of these were subsequently released as a podcast in 2005). It comprised a rather free-format radio show that featured three well-known actors, Ricky Gervais, Stephen Merchant and Karl Pilkington, who would banter about various topics (often at the 'expense' of Mr Pilkington). In keeping with a conversational format, the radio show featured discussions, debates, personal anecdotes and occasionally elaborate fictional tales. It proved to be very popular when it was made available as a downloadable podcast. In order to capitalize on this, it was then made into an animated series.

In each episode of the animated series, at least four different cognitive-animation states are depicted. Firstly, the show would open with a live-action shot of the actors in the radio studio, effectively establishing its real-world audio origins (see Figure 3.5a). Next this scene would become transformed into an animated scene set in an animated radio station (see Figure 3.5b). In this state, the characters would speak and banter with each other, but remain stable in their roles as (animated) radio presenters within a studio space. In this state, they might say things like 'Hello, my name is Ricky Gervais, and that one over there is Karl Pilkington.' However, as their conversations would evolve, they would generally begin to speak about events or places outside of the studio space. For example, in one episode they played out a hypothetical scenario in which they were at a gas station, about to embark upon a road trip; but first had a debate as to whether it would be better to use a traditional map or a GPS device to find their way. As a radio listener we would most likely have envisioned them at a gas station, but still be aware that it was the *presenters* speaking about a particular 'hypothetical' event. Thus, during these moments in the animated

FIGURE 3.5 *Images from* The Ricky Gervais Show *animated series (Series Two). These four frames illustrate the primary different audio states that are expressed through the animation series: (a) a live-action view of the radio presenters, (b) an animated interpretation of the radio presenters, (c) a fictional setting in which the presenters might imaginably be situated and (d) an entirely fictional scenario featuring fictional characters in a fictional location.*

series the presenters themselves were portrayed as being at a gas station and having a debate among themselves (see Figure 3.5c) On other occasions, one of the presenters (Karl Pilkington) might tell a completely fictional tale, for example, about a turkey that 'whistles' when it perceives danger (see Figure 3.5d). During such a scenario the animators illustrated the scene with entirely fictional characters in an entirely fictional location. However, as the show's format was also very much about the banter between the presenters, one would frequently interject while another would be telling a story. During these occasions, the interrupting comments might be seamlessly integrated into the fictional narrative – for example the 'whistling turkey' might be made to lip-synch Ricky Gervais' rather disparaging comment about the general storyline. The animated depiction of these diverse settings seems to emulate (albeit sometimes rather playfully) the same cognitive animation imagery that the listener would have experienced while listening to the original audio-only broadcast.

A similar example can be found in Dennis Tupicoff's *His Mother's Voice* (1996). It is also an animation based on a recording of a live-radio broadcast, and also depicts multiple unique audio-scapes. The original broadcast featured an interview with a mother, Kathy Easdale, who had recently lost her son in a tragic and deadly accident. At the start of the film, an image of a live-action radio was shown in order to establish a real-world audio context (see Figure 3.6a), and the fact that it was derived from an actual radio broadcast. The next sequence (while the mother described the events surrounding the death of her son) illustrated those actual events in a

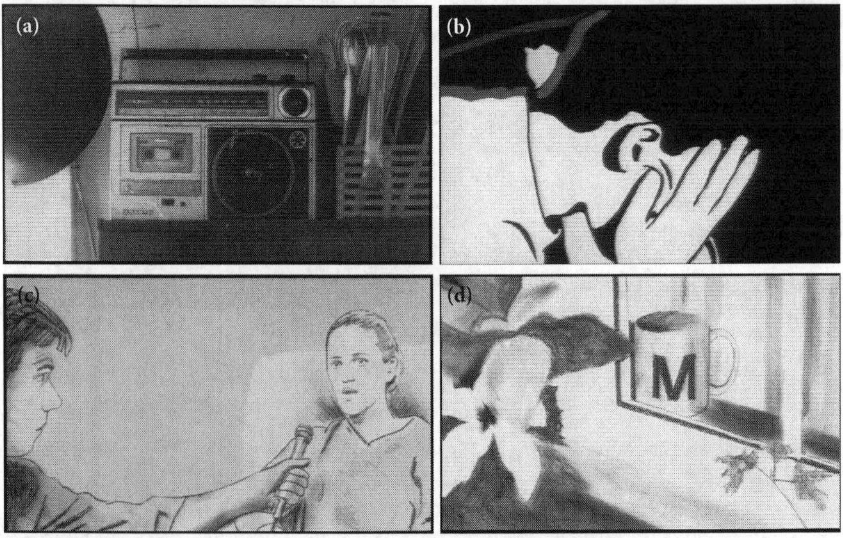

FIGURE 3.6 *Images from the animated film* His Mother's Voice *(1996) by Dennis Tupicoff.*

comparatively graphical style (see Figure 3.6b). Another sequence depicted not the events that she was describing but the mother herself as she was being *interviewed* (see Figure 3.6c). It was a very emotional interview, and the mother's grief was quite evident and palpable throughout her vocal delivery. The most powerful element was, of course, her feeling of great loss and emptiness. To highlight this, in the midst of the interview, and while still hearing the mother describing the narrative, the animated camera began to wander around her house, visualizing many of her son's belongings, including his empty room, and finally an image of a coffee cup that was inscribed with the letter 'M' – presumably belonging to Matthew, her deceased son (see Figure 3.6d). Though very different in atmosphere and content, both *His Mother's Voice* and *The Ricky Gervais Show* are excellent examples of how vocal performances can elicit very fluid cognitive visualizations that can transform through time and space, depending on the perceived audio cues. It is such fluid depictions that seem to correlate remarkably well with our own visualizing experiences which can freely float from one animated context to another.

Non-verbal audio-imagery

There is something exceptional about the intimacy of the human voice and, as demonstrated in the above example, it can generate multiple layers of cognitive animation. Yet, what of the non-verbal sound? How does non-verbal sound impact cognitive imagery? Normally, the non-verbal sounds that we hear are contextualized or 'anchored' to some *thing* (for example a roar of an engine emanating from an accelerating car). In the case of radio, the sound effects do not possess this visual anchor.

It is interesting that, according to Crisell, the non-verbal sound effect often requires precise contextualization for the listener to be able to image it.[120] But once that contextualization is provided, anything is possible. We can believe that a cow mooing is a horn honking, that the head of cabbage being smashed is a foot tromping in the snow. And with cinema, when given a pictorial context, we readily accept a 'boinging' sound to be that of the Roadrunner hopping, or the roar of the rhinoceros to be the sound of a tornado in the movie *Twister* (Jan De Bont 1996). As Andrew Crisell points out, 'sounds require textual pointing – support from the dialogue or narrative. The ear will believe what it is led to believe'.[121] In a radio dramatization one will usually have a sound effects person create particular sounds that purport to be indexes of real life, yet are produced by other means. For example, coconut shells are clapped together to simulate the sound of horse hoofs. This is an iconic representation of the sound of a real horse trot. However, at the same time, it is an actual broadcast of a person clapping coconut shells, which is an indexical representation of coconut shells being clapped. Thus, the combined effect, according to Andrew Crisell, is an 'iconic-index'.[122] Thus, even with the radio sound effect, there is a multiple layering of imagery that may occur; we may envision a horse trotting along, or we may envision a person clopping something on a tabletop.

In 1951 UPA studios produced a short animated film entitled *Gerald McBoing Boing*, which can be considered as an embodiment of the radio broadcast experience. It is about a boy who cannot speak, but instead makes 'sound effect' noises. He is soon employed by a radio station to become their 'sound effects department'. What makes the sound effect noises that Gerald produces so compelling is the fact that he generally pantomimes his actions while 'performing for a radio broadcast', thus the viewer is given the necessary contextualization to make sense of the strange noises emanating from his mouth. Using his thumb and index finger, he pretends to 'shoot a gun' while making a 'gunshot' sound; he pantomimes opening and shutting doors as he makes the 'clicking' and 'slamming' sounds. In *The Ricky Gervais Show*, a number of non-verbal sounds also emerge during the radio show; for example, the presenters will frequently be heard to be banging on the table, or going into fits of uncontrollable laughter. Normally these will be expressed in animation that is situated 'in the studio' (see Figure 3.5b). However, in other cases they may be incorporated into the 'other spaces' (see Figure 3.5c or d) of the animation. However, on top of this, the animators have added supplementary layers of sound effects (that were not part of the original radio broadcast) that serve to emphasize and contextualize the animated imagery.

Thus, by its assimilating sound and image as separate and distinctive processes, our cognitive animation has the flexibility and complexity of the animated image. This complexity is further compounded by the fact that, in many instances, both cognitive animation and traditional animation are produced *in response* to audio.

Abstraction and cognition

There is no singular aesthetic to the animated image, nor could there be said to be a singular aesthetic to the mental image. Yet there are a series of similar processes that can be detailed in relation to the animated image and the cognitive image. And both of these unequivocally must engage in abstraction. As has been argued in previous chapters, *all* animation is inherently abstract in one way or another – that is, in the process of its construction, all elements invariably become (1) simplified, (2) distorted and (3) decontextualized. From a practical standpoint, even if the aspiration is there, it is very difficult to fabricate and emulate *every* realistic detail of image and motion in an animated form. It is normally too onerous and expensive to render every nuance; and such detail is normally unnecessary. It is often the case that only the essentials *need* be visualized. It can certainly be argued that by utilizing simplified lines and shapes, and fewer blocks of colour, the animated image (particularly in the earlier cel animation process) saved enormous amounts in time and resources. Of course there are motivating factors other than economy for creating simplified imagery in animation (including issues of graphical design and aesthetics). For example, it could be credibly argued that the American UPA studio's use of extreme simplification of imagery were for reasons of both economy and style: or that, at least in pursuing one of these reasons, they also successfully realized the other.[123]

Furthermore, our visual perception process does not operate like a camera. We do not 'see' every detail of our surroundings. Not only is our field of vision severely limited to 'just what is in front of us' but also what is *within* our field of vision has an even smaller area of 'focus'. The area that we see in detail, that which we process with the fovea area of the eye, is very small; the rest of the 'field of vision' is perceived in the most rudimentary of detail; light and dark and some large blocks of colour.[124] Our visuo-spatial working memory systems will often engage in a similar process of simplification. We are severely limited in the cognitive load capacity of our working memory (though our long-term memory functions are much less limited). Thus when we recall events, only sections of, or particular elements may be 'visualized'. For example, we may remember a particular past conversation, but recall a clear image only of the orange, horn-rimmed glasses on Aunt Clara's face. It is the limitations of our visual system and the further limitations of our cognitive load capacity that cause us, automatically, to simplify our mental imagery for reasons of economy. However, as with the UPA studios, it could be argued that our simplification of mental imagery is what potentially underpins some of our innate creativity and imagination.

Cycles and cognition

As with animation, the human cognitive system also engages in cycles and in the re-cycling of cognitive components. There are a number of instances in which such a cognitive cycle image is manifest and, as with animation, there are different motivations for the use of cognitive cycles: one is efficiency; another provides for better understanding and comprehension.

In keeping with previous discussions of cognitive loading and of Deleuze's *Difference and Repetition*, it appears that we also seek to find temporal patterns in and of divergent *events*. We respond to cycles because they are seemingly quite common in our world, although if one were to perform a close examination, one might find that most of such apparent cycles actually possess many individual differences which are evident from one revolution to the next. In fact, Taiwo wonders if perhaps the concept of the cycle might actually be a purely cognitive construct:

> When we collectively observe repeated cycles in temporal space, are we in actuality performing a perceptual dance in the act of seeing, conceptualizing and reflecting the rhythmic patterns in the universe's material performance? […] Are we constructing new models using existing principles […] in order to understand nature, that is, what we are essentially wondrously awestruck by?[125]

Arguably, it is much easier for us to consider that today's sun rising and setting is identical to the one that took place yesterday (and that of last Tuesday). Similarly, when we witness someone walking, rather than noticing difference in every step he or she takes, we diminish those differences and see the action as a series of repetitive movements. Such a process is comparable to what Schnots and Lowe call cognitive 'chunking', which entails the condensing of information into easily encoded 'chunks'. It does this by 'subsuming a set of items under a super-ordinate item'.[126] In this way, a cycle can embody the simplification of complex activities into containable and recognizable temporal patterns. An important use of a cognitive cycle is the manner in which it can facilitate understanding of complex concepts. For example, we may 'mull things over', repeatedly enacting out scenarios or imagining a complex process time after time in order to make sense of it. As Deleuze has noted, 'repetition changes nothing in the object, but does change something in the mind which contemplates it'.[127]

It has been suggested by de Koning et al. that the animated diagram of the type used in educational animations utilizes loops to show complex processes repeatedly. These repetitions enable the viewer to better grasp the complexity and understand the processes.[128] Animation is an important tool for this understanding and, although a cyclical process can be illustrated in a still diagram, it requires the subject to infer the dynamics of the process. A common problem that a viewer may encounter in trying to infer an illustrated system (such as how a machine operates) is that most try to conceive (mentally animate it) in a *linear* manner, even though the process may be cyclical. This generates a greater comprehension of the earlier segments of the process, but less (if any) of the later processes. But the viewer, when shown the cycle repeatedly as an animation, will have increased comprehension, considering it less as a linear event, more as a system that occurs *simultaneously*.[129]

Often while watching a cycle, the viewer may focus on absorbing only one facet of it (though all the while keeping in mind the greater cycle); then on the second viewing may focus on understanding a subsequent facet of the process.[130] B. B. de Koning et al. conducted a test in which they showed an animation of a cardiovascular system and found that, on average, subjects needed to view the cycle (which lasted ten seconds) at least six times in order to gain a good understanding of the process. Additionally, it was found that if certain aspects of the cycle were spotlighted during the repetition of cycles, it would sometimes help in the understanding of the complex cycle by, in a sense, breaking it down into smaller chunks, but without distracting from the overall larger system and context.[131] An animated cycle may compress an enormous amount of information. Such a compression of information, even though it requires the viewer to unpack a lot of the information through repeated viewings, maintains an authenticity of temporal and spatial interrelationships that could not occur if the cycle were broken up into many linear sub-processes and viewed sequentially.

4

Reading Animation

This chapter, as with the previous one, considers animation in terms of cognition. However, the emphasis here is on some of the unique ways in which audiences might interpret and in turn be affected by animation. First, it considers how we might cogitate the animated image, including the double cognitive coding that can occur when viewing some more graphical forms of animation. This is followed by an exploration of audience interpretations of a number of relevant topics, such as anthropomorphism, animated performances, stop-motion, video games and various hybrid forms of animation.

Interpreting the abstract and the graphical

Though animated imagery can look identical to live action, traditionally much of it has tended to be rather simplified or graphical in nature, and these graphical images can express a unique set of interpretive possibilities. This section will detail how such animated images have the capacity to: (1) appeal to potentially wider audiences; (2) be less demanding in terms of our direct perception of the images; (3) yet also be more demanding in terms of our cognitive interpretation of the images.

A simplified image lacks descriptive detail and can express a certain amount of 'incompleteness'; as a result, the viewer can interpret these images more broadly and can apply to them a wide range of meaning and identity. In this manner, Rescher suggests, 'for as long as our descriptions remains incomplete [...] when there is any sort of incompleteness, there will always be a plurality of alternatives'.[1] Scott McCloud in *Understanding Comics* describes how, with a diminishing lack of detail in a character's face, there is a lessening degree of information presented regarding gender, race and age. This deficiency can allow the audience the opportunity to interpret the image in many different ways – even leading to a greater individual affinity for the character, regardless of the viewers' demographic.[2] Though McCloud was specifically dissecting the comic book form, it is a discussion that is equally applicable when considering the international success of some of the more prominent Disney's characters, or that of Pokémon or Felix. Simply put, their inherent ambiguity potentially broadens their appeal.

The graphic simplification of many cartoon characters can also allow for a relatively effortless perceptive identification. For example, the traditional cel cartoon image of Mr Magoo or Astro Boy, with its simplified line and limited blocks of flat colour, has a simplicity that does not normally tax our *perceptive* load limit. We often do not have to foveate and repeatedly scan the image to 'perceive' it. In contrast, a 'fuller' image (a photograph, or a detailed drawing) might require a more active vision process (see discussion of 'animate vision' in earlier sections). That is, the viewing process of such a detailed image may require numerous saccadic views to 'see' the image, compared to the larger 'chunks' of imagery that a Pokémon character may afford.

Conversely, the simplified animated image may place greater strain on our *cognitive* capacity. The form and movement of Mr Magoo, for example, is not 'natural'; it is a graphical representation of human form and movement. It represents both a simplified and a uniquely creative interpretation of actuality, which requires the viewer to continually translate and reinterpret it. Eric Jenkins, in his discussion of classical Disney animation, notes:

> Indeed, the low level of detail in the cartoon image demands that viewers become a part of the image. The viewer fills in so much detail that they feel they are participating in the image-world.[3]

Graphical animation requires its audience continually to interpret its pictorial signs, processing them to a semblance of veracity and facilitating a highly engaged viewing experience. Furthermore, because the viewer is compelled to translate and reinterpret the graphical imagery and movement, it can also allow for a personalization of the simplified image. That is, when we look at an image, we bring to it our own memories and experiences, and thereby extend that image (a concept that Bergson referred to as the 'memory-image'[4] and Deleuze the 'recollection-image'[5]). Images can serve as cognitive storehouses and provide us a with a 'memory trigger'. In fact, objects, places and material things may hold the key to the effective triggering of strong memories, which explains why we so fondly cherish things or places from our childhood: we rely upon these to trigger our stored memories. The stronger the trigger cue, the more vivid (and possibly accurate) will be our memory. Because of live-action film's more indexical nature, most would assume that it can function more effectively than animation as a memory trigger when such objects are represented.

However, because of the generally iconic nature of a lot of animation, and because of the simplification of much of its imagery (either of its form or its movement), it has the potential to serve as a more universally accepted memory trigger. Even though animation may not provide as strong a memory trigger as live-action film might to a limited audience, it might serve as a *weaker* trigger, but to a much *larger* audience. For example, animation may not be able to portray the very house that you grew up in (only your personal video footage could do that); but it might portray an effective symbol of a house, with its invitingly warm yellow interior light and other familiar features. The viewers then use their imaginations to replace it with their own home, thus perhaps avoiding a potential confusion that could be caused by the indexical/real portrayal of someone *else's* childhood residence.

Henri Bergson used the term 'memory-image' to describe virtual images (images from one's memory) that enter into a relationship with actual images and extend them, creating a new imagery. For Bergson, these memory images do not conserve 'bygone images', but instead 'prolong their useful effect into the present moment'.[6] The generalized nature of many animated images allows for a greater such extension by the recollection image. And it is this relationship that causes many forms of animation to exact a greater intellectual collaboration with the viewer, for the simplified images and motion of animation require a greater Bergsonian 'extension' of recollection motion/image. In order to comprehend the image, 'we remount the slope of our past'.[7] In this regard, we are required to bring more to the image in order to complete it; therefore, the simplified animation image becomes cognitively transformed into a much more complicated and multifarious image.

There have been several studies that have looked at viewer's responses to animated films. One interesting study by Mar et al. (2007) involved viewer's specific responses to the animated feature, *Waking Life* (Palotta and Linklater 2001). *Waking Life* is a unique animated feature in that it was first shot as live-action video (with real actors) and then by using a proprietary digital rotoscoping process (Rotoshop), the animators transformed the video footage into animation. With permission from the film-makers, a group of researchers were able to obtain not only the completed animated sequences but also the original corresponding video footage. The researchers were thus able to devise an experiment in which participants could be shown both versions of the same scene and comparisons could be made as to how each version affected the viewer. What the researchers found most promising was that each corresponding clip contained essentially the same 'biological movement' (regardless whether it was the 'animated' or the original footage) so that they could focus on the surface aesthetics of the forms.[8] Furthermore, the participants were also shown the sequences while undergoing fMRI scanning to measure their brain activity.

While watching the live-action sequences, the viewers, as might be expected, displayed greater activity in the 'social brain areas' – thereby identifying with the live-action actors in much the same manner that one does with real-life people. However, during the animated sequences, participants showed increased activity in 'the anterior orbitofrontal cortex', which the researchers believed to 'indicate that the cartoon stimuli were viewed as more novel and thus more rewarding'.[9] Most intriguingly, the areas 'that have been associated with subjective percepts, specifically of objects and shapes', were also heavily activated when watching the animated sequences. The researchers believed that this would indicate 'that more [cognitive] effort was required to parse the cartoon presentations into recognizable objects'.[10] Though not entirely conclusive, the study did appear to support the idea that more graphical forms of animation can actually require a greater degree of cognitive activity in order to 'make sense' of and reinterpret the imagery. One could argue that graphical animation is essentially someone else's interpretation of the world: as we watch it we need to translate it into our own interpretive language. Buchan echoes this sentiment:

> Although rooted in an understanding of the world we live in, the mental processes that animation stimulates and activates have much more to do with a set of experiences and schemata located in the imagination, the locus of most artistic production.[11]

Contrastingly, with live action, as with the more common aspects of the actual world, this process needs to occur less frequently since the visual information is generally a more 'realistic' representation of actuality.

But if the imagery of animation requires a high degree of translation (Mr Magoo's face into a real human face), what then is the position when the animation is completely abstract? How do we interpret animation that does not display any resemblance to actuality, such as the 'visual music' animations of Oskar Fishinger? Such works can provide us the opportunity to clearly see the types of imagery and movement that we normally see only in very vague terms. Consider again how we visually perceive the environment around us. We can only foveate (see in detail) a very small area at a time.

> Only details of a small area, about the diameter of an American quarter or a European euro held at arm's length at the point at which our eyes fixate, are available in high resolution to the visual system. About 50% of the optic nerve and 50% of the visual cortex are devoted to information from this small area.[12]

Everything else in our 'field of vision' is hopelessly void of detail. As stated earlier, it is only 'seen' in the most rudimentary manner as large blocks of colour, light, shadow and movement, and only in terms of these simplified 'blocks'. Though it is true that large blocks of colour and simple forms do exist in the real world, the abstract animated film can provide us with a unique perspective of all-encompassing abstraction, and it allows us to then foveate on these dynamic abstract forms in unconventional ways.

There have been several related experiments that have used simple abstract animation in order to test viewer's interpretation and perceived meanings of those animations. The first experiment was conducted in 1944 by Heider and Simmel, which was then recreated and tested more comprehensively in 1985 by Oatley and Yuill. The experiment involved a simple animation of triangles, a circle and a rectangular box-like shape. The triangles and circle were made to move around the screen in different ways and some were made to move in and out of the rectangular box. After viewing the initial sequences, viewers would speak in a rather disengaged manner about the animation. For example, they would explain how 'the circle and small triangle' were simply 'moving downward' along the 'right-hand side of the screen'. Then, as they viewed further sequences, their language and engagement appeared changed – they began to clearly identify with the 'characters' and 'narrative'. The viewers began to use such words as 'escape', 'chase' and even 'loves'. Upon reflection, Oatley suggests that

> All seeing is *seeing as*, and viewers' schemas of personal agency were invoked: The large triangle was seen as leaving his or her house, the large triangle was seen as chasing the circle and small triangle. Viewers' ideas of leaving a house and of chasing were pure projection of their knowledge schemas of social intentions and actions.[13]

It is quite remarkable how we are able to identify with such abstract forms. For Oatley, this identification process is very similar to that of traditional live action:

> In a realist film, you seem to see what you would have seen had you been there in the story. There is immediate elicitation of your interest and you project your understanding onto the film in the same way as did our viewers in our remake of Heider and Simmel's film.[14]

However, it was primarily the movement that enabled the viewers to identify with the animations as they did. Even though the imagery was entirely abstract, the movement was in fact somewhat analogous to real-life movement and the viewers were therefore able to more easily consider the simplistic forms as those having 'intent'.

In a further study a similar series of abstract animations were shown to viewers. In this experiment, however, each animated sequence contained decidedly different animation approaches. In some sequences the shapes appeared to drift around without any noticeable intent; in other cases, they appeared to take on more character-like attributes and were made to move 'with intention'.[15] Also, in this experiment, researchers subjected the viewers to brain scans. The results showed that the viewers had much more brain activity (in specific areas) when there were greater indications of narrative or intent in the movement of the forms. However, when the movement was primarily without intent – for example it was seen to merely drift across the screen – then only the visual areas of the brain were activated, suggesting that it required 'less intentional involvement and [more] passive viewing'.[16] Essentially as the movement of the abstract forms became more character-like, the viewers began engaging those parts of the brain that are involved in social interaction. Remarkably, the data also suggested that the mirror neuron systems were being invoked – those parts of the brain that are normally activated when we perform an action (or when we watch someone else perform an action).[17]

Reading animated characters

Something unique seems to happen when we do accept the animated forms on the screen as identifiable entities and characters. A great deal of this acceptance has to do with matters of performance – the perceived intentional movements of the forms and characters. These movements can be represented through more superficial actions, or more thoughtful and subtle behaviours – each having a varying affect upon the viewer.

Donald Crafton has delineated two significant approaches to animated performance: figurative and embodied. 'Figurative performance is extroverted', and it is essentially reliant upon clichés and 'masklike signs and gestures'.[18] He provides examples from early cartoon animation, where movements were often greatly exaggerated and the character forms highly elastic. Whereas 'embodied acting is introverted. It is the philosophy and practice of creating imaginatively realized beings with individuality, depth, and internal complexity'.[19] This embodied approach is what is commonly taught to animators today – and generally what most character animators strive for – a true sense of believability that emanates from their characters. Because of the complexity of embodied acting, there can be many different expressions of it and, as a result, it can often occupy a shifting liminal space somewhere between the real and the unreal.

> A simplified way to describe these phenomenological states of screen consciousness is to consider embodiment as a belief system. These cinematic, kinesthetic bodies are not material, but they are real. They are beings we believe in, although the beliefs may not be enduring or strongly

> held. They are like imaginary playmates that we pretend are real while knowing in our heart of hearts that they are not.[20]

However, there are some instances in which all disbelief can be completely supressed because the on-screen characters and events are fully believed. For Grodal and Kramer, this can most certainly be the case with live-action cinema:

> Viewers form relations to film characters that in many ways are similar to those experienced in relation to other people. To watch a film is therefore an experience similar to that of participating in a social event and central to this event is empathic participation.[21]

This can also occur in animation, particularly if the narrative context is convincing and the actions are elaborately 'embodied'. In such instances we view the characters as if they are real. This is in part because we project our own emotions and memories onto the characters that are presented to us. And at the same time, if their movements are convincing enough we engage our mirror neuron system. Importantly, such engagement 'recruits and reuses some of the same neural centers and networks as those used when experiencing the phenomena oneself'.[22] Thus, while watching an on-screen performance, 'in peak moments in engrossing films with a strong emotional impact, the viewer's ability to distance him- or herself diminishes and may become a total mirror resonance'.[23]

In such cases, it does not matter whether it is a 'real' live-action character, or an animated one – viewers can become completely overcome by the emotional impact of the characters' actions. For example, viewers have unquestionably become very emotional while watching particular animated sequences: when Bambi's mother dies (*Bambi*, David Hand 1942), or in exceptionally poignant scenes of the animated feature, *Grave of the Fireflies* (Isao Takahata 1988). Especially, it seems that with some contemporary 3D-animated films, such as Pixar's *UP* (Pete Docter & Bob Peterson 2009), *Inside Out* (Peter Docter 2015) or *The Good Dinosaur* (Peter Sohn 2015), the film-makers have become exceptionally adept at eliciting an emotional response from the viewers. For example, during some of the more touching scenes of *The Good Dinosaur*, many theatregoers have remarked how deeply emotional the audience became. This seemed to occur most acutely during the climactic scene in which the human child character 'Spot' and the dinosaur character 'Arlo' parted ways. Audience members (both young and old) were described as sobbing uncontrollably – these emotional outpourings lasting sometimes for more than several minutes.[24] Clearly, such responses illustrate, unequivocally, the emotional potential of animation.

Grodel and Kramer describe how there are several basic facial expressions that can elicit immediate responses in viewers – 'anger, fear, surprise and happiness', which are generally exploited in many forms of media, including, 'in cartoons and animated films and even in such stereotype representations as "Smileys"'. These basic expressions, without any contextualization, can have "a strong impact even when presented subliminally",[25] and 'angry faces have a direct impact on the amygdala'.[26] In addition to our regular macro-expressions, humans also produce (often unconsciously) what are known as 'micro-expressions' – slight split-second facial expressions that might belie our true emotions at that moment (anger, stress, joy). Grodal mentions one commonly occurring micro-expression, known as the 'eyebrow flash', which is 'a 1/3 second lifting and lowering of the eyebrows, is probably a universal trait with cultural variation and is dependent on contextual deduction'.[27]

With the potential exactitude of 3D animation, such micro-expressions can be effectively included into a sequence and the viewer might subliminally pick up on these. Conversely, a live-action actor may provide a convincing performance, but at the same time display contradictory micro-expressions. Such inconsistent 'signals' could (at least hypothetically) weaken the impact of their intended emotional performance. By contrast, the digital animation performance can be worked and reworked hundreds of times down to the most minute detail of each frame, and if appropriate, micro-expressions can be added or neglected as needed. The motion capturing of facial expressions, or 'performance capture',[28] can also add to the detailed presentation of facial expressions in animation. However, much further 'frame-by-frame' animation and manipulation is usually employed in order to get the best performance and it is this laborious intervention by the animator that potentially makes these performances ever increasingly more compelling.[29]

Reading stop-motion animation

Our reception of stop-motion animated performances is often quite different from that of other approaches to animation – this is particularly the case with sequences in which the viewer is acutely aware of the material origin of the on-screen forms. For Wells, stop-motion often exemplifies the idea of 'fabrication', which includes the 'taken-for-granted constituent elements of the everyday world'. Therefore, it is not just forms that move, but it fundamentally represents 'the re-animation of materiality for narrative purposes'.[30] With stop-motion, the viewer finds himself or herself in a strange in-between space where they recognize the forms as real objects made of cloth, clay or wood (that would not normally move on their own) and at the same time as vibrant and lively characters. As Buchan astutely notes, 'The fundamental principle of all puppet animation films – the animation of the inanimate – goes against logic in terms of our experience of the phenomenal world.'[31]

Although we get caught up in the narrative and belief system of stop-motion animated films – we are normally always aware that they are in fact objects pretending to be alive. We understand that they are simply objects that have been made to move through the process of animation. Furthermore, we are generally aware that the objects are, in fact, much smaller than those that they are made to represent. The human figure and animal puppets in *Fantastic Mr Fox* (Wes Anderson 2009) are much smaller than real life humans and animals (as are the on-set chairs, cars and trees). These common practices of miniaturization are usually meant to represent much larger human-scaled forms. For Buchan, the miniature aspect of most stop-motion animation readily adds to its remarkable viewing experience: 'The miniature is perceptually close to our experience of the fantastic. Neither the miniature nor the fantastic exists in the natural world; each is co-created by the observer.'[32] Another reading of stop-motion animation, and one that also involves participation and 'co-creation' by the viewer, comes into play when it both highlights its material nature and at the same time uses that materiality to forge what we could refer to as materialist puns. For example, the materiality found within the stop-motion feature animated film *Fantastic Mr Fox* is continually highlighted. In fact, one of the driving forces behind the Wes Anderson's desire to use stop-motion was his love of the material:

> The thing I've always loved with stop-motion, more than anything else, is puppets that have fur [...] I love the way King Kong, the old King Kong, looked, with his fur [constantly moving] – the animators call it 'boiling'.[33]

Throughout the whole of *Fantastic Mr Fox*, we are constantly reminded that we are watching puppets and material forms. For example, it is fairly easy to perceive that 'the flames were made from pieces of soap and the smoke from steel wool'.[34] And we the viewers will at the same time read the 'smoke' as 'smoke', but also as undulating mounds of cotton or steel wool (see Figure 4.1). And contemporary audiences might also laugh and delight in the fact that it is so obviously made from low-tech physical materials. Of course these effects could have been achieved much more easily through digital effects such as particles, dynamics and through digital compositing, but instead the animators chose not to. This obsession with the materiality of stop-motion is what makes the medium so appealing to the director, Wes Anderson. In an interview he exclaimed:

> The whole magical aspect of stop-motion [is] where you can see the trick. [...] Those effects where you can see what it is, have always been the most fascinating and mesmerizing and moving to me. And with stop-motion,

> the whole film is that sort of thing in a way [...] That magical effect where you can see how it is accomplished – where at one and the same time you are enchanted by the trick [of] the effect and by the story itself.[35]

There are also a number of visual puns that are incorporated into the film that are based on the materiality of the animation. For example, at one point, Mr Fox, marvelling at his wife, says to Mrs Fox, 'You're practically glowing' and then instantly we see that her regular puppet form has been replaced with a cheap blow-mould plastic form that is lit by an actual internal light bulb. At other times, in order to depict that the characters were either inebriated or under hypnosis, their normal eyes are instantaneously replaced with large plastic 'swirly-eyes'. Such visual motifs could have been achieved much more simply and believably through the use of digital visual effects – but that would have resulted in rather anaemic jokes and would have strayed wildly from the film's materialist aesthetic. The film-makers instead chose to direct the gag towards the material nature of the animation, therefore making it much more efficacious and playfully adding a layer of object-based self-reflexivity.

Reading the uncanny

Some of the most remarkable and uncanny screen-based experiences can arise from watching animation. As Buchan notes, 'animated techniques can effect in us a private, personal, and often incommunicable experience: that of the uncanny'.[36] Stop-motion animation seems particularly adept at

FIGURE 4.1 *Still from* Fantastic Mr Fox *(Wes Anderson 2009). Smoke effect is made from cotton and steel wool.*

eliciting such responses because it involves the rather unexpected motion of real objects – things that don't normally move.

However, it is the idea of the uncanny within the realm of 3D digital animation that has sparked the greatest interest – particularly in what is referred to as the 'uncanny valley'; the rather unsettling part of the spectrum of the uncanny experience. The 'uncanny valley' hypothesis was first posited by roboticist Masahiro Mori, in which he suggested that as a robot is made to look and move in ways that are increasingly human-like, the viewer would have a correspondingly positive emotional response – that is until the robot's anthropomorphic nature surpasses a certain threshold. Once this has occurred, the viewer's emotional response would become conflicted and plunge downwards into a dip or 'valley'.[37] In recent years, this theory has been widely applied to computer animation, in particular upon the release of the animated feature *Final Fantasy: The Spirits Within* (Hironobu Sakaguchi 2001). And it was also often bandied around in consideration of the motion-captured performance of *The Polar Express* (Robert Zemeckis 2004), and to a lesser degree in regard to the animated feature *The Adventures of Tintin* (Steven Spielberg 2011). Walker describes:

> As visual consumers of animation and games, we become engrossed with characters of all kinds, but if they approach photorealism we become hyper-critical. Our brains seemingly magnify the slightest imperfections. We note the soul-less eyes, the rigid lips. Our empathy with the character is curtailed, and in some cases we feel a form of revulsion. Oddly, we can empathize more with Woody and Buzz Lightyear in *Toy Story* than we can with their owner, Pete; we feel more empathy for characters in Pixar's *Cars* (who don't even have limbs) than say, the perfectly proportioned Dr. Aki Ross, the main character in 2001's *Final Fantasy: The Spirits Within* – the first animated feature to seriously attempt photorealistic CGI humans.[38]

In 2007 there was a scientific study which asked participants to view a series of animated walk cycles. Some of these were produced with motion capture, others were created using key-frame animation.[39] Furthermore, these varying sources of movement were applied to a variety of different human-like forms – ranging from the very abstract (a simple array of thirteen dots) to a fairly realistic looking 3D human model. In the first instance, the study surveyed the participants to see if they could distinguish between key-framed animation (described as 'artificial') and motion-captured performance (described as 'biological'). Interestingly, when the motion-capture data was applied to the simplest forms, participants generally identified these pairings as 'biological'. However, when motion-capture performances were applied to the more realistic looking human forms, the majority of participants identified these as being 'artificial'. The researchers concluded that this was in large part due to the uncanny valley effect, which likely stemmed from the fact that the motion-capture data was somewhat limited and therefore when applied to a complex model, not all elements (such as hair and clothing) moved as it should. In addition, the participants were subjected to a brain scan (fMRI scan) while viewing the animations. The results seemed to show that the more natural or realistic the human movement appeared to the viewer, the greater the activation of the areas of the brain that are involved in social interactions – which is a result that seems to have been confirmed in a number of other studies.[40]

The uncanny valley syndrome has much more to do with movement and how that movement is attached to a form, than with the form itself. Still images do not normally elicit this response; so, correspondingly, it seems that realistic movement attached to an abstracted non-realistic form does not either. Therefore (as outlined in the above study) it is most likely the incompatible pairing of 'recorded movement' and 'constructed forms' that is most troubling to viewers. However, the recorded movement found in the features *Waking Life* (Richard Linklater 2001) and *A Scanner Darkly* (Richard Linklater 2006) did not receive these criticisms. Walker questions why this is:

> Should this too not arouse unease? The characters move just like us, thanks to the comprehensive use of 2D rotoscope techniques. They are almost human. You could argue that their eyes are soul-less [an oft-repeated characteristic of the residents of 'Uncanny Valley'], yet when reviewers speak about the technique, it is words like beautiful and dream-like that get used.[41]

Perhaps the answer resides in the fact that these films vectorize and simplify the imagery, but only marginally affect (smoothen out) the movement. Therefore the films maintain all of the unexpected minute movements of real life – the accurate timing and placement of eye blinks, the fluttering wisps of hair, unpredictable micro-expressions and the tremors and off-balance faltering of the characters as they move. In the case of *A Scanner Darkly*, its natural 'biological' movement is seemingly 'attached' to very simplified forms – making the movement much more complex than the forms would suggest and thereby avoiding the disquieting effect of the uncanny valley. It does seem that when movement possesses a greater complexity than a form suggests – it succeeds; but when movement is less complex than the form implies, it is more likely to cause an unsettling viewing experience (see Figure 4.2).

However, it is quite possible that many of the concerns surrounding the 'uncanny valley' have been resolved in recent years as both technology has advanced and people's acceptance of a wider range of animated styles (including the vast array of video games) has alleviated some of our unease.

FIGURE 4.2 *Still from* A Scanner Darkly *(Richard Linklater 2006).*

Reading hybridity

Animation, because of its constructivist nature, seems to facilitate the presentation of hybrid characters – that is forms that have been made from a number of constituent sources – including combinations of live action and animation. There are many reasons as to why a film-maker would decide to produce hybrid characters of animation and live action. Historically some productions have chosen this approach as a cost/labour saving, or simply more practical method. While others have done it for aesthetic reasons.

The 'fawn' characters in *The Chronicles of Narnia: The Lion, the Witch and the Wardrobe* (Andrew Adamson 2006) were essentially hybrid forms of animation and live action (the legs were animated and the upper body was derived from live action). The hero characters in *X-Men: Days of Future Past* (2014), *Spider-Man* (Sam Raimi 2002), *The Amazing Spider-Man* (Marc Webb 2012) and *Deadpool* (Tim Miller 2016) were often exchanged back and forth between their live-action and their 3D-animated forms. The live-action forms would normally be deployed during close ups and every-day scenes (and in particular the more emotional sequences); fully animated forms would be utilized for many of the spectacular action scenes. Usually these interchangeable forms can work fairly seamlessly – though more astute viewers have remarked, not about the 'look' of the characters as they are swapped between live action and animation, but about their inconsistent movement. As Lisa Purse describes:

> The comments about the cartoon nature of Spider-Man's actions and the Hulk's bouncing trajectory across the desert also reveal a concern in the reviewers' responses with the veracity of physical *movement*. Motion helps anchor the fictional three-dimensionality of a film's diegesis, including the volume of objects and spaces within the frame, and demonstrates the mass and structural integrity of onscreen bodies and objects.[42]

Importantly, movement can also be thought of as a layer of hybridity. In fact, all motion-capture animations are essentially hybrids of live action and animation – they appropriate live-action movement and combine it with digital animated forms. Furthermore this movement is often in and of itself also a hybrid in that it will normally comprise motion-captured movement along with key-framed movement.

Some particularly remarkable hybrid forms can be found in the stop-motion animated short *Madame Tutli-Putli* (Chris Lavis and Maciek Szczerbowski 2007). This film has a very unique amalgamated aesthetic; it features stop-motion puppet characters that are augmented with seamlessly composited live-action eyes. Appropriately, the use of real eyes also makes thematic sense, as much of the film is about the gaze and communicative properties of eyes. Quite often the main character (Madame Tutli-Putli) seems to be the victim of the rather threatening gazes of many of the other characters, which is accentuated by her own rather fearful wide-eyed responses.

But these live-action eyes also contribute greatly to the overall emotive power of the film. In contrast to the criticisms of the uncanny valley (which often focuses on the 'soulless eyes' of a character), the eyes of these characters seem very alive (indeed very soulful) particularly in contrast to the extremely rough-hewn puppet bodies. Rather than appearing zombie-like, the addition of a live-action element actually seems to elevate the entire character's animated performance. Co-director Marciek Szczerbowski explained his intentions:

> We needed Madame Tutli-Putli to be a very contemplative character. We needed to see into her mind [...] we needed to show her anxiety, her apprehension and the kind of mental process going on inside her head. So, we tried something very crazy which is to composite the eyes of a live human onto a puppet, after the animation. And it worked! [...] It actually seems like you're watching a performance rather [than] of a puppet, which is very important.[43]

Although the set design and the stop-motion animation of the puppet characters is effectively executed, it is unquestionably the live-action performance of the human eyes that conveys most of the expressive power of this film.

Much of this emotive power stems from the stark contrast between the rough-hewn aesthetic of the stop-motion puppets and the live-action eyes. As viewers, we cannot help but to fixate on these eyes, but because they are so seamlessly integrated, they successfully elevate the attached puppets into a realm of greater believability. This effect is analogous to the concept of 'synecdoche', where one small portion or element can indicate a greater whole (see Paul Wells). One common example of visual synecdoche in comics and animation is expressed through the depiction of 'floating' eyeballs amongst a solid black void of darkness. We, of course, read such visuals as an indication that an entire figure is effectively attached to those eyes as we, in effect, cognitively complete the imagery. Similarly, in the case of *Madam Tutli-Putli*, the human eyes imply that there is essentially an entire 'real' body just out of view. In this instance, rather than mere blackness, the 'void' in which the eyes 'float' consists of comparatively crude stop-motion imagery. We therefore cognitively complete the missing live-action bodies upon the skeletal structure of the stop-motion forms (see Figure 4.3).

There have been a number of other examples (though usually less successful) in which live-action facial components have been incorporated into animated imagery. One particularly uneasy pairing could be found in the American television series, *Clutch Cargo* (Haas 1959–1960). This series featured extremely limited cel animation which, as a means to save costs, incorporated live-action mouths to express the characters' dialogue. To achieve the live-action composite, *Clutch Cargo* utilized a patented

FIGURE 4.3 *Still from* Madame Tutli-Putli *(Chris Lavis and Maciek Szczerbowski 2007), which featured composited live-action eyes.*

process which was dubbed the 'Syncro-Vox' optical printing system. Other than the composited live-action mouths, the only animated movement consisted of occasional eye-blinks and even less frequent head turns or camera pans. *Clutch Cargo's* hybrid form seemed to (at least in historical retrospect) highlight a very strong disconnect between the two elements. The divide between the extreme fluidity of the live-action mouths and the almost non-existent animated movement (compounded by the limitations of the 'Syncro-Vox' system) amounted to a very uneasy viewing experience that seemed to accomplish just the opposite of that which *Madam Tutli-Putli* managed to achieve.

Reading anthropomorphism

One way for us to identify more readily with an animated form is through the use of anthropomorphism, which is arguably one of the more intriguing and pervasive conditions found within animation. The anthropomorphic paradigm has a very long and pervasive legacy; as humans, we are naturally inclined to anthropomorphize, or imbue other forms with human characteristics and examples can be frequently found in the folklore, art or literature of most cultures. According to Paul Wells, this inclination stems in part from our desire to make the unfamiliar more familiar. That is, we are able to make better sense of the world through 'the imposition of human character traits that render material and natural artifacts familiar'.[44] In fact, a number of scientific studies have shown that when anthropomorphism is used in language and visual communication we are, for example, more inclined to identify with and become more empathetic towards animals and the environment.[45]

Animation is particularly well suited to anthropomorphic expression and its vital characteristics can arguably be expressed more eloquently and more intricately through the medium of animation. Wells has suggested that because of the unique characteristics of the animated form (namely metamorphosis and condensation) animation naturally encourages the depiction of the anthropomorphic. Most apparent is how 'metamorphosis is used to demonstrate the physical and emotional transitions of animal life'.[46] In fact we can read an anthropomorphic character as concretizing a transitional moment as a character transforms from one state to the next (for example animal into human). Furthermore,

> condensation is used to invoke the maximum of suggestion in the minimum of imagery, moving beyond the literalness of the photographic image to illustrate the flux of animality as it is intensely felt, half-recalled, consciously observed, physically empathized with, or intellectually understood by the animator.[47]

Generally, in the animated realm, when an animal form is imbued with human characteristics it becomes quite removed from any notion of realism, but instead represents a uniquely abbreviated suggestion of human physiognomies. As a result, it can facilitate the creating of 'fresh image forms while still providing an empathetic or identifiable human aspect'.[48]

When we think of the concept of anthropomorphism, we normally focus on the animal kingdom, and much of the literature on the subject also directs its focus towards these creatures. It could be argued that animals, to some extent, are already quite a bit like us humans. They are sentient living creatures that move and think autonomously. However, just about anything can be anthropomorphized, ranging from the inanimate (teacups, toasters, rocks) to the living (plants and animals) to the diminutive (atoms and viruses) and to the immense (stars and planets).

Anthropomorphism is actually a rather complex and multifaceted concept that also has a number of associated terms. Some have sought to define the starting point of an anthropomorphic transformation: if something begins as *non-human*, and then has human characteristics applied to it, it is generally regarded as anthropomorphic; whereas when a *human* adopts animal-like traits, the character can then be described as *zoomorphic*. Similarly, there are more specific terms such as *floramorphic*, where a non-plant form might take on plant-like characteristics. Even more precisely, the term *dendromorphic* can be used to describe how something has adopted tree-like characteristics. Furthermore, we can use sliding scales to designate to what degree something has been anthropomorphized (whether it is mostly animal, mostly human or somewhere in the middle). Wells has outlined a spectrum measuring the degree with which anthropomorphism is applied, which he refers to as a 'bestial ambivalence model'. This model sketches examples from the 'purely animal' to the nearly human.[49] We can actually see a glimpse of such a spectrum in action when, for example, the misled characters in *Pinocchio* (Luske and Sharpsteen 1940) exhibit a progressively zoomorphic resemblance as they become increasingly donkey-like.

Unlike the still image, animation also normally exhibits movement, time and sound. When we consider anthropomorphism in the context of animation, then it too can be dissected into similarly distinct layers and subsets. These multiple layers can be individually assessed for a fuller understanding of what anthropomorphism can mean to the animated form. If we look at the actual derivation of the word anthropomorphism, its emphasis relates to the visual characteristics of a form: 'anthropo-' suggesting human, and '-morphic' suggesting form. So in its most precise meaning, anthropomorphism can refer to things that have visual human features and characteristics in terms of *shape and form*. But, we can also consider precisely targeted terms in order to highlight various layers of animated anthropomorphism. The table below describes how the idea of animated anthropomorphism can be divided

Anthropomorphism	
Anthropo-morphic	Form
Anthropo-kinetic	Movement
Anthropo-sonic	Sound
Anthropo-chronic	Time

up into four constituent elements, which are denoted through distinctive hyphenated terms: anthropo-morphic (form), anthropo-kinetic (movement), anthropo-sonic (sound) and anthropo-chronic (time). Of course, many of these concepts do overlap, and most animated examples exhibit several or all of these, while others may exhibit just a single attribute.

In order to focus the term more precisely upon the form of a character we can utilize a hyphenated form of the word, *anthropo-morphism*, while we can use the unhyphenated term, anthropomorphism, to express its broader meaning. Most examples of anthropomorphism are indeed *anthropo-morphic* in that they do have at least some level of visible human traits incorporated into their form. The distinctly human-like rabbit known as Bugs Bunny, the teapot in the Disney animated feature *Beauty and the Beast* (Gary Trousdale and Kirk Wise 1991), or the plants in the video game *Plants vs. Zombies: Garden Warfare* (2014) are just a few examples in which non-human entities are imbued with varying degrees of human-like physical (-morphic) features.

However, we could also have an animal or plant that might look exactly like its real-life animal/botanical form, yet through animation it may be made to move in very human-like ways. Thus we can use the term ***anthropo-kinetic*** where the emphasis is solely on the application of human-like *movement*. One, somewhat obscure example (but a very good one) can be found in a television advertisement for a local hospital in Arizona, the Phoenix Baptist Hospital, which is self-described as 'Arizona's emergency chest pain experts'. The ad featured a fairly realistic looking cactus that was seamlessly composited into a live-action desert that was also populated with real cacti. For the first few seconds of the ad, the 'fake cactus' did not move; then it could be seen suddenly to lower its 'arms' and clutch its chest as if it were having chest-pains associated with a heart attack. Until the animated movement occurred, most viewers would probably not have noticed that this cactus was not real and not an original part of the photographic scene. Thus, the idea of anthropomorphism resided almost entirely within the *movement* of the cactus: not with the design of the cactus 'character' (see Figure 4.4). A more mainstream example can be found in the Harry Potter movies within an entity known as 'The Whomping Willow Tree', which makes notable appearances in *Harry Potter and the Chamber of Secrets* (Chris Columbus 2002) and particularly in *Harry Potter and the*

FIGURE 4.4 *Image from animated advertisement for the Phoenix Baptist Hospital depicting an* anthropo-kinetic *state.*

Prisoner of Azkaban (Alfonso Cuaron 2004). This *anthropo-kinetic* tree, though appearing in form as a natural tree, had animated actions that exhibited deliberate aggression and was very much human-like in some of its behaviours as it lashed out at passers-by.

A third term, ***anthropo-sonic***, highlights the display of human-like language and sounds. For example the largely realistic looking animals of the animated feature, *The Plague Dogs* (Martin Rosen 1982), generally moved and looked like animals, yet they spoke with human voices. Normally, their mouths moved in synch with the dialogue, however, frequently these mouth movements, and certainly the expressions on their faces, remained very dog-like. Sometimes they would merely open their mouths in a barking motion, yet human words emanated. A further example can be found in the Disney/Pixar feature *Up* (Peter Docter 2009) and the accompanying short film *Dug's Special Mission Dog* (Ronnie del Carmen 2009). In these animated films various dog characters (particularly, Dug) had been fitted with translating collars, so that whenever they would 'speak' their dog-language communications would be translated into audible human language. As a result, the dogs essentially looked, acted and moved like dogs, but they emitted their communication in human-speak. Also, in the live-action/animation hybrid feature film *Babe* (Chris Noonan 1995), the animals (which are essentially live action, but with seamlessly animated mouths) also spoke 'human'. Though their mouths were lip-synched to the dialogue, for the most part, the mouth shapes remained very animal-like, making these characters primarily *anthropo-sonic* in nature.

The term ***anthropo-chronism*** can be used to refer to a human time-scale or a human conception of time. Not all things in our world move at the same rate as we do. Plants for example, live on a very different time-scale. Apart from a few exceptions such as the Venus flytrap, their movement is virtually invisible to us. Yet, when we revisit a plant after a few weeks, we might notice that it has a new growth or a new flower – so movement and growth has unquestionably occurred; we have just not been able to witness it as it has happened. Though not often celebrated, there is a long history of animated anthropomorphic plants, ranging from Disney's *Flowers and Trees* (Burt Gillett 1932) to the walking and talking trees known as the 'Ents' in *The Lord of the Rings* (Peter Jackson 2001–2003) or the enigmatic superhero character known as Groot in the movie *Guardians of the Galaxy* (James Gunn 2014). Animating plants anthropomorphically can be seen as a way of articulating their extraordinary life that resides just beyond our perception of time. Although most animated depictions of plants exhibit essentially the full range of anthropomorphism (including form, movement and sound), there are some cases in which the concept of human *time* becomes most apparent. For example, if we subject a plant to the pseudo-animative process of time-lapse, they suddenly look very much alive because of their visible movement. And even though the natural movement of plants (when sped up) is generally quite different from that of humans or animals, we are able to identify with their liveliness because of the rate with which they appear to move. Thus, the descriptive layer of 'anthropo-chronism' can describe how these plants now move at a human time-scale.

In the animated feature *Epic* (Chris Wedge 2013), there is an interesting assortment of animated plants that exhibit different levels of anthropomorphism and anthropo-chronism. First, there are a number of fully anthropomorphic plants that walk, talk and look quite human. However, there are also sequences that showcase purely anthropo-chronic elements. An example is when the Queen magically 'animates' the normal plants of the forest, imbuing them with human time. We then see these plants grow and coil around things while huge flowers open in bloom as she passes by. (See Figure 4.5) We can see similar examples of this anthropo-chronic treatment of plants in several other animated films, including *Avatar* (James Cameron 2009) and *Princess Mononoke* (Hayao Miyazaki 2001).

Similarly, in the German stop-motion animated film *Das Rad* (Chris Stenner, Arvid Uibel and Heidi Wittinger 2001), there is an interesting shifting that occurs between the film's depiction of 'human-time' and 'geological-time' (the geological rate at which rocks and mountains form and rescind). When the film slips into 'geological-time' we see groupings of anthropomorphic rocks essentially exhibiting all the features of anthropomorphism (they have human facial features, move and speak in human ways), but additionally, because they are depicted as visibly moving, they (and the whole sequence) are imbued with a substantial amount of *anthropo-chronism*. In one remarkable display, a rock character throws a pinecone at the base of a rival rock character, and (because of the *anthropo-chronic* treatment) the pinecone instantaneously sprouts and shoots up into a full-grown pine tree, knocking over the unsuspecting rock character. What would have taken fifty years or more in real time was, through the process of *anthropo-chronism*, achieved in less than a second.

One reading of animated anthropomorphism is to consider that it can represent the process of becoming – of, for example, animal becoming human. If we consider it to be a representation of such a transitional process, it can also be considered to be quite unstable, allowing the form to shift more towards human or back towards animal – or alternately to launch from its amorphous state into something entirely different. Depending on a form's progression, we can think of an anthropomorphic character as a mid-point between the transformation of a human into an animal, or an animal into a human. Thus, Mickey Mouse represents an arrested transformation from a mouse to a human and at the same time a human to a mouse. Anthropomorphism serves both to depict but also to interrogate what it means to be within this liminal state of both human and animal – suggesting what it might mean to become *more animal*, and in return what it might mean to become *more human*.

Ultimately there is an inherent malleability in anthropomorphism and in this way metamorphosis and anthropomorphism are very much intertwined. Wells has clarified that anthropomorphism 'becomes a model of translation in which a metaphysical insight is offered by revealing the relationship between former and current states and their oscillation'.[50] In another words, we might think that we are imbuing a form with human characteristics, but

FIGURE 4.5 *Image from* Epic *(Chris Wedge 2013), which featured both 'antropo-morphic' and 'anthropo-chronic' imagery.*

the inverse is also true, and as a result something completely new has come about. Jenkins has also argued that Disney's anthropomorphic characters exist in a rather ambiguous space, 'they move and sound like humans while looking like animals; they maintain semblance and play. The human becomes mouse as much as the mouse becomes human'.[51] These sentiments are echoed in Deleuze and Guattari's approach to the philosophical concept of 'becoming animal' in which they claim, 'We become animal so that the animal also becomes something else.'[52] Furthermore, they asserted '[one] can not become dog without the dog itself becoming something else',[53] which makes the whole concept of becoming (and by extension animated anthropomorphism) a rather fluid one. Once an animated anthropomorphic transformation becomes percept – neither human nor animal (or plant, or toaster) is present – instead, an entirely new construct is made manifest, which becomes difficult to identify, let alone emulate.

As outlined in the previous chapter, when we engage in the process of 'cognitive metamorphosis' we are generally already mindful of what the object will morph into while we are envisioning it. However, when watching animated metamorphosis we often do *not* know what it will become next – and this is where, in part, the remarkable spectacle of it lies. It can be delightfully puzzling for us as we try to figure out what the image will become. In fact, we might even get it wrong in some cases – as the transformation of the car to the penguin might look momentarily as if it is going to transform into a human or a dinosaur.

We can think of an anthropomorphic form as being part of a transition, though from exactly what it came and exactly where it is going might remain a puzzle. In this light, though the form of Mickey Mouse may seem very stable, we might alternatively focus on the identity of the very human hands, mouth movements and clothing, but then suddenly fixate on the animal-like ears and tail. It is an ongoing moment of plasticity and translation that is at once frozen in the middle – but at the same time we do not know whether it will progress or revert. The anthropomorphic, therefore, highlights the linkages between two things – but importantly, this is always a multi-directional trajectory and can be considered from many different angles. For example, if we imagine a human-like mouse, we also need to imagine a mouse-like human.

One intriguing animation sequence that features anthropomorphic forms that are able to engage in varying amounts of metamorphosis can be found in the Walt Disney feature film *The Three Caballeros* (Norman Ferguson 1944). The sequence involves a choreographed interplay featuring a live-action Brazilian woman and an animated Donald Duck. In addition, there is a supporting cast of dozens of animated cacti that continually change their form.[54] As the sequence begins, Donald Duck emerges amongst a grouping of tall anthropomorphic saguaro cacti, which suddenly begin to move, then dance and metamorphose into different forms. One of the dancing cacti suddenly makes a full transformation into a live-action woman. Donald is immediately enamoured of her, and tries to impress her. Knowing that she is derived from a cactus, he attempts to impress her by doing cacti-impressions. He first strikes a cactus-like pose of a saguaro (arms held up), then as a prickly pear (standing on one leg with limbs akimbo); but these incompetent transformative efforts fail to impress the woman. He then continues to pursue her; this time attempting to closely emulate her human movements, but even this gains only a brief acknowledgement by the woman. As he moves closer to her, the animated cacti proceed to block his way, then they effortlessly transform into a group of perfectly formed representations of little cactus-skinned Donald Ducks. These cactus-ducks then proceed to jump on to him and dance their spikey feet painfully into his back. In a final effort, Donald races towards the woman, but just as he throws his arms around her, she transforms into a realistic looking cactus, causing him to slam painfully into her spikey cactus trunk. This sequence highlights the contrasting conditions of the anthropomorphic form. In Donald's case he proves to be a frustratingly stable entity – perhaps almost a purgatorial construct that restricts him mid-point between human and animal, while everything else showcases the wonderful fluid possibilities of the anthropomorphic state.

Reading animated video games

Video games generally comprise animation, the principal visualizer of most digital games. But, as distinct from other forms of animation, games typically encourage individualized interactive experiences, which articulate much of the basis of their assembly. Although games are interactive, they can also offer frequent (and often overlapping) opportunities for more 'passive' animation spectatorship. Ultimately, games are both played and viewed, and it is arguably the combination of these two activities that can make animated games so compelling. Many past scholars have sought to interrogate video games from differing perspectives, often comprising either narrative concerns (dubbed 'narratology') or more playful concerns (termed 'ludology').[55] Interestingly, much of the recent literature has focused upon the underlying structures of games. For Miguel Sicart, video games are composed of, and defined by, 'a formal system of rules'.[56] Sicart further explains:

> Games engage players by constructing a world into which they pour their being. The meaning of games is found in the way that players live by the rules, playfully and emotionally, within a space of play.[57]

More specifically, Jesper Juul has defined 'four conceptions of game playing' that seek to articulate different levels of engagement, 'They fall roughly on a scale from the assumption that the game dictates the playing of the game to the assumption that the player essentially creates a game by playing it.' The first two states are categorized as submission and constrained freedom where the game structure dictates much of the experience; the final two are labelled subversion and creation in which much of the experience is dictated by the *player*.[58]

Following on from these discussions, it can also be useful to consider games against a slightly more animation-centric and process-based scale – one that focuses attention on the animation process and also specifically between the role of the *player* of the animation and that of the *spectator* of the animation. Of course, most games allow for a limited number of players; anyone else in the vicinity will be consigned simply to watching the gameplay unfold on screen. Even so, a spectator can often find this viewing experience to be an engaging one. Furthermore, the player will normally inhabit a dual position both of 'player' and of 'spectator' – perhaps oscillating between predominately 'passively' watching the animation (during the presentation of cut-scenes, and where there is minimal interactivity available) and impulsively reacting to whatever is animatedly 'thrown' at them. Moreover, there may be moments (or even very long durations) where one is permitted just leisurely to explore a game-space, or quietly to watch elements of the game-world pass gently by. For a spectrum comparable to that which articulates player to spectator we might look to live sporting events, such as a soccer match in which some of the players might play for the full duration of the game, while others may play only for a few minutes – obliged to sit out most of the game just watching their teammates play. Other players may find that they have very little direct contact with the ball as they remain in their designated positions during most of the game, thereby also primarily watching their teammates' more active play. Additionally, there might be a cohort of super enthusiastic fans who sit in the front rows and cheer loudly – some, perhaps, appearing to be as fully engaged as the actual players.

In some cases the interactive characteristics of a video game might be minimized, or even almost completely removed, transforming the generally non-linear construct of the game into what could be better described as a linearized display of animation. Machinima (animation made exclusively from gameplay footage) is one clear example of how games might be transformed into more cinematic forms of animation. Recently, however, there has been a developing trend towards the online live streaming of video games in which people will log in to merely *watch someone else* play a video game. Initially, it might seem strange that anyone would want to watch a video game rather than play it. But the fact is that people like to watch live competitions, especially if they have a vested interest in the outcome. In the world of sports, the Olympic Games, the American Super Bowl and major cricket matches will normally attract vast television audiences numbering in the hundreds of millions. Deninger argues that what makes these televised competitions so appealing to watch (as opposed to a scripted television drama) is essentially 'the unscripted nature of sports, and the fact that the results of the games and events *matter* to you'.[59] An enthusiast of basketball may have watched literally thousands of games, yet to him or her, each new one can be just as exciting as the last. Similarly, even though we may be very familiar with the various scenarios of a particular video game, we will nevertheless like to watch it progress – as each iteration of the game will be slightly different from the last. Quite simply, video games continually provide us familiar yet progressively unique iterations of the animated visuals.

As described in the Introduction to this book, animation is composed essentially of three phases: the *construction phase* (where the animator adds movement to things); the *animative-state* (in which all of the elements of the animation are established, ready to be played back as animation); and the *presentation phase* (where the animation is made visible to the spectator). The animative-state is constructed from separate streams of movement and image; as a result of the fundamental manipulation of these dual streams of stored data, each presentation of the gameplay provides a high degree of visual variance. The 'player' is therefore effectively influencing the animative-state and thereby contributing significantly to its perpetually unique presentation. Thus we might also suggest that the video game player, in effect, takes on the role of a *pseudo-animator*, as they guide and direct various animative processes, which culminate in a plethora of customized animated events.

One modest example can be found in the game *Little Big Planet 3* (2014), in which the player not only can make the character, 'Sackboy', run and jump and move objects around but can also make his head and body sway from side to side, or independently move one arm at a time. The player can also change Sackboy's facial expression and body language to express emotions that range from happy to sad, worried or angry. There are also a number of game systems (and corresponding array of games) that now allow for more direct control through the capturing of the game player's bodily movements. But even these increasingly sophisticated control functions are limited within predetermined boundaries. That is, the player is never in complete control of the game's animation – and in some cases might have deceptively little control. As one games scholar has noted, 'The trick of the trade of game design is indeed to make the player believe she is in control.'[60] However, a player's capacity, at least partially, to manipulate the animative-state has led many to engage in what Meades would refer to as a form of 'counterplay', where one might actively attempt to subvert the rules of normal game play.[61] For example, one may try to make a character walk through a wall, move an 'unmovable object' or unnecessarily destroy something, merely to test the potential boundaries of animated manipulation.

The spectator is, at least on a fundamental level, also aware of the significant and unscripted manipulation that the player may enact upon the animation – which exponentially adds to their unique reading of the presentation. For example, while watching someone else play, we might become so emotionally invested that we may feel compelled to scream 'look out!', 'go left!' or other such utterances. In some cases, we might even feel the need to grab the controller from the player in order to manipulate the animation ourselves. Such spontaneous responses can be indicative of the high level of engagement that one may feel when watching a video game – which can be further considered in terms of our mirror neuron system. As discussed earlier, when watching a traditional film (either live action or animated), our mirror neurons are likely to be activated – for example, if a character is seen to be jumping, it might trigger our own 'jumping' neurons. However, when watching a video game (either primarily as a spectator or as a player), a more complex array of neural activity might also be activated. Conceivably, not only will one's mirror neurons be activated in terms of the action on screen (running, jumping), but for those familiar with the gameplay and the game's controls our neurons may also be activated potentially to 'move' the buttons and sticks on the controller so as to 'move' the on-screen character. For example, if an attacker is coming towards the main character, the *spectator* might try cognitively to 'move' the controller stick to the left in order to avoid a fatal collision.

Ultimately, the participation and spectatorship of animated games involves an interwoven and multilayered array of processes and it is the combination of these complex activities that can make animated games seem so engaging. The underlying structure of a game promises that with each iteration the animated visuals and the structural basis of the animative-state will be in a continual state of flux. It is this inherent fluidity that allows for the transformation of an almost endless array of abstract potentialities into a similarly endless array of on-screen visuals. Furthermore, because the player has a hand in actualizing these new and ongoing animated iterations, the resulting outcomes can often seem to be quite significant to both the player and the spectator.

PART THREE

Animation and Actuality

5

Non-Fictional Animation and the Transformation of Actuality

Because of its generally constructed nature, animation fosters a unique relationship with actuality. Writing in 1946, John Hubley and Zachary Schwartz noted how effectively animation could consider real-world topics:

> We have found that the medium of animation has become a new language. It is no longer the vaudeville world of pigs and bunnies. Nor is it the mechanical diagram, the photographed charts of the old 'training film'. It has encompassed the whole field of visual images, including the photograph. We have found that line, shape, colour, and symbols in movement can represent the essence of an idea, can express it humorously, with force, with clarity. The method is only dependent upon the idea to be expressed. And a suitable form can be found for any idea.[1]

Here, Hubley and Schwartz addressed two of the core arguments with which much of the current discussion on the use of animation in non-fictional contexts, to varying degrees, still grapples. These are: firstly, animation should be taken seriously (it's not 'just for entertainment') and therefore can be utilized for non-fictional purposes; secondly, in some circumstances animation can communicate ideas more clearly and more expressively than live action. It is somewhat surprising that the first point persists as an issue, the reason for which is probably the continued industrial and market focus on the profitability of animated entertainment oriented towards children, particularly through the continued successes of Disney/Pixar. However, in the public discourse and certainly in film studies this conception of animation has begun to change (aided, undoubtedly, by the shift to digital film-making and the blurring of animation and live-action forms). Paul Ward suggests the reason that such a belief persists in relation to the documentary is because of the 'misguided belief that documentary is somehow "capturing" reality rather than offering an *analysis* of it'.[2] The second point, however, will continue to be a subject for discussion because it also advocates that within animation 'a suitable form can be found for any idea'.

To use animation to represent actuality is a very natural tendency – we do after all, as described in Chapter 3, *cognitively animate* our world every day. So, why not also use the process of animation as a means to both represent and to better understand our world? Animation has, in fact, been used to depict non-fictional information since the form began. Even prior to the advent of cinema, animation was used for pedagogical and non-fictional purposes. According to Lutz,

> it is an interesting fact to note that as early as 1860, Desvignes, who invented one form of the zoetrope, is recorded as having made a series of pictures for his optical instrument that showed a steam-engine in motion.[3]

A few years later Marey detailed how these animation devices could be used, for example, to depict accurately the flight-cycle of a bird. The advantage being that it allowed for a very focused and articulated analysis:

> for it enables the observer to follow movements, which would otherwise be impossible to examine, by slowing down the motion to any desired rate. [Therefore] the eye can follow it in all its phases, whereas, in a living bird, only a confused flutter of the wings can be distinguished. In the same way, by slowing down the phases of a horse's paces by means of the zootrope, they can be more easily analyzed than by observations made directly on the animal.[4]

Over the decades, animation has continued to play a very important role in communicating non-fictional information. And, as animation has become more pervasive in recent years, it has been used in every conceivable manner to communicate a wide range of non-fictional information. The one area that has perhaps garnered the most attention has been its use within the documentary film genre. In these films, animation has been used both as seamlessly integrated digital elements and as very graphical animated sequences.

Particularly beginning in the 1990s, a large number of short-form animated films emerged that were not only non-fictional in content but also intentionally adopted many of the conventions of traditional documentary film. These have come to be known as 'animated documentaries'. As a result, a growing amount of scholarship devoted to this area has emerged within animation studies. For Annabelle Honess Roe,

> The convergence of animation and documentary into the cohesive form of animated documentary is a development that transcends constricted

> definitions and binary understandings of what, and how, documentary and animation can show us.[5]

The definition of what exactly constitutes an animated documentary can be a rather fluid one; traditional documentary films have incorporated animation for many decades, and animated films that derive from non-fictional subjects also have a long-standing tradition. Roe suggests that an animated documentary is one that

> (i) has been recorded or created frame by frame; (ii) is about *the* world rather than a world wholly imagined by its creator; and (iii) has been presented as a documentary by its producers and/or received as a documentary by audiences, festivals or critics.[6]

Notably, as Roe also points out in point (iii), the context surrounding the animated documentary has a great deal to do with its positioning. It should also be noted that many animated documentary films 'feel' like they are documentaries (rather than being merely an animation that is derived from a non-fictional subject matter) because of their structure, their editing and quite often their inclusion of indexical (or indexical-like) elements (most commonly, an indexical voice-over).

In line with these evolving discussions, this chapter will consider the form and process of the animated documentary; but the discussion will be focused less upon the animated *representation* of actuality, more upon the *process* of actuality *becoming* animation. This is an important distinction because the 'animated object' of most fictional animations does not derive from any prior existence, whereas the animated documentary normally personifies a prior condition: it begins as actuality, and through a transformative process of generalization, it *becomes* animation.

Indexicality

When considering the animated representation of actuality, it can be useful to revisit the system of semiotics, or the study of signs. Charles Sanders Peirce made his important contribution to semiotics by developing a 'tripartite classification' system which divided them into indices, icons and symbols.[7] For Peirce, an *index* 'signifies its object solely by virtue of being really connected with it'.[8] Indices, therefore, are thought to provide a direct link to the actual object, and the photochemical process of film is often characterized as possessing such a link. Further removed from actuality resides the *iconic sign*, which 'stands for something merely because it resembles it'.[9] A drawing, for example, may fall into this category of sign. Finally, at a still further remove resides the *symbol*, which is 'usually an association of general ideas, which operates to cause the Symbol to be interpreted as referring to that Object'.[10] A national flag is generally associated with the particular country, even though it in no way resembles it. Importantly, Peirce noted that his divisions of sign types were not absolute, each sign often exhibiting the properties of other types. For example, a photograph can be thought of both as an index and as an icon. It is indexical in that there is said to be a photochemical direct link to the object, and it is iconic because it merely *resembles* the object.[11] It is, in part, because of this fluidity of representation that animation is (along with live-action) equally well placed to deal with actuality.

Mary Ann Doane suggests that the index may be considered essentially in two ways: as a 'footprint' of actuality, and as a pointer *to* actuality. On one hand, when the index 'is exemplified by the footprint or the photograph [it] is a sign that can be described as a trace or imprint of its object. Something of the object leaves a legible residue through the medium of touch'.[12] For Doane, the materiality of the medium of film (which is 'wedded to a photochemical base') is what makes this conception of the indexical possible – the process of light hitting the emulsion of the film leaves an indelible trace.[13] Such a perspective requires a medium-specific interpretation because each medium will have a differing effect on how the 'footprint' might be captured. In this regard, the digitalization of cinema has greatly challenged the notion of the indexical, as the digital image is totally devoid of materiality and therefore, according to this reading, is incapable of accepting an indexical footprint.[14] By another reading the index serves merely as an *indicator* and is, in and of itself, vacuous because it is nothing more than a pointer *to* actuality. It tells us what to look at, but does not *describe* it; it is therefore a 'hollowed-out sign'.[15] It is this latter aspect of the indexical, the embodiment of the arrow, which is the most pertinent to this discussion of the indexical as it does not so closely bind itself to any specific medium.[16]

Animation, is always at least partly iconic (either in form *or* in motion), and filmed animation can have a rather complex relationship to the indexical. As Richard Leskosky has articulated, 'There is no pro-filmic event as such, although there is (usually, but not necessarily) a pro-filmic object. Animation thus creates an event where none had existed before.'[17] For example, a stop-motion animation will contain what most would consider to be indexical images of the real-world objects – 'but not of the actual motion of that object'.[18] The movement applied to these forms is indisputably constructed and imposed, situating the collaborative effect well outside the realm of the *purely* indexical.

In regard to the *acoustic* aspect, some have taken a fairly narrow interpretation of the auditory index in animation. For example, Scott Curtis has stated emphatically, 'indexicality is impossible in a cartoon'. He bases his claim upon the observation that although 'through live-action synch speech, the actors leave their indexical mark on the sound track; there is a necessary connection between sound and image that is missing from cartoons'.[19] Curtis does, however, make interesting observations on the link between the distorted vocal performance of many animated cartoons and the distorted character design of the animated character.[20] For him, this relationship (for example the cartoon design of Bugs Bunny and the exaggerated vocal antics of Mel Blanc) pays tribute to the relationship between live-action actors and *their* voices. However, a more appropriate reading of this relationship would be to draw upon Crisell's discussion of radio sound effects and what he terms the 'indirect signifier'.[21] Crisell offers an example found in radio dramatizations: coconut shells clapped together to simulate the sound of horse hoofs. He suggests that this is an iconic representation of the sound of a real horse trot. However, at the same time, it is an actual broadcast of a person clapping coconut shells, which is an indexical representation of coconut shells being clapped. We can borrow from this discussion on radio, and apply it to animation. The voice recording of the actor who performs the voice of, for example, the character Shrek is comparable to what Crisell would call an 'indirect signifier'. For though the recording of Michael Myers (the voice of the Shrek character) is an indexical recording, it is meant to refer to the voice of the animated character, making it an 'indirect signifier'. Conversely, in the case of the animated documentary, the voice of, for example, Kathy Easdale in *His Mother's Voice* (Tupicoff 1996) is an indexical recording, *and* it is meant to refer directly to the actual Kathy Easdale (Matthew's mother). Michael Renov refers to this animation as containing a 'profoundly indexical auditory signifier'.[22]

Of course, the issue of indexicality is a complex one, particularly when it relates to the differences between live-action film and animation: both present their own modes of mediation in screen-audience relations. For Roe, it is animation's ability to perform without any regard to the indexical that tenders its greatest potential:

> By releasing documentary from the strictures of a causal connection between filmic and profilmic, animation has the potential to bring things that are temporally, spatially and psychologically distant from the viewer into closer proximity. It can conflate history, transcend geography and give insight into the mental states of other people.[23]

Certainly, this is one of the strengths of the animated form – it has inherent potentialities to reveal and communicate virtually anything. Stephen Prince also questions whether indexical classifications are still relevant, particularly when we consider the photo-realistic possibilities of digital animation. He asserts that it is essential that we develop a clearer understanding of how these digital simulations can actually provide 'perceptually valid experiences' which can invoke the credibility of the traditional index. He also suggests that rather than an index-based system; we adopt a 'correspondence-based model of cinematic representation' and asserts that these images can

> display a nested hierarchy of cues which organize the display of light, color, texture, movement and sound in ways that correspond with the viewer's own understanding of these phenomena in daily life.[24]

Prince further reasons in the realm of digital and animated imagery we are not required to 'reinstate indexicality as the ground of realism'.[25] Undoubtedly, such theories of mediation are continually expanding, particularly as digital simulations make provision for a greatly enhanced mimetic image.

Even though the capabilities of animation have evolved and our acceptance of a broader reading of documentary has also evolved, the concept of the index likely still has some currency. However, rather than a discussion about extremes (*either* indexical *or* iconic representation), it can be much more useful to focus upon the icon and the index working effectively in tandem to create an innovative documentary effect. Furthermore, the index, when situated in an animated context, can be subdivided effectively into a number of different constituent layers. By dissecting the concept of the indexical into multiple layers or processes it can not only better reflect the intense complexity of the actual world but also embrace the highly flexible nature of animation. When considered in this manner, the index, rather than inflicting any sort of creative limitations, can contribute greatly to both the veracity and the creativity of the animated documentary. Furthermore, we can think of the collective power of the icon and the index in terms of a Deleuzian styled 'inclusive disjunction',[26] in a sense, a form that is simultaneously in opposition and in collaboration: an *icon-index dialectic.*

Becoming the animated documentary

The first stage in any animated documentary's becoming rests within the realm of actuality, as it is a fundamental claim of the documentary film that it describes some aspect of actuality. The documentary film generally refers to that 'which exists beyond and prior to the text, and which has an independent existence beyond the consciousness' of the film-maker.[27] Correspondingly, for Nicholas Rescher,

> to be actual or real is
> 1) to be an item that has footing in a thought-independent realm of some kind;
> 2) to be able to figure in the description or explanation of the world's causal commerce.[28]

Conversely, C. S. Peirce considers that what is *not* actuality can be embodied within the notion of 'incognizables', that is those things which cannot be cognitively understood. Simply put, if one cannot *know* it, then it cannot *be real*. Here Peirce, according to Rescher, delineates an important 'boundary line separation between ontology and epistemology'.[29] Rescher at the same time acknowledges the tension between the actual and the cognitive: 'For the only reality worth having is one that is in some degree knowable. And so it is the very limitation of our knowledge – our recognition that there is more to reality than what we do and can know or ever conjecture about it – that speaks for the mind-independence of the real.'[30] Ultimately, the documentary film offers an epistemological service, providing the viewer an understanding of the actual, and thus serving to blur the 'separation line' of the ontological and the epistemic. For example, in a David Attenborough nature documentary we may be able to see (for the first time) the feeding habits of a particularly rare animal; this, in effect, transforms the previously 'uncognizable' into a clearly cogitative figuration.

Entomologist (and part-time film-maker) Ladislas Starewich (best known for his fictional animation *The Revenge of the Cameraman*, 1911) (see Figure 5.1) was able through his early non-fictional animation experiments to make 'cognizable' the mating habits of beetles. He initially attempted to record the beetles in live action; but because of the technological limitations of the time, he found it impossible to get clear live-action footage of the beetles' night-time behaviour (although he had *witnessed* it, he was unable to *film* it). Thus he resorted to killing the beetles and, having fitted them with armatures, reanimated the dead creatures to perform their original actions. Today, with the arrival of micro low-light video cameras, the documentary film-maker would be much better placed to capture the actual beetle behaviours (without needing to resort to killing them first); however, Starewich did illustrate quite early on that much of actuality is *unfilmable*, and that animation could be an effective revealer of those unfilmable aspects.

For Bill Nichols, the documentary offers us a view of the actual. 'Instead of *a* world, we are offered access to *the* world.'[31] However, the contention that the documentary somehow offers us a pure, unmediated access has been strongly refuted.

> The duplication of the world, even of what we know most intimately – ourselves – can never be unproblematic... Always issues of selection intrude (which angle, take, camera stock will best serve); the results are indeed *mediated*, the results of multiple interventions that necessarily *come between* the cinematic sign (what we see on the screen) and its referent (what existed in the world).[32]

For Keith Beattie, the presence of the documentary film-maker goes beyond mediation and can, in fact, *alter* actuality. 'The presence of a documentary

FIGURE 5.1 *Image from* The Revenge of the Cameraman *(Ladislas Starewich 1911).*

camera and sound and light equipment is likely to affect the world being filmed in multiple direct and indirect ways such as a simple rearrangement of furniture to accommodate a film crew in a cramped space, to alterations of behaviour in which subjects "act" naturally for the camera.'[33] As a result of the continual presence of the film crew and cameras, the production of the documentary *An American Family* (Craig Gilbert 1973) is often credited with *causing* the on-screen divorce of the couple that is the subject of the documentary.[34] Such is the dilemma of much documentary film-making – to what degree does the film-making apparatus impose its presence? If Starewich had turned the lights on to his mating beetles, he would have had sufficient light to film them, but the beetles would most likely have scurried away or, at least, not have performed. Therefore, all documentary film can have an impact on the actual content of the film, on actuality itself. It often requires a participatory role in the actuality as it is being filmed, and therefore there is an undeniable reflexivity that occurs.[35] Animation is usually *not* directly involved in the actuality event, and in some cases is arguably better situated to act as an external assessor.

Further to the imposition of the film-maker, another problem is that the film-maker cannot record *everything*. And though more and more of our world is being continually filmed through surveillance cameras and personal recording devices, it is still impossible to have a fully omniscient recording of an event. Only small portions and aspects of it can be recorded, and thus only a very limited amount of data can be documented. Ultimately, the documentary film-maker demonstrates a bias based upon what he or she points the camera at; and at the same time, the limitations of the filming apparatus impose their own set of biases.

Hollywood producer Robert Evans noted at the start of the documentary, *The Kid Stays in the Picture* (Brett Morgen 2002): 'There are three sides to every story: your side, my side, and the truth. And no one is lying. Memories shared serve each differently.' Indeed, everyone has a unique and personal perception and cognition of his or her experience of actuality. Deleuze notes that each moment of experience presents two unique aspects: the actual (which is perception) and the virtual (which is recollection).[36] In many cases, the documentary film provides us an amalgamation of these differing aspects, integrating aspects of bias and the camera's 'perception'. Grierson suggests of the documentary film, 'in its use of the living article, there is also an opportunity to perform creative work'.[37] He continues, 'You photograph the natural life, but you also, by your juxtaposition of detail, create an interpretation of it.'[38] It is this recording *and* interpretation that collides with the simultaneous Deleuzian aspects of the virtual and the actual.

Grierson's oft-referenced definition of the 'creative treatment of actuality' clearly suggests just such a schism in which 'creativity' and 'actuality' are functionally distinct. Paul Ward similarly argues that the documentary does *not* come from a position where 'facts are presented "impartially" and "balanced" in order to reach an external truth'.[39] But it is Michael Renov who delineates four fundamental tendencies of the documentary form which, one could argue, extradite the documentary from the burden of providing us with a single 'truth' about actuality. Renov suggests four tendencies or 'four functions [which] operate as modalities of desire, impulsions which fuel documentary discourse:

1 to record, reveal or preserve
2 to persuade or promote
3 to analyze or interrogate
4 to express'.[40]

These four functions help to articulate a logical pathway from the actual towards the documentary film. Only the first function ('to record, reveal or preserve') intimately deals with the actual, while the other three operate in a much wider discursive field *around* the actual.

To merely record actuality does not make a documentary; in fact, there is an important distinction between the historical *understanding* of actuality and its *recording*. The documentary can put into perspective, contextualize and structure that which has been recorded. All documentary footage requires explication, without which we may not know what we are looking at, or *why* we are meant to look at it. Nichols claims that the documentary must incorporate an 'organizational backbone' which 'constitutes a "logic" or "economy" of the text. This in turn, guarantees coherence'.[41]

It can be argued that the more 'indexically direct' the documentary footage, the more organization must occur. 'The closer the image comes to being reduced to pure presence, the more it threatens to become unreadable and requires explication.'[42] Whitehead echoes this when he argues: 'The pure mode of presentational immediacy gives no information as to the past or the future. It merely presents an illustrated portion of the presented duration.' Such a pure observation may provide a 'cross-section of the universe', but it does not provide us with a context, which is essential for comprehension.[43] Actuality is simply too vast to be represented without mediation, which is also an important aspect of our own cognitive processing (we focus only on the relevant). For Whitehead, this comes in the form of 'causal efficacy', a process by which our previous knowledge and memory assists us to contextualize our experiences.[44] In a sense, the documentary film must serve to cogitate and interpret actuality for us. Because we are not, in fact, experiencing actuality, and are only being privileged to a very narrow view of it, we are unable to utilize the full scope of our *own* perceptive and cognitive abilities. Thus, at some point the *document* (the raw recording of actuality) needs to be converted into the *documentary film*. When this occurs, the film-maker asserts 'his social position as synthesizer of reality against the unmediated, unorganized index'.[45]

The approach to the *animated* documentary is often quite different because the structuring and the creation of the imagery are habitually performed concurrently. Due to the generally constructed nature of animation, the editing and the animation process occur in tandem, and normally the necessary explication also occurs simultaneously. Its detailed construction process will often provide an initial structural impulse. The documentary film is able to represent, and relies upon, the substantive properties of actuality. Nichols explains that the representation of documentary is 'taken' from actuality, noting that 'this *taking* is nonsubtractive: the thing remains, imparting information to the representation, but not at the expense of any of its own matter or energy'.[46] In this same manner, it could be understood that the animated documentary *gives* to actuality, in the sense that new images and motion are constructed and 'given' or added to it. Here, too, the original actuality remains unaltered, but the resultant product (the documentary) comprises a new representation, more complex because of this additive process. However, because animation ultimately simplifies the image and motion it embodies, there is a *simultaneous addition and reduction* of the total construct.

Consider Bob Sabiston's animated documentary *Snack and Drink* (1999), which Paul Ward describes as 'an amusing and strangely touching visual rendering of just how obsessively focused an autistic person can be',[47] simultaneously presents simplified forms as well as a further visual commentary. Ward locates this animation within what Paul Wells describes as animation's ability to provide us a 'penetrative' view into the subject's thought process.[48] In one scene the main character is seen pouring a soda for himself; the soda dispensers momentarily come to life with wiggling arms and goggling eyes that help to comment on the character's autistic mental state (see Figure 5.2). Through a remarkable range of techniques, the animated documentary can provide both a focused presentation of actuality (in this case, a graphic simplified image) and a simultaneous explication of the event.

Importantly, Wells and Hardstaff have suggested that some animated documentaries, rather than seeking a Griersonian 'creative treatment of actuality', are instead concerned with the possibility that 'actuality is created for treatment'.[49] By progressing actuality into the realm of the generalized, we avoid fixating on issues of aesthetics and traditional documentary stylings and instead are able to focus on the documentary *process* at work in the construction of the animated documentary. Once actuality is

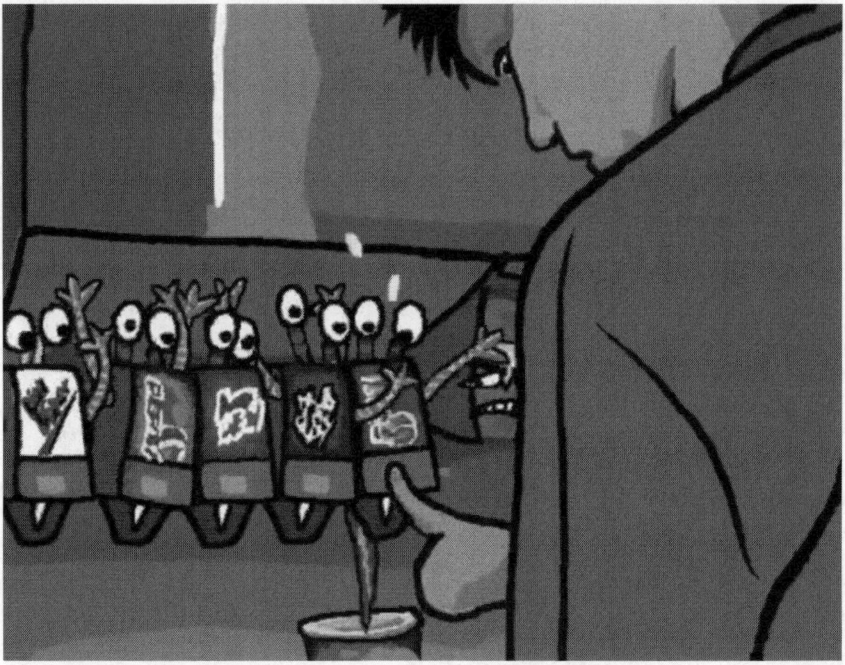

FIGURE 5.2 *Image from* Snack and Drink *(Bob Sabiston 1999).*

transformed to a new state through the animated documentary, the viewer may be better placed to understand more fully the real-world information that is presented.

The tendency of animation is towards the simplified and the iconic, which inherently embodies a multiplicity of significance. The further an image shifts away from the indexical and towards the iconic, the wider the *possible* range of its representation. For example, a photograph of one's smiling next-door neighbour can really represent only that one person, whereas a 'smiley face' icon could simultaneously represent every person on the planet. An icon is always a generalized signifier which can represent the specific event in question, but at the same time could also represent *other* events. Thus the animated documentary must balance two conflicting tendencies: first that the image is not absolutely specific in its appearance and therefore could represent many different things; second that the image refers to a *specific* aspect of actuality and not to any other aspect of it. It is therefore less important to consider the animated documentary image as a simplified rendition of actuality, but instead as a *generalized* rendition of a specific event.

However, we understand that the simplified image of the animated documentary is intended to represent a specific event because we are *told* that it does. This is not unlike the situation that some live-action documentary encounters when it considers certain indexical filmic recordings. Even although these recordings are of specific events, the viewer may not recognize which event it is, and therefore may need to be told this. Rosen discusses the amateur footage that captured the assassination of John F. Kennedy and how, without additional explication in subsequent (early) documentaries and broadcasts, such imagery could not adequately describe the event.[50] The footage alone, even though it describes a singular event, could be erroneously interpreted as something other.[51]

Jim Moran claims that 'documentary authority never lies within the image, but always in the discursive field around it: its narration, site of exhibition, reputation, intention, interpretation – even its category'.[52] Thus, there is a common deficiency to be found in the imagery of both the live action and the animated documentary film; the image alone may not be able to convey satisfactorily its intended meaning. That the image refers to an actual event that took place is of paramount importance, as is the fact that the imagery was made as a result of that event (either by camera or by construction). Thus, the iconic image found in an animated documentary is always a generalized representation that becomes a specific image representation. This results from both a preceding actual event and this event's documentary explication and contextualization.

By contrast, the imagery of the animated fictional film contains iconic images that have only existed as generalized icons, and are not the result of any particular actuality. Mickey Mouse is not meant to represent an actual creature of the animal kingdom, let alone represent a *specific* actual mouse. Sometimes, though, this condition becomes inverted, and the animated image presents us with a *specific* generalization, rather than a *generalized* specificity. Consider how animation is often used to visualize abstract or theoretical ideas or those generally discussed occurrences that cannot be specifically filmed – the breaking of atomic bonds, or of solar windstorms in space. In these cases, general ideas are given specific visual images. In relation to the visual complexity that digital 3D animation can afford, Wolf has noted that 'by translating invisible entities (beyond the range of human vision) or mathematical ideas into visible analogues, computer simulation has allowed the conceptual world to enter the perceptual one'.[53]

The animated documentary is thus able to reify the abstract, making it more concrete, but at the same time remaining non-specific. For, according to Rescher, science and theory must always 'deal in generalities', while events and experiences always result in specifics.[54] Interestingly, the documentary film may feature generalized ideas, but it is best serviced by the generalized image of animation to directly reference these concepts. Thus, in a reversal of the photograph's sole claim to represent the visual index of specific actualities, it might be appropriate to consider the visual indexical referent of generalities as existing only within the animated form.

The animated documentary image

The animated documentary ultimately relies heavily upon iconic imagery, which Rescher would refer to as *fictional objects*. It is because a fictional object is not actuality and, in fact, must fundamentally remain external to actuality, that it is often able to utilize such a privileged position to its advantage. One advantage of this process is that it allows for an enhanced focus upon particular aspects of actuality. Rescher surmises that 'Nature presents many things together: it conjoins, but does not prioritise; its favoured connective is *and* rather than *and next*; it has no point of view, but is all at once.'[55] The fictional object (or in our case, an iconic animation image) is able to make us aware of truths about actuality of which we would not otherwise be conscious. Even though such an image may convey an impoverished nature, it 'enables us to achieve a clarity of focus' unavailable to us in the real world.[56]

The animated documentary allows the viewer (and the film-maker) to focus on the essential particulars of actuality, just as our cognitive imagery allows the mind to focus on what is most important and avoids being diverted by an over-abundance of information. Further to this it serves to visually order and structure the visual data. One way in which it achieves this is through what Shnotz and Lowe refer to as animation's 'directive function'. By literally highlighting, exaggerating or simplifying specific key elements, animation can 'increase the perceptual salience of parts as well as their attributes or relations'. Furthermore, it can physically realign 'relevant corresponding features so that their spatial arrangement better reflects their underlying conceptual relationship'. This results in a clearer sense of the correspondences and differences between the features.[57]

Even so, the animated documentary is well placed to *add* to the epistemic realm and it is also capable of aiding in the cognitive process: new ideas are still possible even within the finite borders of the iconic image (fictional object). For example, it is relevant to consider the inherent visual evidence of the animated film itself. Prior to cinematic animation the magnified, temporal and quivering pencil line on paper, or the quivering etched line onto film stock, would have been an 'uncognizable' phenomenon. Consider for example the early direct animation films of Len Lye, such as *Colour Box* (1935), *Colour Flight* (1938) and *Swinging the Lambeth Walk* (1939), each of which exhibits a form of frenetic motion that most contemporaneous viewers had likely never seen or imagined before. It was the very form and process of animation that permitted the viewer to witness such visual manifestations that defied traditional physics, yet at the same time were the very embodiment of quantum physics with their spatial and temporal popping and quivering. Quite simply, animation, because of its inherent structure, could depict images and movements that had never been seen before. Often, scientific exposition benefits from the contrivance of an imagery of the abstract. Consider the graph, the weather map, the description of atomic bonds and energy waves. Animation is often used in scientific documentary films to visualize such concepts and theories that have not yet been made concrete. For example, complex quantum theorems or prospective nano-machines (which are built atom-by-atom) may be explored. Before being set in animation such concepts were in some cases 'uncognizable' and were certainly *unenvisionable* in the temporal form. In this way, van Dijck proposes that such 'Models and representations' are able to 'demonstrate how scientific claims are intrinsically dependent upon their visualizations. Computer animations are concurrently instruments of mediating and constructing science'.[58] Wolf regards this form of documentary as the 'subjunctive' documentary, that which might be, or is, probable.

These subjunctive elements, once concretized into the animated form, inevitably have a perceptible effect on the real world as well. For example, though scientists had a good idea of the general size and shape of the featured dinosaurs in the animated *Walking with Dinosaurs* (Tim Haines and Jasper James 1999), there would have been other details such as colouration and texture (and exactly how they might have moved) that were largely conjectured. However, once made concrete (that is seamlessly integrated into the live-action backgrounds), these articulated dinosaurs also became, at least metaphorically, seamlessly integrated into our world as well. Their detail and presented behaviours inevitably contributed to how we think about dinosaurs. It has also had further influence upon such diverse areas as the design of museum displays, educational programmes, research funding and a variety of popular culture and entertainment experiences. Brian Winston suggests that the ultimate effect of the documentary is a process of scientific collection of data: 'the apparatus becomes transparent; the documentary becomes scientific inscription – evidence'.[59] Within the animated image, this evidence can be interrogated with precision, and can adjoin supplementary meaning to the image; and it has the further cognitive ability to signify previously unnoticed associations. Moreover, it can present us with visualizations that before were *uncognizable*, thus opening up new realms of possibilities.

According to van Dijck, we are witnessing a new era of 'picturizing' where we can 'create moving images out of pixels that look like analogues of video footage'.[60] As such examples of digital simulation become more common, it becomes increasingly irrelevant that one form of cinema can be transformed into an emulation of another. Thus we have animated films that look exactly like traditional wildlife documentaries (beginning with the *Walking with Dinosaurs* series, 1999), and we see live-action films such as *Sin City* (Robert Rodriguez and Frank Miller 2005), which take on many of the stylistic affectations of animation. For Beattie this might suggest that the 'potential of digitalization to erode the bond between image and referent jeopardizes notions of realism, thereby disrupting the basis of the entire documentary tradition'.[61] However, as we have observed, even the most indexical photographic film images can lack meaning (for example, if poorly shot or of an extreme close-up) and may therefore contain little inherent basis into which the viewer can place their 'faith' – unless, of course, these are further explicated by the film-maker, in which case it then becomes the film-maker in whom one puts one's trust. And ultimately it becomes a matter of trust since even the most traditional of film processes allow for deceit.

The animated documentary need not, of course, be restricted to the depiction of the unfilmable. This is illustrated by Tamara Meem's animated documentary *The First Thing I Remember* (2005), which seeks to subvert the expected paradigm of logical animation usage in a documentary film. Here she uses rotoscoped animation to substitute the *only* truly indexical footage that she was able to record, and uses re-enacted live-action footage, affected by a home movie aesthetic, to depict the most unfilmable portion of the documentary, namely the interviewees' 'first memories' (see Figure 5.3). The subverted image of this film allows us to question the verisimilitude of the 'memory' imagery, immediately recognizing it as a stylistic device. Additionally, if the interviewees were *not* featured as animated images, then it is likely that the 'home video' style memory sequences would not

FIGURE 5.3 *Image from Tamara Meem's animated documentary* The First Thing I Remember *(2005).*

successfully signify the intended cognitive imagery. But instead, the viewer is fully aware that the film-maker has made carefully plotted stylistic choices without bringing into question the veracity of the rotoscoped interview footage.

Animated documentary layers

Much of the complexity of the animated form is derived from a multiplicity of apparently simplistic layers which, through collaborative interactions, are brought to an advanced complexity of composition. Similarly, collaborative interactions allow the *animated documentary* to achieve a far greater level of complexity in its representation of actuality. Actuality is incredibly complex, drawing Whitehead to claim that it 'is the fundamental exemplification of composition'. Thus, innumerable layers of processes converge in 'the composite constitutions of the individual occasions' to become a moment in time and manifest as actuality.[62] As Rescher clarifies:

> Of course, when any one of these 'events' is examined in detail, it soon becomes clear that, in fact, a long and complicated process is involved, a sequence of activities and transactions that in each case constitutes an elaborate story of interconnected developments. On closer inspection, the idea of discrete 'events' dissolves into a manifold of processes which themselves dissolve into further processes.[63]

However, the inherent complexity both of actuality and of animation should not be deduced simply because it can be deconstructed into *many* discreet layers. For clarification, we could look towards the concept of 'collective intelligence'. This is illustrated by the collaborative and ostensibly intelligent nature of an ant colony – a phenomenon which is achieved, not as the result of *each* ant's possessing a high intellect (individually they possess a very *limited* one), nor because there are merely large numbers of them in a colony (as this would simply provide a random complexity): it is because they can successfully *work together*. Each ant has just sufficient intelligence to allow it to react in a particular manner to other ants or to a certain number of given situations. Yet, when compounded, these re-actions begin to resemble a carefully constructed intelligence.[64] Similarly, the single iconic image (or the fictional object) can in and of itself never reach the complexity of actuality; but with a carefully orchestrated layering of sub-frame elements, the animated documentary image can begin to personify a complexity that edges *closer* to our perception of actuality.

To represent the infinite complexity of the real world in a single-view camera image inevitably *flattens* it; despite its being able to record much of the visible interaction of objects, it can only depict a single dimensional facet at any one time. However, the intricacy of layering that can be achieved through the animation process provides the potential to exploit an exponential complexity of interplay between the layers. The resulting complexity is not necessarily a direct index of actuality, but a representational schematic of this complexity. Essentially, it is a generalized symbol of how the elements of actuality are interwoven. By segmenting representations of actuality into such distinctive layers, we are better able to see both the cohesion and the disjunction between these. Another means by which to consider the investigation of actuality is to view it from a forensics perspective. One of the central strategies of forensic investigation is the recognition that an event cannot be truly analysed by any single measuring device. Every event exemplifies numerous micro-events, and thereby leaves behind an evidence trail of many layers, each of which contains a segment of information. When combined with other segments – exponential amounts of information can be inferred.[65]

Writing back in 1999, at the earlier stages of the digital revolution, Wolf makes the claim that the assemblage process of digital imagery will eventually provide near equivalence to the traditional indexical recording. The process of constructing a computer simulation requires the compositing of vast amounts of data and, 'as the data set becomes larger and more comprehensive, its indexical link to the physical world grows stronger' eventually becoming a sufficient representative.[66] Thus through the additive process, the animation is, in many cases, sufficiently placed to visualize an event more complexly: it is not restricted by the narrow specificities of the filmic camera's point of view and can potentially provide us with a broader panoptic view of the event.

With the increasing prevalence of new digital technologies, Stephen Prince suggests that the conception of the index should be replaced by a sliding scale of 'equivalence', for there is no longer a direct photochemical relationship between the illumination of actuality and the film camera.[67] Although Prince is most certainly correct in that, as increasingly complex technological mediation is developed, so there occurs a greater and greater loss of *directness* in the images we capture of actuality, it could be argued that such a conception places too much primacy on the idea of an *indivisible* indexical image. If we are to follow Whitehead's conception that 'actuality is the fundamental exemplification of composition',[68] then it should also follow that the *index* of actuality should also be a 'fundamental exemplification of composition', and we should therefore be able to divide the index up into layers and constituent parts.

In her discussion of Charles Sanders Peirce, Mary Ann Doane notes that the index in and of itself is vacuous, as it is nothing more than a pointer *to* actuality. It tells us what to look at, but does not *describe* it, and is therefore a 'hollowed-out sign'.[69] Accordingly, indices are nothing more than arrows which *point* at particular aspects of actuality. However, an arrow does not need simply to point in a general direction 'somewhere over there'. It can also point in a very precise manner: to a forest, to a tree, to a leaf or to a cell. On the other hand, it can also point to more conceptual layers of actuality – to the green of the leaf, the texture of the tree trunk or the sound or the motion of the branch creaking in the wind.

It can be argued that the notion of the index might be considered in a similar manner to that by which we have previously dealt with the form of animation and the form of perception and cognition, that is as a multilayered, multifaceted construct. Initially, the idea of the index could be divided into four primary layers: sound, motion, image and time.

Index
Sound-Index
Motion-Index
Image-Index
Time-Index

The still photographic image has long been considered to be an indexical representation, yet it clearly lacks motion, which the *other* indexical image (the live-action film) contains. It could be argued that the contemporary motion-capture systems could also be considered in their own right to be *motion-indices*. The still image also lacks sound: and sound alone can clearly be considered as a recorded index of an event. Michael Renov, for example, in his discussion of Tupicoff's *His Mother's Voice*, refers to the audio recording as an 'acoustical indexicality'.[70] Even time, as will be discussed later, can be considered (at least tangentially) as an indexical layer when we consider the isochronal possibilities of the animated image. Furthermore, the primary layer of the indexical image could be further subdivided into such corresponding indices as form, colour, texture and qualities of light.[71]

Image-Index
Form-Index Colour-Index Texture-Index Lighting-Index

Movement and image

It is pertinent that most discussions of the documentary form do not dispute the fact that the black and white photographic image provides us with an index,[72] even though it lacks an important indexical perception: colour. Yet there are cases where the colour of an object may be the most important aspect of an event: for example, the person in the *yellow* hat committed the crime! Suppose that, in addition to a black and white photograph of the event, there had been an eyewitness to this crime and he or she had noticed that the person in the *yellow* hat (as distinct from any one of the others who were wearing *lime-green* hats) was the one on the left. In order to clarify the footage for subsequent viewers, the indexical black and white images could quite easily be tinted so that the yellow hat was chromatically visible. In such a case, there would be a resulting image that contained a percentage of indexical information, and a percentage of iconic (or at least 'imposed') information – namely the layer of the colour yellow.

One could consider the reverse case, that one was able to record the *actual* colour spectrum of a star (but not its actual form): could we not then say that this was an *isochromatic* index of an event? As more and more sophisticated devices emerge, which can directly record *particular* aspects of our world, including those which may have gone unnoticed in the past, it would make sense also to consider these as separate indices. Before sound-recording devices emerged, audio-indices did not exist: yet their verisimilitudes are readily accepted today. There will likely be many other aspects of our world that may one day be able to be 'live-recorded', that although inconceivable now, will become commonplace in the future.

Bob Sabiston has created a number of 'Rotoshopped' documentaries such as *Snack and Drink* (1999) and *Grasshopper* (2003), which feature primarily indexical movements. However, their imagery could be classified as being only partly indexical. For even though the forms of the figures generally remain 'true to form' (though they do fluctuate more in some sequences), their colouration and texture are highly manipulated and overtly trend towards the iconic. In contrast, the early stop-motion films of Ladislas Starewich were made using actual beetles that were then animated frame-by-frame by Starewich. Thus the forms certainly denoted an indexical tethering, even although their movement clearly represented an imposed iconic layer of generalized motion.

There has been an increasingly common practice of animating still photographs for documentary films, particularly where there has been a shortage of archival live-action footage. This practice can readily be seen in such documentary features as *The Kid Stays in the Picture* (Brett Morgen 2002) and *Jean Cocteau* (Jacques Barsac 1996) (to name but two). In these films the directors will often choose to animate only certain elements within each photograph. But rarely will the animators choose to substantially reanimate a *person* that is featured in the photograph, as there would probably not be enough information to accurately reify them. Instead, the animators will generally choose to add in movements that are less specific and less historically important. For example, in the primarily live-action documentary film *The Kid Stays in the Picture* (2002), numerous archival photographs become animated. The most typical animated elements included plants made to blow in the breeze, the rippling of water and pipe smoke slowly rising upwards. And although they are not *specifically* accurate movements, they do represent *generally* accurate movements. This procedure is perhaps a kinetic analogue to the common use of 'generic images' that the traditional documentary film-maker will use to 'approximate representation' when there is a lack of actual footage.[73] Such movements are emblematic of how such elements generally behave based upon the perceived laws of the physical world. Wolf refers to these as 'conceptual indices (like gravity or the laws of physics) to govern simulated events'.[74] In other films, human figures within photographs have been animated in somewhat subtle ways. For example, in the 1996 documentary *Jean Cocteau* (Jacques Barsac 1996), there were many examples in which a person in a photograph would turn his or her head, or arms and legs would move subtly. These movements represented generally iconic movements that gave 'life' to the otherwise motionless indexical figures, but were in no way representative of actual movements that would have occurred at the time of the photograph (see Figure 5.4).

Brett Morgen's feature-length documentary film *Chicago 10* (2007), about the trial of a group of political activists including Abbey Hoffman, utilized a great deal of animation to compliment the live-action archival and interview footage. Most of the animated sequences utilized motion-captured performances. In this case, both the motion-capture movement

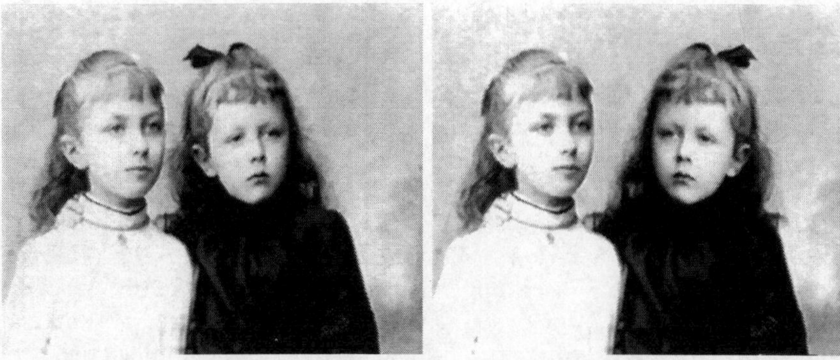

FIGURE 5.4 *Two images from the documentary* Jean Cocteau *(Jacques Barsac 1996), which describe movement that has been added to an archival photograph.*

and the forms were entirely removed from the real-world events described in the documentary – that is the forms were constructed (although modelled closely after the real-life persons), and the movement was created by actors. Similarly, in the short animated documentary *Tussilago* (Jonas Odell 2010), much of the animation is derived from the rotoscoping of actors who engaged in re-enactments of the tumultuous events in Germany in the 1970s (see Figure 5.5). Both of these films provided 'indexical-like' movement to the animated forms, and these layers of movement would correspond to what Crisell refers to as an 'indirect signifier'.[75]

FIGURE 5.5 *Image from* Tussilago *(Jonas Odell 2010).*

Sound

Traditional live-action documentary films often contain voice-over narration, which may be used to structure the film, interpret and contextualize the images being shown and, particularly, to drive home an argument.[76] Most of these voice-overs are interpreted as the voice of 'authority' as they represent an off-screen voice from another realm, one possessing a greater knowledge of the subject than the viewer. Bruzzi refers to it as 'an extra-diegetic soundtrack' which has been appended *after* the documentary evidence-gathering process.[77] The use of sound in the animated documentary shares a number of conventions with the traditional documentary film, albeit there are a number of significant aspects of differentiation. The bulk of the differences can be traced to the constructivist process of the animation form, particularly in how the animated visuals are enacted in careful response to the audio track in a significantly deliberative manner. In animated documentaries such as *His Mother's Voice* (Tupicoff 1996) and *It's Like That* (Southern Ladies' Animation Group 2003), the extra-diegetic, audio track is, in fact, these films' *starting point,* rather than an added construction. In these cases, both audio tracks began as broadcasted radio interviews that had an undeniably profound effect upon the animators who later visualized them.

One essential convention of the use of sound in animation is that it is unavoidably extra-diegetic in nature (while this approach is optional in the traditional film), which may become even more conspicuous in the animated documentary with its heavy reliance upon the *indexical* soundtrack. Arguably, most animations that are considered as animated documentaries feature an imposed 'indexical' soundtrack. Ultimately it is this that provides it with a documentary aesthetic, locating it within this genre. Such animated films as *Going Equipped* (Aardman 1989), *Abductees* (Vester 1995), *His Mother's Voice* (Tupicoff 1996), *It's Like That* (Southern Ladies' Animation Group 2003), *Ryan* (Landreth 2004), *The First Thing I Remember* (Tamara Meem 2005), *Nothing Like the First Time* (Jonas Odell 2005), *A Very Nice Honeymoon* (Simmonds Brothers 2006), *The Wrong Trainers* (Kez Margrie 2007), *I Met the Walrus* (Josh Raskin 2007), and *The Stitches Speak* (Nina Sabnani 2010) and the *Modern Love* series (The New York Times 2013) are just a few of the countless animated documentaries that combine fabricated visuals with indexical audio tracks. For Paul Ward, such a stark contrast between the graphical visual-track and the indexical audio track suggests that 'the viewer can be under *no* illusion that what they are looking at is, categorically, a construction'.[78]

The animated documentary short *It's Like That* is based on a radio broadcast, an ABC radio documentary of a phone conversation with some child detainees at an Australian Immigration Detention Centre. The speakers are depicted as small, cute, knitted baby-bird sculptured dolls. The rather cute visuals seem to illustrate appropriately the innocent sounding voices of the child-speakers. But in this instance, knowing the speakers to be imprisoned children, one is unequivocally led to question the governmental system that holds them. And, it is the tacit knowledge that the government would never permit a film or a video camera documentary interview with these children in the detention centre, and that animation is the only feasible way to visualize this conversation – the very fact that it *is* an animated documentary – that generates the power of the message.

Such an obvious conflation of sound and image compliments a further convention: that the soundtrack often deeply *influences*, even *dictates,* the visuals of the animation. During the production process, the animator will frequently *create* the visuals in *response* to the pre-recorded audio track. Thus, in the case of the animated documentary, the viewer does not believe that the animated imagery *actually* occurred; instead they understand it to have happened as a *result* of the indexical soundtrack. Sometimes the animation will explore a playful interaction between the literal meaning of a word or sentence and the narrator's intended metaphorical usage. For example, *I Met the Walrus* (Raskin 2007) is an animated documentary that takes an emphatically literal approach to the visualization of an unscripted interview – every word is quite literally described, which creates a number of surprising audio/image collaborations.

Another unique manifestation of this condition can be found in the animated documentary *A Very Nice Honeymoon* (Simmonds Brothers 2006). In this example the animation also relies upon the audio track of an interview – of a man who is recounting the events of which his grandfather had experienced many decades earlier. The animated visuals jump back and forth between the present interview and the historical events involving his grandfather. Interestingly, it is always the voice of the interviewee that is used as the source for both the lip-synching of the interviewee and of the historical grandfather. For example, the interviewee begins speaking (in lip-synch): 'And when his first wife died, he said to grandfather' – at which point the image then jumps back in time, to where a representation of the grandfather as a young man continues speaking in the same interviewee's voice: 'Why don't you go back home and bring out a wife?' The result is that the audio seamlessly transcends characters and time, all the while precisely controlling their every move.

Similarly, a recent three-minute long animated documentary *Vital Voices, Hawa Abdi* (Aaron Kisner 2013) tells the story of Somalia's first gynaecologist and her remarkable efforts in founding a women's clinic and hospital despite the ongoing conflict and turbulence within her home country of Somalia. Her voice also controls the flow of animation and is also sometimes transferred to others. For example, when she recounted how on one occasion the soldiers of an invading army had come up to her and said, 'You are an old woman and you can not be in charge!' – at this point the soldiers were made to 'speak' these words, even though they are actually

FIGURE 5.6 *Image from* Vital Voices, Hawa Abdi *(Aaron Kisner 2013).*

spoken with the indexical intonation of an 'old lady' (see Figure 5.6). For Renov, referring to such animated documentaries, 'all [the] images, fantasies and figurations appear only in relation to the profoundly indexical auditory signifier'.[79] This is in stark contrast to the standard documentary's use of the voice-over in which 'the visuals corroborate the narration but are not subservient to it'.[80]

Time

As previously discussed, many documentary theorists have placed importance on considerations of the visual index (and to a lesser degree, the audio-index), but there has been very little discussion of other potential indices. This section will consider the somewhat unorthodox idea of *indexical time* within the documentary form.

By drawing from narrative theory texts, we have previously considered several different time-states within the animated film (also within cognition). These are, 'narrative time' and 'discourse time'; and because of the often intensive construction process of the animated form, we have suggested a further time-state which can be identified as *production time*. When we are presented with a text in which the 'narrative time' and the 'discourse time' are equivalent, it can be considered to be *isochronal* in nature. When we consider the documentary film's engagement with actuality, isochronality could also be described as *indexical time* as there is a point-to-point referent between actuality time and duration time. Every event and every recording of an event will comprise a precise amount of time. Thus, if it takes someone twenty seconds to walk up a flight of stairs and this particular event has a screened duration of twenty seconds, then the documentary portrays (at least a sense of) *indexical time*. Conversely, if this event had a screened duration of only *five* seconds, perhaps then it could be described as *iconic time*. Time and the timing of movement are essential to creating compelling animated movement; it could also be argued that it is essential to the authentic depiction of actuality.

Macdonald and Cousins claim that the manner in which the documentary presents actuality has a unique relationship to time, for reality is 'itself still in the making while the presentation is being prepared'.[81] Here the authors describe a kind of indexical time in which the image (and event) unfolds in a direct time-bound manner. However, when we move beyond such live indexical recordings this mode of experiential documentation no longer transpires. Instead, the iconic nature of the animated image is timeless; it is made independent of actuality and of its screen time, and is therefore not bound to actuality time. Additionally, the animated documentary image, though often a referent of the past, can simultaneously embody an impending future. This is because, in the same way that the animated documentary image can always represent its intended actuality referent as well as representing something other, it also possesses an ambiguity of time. The animated documentary time-image also can simultaneously represent the referent time, and all other times as well.

The animated form often lends itself towards such a compression or 'condensation' of time[82]; yet many animated documentary films gain some of their documentary film 'credibility' when they opt for a more isochronal approach. Similarly, as described in the previous chapter, it is when our working memory processes adhere to 'real-time' cognitive imagery that they convey their most convincing effect. Thus, for example, part of the 'realism' achieved in such animated documentaries as *Walking with Dinosaurs* results from the apparently real-time depiction of their movements and behaviours. By contrast, many other animated documentaries will take on the condensed duration of conversational speech, rather than the duration of the actual event in question.

In general, the animated documentary is less concerned with capturing *moments* as it is with capturing *change*; for animation is incapable of directly capturing an event, but it is capable of showing the processes of evolution. Processes can be thought of as the *enduring* entities of actuality 'events occur … processes go on'[83] and by presenting these, the animated documentary is given a greater sense of timelessness. Many animated documentary films seem to operate on multiple time intervals. On one hand they might visualize the recounted memory of a past event as told by a narrator; yet at the same time they will expressly visualize the fluidity of that narrator's conversational speech. Such fluidity is visible, for example, in Jonas Odell's animated documentary *Tussilago* (2010), which features an interview with a woman who was marginally involved with a group of activist/terrorists in Germany in the 1970s. In this film the interviewee describes a number of incidents that occurred, yet it also became quite clear that in hindsight she thought these actions were, at the very least, foolish. And this perspective comes through visibly within the context of many of the scenes as they are visualized through the curious mix of animation and live-action elements.

With the advent of live-action cinema, it became possible to not only capture an image but to also capture a section of time and movement. For Doane, 'the cinema made achievable duration itself'.[84] In a sense, the animated documentary inverts the notion of 'capturing', and instead strives to recreate or recapture it. For rather than capturing time, it strives to imbue constructed images with a sense of *actual duration*. Thus, an invisible event (one too small, too far away or too long ago) when given a presence via animation is then given a genuine duration. Not only is the documentary event given a duration (either indexical or iconic) but the symbol itself is also given a genuine duration. In the somewhat speculative documentary *My Pet Dinosaurs* (Mark Everest 2007), a number of animated dinosaurs (seemingly removed from their ancient existence) were 'placed' into contemporary time by compositing them into present-day live-action footage. However, unlike the scenario of *Jurassic Park* (Steven Spielberg 1993), these dinosaurs had been allowed to further evolve. The documentary asked the question, what would the ancient dinosaurs look like today if they had continued to evolve, and not become extinct? Based upon fossilized evidence, scientists mapped an evolutionary path for the dinosaurs, thereby creating a trajectory which extended to the present day. The iconic dinosaurs were amalgamated into indexical environments, creating an assemblage of forms, movements and durations.

There are enormous time-based possibilities within the animated documentary, and it could be said that this form can simultaneously both capture and re-capture time. Also, that it can suggest impressions of both actuality (what it was) and potentiality (that which it is becoming). This duality has the potential to provide us a more complete conception of actuality since, not only can it fundamentally consider the progression of history, but consider also the succession of our own cognitive processes as we imagine the various flows of time and space.

Icon-index dialectic

Paul Willemen takes note of the ambiguity within Pierce's definition of signs, particularly between the icon and the index, and situates within this ambiguity a confliction which he considers to be 'the indexical dimension of the photochemically obtained image and the correlative spread of iconic and symbolic imagery'.[85] Thus, every indexical image simultaneously contains some conception of the iconic. Similarly, as has been discussed earlier, because of increasing digital capabilities, it could be argued that the fully constructed image of animation is ever-edging closer to the indexical in its detail and appearance.

Thus, not only is there an internal dialectic within the concepts of the index and of the icon; a more functional form of a dialectic may be found in the intentionally hybridized construct of animation and *recorded* sound and/or image. The iconic form of animation can be divided into a number of different conceptions (motion, image, sound) and, as has been argued above, the indexical referencing of *actuality* can also be considered to be composed of similar elements. What can provide each of these forms their cognitive complexity is the manner in which the various layers of information interact with each other. We can also consider how this complexity could be further augmented by interplay *between* sets of the animated image *and* the indexical image. By literally combining within the same animated documentary both indexical and iconic elements, one can achieve a vigorous form that can be regarded as the *icon-index*. For example, iconic motion might be applied to a still photograph; or one animated (iconic) dinosaur could interact in frame with indexical live-action elements (trees, lakes, rocks), as was the case in *Walking with Dinosaurs*. Ultimately, there are quite a number of combinations that could be applied.

In many regards, the iconic image is often bereft of complexity because it can only convey a *limited* quantity of information about its referent. On the other hand, indices, according to Doane, can 'provide no insight into the nature of their objects: they have no cognitive value but simply indicate that something is "there"'.[86] Thus, one could make the claim that the index can benefit from the cognitive, contextualizing powers of the icon, while the icon can benefit from the complexity of detail which is indicated through the index. The icon-index is well positioned to achieve this; by combining indexical and iconic imagery, we can attach greater significance as a result of the image's increased complexity. An icon-index can provide a number of cognitive functions, one being that it can fundamentally *allow for greater complexity of image*. The iconic elements have the potential to expressly clarify the indexical and, conversely, the indexical elements are able to direct and contextualize the more iconic aspects. Ultimately, the indexical information can be simultaneously explicated and analysed through this amalgamation.

In such films as *My Mothers Coat* (Marie-Margaux Tsakiri-Scanatovits 2010), *Vital Voices: Hawa Abdi* (Aaron Kisner 2013) and the feature *Waltz with Bashir* (Ari Folman 2008), each concluded with a brief live-action sequence that starkly contrasted with the highly stylized animation of the rest of each of these films. The live-action element also served to reify these animated documentaries and tether them to actual persons, places and events – and to a specific time. The short film *Vital Voices: Hawa Abdi* ends with about fifteen seconds of live-action footage of the woman, Hawa Abdi, who was only heard as a narrator throughout the duration of the animated sequences. By seeing her, we are able to verify her identity (an elderly woman from Somalia), thereby giving further credence to her remarkable story. But equally as important, we are able to understand better the current time context that the interview took place in and how this might contrast with the specific time frame of her interview. Similarly, *My Mothers Coat* also concluded with about fifteen seconds of live-action footage that was evidently derived from super-8 filmed home movies. The footage depicted 'the mother' with her young daughter, and significantly, she could be seen wearing her fur coat (the subject of the film). This footage not only verified that the subject matter of the animation was indeed based on actual circumstances; it also located the dialogue of the interviewee into a particular historical context. Likewise, in the animated feature-length documentary *Waltz with Bashir* (Ari Folman 2008), the concluding live-action sequence also served to link the subject matter definitively with a real-world war. This incredibly powerful live-action conclusion depicted a Lebanese woman, overcome with grief as she surveyed the death and destruction that, ultimately, the 'narrators' of the documentary had been (at least tacitly) involved in inflicting upon her. This moment of raw emotion (live and unscripted) contrasted starkly with the graphical beauty and sometimes dream-like musings of the rest of the animated film. Importantly, it also tethered the entire animated feature film to a very specific moment in time.

A number of feature-length documentaries, such as *Chicago 10* (Brett Morgen 2007), *The Life and Mind of Mark DeFriest* (Gabriel London 2014) and *Poor Us: An Animated History of Poverty* (Ben Lewis 2012), feature alternating sequences of live action contrasted with quite graphical animation sequences. The animation sequences are generally employed to illustrate particular events (of which there may be no live-action footage) or to illustrate more clearly what an interviewee might be expressing. These will often fluidly shift between didactic explications, visual interrogations and playful counterpoint. *Poor Us: An Animated History of Poverty* is a feature-length documentary with approximately thirty minutes of graphical animation – primarily used to illustrate various historic events, and in some cases the more abstract concepts of global economics. While the documentary film *The Life and Mind of Mark DeFriest* initially relies quite heavily upon animated sequences to illustrate the many sensational aspects of the story – prison breaks and ensuing manhunts (again of which there would be no accessible footage); but as this documentary progresses, more and more time is dedicated to the live-action interview with Mark DeFriest. It is from this live-action interview footage that one is able truly to get to know and sympathize with this man who, to say the least, had been the victim of a tremendous injustice.

A hybrid *icon-index* is one that at once contrasts and unifies. When the contrast is visible, it means one thing: when it is unified, it becomes another. It is at once a new image, and also a composite of oppositional states. Furthermore, its dialectical state allows for a form of reflexive feedback, as the icon comments on the index, and the index contextualizes the icon. Such a dialectic condition allows for an ongoing inquiry since it has an unlimited cognitive possibility: 'It can produce a steady stream of new data – "new" not necessarily in kind but in their functional interrelationships and thus in their theoretical implications.'[87] We could think of the icon-index as a self-contained cognitive entity; the index benefits from the cognitive powers of the icon, while the icon can benefit from the context and complexity of detail which is indicated through the index.

6

Investigative Animation

While the previous chapter concentrated on the presentation of actuality within animation (and the underlying process of actuality *becoming* animation), this chapter will focus upon a more comprehensive role that animation can play in the *investigation* of actuality. Two different (but interrelated) expressions of this role will be explored. First, this chapter will consider the uses of digital simulation and virtual reality, and how these can act as valuable investigative tools, potentially leading to an enhanced comprehension of the actual. Second, it will consider how the process of animation can more directly interrogate actuality through its analysis of real-world objects, spaces and photographic evidence. In doing so, it will propose a unique *forensics approach to animation*, which asserts that all things contain scaffolds of movement, and that the process of animation can be used to determine how something might have *previously moved* as well as its potential for *future movement*. This consideration parallels the more general process of animating – that is determining how any object or image might most effectively be made to move.

Part 1: Simulation

Digital simulations are comprehensive constructions which rely upon real-world data as the blueprint for their design. A simulation might be used for visualization in such diverse fields as medicine, geoscience, meteorology, astronomy, mechanical engineering or security and risk assessment (to name just a few). What sets the concept of simulation distinctly apart from other forms of non-fictional animation is that not only does it seek to replicate the visual aesthetics of some aspect of actuality; its resultant imagery is unequivocally tethered to the *physical laws* of our world. This strict adherence may place limitations upon how the imagery can *creatively* interrogate actuality (unlike the freedom generally afforded to the animated documentary), yet it does allow for it to be used more directly in the study of actuality. Philosopher Lambert Wiesing distinguishes between animation (where anything is possible) and simulation (where only plausible things are possible), noting that

> Because in simulations the imaginary object is artificially subjected to a physics, it can become the object of scientific observation. This means concretely that in a simulation the imaginary image object becomes a visible object that can be used for scientific experiments.[1]

Since simulations are able to envisage an almost unlimited array of possibilities, they allow the viewer to employ them as an effective *tool* in the cross-examination of actuality. Such potentialities can therefore be used not only to simulate what has already happened but also what is currently happening, and what *could possibly* happen in the future. From this, one could argue that the simulation of actuality may be able to provide (in some instances) a more encompassing form of analysis than a basic recording of actuality. This is particularly the case when we factor in a simulation's predictive potentials. If, for example, one wants to consider what might happen if two structures were to be smashed together, how melting glaciers might affect sea levels or how weather patterns might affect future bird migration (or any variety of scenarios), the use of digital simulation and its visualization of data (with its inevitably strict adherence to the laws of nature) can provide a very useful prognostication.

Simulations are ubiquitous structures and 'do not come with an inherent visual point of view'.[2] They can be viewed and tested from every conceivable angle. And although these 'fictional objects' can become increasingly complex (thanks to advancing technology), they still have *finite* borders that are not found within actuality. Rescher notes that '[Fictional objects] are of finite cognitive depth [...] A point will always be reached when one cannot say anything further that is characteristically new about them.'[3] But the reasons why digital simulations are useful to our consideration of actuality is that, even although the world is comprised of unique events (none of which can ever repeat), it is also made up of conceivable *patterns of processes*.

> The very idea of a process involves trans-temporal constancies. Water evaporates. That is to say, water evaporates is a generic process. It has many instances, occurring alike after rainstorms in the 16th century Lima and in 20th century Atlanta.[4]

Every process is at one level an 'abstraction capable of repetition'.[5] A digital simulation, therefore, is very adept at providing a comprehensive *overview*, and because it would normally also contain a useful amount of specific detail, it can be used to predict potential outcomes and outline plausible historical scenarios. Simulations can further benefit from their incorporating the generic data of physics, which pervade over virtually all instances (past, present, future), and therefore can be transposed from one instance to another. This transferability corresponds to what Whitehead referred to as the 'eternal object' as a means of defining those aspects that are not specific to any particular thing, but can span 'eternally' over a number of similar things. Thus, by extension, gravitational forces applied to a simulation of a high-speed car crash will operate in the same manner as when applied to an ancient volcano eruption two million years ago. Because of this, simulations are particularly useful in analyses that actually seek to *find* connections and patterns. For example, animated simulations are being used heavily in the emerging discipline of connectomics, which is 'a field of neuroscience that analyses neuronal connections' and cognitive patterns.[6]

However, the inherent generalization of a simulation does have its practical limitations, and there is a continuing quest to make some of these as specific as possible. Interestingly, it is not just the computational power and improvement of 3D animation that is advancing the specificity of simulations; it is also the corresponding advancements in real-world measuring and data collection capabilities. For example, in the field of medicine, Vilanova et al. described how the development of more precise measurements of the flow of blood within the human circulatory system is aiding in the advancement of more specific animated models:

> Although research on blood flow simulation has been performed for decades, many open problems remain concerning accuracy and patient-specific solutions. Possibilities for real measurement of blood flow have recently increased considerably by new developments in magnetic resonance imaging which enable the acquisition of 3D quantitative measurements of blood-flow velocity fields.[7]

In this way, a simulation can be devised that will be tailored to a specific patient and to their specific medical conditions.

Another related example of 'specific simulations' can be found in the area known as virtual autopsy (or VA) which involves a cadaver that has been scanned to create a virtual 3D model. This is particularly useful in that it allows for an overall analysis that would be very difficult to achieve manually with a physical cadaver.

> There are several reasons for the rising interest in VA. First, the VA can be a complement to standard autopsies enabling broad, systematic examinations of the whole body which are normally difficult and time consuming, for example, examination of the entire bone structure or searching for the presence of air in the body.[8]

The researcher is then able to switch back and forth between the two in order to gain a superior global perspective and a complimentary detailed perspective. The virtual cadaver also provides an enduring and undisturbed entity that can be referred back to for comparison as the physical cadaver becomes degraded.

Virtual reality

Alongside of the concept of simulation resides the idea of virtual reality. Simulation and virtual reality, though overlapping concepts, have somewhat different agendas. Simulation focuses on the replication of the visuals and of the physics of actuality, while virtual reality is usually intent on creating an *experience* that appears to be real, particularly in the manner in which the user can interact with it. Grau notes that

> In contrast to simulation, which does not have to be immersive and refers primarily to the factual or what is possible under the laws of nature, using the strategy of immersion virtual reality formulates what is 'given in essence', a plausible 'as if' that can open up utopian or fantasy spaces.[9]

Grau does clarify that, although virtual reality needs to be at least plausible, it can indeed provide a purely fantastical experience.

What is important, of course, is to make the virtual reality experience feel like a real-world experience – to make the viewer feel as if he or she is actually *present* in the space. Because of our bodily structure and cognitive functionality, we find virtual reality experiences that provide at least a plausible simulation of actuality (following the basic laws of physics) to be most endurable. As one VR game designer noted:

> Presence is the key component to ensuring that the user has a positive experience in the VR headset. [...] When the user straps on the headset, they are literally strapped into the world we as artists helped create. So when certain aspects of that world don't feel or look right, it can make the user uncomfortable or even sick and ultimately they will become disengaged from your game, and possibly from VR forever.[10]

Significantly, virtual reality is generally not about trying to trick the viewer/participant into believing that they are in the real world, but to provide them with an authentic experience so that they can comfortably imagine that they are in a specific space. Therefore, even the most fantastical VR world must at least constitute a *plausible* world.

Total simulation (or the animation of everything)

It now seems remarkable that just a few generations ago one could exist an entire lifetime without ever being filmed or videoed. Not surprisingly, this lack of extant video footage has been the impetus for many creative methods (including animation) by which to create a convincing visual documentary of past events. However, as more and more video footage is recorded – ranging from the increasing interest in documentary, increasing use of both public and private surveillance and our increased personal use of mobile recording devices – we are fast reaching a point in history where there will be near total visual recordings of most human endeavours.

Similarly, considering the breakneck speed of technological advances, it is quite possible to envision a future in which vast sections of our real world will also be digitized in the form of real-time animated simulations. For anyone who has participated in such online worlds as Second Life, or has played such video games as *Grand Theft Auto V*, which involves a comprehensive modelling of an entire city, its inhabitants and surrounding landscapes (loosely based on the real-world Los Angeles County), one could surely envision this occurring on an exponentially grander scale.

Unquestionably, it is becoming progressively simpler to create accurate 3D models of people, cars, buildings and nature – which can be achieved by using increasingly prevalent (and portable) 3D scanners; alternatively, modelling information can simply be gleaned from a series of photographs or a sequence of video. As further sections of our environment become virtualized (animated), there will also be the inclination to link many of these together, potentially creating vast simulation databases. In fact, in 2016, Singapore became the first country in the world to be completely represented as a simulated, high-resolution 3D animated map. The project, initiated by the Singaporean Government, 'encompassed all of Singapore, an area of more than 700 square miles'. This mammoth simulation is projected to continue to evolve and grow in complexity; but initially the 3D simulation was intended to 'support activities including daily operational requirements, planning and risk management'.[11]

Furthermore, we are generating increasingly more *motion data* every day. Consider the location data and gyroscopic recordings available within every smartphone, and (increasingly) other smart 'wearables'. As this movement data becomes progressively more precise, it is conceivable that it could soon become as comprehensive as the data that can be generated currently in a state of the art motion-capture studio. When all of this information is amalgamated with increasingly intricate simulations of real-world physics (Whitehead's eternal objects), one could certainly envision a comprehensive visual simulation that parallels the real world – essentially the *animation of everything*.

Part 2: A forensics approach to animation

There are a number of ways in which one can philosophically consider animation. One useful way, as this book advocates, is to consider it in terms of process philosophy; namely placing emphasis on the broader connections between instances and the general concepts of *movement* and *transformation*. However, in some regards, the meticulous process of *animating* can seem (at least in part) to represent the antithesis of this vision. Therefore, it can also be useful to dissect the form of animation in a complementary poststructuralist manner in order to understand the differences *between* the broader processual connections. These differing perspectives actually parallel the conventional processes of animation: for on one hand, the animator must seek to make things move, yet at the same time, the animator is obliged to consider the many granular 'instances' that are required for the animated movement to succeed.

In the light of this more detailed analysis of animation, it is appropriate to consider some of the methodologies that animation may share with the highly meticulous field of forensic science. In its most common conception, forensic science (or forensics) involves a systematic investigation of evidence to determine the manner in which a crime was committed, however, this term has also been used more broadly (outside of the legal system) to suggest a variety of systematic investigations of evidential remains. Forensically based approaches are generally employed whenever there is a perceived deficit of knowledge or information. Often when we are animating, particularly if we are attempting to recreate the movements and actions of a past real-world event, we will be faced with a rather large deficit of information.

The following sections will outline a unique *forensics approach to animation*, which suggests that through careful analysis (and the processes of animation), we can determine how presently immobile things might have previously *moved* or *evolved* as well as their potential for *future movement*. On one level this approach will provide an alternative close reading of the animation *process*; on another level it suggests that animation may be used as a vital epistemic tool for the direct discovery of new knowledge. The exploration of animation in this manner draws some initial inspiration from Michael Leyton's theorem of a *forensics theory of geometry*, in which he suggests that all things with asymmetrical properties contain essential information on that thing's *becoming*.[12] For example, we could infer that the originating state of a crumpled piece of paper would have been a flat symmetrical sheet.

In recent years, the notion of forensic science has been pushed to the forefront of public consciousness. There are now countless forensics-themed television dramas – *CSI*, *Bones* and *NCIS* to just name a few. Although they all employ forensic investigative methodologies, many stray into the realm of pure fantasy, which has helped to create unrealistic expectations of what forensics are capable of achieving. This condition has been described as 'the CSI effect', which has had a far-reaching impact on the criminal justice system.[13] Given such heightened expectations, it is important to keep in mind that forensic science (and a forensics approach to animation) is not infallible, but it does usually endeavour towards the most accurate findings possible.

Derived from standard approaches to forensic investigations, this text has appropriated several core fundamental methodologies that are relevant to the discussion of animation. Collectively these approaches enable the animator to proceed towards the most precise findings possible. The first essential aspect is *process*, which principally asserts that all things are foregrounded by and composed of movement and change. Correspondingly, all things contain clues and traces of this movement – essentially a scaffolding of prior and future movement. The second considers the idea of *difference*, and asserts that movement can always be found between two differences. The third concept claims that from the notion of *asymmetry* we can deduce prior movement. Finally, through the careful use of *inference* future movement can also be projected.

Process (everything is movement)

Forensic investigations comprise a systematic analysis, which seeks to detail all of the processes and actions that transpired within a particular event. Interestingly, forensics-themed television dramas such as the *CSI* shows have been described, not as *who-dunnit* shows (which is how we have traditionally described earlier crime dramas), but instead as *how-dunnit* shows, which places emphasis upon the detailed procedures of the crime.[14] Similarly, a *forensics approach to animation* places emphasis upon the *process* and *actions* of animation, as it seeks to uncover the manner in which an object has previously *moved*. This becomes critical in cases where there is evidence that an event has occurred, but there is no direct indexical motion recording of that event.

One of the underlying assumptions of this approach to animation is the belief that everything, whether outwardly exhibiting motion or not, contains movement (both prior as well as potential future movements). New Zealand animator Len Lye suggested that movement is essential to our understanding of static forms: 'When we look at something and see the particular shape of it we are only looking at its after-life. Its real life is the movement by which it got to be that shape.'[15] We can recognize that every apparently still object *has previously moved* and this recognition acknowledges the processual nature of actuality, that everything is in flux, that everything has a history of development – there can be no fallen tree without its first having stood upright: there can be no person standing on a mountain top without their having first climbed the mountain. Henri Bergson echoed this sentiment when he noted that 'In reality, life is a movement.' He then directly added 'materiality is the inverse [of] movement'.[16] And we could interpret this to imply that by declaring materiality to be the 'inverse' of movement, it could thus be (at least conceivably) *reverted back* into movement.

By determining the movement that led to a form's current state, or the actions involved in a past event, we inevitably gain a better understanding of that thing or event. For example, we may know that in the past Mount Vesuvius erupted, but if we are able to actually see it occur, then we will have a much clearer comprehension of the event. If we can witness how the lava flowed down into the city of Pompeii, and if we can visualize how quickly it flowed and see how the resulting ash clouds behaved, we will be likely to gain an enhanced and more accessible comprehension of these events. Similarly, if an engineer is able to see how a hillside or a building collapsed (that is, to witness its actual collapsing), he or she will be likely to attain a much better overall comprehension of structural design and structural integrity.

Of course, a collapsing building or an erupting volcano (and their resulting destruction) constitute very complex events. One of the central strategies of forensic investigation is the recognition that an event cannot be reliably analysed by any *single* measuring device. Every event exemplifies numerous micro-events and thereby leaves behind a multilayered evidence trail. Each layer contains a segment of information; when combined with other segments – exponential amounts of information can be inferred.[17] According to process philosophy, all processes, events and movements are multilayered, and all instances of actuality are manifestations of such a complex composite. Deleuze also suggested that 'movement…implies a plurality of centers, a superposition of perspectives, a tangle of points of view…'.[18] A *forensics approach to animation* seeks to emphasize and disentangle the composite complexity of this prior movement.

Difference – A movement between

Comparison and the resulting assessment of difference mark an essential strategy of forensics. By comparing two different sets (for example DNA sequences, finger prints, bone densities or chemical structures) not only can one determine whether a particular *person* was involved but, importantly, it can also provide clues as to *how* an event transpired. We normally can look at two things and perceive that they are different – but being able to understand what that difference means in terms of *movement and flux* can be a very enlightening piece of information. For example, the engineer might have available to him a 'before' and an 'after' photograph of a building that has collapsed, but it will probably be the comprehension of the movement during the collapse that will be of greatest epistemic value.

Difference is unquestionably one of the key components of animation – without difference we would not be able to detect any movement or transformation when we view it. If the difference between two states (or things) is slight, then movement can be deduced simply by subjecting these to the process of animation (for example playing them successively in a looped sequence). However, if the difference is large, the two images will simply appear to jump or 'glitch' in their playback. Therefore, an in-betweening process (a more analytical study) will be required in order to determine exactly *how* movement occurred between the two states and what it ultimately looked like.

Difference – Repeat photography

There is a well-established practice known as repeat photography (or 'rephotography') that in essence involves taking repeated photographs of the same location. However, it is rather different than the concept of time-lapse photography in that the lapses between each repeat photograph might comprise several weeks or several decades. Repeat photography's goal is 'the visualization of change as represented through photographs made of the same subject taken at different times'.[19] Quite often the process will begin with the discovery of an archival photograph (perhaps as much as 100 years old); after determining its original camera position, a new photograph will be taken of that same view.

> As a scientific tool, repeat photography is unique in that it can be used to both generate and test hypotheses regarding ecological and landscape changes, sometimes with the same set of images. From a cultural perspective, it provides a time capsule showing how towns, favourite places, archaeological sites, historic buildings, and even people have changed. Rephotography has long been used medically to monitor a variety of conditions, ranging from tuberculosis to retinal deterioration.[20]

Because of the vast lapse of time between the images (sometimes as much as a century), most often the resulting photographs will be viewed as side-by-side comparisons. However, some have begun to use the process of animation as a means of playing back or displaying the images (rather than through simple side-by-side viewing). There are of course some problems with this technique as was noted by one researcher:

> While we found this technique was effective, we also found that it required a greater degree of precision in making the repeat views than was required by side-by-side comparisons. If the rephotographs were not

> exactly remade from the original vantage points, or if the lighting was significantly different between photos, the changes [...] became glaring, immediately recognizable and distracting.[21]

As with virtually all animation, substantial changes are more easily interpreted when seen side-by-side; subtle changes emerge only through the animation process of 'sequential comparison'. We see this particularly with regard to animated 'boiling', where the images might look perfectly identical when viewed side-by-side, but animatively distinct.

There have been several automated systems that have been produced in recent years that are capable of detecting very minute differences between two images or forms. These have been marketed as both security devices (for the detection of slight alterations that might compromise security) or as diagnostic systems (for example charting minute geological changes). Generally, the human eye would be incapable of detecting such slight variations, and only the process of animation, or an electronic device that emulates the animation process of 'sequential comparison', would be capable of doing so. In a way, these systems are also engaged in a very high-tech version of the classic children's game known as 'spot the difference', in which two nearly identical images are printed side-by-side but with several minute differences between them. The challenge is to identify and circle these discrepancies. Some more advanced versions of this puzzle can actually be very difficult to solve, but one simple way to find all the differences in a matter of seconds is to photograph each image and then animatively flip between them. By creating an oscillating cycle of animation, all the 'hidden' differences will become immediately revealed.

A more subtle form of repeat photography can be found embedded within the image of stereographic cards (see Chapter 2). However, rather than being a lapse in time, it features only a lapse in space. Deleuze has noted:

> Stereoscopic images form no more than an even and flat opposition, but they depend upon something quite different: an arrangement of coexistent, tiered, mobile planes, a 'disparateness' within an original depth [...] they presuppose in their real depth far more voluminous, affirmed and distribute differences which cannot be reduced to the banality of the negative.[22]

The stereograph image (or any 3D image) represents an optical composite of two similar, but marginally different photographs; their difference is derived merely from a slightly shifted camera angle. When viewed through the stereograph device they appear as if they are one 3D image, and when viewed side-by-side the two images look virtually the same. However, when subjected to the process of animation, that is when the two images are sequentially compared in a repetitive cycle, they begin to 'boil' and one can see a surprising amount of movement difference (see Chapter 2). Not only does this approach highlight the slight perspective difference between the two frames but it also lays bare the process by which the stereo effect is produced, and furthermore, gives us an indication as to how our brain perceives the 3D effect. This, incidentally, is similar to how our own binocular vision perceives the dimensional world – and can be experienced by alternately winking the left and then the right eye in a repeating sequence while viewing something. In her analysis of the stereograph, Flores has suggested that it expresses

> no actual movement, no 'movement-image': but the two images of the pair, mentally fused one with each other, and their effects upon the consciousness of time, space and the gaze enable us to think of a kind of 'time-image'.[23]

However, as described previously, we can also think of the stereograph as a compression of movement. For when it is subjected to the animation process, a very observable discharging of movement does occur – a hidden 'movement-image' that is only accessible through the process of animation.

Difference – Replacement images

A significant aspect of the replacement animation process is that it converts difference of forms into movement. For example, Joanna Priestley's film *Utopia Parkway* (1997) features sequences that are composed of individually different ceramic forms that are sequentially replaced under the camera. Though each sequence is composed of distinct, utterly immobile and rock-hard forms, an incredible sense of plasticity is achieved. These forms ultimately generate a dramatic pulsating and metamorphic movement (see Figure 6.1). Similarly, Paul Bush's short animation *Furniture Poetry* (1999) also seeks to highlight difference (and generate movement) through the sequential comparison of objects. But in *Furniture Poetry* specifically selected objects were used that had either similar shapes or similar themes. For example, a series of teapots – each only marginally different in shape and design from the next – were sequentially replaced, creating an almost metamorphic effect as they grew, shrank and undulated their forms. In another sequence, he chose different sized shoes, which he sequentially replaced – beginning with large work boots, scaling down to child-sized shoes, then down to miniature doll shoes. Even though the shoes appeared to shrink, each one was sufficiently dissimilar that the viewer would be aware simultaneously of an overall shrinking effect, and of the individual nature of each featured shoe.

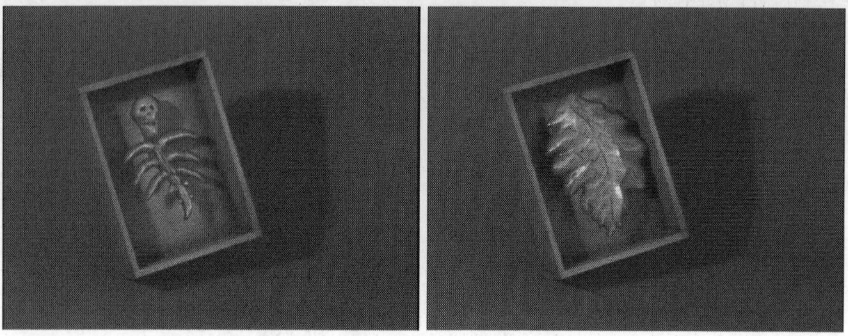

FIGURE 6.1 *Images from* Utopia Parkway *(Joanna Priestley 1997), featuring sculpted replacement forms.*

One thing that is unique about the concept of the animated boil is that, normally, when the images are viewed side-by-side there will be little if any discernable difference; it is only when they are viewed in succession the effect can become visible. There are, actually, many forms within the real world that display little if any discernable differences, and it is *only* when these are subjected to the animation process that their inherent difference will be made visible. Such examples can be found in abundance within industry, manufacturing and, in particular, the resulting mass-produced consumer items. Most of these consumer items are produced under strict quality-control methods so that, when viewed side-by-side on display in the shops, they will look identical. Individual differences are almost always discouraged in the production of mass-consumer goods. Yet, even here, differences can be detected when the items are subjected to the process of animation.

In the experimental short animation *Hard Boiled* (Torre 2015), these themes are playfully explored. However, in a distinctly different approach to *Furniture Poetry*, all of the objects that are used in this animation are mass-produced and purport to be *absolutely identical*. This animation was created by sequentially replacing multiple, yet 'identical', mass-produced objects in precisely the same place, thus minimizing any perceived movement of the forms in space. Upon playback, the minute differences due to the manufacturing process or to subsequent postmanufacturing wear and tear (slight scratches, staining, fingerprints) appear to wriggle and undulate with a surprisingly dramatic difference. As with the traditional line-drawn boil, because the actual objects do not appear to 'move' or transpose in space, the viewer's attention is focused on the form's more superficial fluctuations. The initial sections of *Hard Boiled* primarily consisted of commonly available, hand-painted (though now increasingly robot-painted) PVC plastic figurines. Many of these hand-painted figures were representations of popular animation characters (for example, Bart

Simpson or Shrek), which is apropos since these could be considered to be one of the last vestiges of the animation cel-painting production model. In both cel animation and in the mass production of these cartoon character figurines, each would be painted with as great a precision as possible, and then would have to pass strict quality controls (careful visual inspection). In the case of cel animation, it would not be until the cels were photographed into an animation sequence that any errors would be discerned (for example paint pops and colour flashes), and by then it was generally deemed to be 'too late' to fix them. Similarly, it is only after the cartoon figurines are exposed to the rigorous scrutiny of animation that their difference can be discerned. The final sections of *Hard Boiled* also featured many larger forms and consumer items – such as garden statues, tools and housewares. Ultimately, the film, by highlighting the traditional animation process of boiling, sought to expose the hidden inconsistencies derived from the manufacturing process as well as expressing the object's postmanufacturing movement and vivacity.

Difference – In-betweening

In conventional approaches to animation, the animator is often faced with the task of having to find the difference between two states – a process that is commonly referred to as in-betweening. The process requires the animator to perform a certain amount of forensical deduction in order to determine the ideal placement of the in-between in relation to the following and preceding images.

Just finding the 'exact middle' of the difference of the two states or drawings will not usually suffice. For example, if a character is turning their head from left to right, placing the in-between drawing directly in the middle of the turn will produce not only a very mechanical head-turn but also a potentially highly distorted effect. Veteran animator Richard Williams has advised that one of the most important considerations in animation is that the animator correctly places the intermediate drawings, as this will have 'a profound effect on the action and character'.[24] An understanding of proper timing and natural variance is essential to understanding movement (and good animation).

Another important factor is that real-world movement is full of variance – rarely will something move or grow in an absolutely regular manner. There will be great variance in the speed at which things move (perhaps first slow, then fast, then slow again), and how they move (one part may move first, other parts might follow). One way to express these vital inconsistencies is through the animation technique known as *overlapping action*, which, says Williams, 'is where things move in parts, and everything does not happen at the same time'.[25] When something moves it normally

> unfolds, one part starts first, generating the energy for other parts to follow – which then 'follow through'. When a figure goes from one place to another, a number of things take place and everything isn't happening at the same time. Things don't start or end at the same time. Various parts of the body overlap each other, so this is what's called in the craft – 'overlapping action'.[26]

Neither does metamorphosis and growth within the natural world happen uniformly. One part of a plant may grow faster than another and at differing rates. Similarly, if one wants to create a compelling metamorphic effect, substantial variance in the rate, direction and flow of the change is essential. Thus any two successive images are likely to tell us the degree of change between two states; but additional information is often needed to tell us the timing and rate of this change. The animator will need to take such inconsistencies into account wherever the process of in-betweening is needed. This information is sometimes inherent within the forms, or it may be available in the discursive realms which surround the imagery (see following sections on asymmetry and inference).

Asymmetry – Prior movement

Asymmetry, like difference, can provide clues to how something might have moved. While difference normally describes the inconsistencies that we find between two things, asymmetry can describe differences within a single thing. Forensic investigations may also search for the asymmetries *within* a particular piece of evidence. For example, a dent or a scratch on a piece of furniture may provide essential information about a crime or other traumatic event.

Michael Leyton in his text *Shape as Memory* argues that everything in the universe contains a 'storehouse of memory': that is everything with asymmetrical properties contains information on the thing's becoming.[27] For example, a scar on someone's face tells us that previously the skin has been cut; a dent on a car suggests that it has been involved in an accident. Leyton's consideration of the asymmetrical echoes Deleuze's assertion that the imperfections of 'disequilibriums' suggest 'the dynamic process of [a thing's] construction'.[28] Without such imperfections, very little processual information is readily conveyed. Leyton develops his argument into a 'process-grammar of shapes', and later proposes (from this) a 'forensics theory of geometry' which claims that all forms containing asymmetry can be inferred back to a previous symmetrical form. Leyton's theories are based upon two fundamental tenants: the first that 'Memory is stored in asymmetries'; the second that 'Memory is erased by symmetries.' That is, the asymmetrical part of a form contains information on the form's construction; the symmetrical portions lack any such information.[29] In his 1982 studies, Leyton found that when participants were presented with the image of a skewed or rotated shape, they would mentally infer it back to a symmetrical shape (for example from a rotated parallelogram back to a square).[30] Even the most simplistic form contains evidence of process that is embodied within its asymmetry: for example a twisted strip of paper can be inferred back to a flat untwisted plane, while an unevenly squiggly curved shape can be inferred back to a previous state of a perfect circle.

Actuality is unquestionably extremely complex, but if we accept Whitehead's claims that it is a composite of layer upon layer of movements and flux, then regardless of how complex the image or event may be, its processes of becoming can (at least in theory) be regressed. A grown tree, for example, is composed of thousands of distinctive asymmetrical manifestations each of which could, through processes of inference, be reverted back to its previously symmetrical state. Thus such a fully grown tree can be visually transformed back to a state of a seed-like form. We can think of this in the light of Nicholas Rescher's elucidation of the concept of regression (what he terms 'infinite regress'). The basic concept of infinite regression 'is a matter of taking sequential steps backwards to what has come before'.[31] To distinguish between regression and the normally forward looking processes of actuality, he notes: 'A regress moves "backwards" into the preconditions or prerequirements of things, a progress moves forwards into their consequences and elaborations.'[32] Although all aspects of our world are engaged in a forward-moving process of change, we as cognitively complex beings can infer these processes back to infinitely earlier states, giving us the capability not only to better understand them but also to visualize their evolution and movement. We can therefore identify all things as being made from process, and we can sometimes better understand the nature of those things by 'regressing' their inherent progressiveness.

Using this approach, we can also forensically consider the transpositional movement and locomotion of a form – even those as complex as human movements. Thus, rather than considering only asymmetry of shape, we can also examine states of rest and states of motion – that is a type of temporal and positional asymmetry. Accordingly, from a single photograph of a person frozen in mid-air it can be deduced that they were in the process of leaping; we can further infer the figure regressively back to a state of rest in which their feet were firmly planted on the ground. Additionally, we can infer the recession from a state of exertion back to a pose in which the body's muscles are relaxed (a clenched fist to a relaxed open hand). In fact any kinetic state can be inferred back to a state of stasis. Such inference is common in the standard animation process whereby the animator will often commence by marking out the *extreme poses* of a character in a scene (either by 3D model or drawing), and then infer how it would move in order to reach that particular pose. When a form displays extreme levels of asymmetry, it contains essentially a scaffold of movement that can be readily discerned.

Another manifestation of asymmetry can be found in the movement-induced distortion of a form. Consider, for example, a photograph of a person caught leaping in mid-air: the body will often appear contorted – hair and clothing will appear billowed, flesh may be undulated and there could be an unnatural grimace on the face. In the process of inference back to a state of rest, all of these complexities and resulting distortions will need to be stripped away. So, not only must the animator be able to infer the figure back to states of stasis, but they must also be able to infer away motion-induced distortions that have become part of the form. We could consider that this forensics analysis essentially constitutes an inverse unravelling (or infinite regression) of the essential animating technique of *overlapping action*.

Inference and future movement

No matter how methodical one tries to be while undertaking a forensics investigation (including animative investigations), one will inevitably need to rely upon some level of inference, as there will always be informational gaps in the available evidence. There are at least two logical methods by which we can infer something based upon given information. Ideally it will involve a systematic *deductive* inference, based upon the given evidence; but more often than not, it must rely upon some level of *induction*. Induction is described in its broader sense by philosopher Nicholas Rescher as the process of transcending 'from informatively lesser data to relatively larger conclusions'.[33] Such a process is perhaps most notable in the forensical study of cranial-facial reconstructions, which rely upon a *prediction* of the shape and look of a face based solely upon the skull.[34] Similarly, in the dinosaur forms depicted in the animated documentary *Walking with Dinosaurs* (1999), a great deal of induction was required to articulate from the available evidence (namely skeletal remains and fossilized footprints) the dinosaur's specific form, their skin texture and colouration. Charles Peirce describes *deduction* as an *analytic inference*, and as being grounded in the specific. In contrast, he describes *induction* as a *synthetic inference*, which must delve into generalizations. According to Peirce, induction is where we look at specific cases, and then make generalizations or predictions based on these.[35] Because of its generalizing nature, *induction* has been described by some as an 'aspiring to, but failed, deductive inference'.[36] However, for Nicholas Rescher, rather than seeing induction as *less* significant, he suggests that it has the facility to transcend 'from informatively lesser data to relatively larger conclusions'.[37] In effect, it is able to amplify and transcend *beyond* the visible evidence, conveying important new information. It is from this cognitive process that the animation of actuality can ultimately succeed – it is most adept at making visible past events and complex processes as epistemologically useful *generalities*.

There are essentially three scenarios of inference in which the animator will need to determine an object's movement. One scenario relies upon *connective movement*, that is, how something moved in-between two sets of available evidence or available images. These conditions of movement may involve either trans-positional movement (how something moved from point A to point B) or evolutionary movement of growth and metamorphosis (how something changed from *state* A to *state* B). A second condition is its *prior movement*, that is, how something moved prior to the available set of evidence or available image. And the third situation is its *future movement*, how something moved after the available set of evidence or available image. In some cases (as previously discussed) the in-betweening process will be fairly deductive. If we have two roughly similar key frames, we can be reasonably certain as to how the object would have moved from one key frame to the next. And it could be said that when they are similar enough, then essentially no induction is needed whatsoever – in fact, when subjected to the form of animation (and played through the animation apparatus), the inference process will be fulfilled as it animatively reveals the exact movement between the frames. However, key frames that are further apart or more dissimilar will require a certain amount of induction. And when the animator is faced with just a single image, a much larger amount of induction is likely to be necessary in order to define its future or prior movement – although, depending upon the amount of inherent information contained in the image, some degree of concrete, deductive reasoning may be extracted.

In order to begin to *infer forwards* (or to go beyond the mere removal of the asymmetrical), the animator must be able to apply previously gathered knowledge to the currently perceived form. In the process of animation's investigation of actuality, this knowledge transfer can occur in two primary modes. One is the *personal* transfer mode, which draws upon our own previous experiences and observations of the animator (basically, we know how other people walk because we also walk); the other is the *scientific* transfer mode which draws upon the collective observations of science and documentary, or to what some have referred as our 'collective knowledge'.[38] Quite often these two will be employed concurrently. For example, we understand how a ball bounces because we have bounced a ball many times, but there is also a wealth of available scientific knowledge regarding the physics of movement and forces of impact that can be applied.

There are a number of general movements based upon scientific laws of physics that can be inferred upon a form, such as how inertia, friction, acceleration and gravity affect matter. Such movements would also fall into the category that Whitehead would refer to as 'eternal objects' and which

Rescher terms 'historically generic' (colours, numbers and fundamental physical laws); these 'have historical instantiations and exemplifications but they themselves are outside of space and time'.[39] Although each form is unique (in mass, density and shape), we can rely on these laws to provide a certain degree of consistency and predictability in their behaviour. Thus a person in mid-air will have to come back down again, and will do so adhering to their current trajectory. Similarly, there are a number of atmospheric elements that can often be scientifically inferred and thus animated. Wind, rain, gravity, smoke, can all be inferred based upon scientific knowledge of these phenomena. Most 3D software contains prefabricated manifestations of such scientific knowledge (animated dynamics) that allows for the creation of accurate depictions of liquids, smoke or combustion making their implementation quite feasible. Obviously such animated inferences will be subject to a certain level of abstraction and generalization, which clearly places them into the category of what Mark Wolf calls the 'subjunctive' (that which possibly could be).[40] However, because these are often deemed as non-essentials (atmospheric elements like smoke and snow), and they clearly follow the laws of physics (smoke rising up from a cigar, and snow falling down from the sky), we do not interrogate their veracity and specificity in the same manner that we might a human's movement.

The purely *personal* transfer mode, which draws upon our personal experiences, may be less systematic than the *scientific* transfer mode, but it is a methodology in which we engage constantly. One could argue that every still image and every static object contains within it a *scaffolding of movement*; and through the use of our animate vision and our animate envision, we are well placed to apply to each movement based upon our previous knowledge of events and motion. It is through this methodology that we are able to achieve the most sophisticated of movements, because our cognitive functioning deals with motion and form as separate and unique processes in a manner similar to the process of animation. This separation of process may lack an indexical accuracy, but it provides the animator an essential key to a deep understanding of images and forms – namely their inherent movement.

7

Animating the Real World

This chapter will build upon the previous discussions of animation process, how animation is uniquely placed to consider actuality; it will look, in particular, at the way in which animation can be used to directly animate our environment. The chapter is divided into three main sections that revolve around the processes of animating the real world: Landscape Animation, Projection Animation and Actualizing Animation.

The first section (Part 1) examines the growing trend of large-scale animations of the landscape or cityscape (referred to as landscape animation) in which the animator will normally work with found-objects and with *found-spaces* to create site-specific animations. This particular approach to animation is greatly influenced by the location and by the natural materials found at the site. Because the animator is often so strongly guided by these influences, it is possible to consider that, in addition to working with *found-spaces*, he or she is also working with a suggestion of *found-movement*. Furthermore, because these animations take place outside the controlled environment of a traditional studio, unique manifestations of the animation process and the passage of time can occur. The second section (Part 2) deals with projection-mapped animation, which signals a very different concept of real-world animation. Rather than directly manipulating the environment, large-scale animations are overlaid *onto* the real world, effectively changing our perception of it. The final section (Part 3) amalgamates the ideas of the previous two into a more concrete expression of the 'animation the real world', looking at several different ways in which animation can 'become actuality', in particular through a discussion of the process of robotic animation. Interestingly, many people do not think of robots as true animation; but in terms of the process of animation, the 'programing' of robotic movement and the animating of screen-based digital forms are becoming increasingly integrated.

Part 1: Landscape animation

'Landscape art' (also referred to as 'land art' or 'environmental art') is a well-established genre of fine art in which sections of the environment are sequestered for use as the artist's canvas – the large-scale man-made structures of Christo, the huge earthworks of Robert Smithson and the more subtle manipulation of natural forms by Andy Goldsworthy or Chris Drury are a few prime examples of this category.

Similarly there is a developing genre of animation that can be referred to as 'landscape animation' in which real-world settings are appropriated for use as the animator's stop-motion set. In landscape animation, rather than relying on a more allegorical definition of place (such as a small scale stop-motion set or a painted background to reference a particular place), the animation is produced directly within the real world – in *found-spaces*. Although *pixilation animation* could be considered to be a close cousin of landscape animation, pixilation has historically highlighted the animation of *people*, whereas landscape animation generally detaches itself from the human form, focusing on the environment itself.

Of course, the animation of one's surrounding environment is by no means new, as is evidenced in such early animations as *The Automatic Moving Company* (1910) by Italian animator Romeo Bossetti, in which a truckload of furniture arrives at a new house and systematically arranges itself within the various rooms. Yet, we are currently witnessing an expanding use of this technique, one that places an increasing emphasis on real-world *found-spaces* – fuelled, no doubt, by the portability and accessibility of digital still cameras, the greater influx of trained (and non-trained) animators to the medium and, of course, readily available online distribution networks. One could also speculate as to whether the rising interest in this technique (and in traditional stop-motion animation in general) is partly being fuelled by a reaction against the current prevailing digitalization of animation.

This section examines a number of recent examples of landscape animation, describing some of the principal characteristics found in this emerging genre. It also explores the animator's working process, how real-world *found-spaces* impact, not only on the visual design of the animation, but also on how it might move. In articulating these perceptions this section will continue to draw upon concepts underlying process philosophy to propose the possibility that from these *found-spaces*, *found-movement* might also emerge. Finally, it will consider how landscape animation, due to its scale and location, encourages a high level of self-reflexivity – or an imbedded documentation of the production process (the process-document). This process-document subsequently unveils a duality of time: *animation time* and *environment time*.

Animation of the environment

Some of the most prominent landscape artists include Andy Goldsworthy, Chris Drury, Christo (1935–2009) and Robert Smithson, each of whom represents a distinctively different approach to landscape art, which can be translated into the possible differing approaches to landscape animation. For example, Goldsworthy's work tends to take a more understated approach to the manipulation of the environment. Some of his works involve simply the collection and reconfiguration of fallen leaves or the breaking of seasonal ice sheets to create new forms and patterns. Similarly, Chris Drury is known for his stacking of large rocks (*Seven Sisters Cairns,* 1995) or his twisting and weaving of branches and grasses into spherical shapes (*Four Spheres*, 1984). By contrast, Christo's approach tended to be a much more intrusive one. Quite often he would introduce large artificial elements into his found-spaces. In his work *The Umbrellas* (1991), he covered a hillside in California with 1,760 giant yellow umbrellas and simultaneously placed 1,340 blue ones in Japan; in another work he wrapped an enormous cliff located on the coast of Australia in brown fabric (*Wrapped Coast, 1969*). Robert Smithson (1938–1973) created work that quite often involved the manipulation only of site-specific materials; however, his work was on such a large scale that it dramatically altered the environment. His massive *Spiral Jetty* created within the Great Salt Lake in Utah, USA, in 1970 still exists today. This colossal project spans over 460 metres and consists of thousands of tons of rock, earth and salt. Despite these artists' varying approaches, what links nearly all 'landscape artists' is that their work is very dependent upon the found-spaces and quite often composed of the materials found within a specific environmental space. Art theorist William Malpas notes that

> The land artist does not use oil or pastel or ink to 'represent' nature. Rather, s/he works directly with nature, getting her/his fingers dirty with mud, snow, sheepshit, stone, ferns, wood.[1]

This is the central feature of the works of the landscape artists, works which exist within found-spaces and which, through the manipulation of those physical elements, transform the spaces into concrete works of art rather than representing them elsewhere in another medium. Both the place and the materiality of the place become the work of art.

Landscape animators may also practice a variety of approaches, but all are deeply affected by the space itself, and this in turn has a profound affect on their animated outcomes. For example, the animator known as 'Blu' has produced a number of animations set directly on the streets and beaches of various parts of the world, all of which are inextricably connected to the places where they were filmed. In his animation *Big Bang Big Boom*

(Blu 2010), massive graffiti-painted images (some so large that they cover entire sides of buildings) and large quantities of urban debris (bottles, cans, dustbins, beach chairs) are animated with a frame-by-frame stop-motion technique. And, although he could have made a comparable animation elsewhere, it would be impossible for it to be identical to this one if it were set anywhere but in this particular location. The shape of the buildings, the presence of rubble, the form of pipes and bridges, all affect how his animated forms will move and progress.

In, perhaps, a more subtle approach, Australian animator John 'Hobart' Hughes animates found-objects within found-spaces: his work involves manipulating *only what is already there*. In his short animation *Earth Shiver* (2006), he visited a number of abandoned industrial sites located in remote areas and animated the items (both natural and manmade) that he found there. Much of the animation is simply of the objects 'shivering' back and forth in their found location. Many of the items have clearly not been touched by human hands for many years prior to his actual animation process, as is evidenced by the visible thick layers of dust and cobwebs. In his 2004 animation *The Wind Calls Your Name*, we also see a number of very subtle manipulations of the environment, such as when the bark 'self-peels' off of a eucalyptus tree.

Similarly, much of the work of animator Eric Leiser also generally involves the temperate manipulation of nature. There are extensive sections in his film *Land* (2012) that involve the reconfiguration of found-leaves and sticks into choreographed patterns and evolving geometric forms. One sequence, for example, featured an animated pile of leaves that formed and reformed into mounds, and then scattered and reformed into geometric patterns and again into meandering lines. In other portions of the film Leiser highlighted the structural forms of bridges and trees through the introduction – and then the removal – of brightly coloured animated ribbons. In other sequences snow was manipulated (trampled and cleared) over large hillsides; and on large empty beaches footprints appeared and large abstract designs 'drew themselves' into the sand. Through these varying techniques each of the sequences creatively engaged with each specific real-world location (see Figure 7.1).

Kirsten Lepore's short animation *Bottle* (2011), which represented a more narrative approach to landscape animation, utilized the manipulation of two distinct environments – snow and sand. Amid this manipulation of the existing environment two 'characters' were introduced, a snowman that resided in a frozen winter world of snow and ice, and a sandman that inhabited a more temperate sunlit beach. It was a tale of unrequited love as the two characters, not only from, but actually composed of, very different environments, endeavoured to meet each other. Yuval and Merav Nathan similarly manipulated sand on a night-time beach in an ethereal music video clip for the group *Eatliz* (2010). Here the sand was used to form dozens

FIGURE 7.1 *Image from* Land *(Eric Leiser 2012).*

of animated sea turtle hatchlings that attempted to reach the safety of the sea, but were terrorized by menacing sand creatures along the way. Darcy Prendergast's animation, *Rippled* (2010), was also somewhat character based as it featured a strange fluffy creature (a large stop-motion puppet) who could be seen traversing the vast abandoned industrial site in which the animation was set. The site (overgrown with weeds, littered with debris and defaced by graffiti) was brought to life through the use of animated lights, animated rubble and other animated forms that interacted dramatically with the ruins of the derelict site; sometimes they would emerge from behind structures, sometimes they would traverse the undulating surfaces of the walls and rusted machinery.

Found-spaces

Most stop-motion animation involves a meticulous construction of characters and sets; for example the puppets used in the *Wallace and Grommit* films were constructed out of armatures and plasticine. Similarly the puppets used in the feature *The Corpse Bride* (Tim Burton and Mike Johnson 2005) were carefully moulded out of latex and possessed intricate armatures and clockwork adjustments. In other cases of stop-motion animation the animated elements will derive from found-objects – objects that have previously been formed for some other purpose, and then merely recontextualized as animated elements. Jan Svankmajer, the Quay Brothers and Jiří Barta have quite often employed such an approach, using a range of objects – toy dolls, bricks, light bulbs, screws and hammers. The majority of these stop-motion films also utilize constructed *environments* for their characters and forms to exist within. This approach generally works quite well as these environments will be constructed to a suitable scale, perspective and design. For example, a ten-inch tall stop-motion puppet of Wallace or Grommit requires appropriately scaled sets. Inevitably, stop-motion puppets 'occupy a space constructed to accommodate their relative size. They walk through doorways, sit on chairs, look through windows, and sit at tables that have been built to scale'.[2] And if a found-object were to be introduced to this diegesis, it too would most likely become narratively transformed to such a space. A small stone, therefore, would probably no longer be identified as a small stone, being more likely to fulfil the role of a large boulder.

The spaces within which landscape animation takes place are always *found-spaces*: spaces that were originally constructed (or evolved), not for animation, but for entirely different purposes (a forest for trees to grow in, a parking lot for cars to be parked in). With *found-spaces* the scale and identity of the objects that move about within them are always adherent to those spaces. Thus (in terms of visual form) a small stone would always be identified as a small stone. Even when the elements that are to be animated are entirely imposed, the landscape will always have a profound effect upon the animation. This is an essential distinction that defines the process of landscape animation – the animator must always respond to what is already there, thus giving the *found-space* definitive power over the proceedings of the landscape animation.

Mobius (Benjamin Ducroz 2011) is a landscape animation that features entirely imposed elements of large, bright green, three-dimensional geometric forms. It features twenty individual sculptural forms, each slightly different, that were sequentially replaced to create an undulating animated form that would appear to sink into the ground and then rise up again. In this unique film, all twenty sculptures remain visible throughout the film, forming a constantly moving and constantly shifting formation. The result is a rolling animated cycle that is repositioned into different formations (meandering lines or circular patterns) and importantly into different cityscape locations. From sequence to sequence, the movement remains essentially the same, but the formation and context dramatically transforms. Ultimately, each new location has a profound affect upon the form's design and its collaboration with the surrounding environment (see Figure 7.2).

In 2009, Frank Budgen directed an animated advertisement for Sony television that was set within large public spaces of New York City. The ad featured hundreds of sculpted life-sized rabbits, brightly coloured cubes and countless other large forms that were introduced throughout the streets, sidewalks, parks and public squares. And although all of these elements were imposed, their movement was very much influenced by the contours of the ground and the positioning of various cityscape features: lampposts, steps, rubbish bins, walls, hedges and trees. Not having the City Council's

FIGURE 7.2 *Image from* Mobius *(Benjamin Ducroz 2011).*

permission to close off the area, thousands of people, and countless dogs and birds, unwittingly traversed the shoot (many of these caught momentarily within the frame). Most of the sequences in this animation were quite spontaneous and the animators were given free rein to move their designated character or form throughout the cityscape. Often, while in the midst of animating, the animator would be required to revise their trajectory when they encountered different obstacles (even in some cases having to deal with pedestrians picking up the rabbits mid-stream).

Another remarkable landscape animated advertisement *Pen Giant* (Florian Giefer, Peter Göltenboth 2010) was also was set within a large open section of a cityscape. The process for this animation first involved animating a human actor in a pixilated (stop-motion) manner within the city spaces; each of a resulting 350 frames of animation were then printed as mammoth-sized billboards (each approximately 3.5 metres by 2.5 metres). These giant billboards were set up and animated (replaced sequentially) throughout the streets, each occupying the same specific location and perspective that the original pixilated human had occupied – although at about three times the size of the human actor. In many sequences, the previous billboard would remain fixed in its location, while the next in the sequence would be positioned ahead of it. This created a long winding 'domino chain' of huge billboards that appeared to traverse the city, racing along streets, scaling buildings and navigating rooftops.

Both the directors of the Sony advertisement and of *Pen Giant* had very little control over the encroachments into their 'sets' and were clearly resigned to these unpredictable intrusions. Also both were acutely aware of the shifting daylight and corresponding cast shadows that were evident within each frame. The director of *Pen Giant*, Peter Göltenboth, described how each billboard took approximately ten minutes to set up, but would remain on screen for approximately 1/10th of a second, providing a consistent array of animated shadows. Similarly, Frank Budgen carefully scheduled each exposure to occur every few minutes so that the shadows would always travel across the set in a very even manner (see Figure 7.3).

Found-movement

When animators apply movement to the world *as they find it*, the animating movement is likely to be very much influenced by what is there. For example, when Eric Leiser animated a grouping of sticks and pinecones along the surface of the rocky ground in *Land* (2012), he intuitively animated them in accordance with the surface of the ground – that is they were rolled, slid and bumped along the natural terrain. When John 'Hobart' Hughes animated his landscape animations (such as *Earth Shiver*, 2006), he simply entered into the spaces, camera in hand, and intuitively began manipulating what was before him – in deference to what is already there.[3] Others, such as the animator Blu, may have entered into his spaces with definite plans as to what sort of imagery he wished to create, what stories he wish to tell; but these ideas were inevitably altered dramatically by the dominance of the found-space. Darcy Predegrast, the creator of the landscape animation *Rippled*, noted that

FIGURE 7.3 *Image from* Pen Giant *(Florian Giefer and Peter Göltenboth 2010).*

> Whilst the blueprints were all laid out, the composition of the shots formed in a visceral manner – the dynamic elements in the location were often too beautiful to not include. We kept on adding new shots…'One more shot' was my catch phrase.[4]

And, clearly, much of the movement of elements in *Bottle* (Lepore 2011) is affected by the landscape. For example, as Lepore animated a snowball rolling over a snow-covered field, it grew larger and larger due to the natural accumulating properties of packed snow (see Figure 7.4).

The landscape animator, in addition to working within a found-space, is also tapping into the 'found-movement' of that space. In a sense the animator is able to extract movement, or at least *indications* of movement, that already exist within the spaces and then appropriate these for the purpose of animation. In describing his fine art practice, Andy Goldsworthy noted:

> Nature contains so much pent-up energy waiting to be released. Most boulders are either on or resting from a journey. I enjoy visiting stones marked on maps as 'Hanging', which appear ready to fall but can remain like this for hundreds of years – balanced between an instant and timelessness. I am drawn to the tension that accumulates at the tip of a rock or the peak of a mountain. A rock balanced on a point feels supported by that tension. A good work releases a build-up of energy with only the slightest of touches. It is sometimes less about how much I touch than where – like plants with seed heads that become taut as they ripen and need only a stroke to make them explode.[5]

FIGURE 7.4 *Image from* Bottle *(Kirsten Lepore 2011).*

Here Goldsworthy is articulating something very close to the intuitive process that encompasses many aspects of landscape animation. It is entirely possible that landscape animation can recognize, and indeed exemplify, the concept that the world is in a state of continual flux and can serve as a concretization of the processual nature of the environment.

Stop-motion animator Barry Purves has noted that:

> Animation excels in…being a medium where everything is fake and has to be created from scratch. It would be a waste not to exploit this artificiality.[6]

And, although this is a perspective with which most would agree, one could also rewrite and essentially invert this claim to argue that

> Animation excels in the manipulation of the natural world and of *that-which-is-already-there*. And it would be a waste not to tap into such a reservoir of potential movement.[7]

As discussed in Chapter 6, all things are composed of movement, and we can think of them as possessing a scaffolding of movement; the job of the animator can be to coax out this potential movement. We can consider again the claims of Michael Leyton who argued that everything in the universe contains a 'storehouse of memory': that is every 'thing' with asymmetrical properties contains information on that 'thing's' becoming. Ultimately, the real world is full of asymmetrical storehouses of information. When we enter into a found-space, such as an industrial ruin or a natural landscape in the aftermath of a flood – particularly a space that shows obvious traces of flux – we are confronted with a vast reservoir of memorialized movement which in turn provides us hints about future movement possibilities. It is true that in animation any type of movement is possible; however, with landscape animation, quite often the movement can be found, or at least directly inspired, by the spatial and kinetic properties of the found-spaces. And when we consider that real-world forms contain stored past movement and potential movement – the landscape animator will most likely be influenced (either consciously or unconsciously) by the movement that is already *there*.

Landscape animation presents the opportunity for the exploration and reification of the processual nature of the world, and in this is aided by the vast wealth of materials and movement information that is inherent within the environment. Part of this perception involves a recognition of the processual nature of the world – that absolutely everything is in the process of movement, and potential future movement, while at the same time containing the traces of prior movement. When we animate the environment as we find it, we are able to tap into the natural world's vast storehouses of movement, and to use our deductive and inductive reasoning to determine how something might have moved previously and how it might subsequently move.

Interestingly, many landscape animations have tended to take place in abandoned spaces and industrial ruins. There are a number of reasons for this. One practical reason is that such spaces are *abandoned* and can often be easily co-opted as an animation set. Another is that within the spaces of industrial ruins lie a vast amount of accumulated kinetic information – their ruinous state is replete with asymmetry including rusted metal, decaying walls and broken machinery. Such asymmetrical states could be thought of as the extreme key-frame pose in the clearly imagined 'before' and 'after' states of a dilapidated structure. This information provides the animator with a wealth of movement possibilities. Furthermore these spaces allow for a certain amount of amusement and play. When we enter into a decaying space, a ruin, we are presented with a degree of liberation and freedom because we are no longer bound to follow the original conventions of that space. In his theoretical exploration of derelict spaces, Tim Edensor remarks how

> Instead of moving towards objects and objectives, bodies tend to move arbitrarily in ruins. With the demolition of guided pathways, and social and physical barriers between spaces, as walls and doors collapse, large ruins evolve into a labyrinthine structure which permit the making of a multitude of paths [...] Thus movement through a ruin is determined by whim or contingency in an improvisational path-making, according to what catches the eye or looks as it might promise surprises or appears pleasurably negotiable[8] [...] Actions carried out for their pure kinaesthetic pleasure are enabled through the lack of any regulation and by the affordances of ruined structures.[9]

As animation director Darcy Prendegrast has described it, such areas provide the capacity to 'create magic in a derelict space'.[10] (See Figure 7.5) Blu's animations quite often exist in urban ruins – it is here that the graffiti images that he paints on a surface, or even the demolition of a wall, can occur without incurring too much legal trouble. John 'Hobart' Hughes, also, clearly revels in the animation of the derelict space as he exploits the patina of time through the manipulation of cobweb and dust-covered objects.

Regardless of whether the landscape animator is working within a natural landscape, a cityscape or an industrial ruin, it could be argued that they all recognize that these spaces are teeming with processual movement. Landscape animation transcends simply the animation of the inanimate, and becomes a revelation of the kinetic forces of sticks, stones and pinecones that exist in a *particular place* within our world. In this regard, an apparently tranquil space is merely one that is waiting for its truly fluid nature to be

FIGURE 7.5 *Image from* Rippled *(Darcy Prendergast 2010).*

revealed, and it can be fascinating to be able to tap into such a reservoir of potential movement.

As discussed in Chapter 1, because of the open set of landscape animation the process of animating will often be made highly visible. Animations that are created on soft earth, sand, grass or snow will showcase the footprints of the animators as they embark on modifying the elements or forms 'frame-by-frame'. Thus we can see not only the intentional differences manifested as movement but also the unintentional movements made manifest. Clearly this becomes an important part of the aesthetic of the films. Furthermore, unlike most animations, these uncontrollable elements actually serve to authenticate the animation – proving to the viewer that the animation was indeed shot on a grand scale, and in the real world without any digital interventions. Additionally, landscape animation is the ideal place to witness animation's duality of time. For example, because of the shifting position of the sun and the resulting moving shadows, we can actually chart each passing day in such productions as *Land* (Eric Leiser), or the animated advertisement *Pen Giant*. Most remarkably, in Blu's 2010 graffiti animation *Big Bang Big Boom*, one can actually chart how many days it took to complete one particularly large-scale fifteen-seconds long sequence. In fact, in most landscape animations we are able to witness a multiplicity of represented timescales. Firstly, the intentionally animated sections typically will move in a predictable and calculated manner, while the surrounding elements might pop and flicker randomly. Both of these representations will often be set against the more consistent time-lapsed movement of shadows that can be seen to traverse the ground or cloud formations that billow across the sky.

Part 2: Projection-mapped animation

This section takes another approach to the animation of the environment, a site-specific form known as projection mapping. This involves the production of location-inspired animation that is then projected, often outdoors on to specific structures – buildings, bridges or other monumental constructions (and which in some cases can involve the projection onto moving structures through a match-moved, real-time mapping process). The result is a unique type of (real world) *situated animation* that is an animated form custom made for a particular location, unquestionably anchored to it, and fully integrated into that specific real-world architectural landscape.

The process of most animation generally involves distinct phases. One of these is its actual making and construction; another is its presentation. There are, of course, numerous different methods by which to create animation (including a wide range of digital, traditional and hybrid practices), but generally the presentation phase involves a fairly predictable display upon a rather innocuous screen. Projection-mapped animation requires a very exact production process, in terms both of its construction and its presentation. Importantly, the real-world landscape always plays an integral role in *both* of these phases. This section, while analysing projection-mapped animation from both perspectives, will place particular emphasis upon the presentation process – the precisely mapped projection that is displayed onto actual physical spaces. There is probably no other form of animation in which the process of display plays such an integral role in the realization, and again in the ultimate manufacture of the imagery and content. This process goes beyond merely making visible the movement of the recorded animation; it also situates and further constructs the animation into a real-world space.

Situated animation

The group *Urbanscreen* is one of many studios that have produced projection-mapped animations. These artists normally create their situated animations first by creating a precise 3D model of the real-world landscape or building, before creating an animated sequence that adheres to the surfaces of the 3D model. The animation is then rendered and readied for projection, sometimes being split into different sections so that different projectors can display separate sections from different angles. The result is a precise projected display that is meticulously mapped to the actual physical surfaces. For example, in 2009, they projected a work entitled *555 Kubrik*, on to the side of the *Galerie Der Gegenwart* building in Hamburg, Germany. Its imagery was so exactly mapped to the building that the effective transformation was highly dramatic (see Figure 7.6).

FIGURE 7.6 *Still image from* 555 Kubrik *(Urbanscreens 2009).*

Windows appeared to be carved out of the solid walls; the large stone bricks of the building were made to protrude outward, then be pulled back in – complete with animated shadows; bold colour patterns of motion graphics appeared to paint themselves upon the walls, then to move in a very dynamic manner. The animation and projection were so seamlessly composited on to the building that, regardless of the angle from which the spectators were to view it, the illusion would still be convincing. Music and sound effects also helped to underscore many of the animated movements; for example the sound of scraping concrete could be heard as the stone bricks began appearing to protrude.

Fundamentally, there can be only a single location in which a projection-mapped animation can be displayed, whereas traditional cinema (be it digital or analogue) facilitates duplication and widespread distribution. Thus a traditional animated movie can play simultaneously on 3,000 cinema screens anywhere in the world, and thanks to the generic nature of the screen (being smooth, flat and white) the movie will look more or less comparable regardless of where it is shown. Some films, of course, have been made with a specific type of venue in mind (particularly some of the large format films – the cinemascope films of the 1960s or the more contemporary Imax films), but even so there have been enough venues of this type to allow the films to be easily distributed from one location to another without affecting their presentation. Many instances of installation art and 'expanded cinema' are also site specific, but because of their comparatively modest scale, many of these could be packed up and relocated to another gallery or exhibition space in another city on the other side of the world. Simply put, traditional films and animation, in terms of their presentation, are not site specific; they embody an inherent presentational ambiguity. In addition, these films can either be made for or be scaled and transferred to the small screen – be it a television, a computer or a mobile device, their meaning and content remaining more or less intact since there is also an ambiguity of scale inherent to most cinema that allows for this conversion – we tend to accept and recognize Mickey Mouse or Bruce Willis as themselves, no matter what their cinematic size may be. But with projection-mapped animation, the movie is made specifically for a single venue (such as the west side of the Sydney Opera House). And because the movie was made specifically for that façade, it cannot be distributed or transferred or scaled to any other site (without actually scaling down and transporting the Opera House as well) and therefore is exclusively a *situated* animation.

Although movies and animation can have a very real impact on the audience, traditional cinematic works are not concreta and do not possess the same physicality as things that reside within the actual world; they remain very fluid in nature, and it is this that enables them to be replicated and screened anywhere. Animation in particular, because of its construction process, encourages an abstraction and invariably provides a decontextualization of time, image and motion. Even when animation does achieve a certain level of realistic effect, behind it lies an array of distortive processes: for example the process of imposing external movement to the form, distancing it quite firmly from actuality. Since animation is not actuality, it could be located in the realm of what Rescher refers to as the 'irreal'. According to Rescher, the primary difference between actuality and irreality is that the irreal lacks 'specificity and concreteness' and is resistant to 'individualization'.[11] By contrast, real things possess a definiteness of detail: 'A leaf cannot lack a more or less definite shape, a flower cannot lack a more or less definite colour, [and] a [particular] building cannot lack a more or less definite height.'[12] Animation – because it is not actuality nor even a direct recording of actuality – always tends to be non-definite in nature.

Projection-mapped animations are composed of two integral but contrasting parts: the concrete physical structure of the building, and the irreality of the animated projection. Once the final projection-mapped animation is completed, the animation will only be successfully actualized if it is projected upon the intended building. The specific building limits the projected animation to a particular location; it also ties the animation to a particular scale, giving some of the irreal aspects of animation a much more real context. Some might refer to this merged form as a type of *augmented* reality, but perhaps a better description would be *concretized* animation[13] because the animation is utterly dependent upon the specific site – and is, in fact, nothing without it. The building fixes and actualizes the projected image, giving it a very *specific* and unique physical presence. Augmented reality is a term that privileges actuality, whereas concretized animation biases the animated form.

But at the same time that the buildings are concretizing the irreal nature of animation, it could be argued that the projected animation is also serving to *abstract* and transform the real world. When the projected layer of animation – or what we could also think of as projected abstraction – is overlaid upon the concrete form, it works to obscure the explicit detail of the real. It serves to de-specify that space, transforming the site into the more abstracted realm of the irreal, and in doing so *absorbs* the specific building into the diegesis of animation. A good example of this is the projection-mapped animation that was made to commemorate the 800th anniversary of Santiago de Compostela Cathedral (Improbable Films 2012), in which the building was transformed and made to move in remarkable ways. The turrets appeared to spin around and columns appeared to grow and shrink with remarkable plasticity. In fact, the projected image was so exact that it blended in precisely with the real structure, making it impossible to tell where the real building stopped and the animation began. Once the actual had entered into the animated realm it was then able to engage in an animated act of extraordinary movement and metamorphosis.

Metamorphosis of place

Metamorphosis is an essential structure within the animated form that provides 'the ability for an image literally to change into another completely different image'.[14] Concrete things in the real world also go through a continual process of metamorphosis, but they normally transform at such a slow rate that we are not usually witnesses to their change. We might see the effects of real-world metamorphosis, but not the actual occasion. We can see the butterfly, but not the caterpillar changing into it; we can see the ruins, but not the process that slowly turned the ancient structure into rubble. However, the actual conception of metamorphosis can be made dazzlingly visible through animation and is something in which the medium truly excels. Metamorphosis is also very common in projection-mapped animation, but here we don't see just animated images morphing into other images: we also see (what appears to be) the actual buildings and spaces firstly becoming animation, and *then* morphing into other forms, creating a uniquely *situated* concept of metamorphosis. The abstract overlay of animated light partly obscures the concrete forms, appearing to transform them from the specific to the abstract. Once the building has become abstracted, it can then freely engage in animation's metamorphic conventions.

All real-world buildings have an evolutionary history: they were constructed, they might have begun to deteriorate somewhat, they might have been extended further and built upon, and one day they will either be demolished or reduced to ruins. And this seems to be a recurring narrative that is presented through the use of projection-mapped metamorphosis. As an example, we are presented with a true documentative history of the Prague Clock Tower (2010) through the projection-mapped animation that was used to commemorate its 600th anniversary. At one point in this animation, the current aged state of the building is highlighted, before a younger version is then overlaid – capturing a moment of stark visual contrast as the transformation takes place. At another point we see the building affected by an accelerated deterioration and subsequent hyper-reclamation by nature of the building's ruinous state as it is quickly overgrown with vines. Still later we see a fantastical deconstruction of its form. Thus, the Prague Clock Tower is transformed into the animation state, then morphed into new abstract shapes – it becomes a different historical construct from one moment to the next.

And all the while that we are watching the animated display of metamorphosis, we are constantly aware of the underlying pre-transformative form and are always conscious that, regardless of its transformations, it will always at some point revert back to its original pre-metamorphic state. That is, the animation will cease, or at least diminish in prominence, allowing the viewer once again to see the original building. This idea of being aware of the actual, even when confronted with the irreal, is analogous to Whitehead's consideration of the interplay between the actual and the abstract when he observed that 'abstraction may misdirect us as to the real complex from which it originates. But, in the dim recesses behind consciousness there is the sense of realities behind abstractions ... [which] points back to its origin'.[15] We know that the building is there and will always be there, but we also delight in the entertainment of the transformative spectacle.

In 2010, an animation by Fernando Salis was projected onto the Christ the Redeemer statue in Rio de Janeiro, Brazil. The statue stands at a colossal height and is posed with its enormous arms outstretched. The brief projected animation included a variety of images and abstract forms – and towards the end, a simple animated butterfly was projected onto the surface of the statue and appeared to gently flutter about it. Then, as a finale, the Christ figure apparently folded his colossal arms to his chest (reminiscent of a grand 'hugging' action). Although the illusion is not perfect (the viewer is still partly aware that the real arms remain outstretched), it is a spectacular effect. In terms of animation, it is a rather simple movement, yet it represents a mammoth transformation of the real-world space (see Figure 7.7).

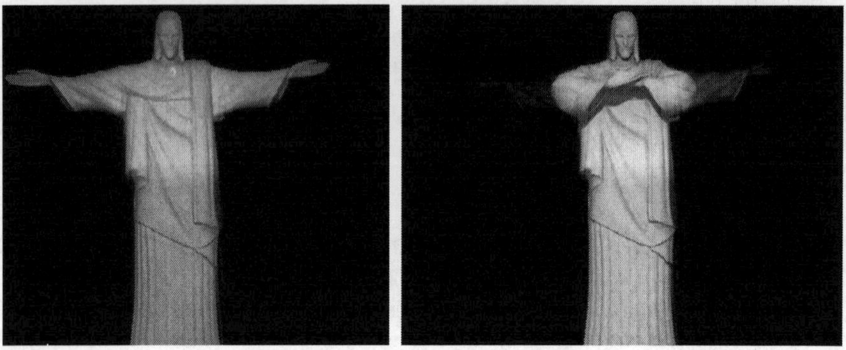

FIGURE 7.7 *Images from Christ the Redeemer projection (Fernando Salis 2010).*

Visual layers

As discussed previously, an important aspect of animation is the manner in which it can be layered and composited, which helps to describe its general constructive nature. 'Compositing', notes Thomas Lamarre, 'is what makes for a sense of the coherence of the image under conditions of movement in animation'.[16] Many forms of animation, from traditional cel animation to various kinds of digital animation, all actively utilize layering and compositing as a method for building up the imagery and the movement of the animation. At the very least, it might involve the placement of animated characters onto a separate background or landscape or, quite plausibly, hundreds of layers all working together. The interplay between the layers can be a vital strategy of the animated form, which can allow for incredibly complex narrative information, intriguing juxtapositions of imagery and movement, and even multiple representations of time. This practice of layering in animation can be furthered substantially through the projection of the imagery onto the architectural forms. Because this type of animation is 'situated' upon recognizable structures, the projected image and the display surface become inextricably linked in visual and narrative dialogue. With most animation it is the moving image alone that provides us with the narrative content (the screen merely serves as a facilitator of this content). But with situated animation, the 'screen' can contribute, quite literally, a large share of narrative information and its visibility and tactility become essential to this narrative. Many projection-mapped animations will directly reference the physical materials and construction of the building – we might see bricks move or crumble, windows and doors open and close. The contours of the building might be outlined, or particular sections exposed or obscured.

There are many different approaches to how the animated layers might interact with the landscape. More often than not it will involve a type of dialectic – a continual point and counterpointing between the actual physical building and the animated overlay. For example, in the previously mentioned projection-mapped animation that commemorated the 800th anniversary of the Santiago de Compostela Cathedral, we see an intriguing dialogue between the two layers during its nearly fifteen-minute display. Initially we see a vine covered building, with giant butterflies fluttering about it, only portions of the real building being visible. Then suddenly a fantastical dragon emerges and appears to burst through the wall (bricks can be seen shattering and crumbling as the dragon traverses the façade, breathing fire and destroying sections of the building). Later, the full building is illuminated and revealed but, almost instantaneously, parts of it begin to move. Some elements appear to spin on their base, and columns and protrusions appear to slide up and down. Then we see portions of the wall slide back to reveal an array of giant clockwork gears, which are implied to be the source of this new movement. The gears move in seemingly choreographed time with the movement of the building. Still later we can see symbols of religious ritual precisely placed and animated upon various sections of the cathedral.

Another thing that occurs in this building's animation (also in a number of others) is a dialectical display of both the interior and exterior spaces of the building. The audience is afforded a view of the actual exterior of the building while at the same time seeing an animated view of its interior. This is something that Paul Wells would refer to as the penetrative property of animation: its capacity to reveal the unseen – in this case the interior of a building. However, this is a unique embodiment of Well's idea of penetration, for not only does the animation allow us to see a representation of the interior spaces – we are able to see the physical exterior spaces simultaneously.

Situated soundtracks

Sound can often play an important role in projection-mapping. The soundtrack can work in a number of different ways in situated animation, quite often being used to underscore the spectacle or metamorphic illusions of the projected display. Thus when we see an animated brick apparently protrude from the side of the building, we will hear a loud scraping sound. Or, we might hear the sound of pencil sketching on paper as the building is transformed into an architectural diagram (as was depicted during one sequence in the 800th anniversary of Santiago de Compostela Cathedral). Additionally, thunderous music will often accompany the animation. This musical track helps to structure the often graphical and rather non-linear moving imagery of many situated animations.

As with all animation, sound is normally an imposed element. However, because these animations often take place in large, outdoor spaces, the sound must be very loud so that it can be heard through the roars of the crowd and the general ambient noise of the urban landscape. Thus, the sound effects and music often echo around the space and, in a sense, become part of the real-world diegesis. It is sound that is not only synchronous to the animation, but also synchronous to the space. By contrast, the sound in a traditional cinema (or even in a lounge room) will generally be attuned to surround the viewer, but it cannot actually surround the cinematic space represented on the screen. Yet the situated sound of projection-mapped animation can take advantage of the large eclectic space. Invariably the sound will reverberate off of the surrounding structures (that are essentially the animation) accentuating the very real expansiveness of the landscape.

One particularly novel use of sound can be found in *Perspective Lyrique: An Interactive Architectural Mapping* (2010), which was produced by 1024 Architecture, and which was presented at the Fete des Lumieres that took place in Lyon, France. The ornate building façade was animated so that it appeared to warp and transform radically until, finally, a giant face appeared. At this point the audience was invited to step up to a microphone and speak into it. Their speech was manipulated into non-verbal grunts and tones, which then activated the 'mouth' of the animated face. The building seemingly roared and bellowed out into the space and created a uniquely situated form of lip-synched animation (see Figure 7.8).

FIGURE 7.8 *Still image from* Perspective Lyrique: An Interactive Architectural Mapping *by 1024 Architecture (2010).*

Light and shadow

Throughout this section we have examined the dichotomy surrounding the actual concrete building and the irreal nature of animation. Light, which is the basis of projected animation, also embodies an oppositional state: light is on one hand composed simply of waves of energy, and on the other hand light is composed of photon particles that exhibit a true physical mass when they are activated. It is this physical presence, the materiality of light and its active processes which create the incredible spectacles of projection-mapped animation, taking it beyond the current technologies of mobile screen overlays or even augmented reality glasses which appear to superimpose imagery over real spaces. With projection, the light actually interplays with the concrete structures, the photon particles literally penetrating and bouncing off the physical building materials. And, according to Whitehead, it is such interaction – in fact, the interaction of all matter down to the smallest particle level – that pervades and constitutes the very nature of actuality.[17] In this manner, the projected light edges the experience closer to the actual – and for the audience, promotes a visibly and equally shared experience.

Such a display also showcases the Deleuzian concept of the fold – a concept that Deleuze used widely, but which we might think of simply as a way to describe the relationship that something has with itself (for example the interior of a form is merely the folding of its exterior). The fold expresses a logical and fluid interconnectivity that some theorists have applied to the consideration of architectural forms.[18] As Greg Lynn notes in his discussion of contemporary architecture, 'If there is a single effect produced in architecture by [the Deleuzian concept of] folding, it will be the ability to integrate unrelated elements within a new continuous mixture.'[19] And if architecture, with its combined construction materials and adornments, can do this on its own, then this construction can arguably be compounded further by the addition of projection-mapped animation. Thus, not only does light add visually or phenomenologically to the building, it also adds physical materiality and in turn creates new kinds of fused interconnections. Simultaneously, light is concretized by the building, while also serving to transform the building; and is further both absorbed by and reflected off the building.

Cinema has always been about light and shadow. In traditional cinema, light is generally used to display images, and shadow (or the absence of light) to hide images. This is most obvious, for example, in the Film Noir genre where, if it were necessary to obscure the face of Orson Wells in *Citizen Kane* (Wells 1941), shadows, or the absence of light would achieve this. Projection-mapped animation can utilize light and shadow to reveal and obscure particular elements. But outside of the dark controlled cinema space, with its flat textureless and colourless blank screen, it is impossible to create a totally black shadow that would truly conceal the façade of a building. So in the non-blackness of outdoor spaces – *light* is often used to *conceal*.

As an analogy as to how this technique might be used we can look to the humble squid. The common squid that lives in relatively well-lit shallow waters uses ink to hide itself. When it feels threatened it squirts out a large cloud of black *shadowy* ink and then scurries off, well hidden behind it. By contrast, the vampire squid (*Vampyroteuthis infernalis*), which lives nearly 1,000 metres below the surface in very dark water, is able, as with many creatures that live in these depths, to produce its own illumination. So when it feels threatened it squirts out a thick cloud of bioluminescent mucus containing masses of particles of blue light that lasts for several minutes. It hides behind this cloud of *light* and then scurries off.[20] Similarly, in projection-mapped animation, light (and its constituency of colour) is often used to obscure the building so that only the projected animated imagery can be seen clearly; in other cases, light is used simply to reveal the building. So, light is used both to reveal and to obscure, and to transform the background structures.

Another exceptional quality of projection-mapped animation is that light is often used to generate artificial *shadows* and, as with traditional animation, it is the use of shadows that helps substantiate a character's or an object's being grounded in a particular place – just as animated shadows in traditional cel animation serve to 'break down the division between foreground and background', helping to create 'a unified visual world'.[21] That is, shadows help to anchor the character to the ground – so they do not look, for example, as if they are floating in the air above the ground. Shadows can also help to substantiate the perspective of the background itself and are essential elements of most realistic visual landscapes. A well-lit landscape with clear visibility but without shadows can seem very artificial. Shadows can sometimes be a challenging element for the animator to produce effectively. Particularly in traditional cel animation, as Donald Crafton has noted, 'creating shadows within cinema posed special problems for animators'.[22] As a result, a number of unique techniques such as the shadowgraph were developed to create convincing semi-transparent shadows.[23]

The use of shadows becomes a doubly difficult problem in projection-mapping as the animated shadows must both place the animation and also displace the actual shadows that are created by the intensely bright projectors. Quite often these shadows will also be animated – as in the above-mentioned commemorative celebrations of the Prague Clock Tower, the shadows can be seen alternately to shorten, elongate and then travel from left to right. This use of animated shadows provides a simulation of a hyper-speed trajectory of the sun passing overhead. Of course, these were not real shadows, but computer-generated animations that over-power the real-world night-time: projected light is utilized to create purely simulated shadows in real spaces.

Part 3: Actualizing animation

Previously we have discussed how actuality could become animation (particularly through the animated documentary and digital simulations), and this section will consider the inverse of this, that is, how *animation can become actuality*. We can use the term 'actualizing animation' to refer to the potential transformation from screen-based digital animation into a more physical form of animation – with particular emphasis on 3D printing and robotics. Of course there have been numerous animated films that have thematically considered the blurring of the animated world and the actual world; perhaps the most notable of these was *Who Framed Roger Rabbit* (Robert Zemeckis and Richard Williams 1988), which playfully considered what might happen if the animated world were to merge with the real world. This final section will consider some of the more plausible aspects of such a merger.

Becoming actuality

An increasingly common method by which to bring digital animation 'into the real world' involves the use of 3D printing. This approach first entails the creation of a 3D-animated object or character. Once the animation is completed, each individual frame of the character's movements will then be 3D-printed. The resulting 'printed' plastic sculptures can then be photographed one at a time using the replacement stop-motion technique. This process was used to, for example, create the different mouth shapes for the stop-motion puppets in the animated feature *ParaNorman* (Chris Butler and Sam Fell 2012). Two particularly interesting animated short films that have utilized this approach are *Bears on Stairs* (DBLG 2014) and *Chase Me* (Gilles-Alexandre Deschaud 2015). *Bears on Stairs* is a brief cyclical animation that was created out of approximately fifty 3D-printed forms that represent a cycle of a bear climbing up a continuously moving set of escalating stairs. What makes this experiment so remarkable is that the traces of the 3D digital animation process remain quite evident throughout the entire process. For example, the blocky low-polygon-count model of the CG animation was faithfully transposed to the plastic printed forms, and furthermore the somewhat 'spliney' nature of the CG-generated movement was also transmitted into the stop-motion replacement forms. However, in contrast to the smooth textureless quality of the on-screen digital model, the 3D-printed forms exhibited a number of imperfections that are commonly seen within the 3D printing process. These imperfections can be perceived as flickering rough patches, oscillating etched lines and alternating dimples and protrusions. (See Figure 7.9) Deschaud's *Chase Me* represented a much more ambitious 3D printed endeavour involving the production of 2,500 individually printed pieces. The resulting 3D-printed stop-motion animation exhibited a strong stop-motion aesthetic (a bit rough and jittery in sections), but this was contrasted with a very complex and fluid movement of the clothing and hair of the characters – something that would only have come about because of the cloth and hair simulations inherent within the 3D software.

The resulting imperfections of the 3D printing process seem to directly emphasize Nicholas Rescher's assertion that virtual or fictional forms (such as digital animations) will always be limited in their detail and complexity. However, in contrast, the real world is infinite in its complexity. When we transition from actuality to animation, a simplification and a generalization inevitably occur. Yet, when we transition from digital animation to material-based stop-motion, just the opposite seems to occur. Once such a transition occurs, the resulting forms become part of the real-world diegesis and also become infinitely more complex (even if those complexities are the resulting imperfections of the 3D printing and stop-motion process).

Animated robots

Perhaps the most visible aspect of actualized animation can be found in the realm of robotics. Both in terms of process, and because of their increasing pervasiveness, robots are set to revolutionize how we think about animation – and probably how we think about our world. When tracing the history of animation, many will point towards the development of

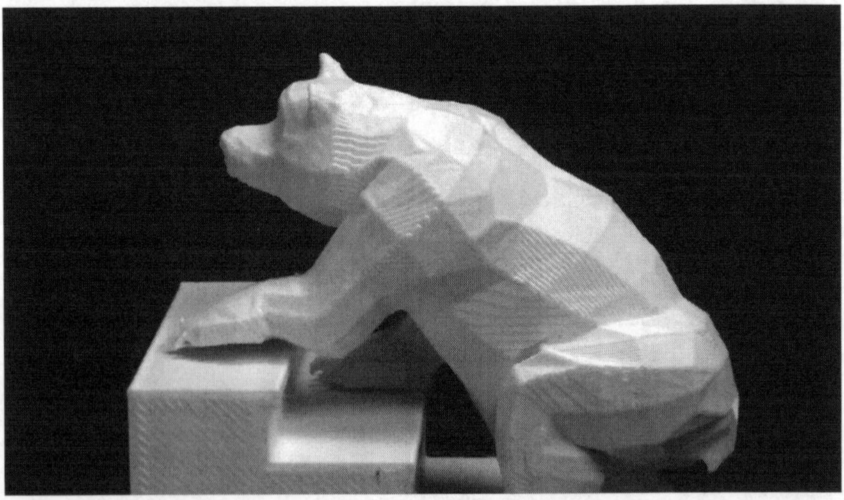

FIGURE 7.9 *Image from* Bears on Stairs *(DBLG 2014) featuring 3D-printed replacement forms.*

automatons and other robot-like machines of the eighteenth and nineteenth centuries as an important part of early animation history. For example, French designer Pierre Jaquet-Droz and his son Henri-Lous Jaquet-Droz created *The Draughtsman* (*c.* 1770), a remarkable automaton that took the form of a small child who seated at a desk displayed extraordinary clockwork movement. Holding a pencil in its hand, when activated, it was able to draw four different complex illustrations and write three different poems on sheets of paper. This example (as well as a number of others) still exists today and remains fully functional. Similar examples were also produced in other parts of Europe and also in Japan around the same time. Much later, Walt Disney dedicated substantial resources to bring animation 'off the screen' through his development of animatronics. Disney has, to this day, widely used these programmable animatronics throughout the company's theme park exhibitions and rides.

On one level, it is unmistakable that robots are 'animated' – they are inanimate objects that are made to move through pre-programmed actions. Yet, many people do not instinctively consider them to be 'animation' since they are not screen based and their movement has tended to be very limited, mechanical and primarily of a utilitarian nature. However, due to emerging technologies and broader conceptions as to what animation can be, many are beginning to reconsider this perspective. There are many approaches and techniques that can be used to animate a robot. Increasingly, however, a 3D digital representation of a robot will be animated in the computer, and that movement information transferred directly to the robot. This movement data might be derived either from key-frame animation or from motion-capture performances (or a blend of the two). Alternatively, some robots can be physically manipulated in much the same way that a stop-motion puppet can be manipulated, and these incremental movements can then be recorded and ultimately 'played back' through the robots' actions. Importantly, however, because robots are situated in the real world, they are subject to the strict physical laws of nature (something that screen-based animation can easily eschew). Additionally, a robot might have a rather limited range of movements (restricted, of course, by their complexity of design and construction). Both of these considerations will need to be taken into account when animating, and the data will need to be fed through what amounts to a 'physics filter' in order to prevent, for example, the robot losing its balance. Here one research team describes some of the challenges involved in animating a robot:

> Humanoid robots for entertainment are designed to imitate human or animal movements. Their motions are usually choreographed by hand to move in synchrony with prerecorded speech or music. Animating such robots is a time consuming process. For instance, it took several weeks for an animator to finish the 255-second long animation for the

> 37-joint humanoid robot used in this work. Furthermore, once the robots are deployed, their animations have to be periodically re-examined and fine-tuned with minimum downtime to adjust for robot wear and part replacements.[24]

As robots become more sophisticated, the process of animating them will also become more accessible, making the divide between a screen-based character and an animated robot a much more fluid space.

As with all forms of 'actualized animation', when digital animation is actualized into an animated robot, a unique transformation occurs. Namely, the generic aspects of the digital animation become specified and contextualized within that actual robot and to its unique iteration of a particular movement. Furthermore, unlike conventional animation that can be 'played back' indefinitely, a robot may be restricted due to mechanical failure or other real-world interruptions. Thus the physicality of the robot can also profoundly affect the digitally fabricated movement that it absorbs.

Some researchers are now advocating that it would be useful to apply many of the traditional animation principles (such as the essential 'twelve principles of animation' pioneered by early Disney animators) to the animating of robots.[25] It has been suggested that not only would such principles improve the general aesthetics of robotic movement but could also conceivably aid in the 'human understanding of the robots' emotions'.[26] For example, if a robot's movements were to be imbued with the animation concept of 'anticipation', then it would help us to understand and predict what a robot was 'going to do'.[27] Some have also suggested the benefits to adding more complex 'layers' of movement as these can provide the robot with sought after life-like qualities. These layers might range from random eye blinks to perhaps grimacing while lifting something heavy.[28] Similarly, a robot could be designed to continue to be 'animated' even when not actively completing a task – perhaps drawing inspiration from the concept of the 'animated boil' the robot could be given a repeating breathing movement or slight 'fidgeting'.

Metamorphosis and animated robots

Metamorphosis is one of animation's most unique manifestations of movement; but how might it be incorporated into the animation of robots? Perhaps when we do reach the point where robots (or other real-world structures) are truly able to express metamorphosis as a result of pre-determined animation, then robots would certainly be considered to be on par with screen-based animation. Traditionally, there are two primary means by which animation can achieve a metamorphic effect, either through the process of 'replacement animation' or through the process of 'manipulated animation'. However, since replacement animation would not generally be feasible with physical robots (it requires the process of subsequently replaced images with interstices between), a form of manipulated animation would be required.

Rudimentary example of robots that can transform their shape (perhaps inspired by the *Transformers* animated series and feature films) have been developed as well as more flexible robots with rubbery skins that can adjust their form (albeit in somewhat limited ways). Though such transformative robots are in their infancy, these technologies do appear to edge closer to a metamorphic capability. However, a more viable approach to creating metamorphic robots will likely involve not a single malleable robot, but instead swarms of micro-robots that will collectively form and re-form recognizable structures or alternatively dissipate into an amorphous mound – perhaps not too dissimilar to those envisioned in Disney's animated feature *Big Hero 6* (Don Hall and Chris Williams 2014).

Recently, a number of researchers have experimented with basic groupings of choreographed robots as a means of making real-world animated images. The robots (each about the size of one's fist) were made to swarm along the floor and form different configurations. These 'robot pixels' created both formations of intricate graphics and of simple moving animations. Hauri et al. described one of their 'multi-robot pattern formation' systems:

> The drawn input could be a stick figure, with the robots automatically adopting a physical configuration to represent the figure. Or the input could be an animation of a walking stick figure, with the robots moving to represent the dynamic deforming figure. Each robot has a controllable RGB LED so that the swarm can represent color drawings.[29]

Though these examples of choreographed robot swarms are still quite basic, some researchers have developed systems capable of controlling as many as 1,000 individual 'robot pixels'.

As miniaturization progresses, the development of micro-scaled 'robot pixels' is increasingly plausible. By massing together large numbers of these, they could then be transformed into any imaginable form. Even *more* speculative, some scientists have envisioned the manufacture of 'utility fogs' comprising literally millions of *nano-scaled* machines, each referred to as a 'foglet' that could be controlled or programmed to flock and move together in the same way as particle systems in 3D digital animation. The term 'utility fog' was invented by J. Storrs Hall. He named it after Batman's 'utility belt' in which, whatever Batman needed or wanted, it was always there ready for use – an endless supply of amazing tools and objects. If such a robotic future were to eventuate, the spectacle of animation would become a matching spectacle of physicality. In one visionary book, *Nanofuture: What's Next for Nanotechnology*, the author compares the idea of the utility fog to that of animated cartoon characters having the ability to reach out and grab anything they wish from thin air,[30] be it a frying pan or an Acme anvil. While, of course, still entirely speculative today, some radical 'actualizations' of what has previously been only screen-based imagery could be on the horizon. Perhaps some aspects of the zaniness and the 'anything-is-possible' conception of animation, as exemplified in *Who Framed Roger Rabbit*, might actually become percept one day. But certainly we are already at a point where it is feasible to consider robots to be more than just mechanical machines, but as a form of *actualized animated movement*.

Conclusion

This book has advocated a process-based analysis of animation in order to provide a more unified perspective of what animation is, and of what it is capable. One of the aims has been to find common ground between the many disparate forms and expressions of animation; simultaneously to broaden the conventional discourses that surround the practice and theory of animation.

This text has consisted of three diverse but interrelated sections: *Processing Animation* (focusing on the theorizing of the animation process); *Cognitive Animation* (which looked at links between the process of animation and the process of human cognition as well as some of the ways in which we might interpret or 'read' animation); and *Animating Actuality* (how the process of animation can interrogate, and be applied to, the real world).

The first section outlined an important process-based model which can be used to facilitate a more detailed understanding of animation. It charted nine different aspects of the animated form: movement, metamorphosis, frames and forms, layers, sound, time, abstraction, cycles and the process-document. Viewed together, these considerations unequivocally distinguish animation from many other forms. The second section introduced a 'cognitive animation theory' that looked at relationships between animation and human cognition in order to describe some connections between the processes of animation and the processes of human cognitive imagery. Importantly, this linking of animation to human cognition was intended to stretch beyond mere comparative analogy and to provide a unique perspective of the animated form. Further to this, the text examined some of the exceptional ways in which audiences might receive animation. First, it was considered how we might cogitate the animated image, including the double cognitive coding that can occur when viewing some more graphical forms of animation. This was followed by an exploration of a number of relevant topics, such as anthropomorphism, animated performances, stop-motion, animated video games and various hybrid forms of animations.

The third section looked at non-fictional animation and the representation of actuality from a perspective of process. Here it considered the process of actuality becoming animation, and how this becoming could, in part, be considered through a revised reading of indexicality. It also considered how animation might be used to investigate directly the real world through the use of digital simulations and virtual reality. Additionally, it introduced a *forensics approach to animation* as a methodology for discerning movement within things (even when it may not be overtly apparent) by tapping into the scaffolding of movement contained within most things. Finally, it considered how animation could be used directly to animate the real world. This involved an analysis of projection-mapped animation, landscape animation and lastly a consideration of how animated movement can be 'actualized' through various processes, including the animation of robots.

This text has positioned animation onto a rather expansive geography. In addition to the widely celebrated realm of screen-based animated 'cartoons', animation can encompass documentary, visualization, virtual reality, visual effects, motion graphics, video games, apps, moving signs and billboards and we can also consider many examples of robots and animatronics to be animation. But what does the future hold for animation? On one hand, it is very likely that it will continue to become more and more pervasive. Animation will undoubtedly play an increasingly large role in all aspects of screen-based media. We shall continue to see more animated feature films, more live-action films that contain an increased proportion of animation (elements that are both overtly graphical and seamlessly integrated) and further sophisticated uses of animation in games, in apps and on websites. It will become more pervasive throughout our environment: on billboards, building facades and on wearable items (perhaps even on our clothing). Augmented reality and virtual reality will continue to exude animation onto the real world and provide seemingly real-world experiences. Probably we shall continue to see more elaborate forms of projection mapping (both on the large scale and perhaps down to the very minute and intimate scale.)

While 'screen-based' animation becomes more pervasive, off-screen animation in the form of robots (and other devices that can be programmed to move) will also be likely to become increasing commonplace. As has been argued throughout this text, movement is the most essential aspect of animation, and with digital technologies it can easily be transferred from one form to another. In the digital realm, movement is nothing more than data and as every device becomes increasingly networked, particularly through the forthcoming internet of things (which will include robots), movement data will be able to be transferred easily from one networked object to another. Currently we think of 'viral animation' as being a YouTube clip or an animated GIF that gets quickly shared from screen to screen. In the future, perhaps we could expect that pure movement data might 'go viral' and be quickly shared from robot device to robot device, enacting some clearly identifiable movement or dance step.

The wide-ranging theories and critical examinations (underpinned by aspects of process-philosophy) that have been explored in this book essentially mirror animation's wide-ranging potential, and therefore can help to address its heterogeneous nature. Movement is unquestionably one of the unifying aspects of animation, and it is an equally unifying aspect of actuality (and our cognition of actuality). Our world is in a constant state of flux – brimming with movement and metamorphosis. Yet, there is much of our world that we still do not fully understand – even in terms of movement. For example, we are only beginning to comprehend the remarkable idea of quantum entanglement in which two linked particles (even separated by great distances) can affect each other's movement – each, in effect, animating the other, but through no visible connections. As we discover more and more about the extraordinary nature of our world, perhaps animation can also play a role in its comprehension. Animation is very adept at simultaneously pronouncing differences and at finding connections between differences. Fortunately our brains are well adept at being able to visualize, to cognitively animate and to ultimately make sense of much of these persistent changes. Fortunately, also, we have the medium of animation, which happens to be a very proficient method through which we can not only reflect upon but also act upon our world's perpetual instability. In this regard, perhaps we could think of the world more in terms of animation, and animation more in terms of the real world.

NOTES

Introduction

1 Furthermore, some have utilized the term 'animation' as a means of making particular concepts more lucid, such as evidenced in the book titled, Edward Packel, *Animating Calculus*. New York: Springer-Verlag Telos, 1996, which is intended to make the difficult subject of calculus clear and lively to the novice.
2 Gilles Deleuze, *Cinema 1: The Movement-Image* (Minneapolis: University of Minnesota Press, 1986), 5.
3 Suzanne Buchan, 'The Animated Spectator: Watching the Quay Brothers' "Worlds"'. In *Animated Worlds*, ed. Suzanne Buchan (London: John Libbey Publishing, 2006), 36.
4 Paul Wells and Johnny Hardstaff, *Re-Imagining Animation: Contemporary Moving Image Cultures* (Switzerland: AVA Academia, 2008), 16.
5 Wells and Hardstaff, *Re-Imagining Animation*, 6.
6 Kenny Chow, 'The Spiritual-Functional Loop: Animation Redefined in the Digital Age'. *Animation: An Interdisciplinary Journal* 4, no. 1 (2009): 80–81.
7 Eric S. Jenkins, *Special Affects: Cinema, Animation and the Translation of Consumer Care* (Edinburgh: Edinburgh University Press, 2014), 94.
8 Lamarre, Thomas, 'Coming to Life: Cartoon Animals and Natural Philosophy'. In *Animating Film Theory*, ed. Karen Beckman (Durham and London: Duke University Press, 2014), 127.
9 Donald Crafton, *Shadow of a Mouse: Performance, Belief, and World-Making in Animation* (Berkeley: University of California Press, 2013), 4.
10 Dr David McDowell.
11 Alan Cholodenko, 'Introduction'. In *The Illusion of Life II*, ed. Alan Cholodenko (Sydney: Power Publications, 2007).
12 Berys Gaut, *A Philosophy of Cinematic Art* (Cambridge: Cambridge University Press, 2010), 148.
13 See Thomas Lamarre, *The Anime Machine: A Media Theory of Animation* (Minneapolis: University of Minnesota Press, 2009), Jenkins, *Special Affects*, Bukatman Scott, *The Poetics of Slumberland – Animated Spirits and the Animating Spirit* (Berkeley and Los Angeles: University of California Press, 2012), Crafton, *Shadow of a Mouse*.
14 Nicholas Rescher, *Process Metaphysics* (New York: State University of New York Press, 1996), 6.
15 Rescher, *Process Metaphysics*, 5.
16 Nicholas Rescher, *Process Philosophical Deliberations* (Frankfurt: Ontos Verlag, 2006a), 7.

17 Rescher, *Process Philosophical Deliberations*, 49.
18 Nicholas Rescher, 'On Situating Process Philosophy'. *Process Studies* 28, no. 1/2 (1999): 37.
19 Douwe Draaisma, *Why Life Speeds up as You Get Older: How Memory Shapes Our Past* (Cambridge: Cambridge University Press, 2004), 56.
20 Rescher, *Process Philosophical Deliberations*, 22.
21 Alfred North Whitehead, *Process and Reality (Corrected Edition)* (New York: The Free Press, 1978), 40.
22 Alfred North Whitehead, *Adventures of Ideas* (New York: The Free Press, 1967), 354–55.
23 Gilles Deleuze and Felix Guattari, *A Thousand Plateaus: Capitalism and Schizophrenia* (Minneapolis: University of Minnesota Press, 1987), 293.
24 John Dewey, *Experience and Nature* (New York: Dover Publications, 1958), 166.
25 Rescher, *Process Philosophical Deliberations*, 3.
26 Catherine Keller, 'Process and Chaosmos: The Whiteheadian Fold in the Discourse of Difference'. In *Process and Difference: Between Cosmological and Poststructuralist Postmodernisms*, eds. Catherine Keller and Anne Daniell (New York: State University of New York Press, 2002), 55.
27 Both Catherine Keller, 'Process and Chaosmos' and Tim Clark, 'A Whiteheadian Chaosmos? Process Philosophy from a Deleuzean Perspective'. In *Process and Difference: Between Cosmological and Poststructuralist Postmodernisms*, eds. Catherine Keller and Anne Daniell (New York: State University of New York Press, 2002) have iterated that Deleuze spans both the areas of process and poststructuralism.
28 Or, quite often, the emulation of such 'framic' conventions in the digital animation software.
29 Gilles Deleuze, *Difference & Repetition* (New York: Columbia University Press, 1994), 1.
30 Deleuze, *Difference & Repetition*, 56.
31 Rescher, *Process Philosophical Deliberations*, 49.
32 Dewey, *Experience and Nature*, 71.
33 Whitehead, *Process and Reality*, 21.

Chapter 1

1 Deleuze, *Cinema 1*, 2.
2 Len Lye, *Figures of Motion: Len Lye/Selected Writings* (Auckland, New Zealand: Auckland University Press, 1984), 39.
3 Greg Lynn, 'Introduction'. In *Animate Form*, ed. Greg Lynn (New York: Princeton Architectural Press, 1999), 11.
4 Henri Bergson, *Creative Evolution* (New York: Henry Holt, 1911), 272.
5 Marta Braun, *Picturing Time: The Work of Etienne-Jules Marey (1830–1904)* (Chicago: The University of Chicago Press, 1992), 143.
6 Braun, *Picturing Time*, 81.

7 Midori Kitagawa and Brian Windsor, *Mocap for Artists: Workflow and Techniques for Motion Capture* (Oxford: Focal Press, 2008), 8–12.
8 Deleuze, *Cinema 1*, 2.
9 Brian Salt, *Movements in Animation: Volume 1* (Oxford: Pergamon Press, 1976), 110.
10 Nicholas Rescher, *Process Philosophy* (Pittsburgh, PA: University of Pittsburgh Press, 2000), 10.
11 Rescher, *Process Philosophy*, 10.
12 Howard Beckerman, *Animation: The Whole Story* (New York: Allworth Press, 2003), 23.
13 Paul Ward, '"Rotoshop" in Context: Computer Rotoscoping and Animation Aesthetics'. *Animation Journal* 12 (2004): 35.
14 Gregory Singer, 'Dream Is Destiny: Waking Life'. *Animation World Magazine,* www.awn.com/animationworld/dream-destiny-waking-life, accessed 1 June 2015 (2001).
15 Paul Wells, *Understanding Animation* (London: Routledge, 1998), 69.
16 Vivian Sobchack, 'At the Still Point of the Turning World'. In *Meta-Morphing: Visual Transformation and the Culture of Quick-Change*, ed. Vivian Sobchack (Minneapolis: University of Minnesota Press, 2000), 136.
17 Michael Frierson, *Clay Animation* (New York: Twayne Publishers, 1994), 22.
18 Peter Lord and Brian Sibley, *Creating 3D Animation: The Arardman Book of 3D Animation* (London: Harry N. Abrams, 2004), 53.
19 Philip Brophy, *100 Anime*, Bfi Screen Guides (London: BFI Publishing, 2005), 6.
20 Paul Wells, *Animation and America* (Edinburgh: Edinburgh University Press, 2002), 24.
21 Deleuze, *Cinema 1*, 5.
22 Sobchack, 'At the Still Point of the Turning World', 130.
23 Wells, *Understanding Animation*, 69.
24 Caroline Walker Bynum, *Metamorphosis and Identity* (New York: Zone Books, 2001), 19.
25 Brophy, *100 Anime*, 6.
26 Rescher, *Process Philosophy*, 10.
27 Anne Daniell, 'Figuring Subjectivity for Grounded Transformations: A Critical Comparison of Rosi Braidotti's and John Cobb's Figurations'. In *Process and Difference: Between Cosmological and Poststructuralist Postmodernisms*, eds. Catherine Keller and Anne Daniell (Albany: State University of New York Press, 2002), 155.
28 That is, when the movement is considered *separated* from form.
29 Norman Klein, 'Animation and Animorphs'. In *Meta-Morphing: Visual Transformation and the Culture of Quick-Change*, ed. Vivian Sobchack (Minneapolis: University of Minnesota Press, 2000), 24.
30 Gilles Deleuze and Felix Guattari, *A Thousand Plateaus: Capitalism and Schizophrenia* (Minneapolis: University of Minnesota Press, 1987), 25.
31 Wells, *Understanding Animation*, 69.
32 Gilles Deleuze, *Bergsonism* (New York: Zone Books, 1991), 41–42.
33 Sobchack, 'At the Still Point of the Turning World', 136.

34 Deleuze and Guattari, *A Thousand Plateaus*, 245.
35 Deleuze and Guattari, *A Thousand Plateaus*, 245.
36 Wells, *Understanding Animation*, 69.
37 Harlan Tarbell, *Chalk Talk Stunts* (Chicago: TS Denison & Company, 1926), 21.
38 Wells and Hardstaff, *Re-Imagining Animation*, 16.
39 Esther Leslie, 'Animation's Petrified Unrest'. In *Pervasive Animation*, ed. Suzanne Buchan (London: Routledge, 2013), 76.
40 Alan Cholodenko, 'Still Photography?' *Afterimage* 32, no. 5 (2005): 5.
41 Mary Ann Doane, *The Emergence of Cinematic Time: Modernity, Contingency, the Archive* (Cambridge: Harvard University Press, 2002), 87.
42 Tony Schirato and Jen Webb, *Reading the Visual* (Sydney: Allen and Unwin, 2004), 193.
43 Brian Massumi, *Semblance and Event: Activist Philosophy and the Occurrent Arts* (Boston: MIT Press, 2011), 106.
44 Deleuze, *Cinema 1*, 5.
45 Tom Gunning, 'Animating the Instant: The Secret Symmetry between Animation and Photography'. In *Animating Film Theory*, ed. Karen Beckman (Durham and London: Duke University Press, 2014), 41.
46 Dorothy Emmet, *The Passage of Nature* (London: Macmillan, 1992), 1.
47 Norman McLaren quoted in John Halas, *Computer Animation* (New York: Hastings House, 1974), 97.
48 Deleuze, *Difference & Repetition*, 56.
49 John Mullarkey, *Post-Continental Philosophy* (London: Continuum, 2006), 13.
50 Maureen Furniss, *Art in Motion: Animation Aesthetics* (London: John Libbey, 1998), 135.
51 Deleuze, *Cinema 1*, 58.
52 Deleuze, *Cinema 1*, 3.
53 Thomas Lamarre, 'From Animation to Anime: Drawing Movements and Moving Drawings'. *Japan Forum* 14, no. 2 (2002): 329–67 and later Caroline Ruddell, 'From the "Cinematic" to the "Anime-Ic": Issues of Movement in Anime'. *Animation: An Interdisciplinary Journal* 3, no. 2 (2008): 113–28, differentiate this commonly occurring aesthetics of motion from live-action movement (and full animation movement) by as being 'anime-ic' (coined by Lamarre). Such apparently 'jittery' movement is distinct from the smoother appearance of 'cinematic' movement.
54 Scott McCloud, *Understanding Comics: The Invisible Art* (New York: HarperCollins, 1994), 112.
55 Harold Whitaker and John Halas. *Timing for Animation* (New York: Focal Press, 1981), 111.
56 William Kentridge, cited in N. Benezra, 'William Kentridge: Drawings for Projection'. In *William Kentridge*, ed. M. Sittenfeld (New York: Harry N. Abrams, 2001), 114.
57 Whitehead, *Adventures of Ideas*, 355.
58 Deleuze and Guattari, *A Thousand Plateaus*, 293.
59 Sabine Heller, cited in Jerry Schmitz, *The Art and Making of Blue Sky Studios the Peanuts Movie by Schulz* (London: Titan Books, 2015), 26.

60 Schmitz, *The Art and Making of Blue Sky Studios the Peanuts Movie by Schulz*, 26.
61 Tom Snyder and A. Lyman. 'USA Patent No. 6252604' (U.S., 2001).
62 Deleuze, *Difference & Repetition*, 76.
63 Richard Williams, *The Animator's Survival Kit: A Manual of Methods, Principles and Formulas* (London: Faber and Faber, 2001), 11.
64 R. Layton, *Australian Rock Art: A New Synthesis* (Cambridge: Cambridge University Press, 1992).
65 Rescher, *Process Metaphysics*, 29.
66 Alfred North Whitehead, *Concept of Nature* (Cambridge: Cambridge University Press, 1978).
67 Rescher, *Process Philosophy*, 31.
68 For further information on the film frame and its basic components, see David Bordwell and Kristin Thompson. *Film Art an Introduction (Eighth Edition).* New York: McGraw Hill, 2008), 276.
69 For more, see Deleuze's, *Cinema 1*, 61–66.
70 Sergai Eisenstein, *Eisenstein Volume 2: Towards a Theory of Montage* (London: BFI Publishing, 1991), 330.
71 Eisenstein had by this time met Disney and was reportedly very impressed with the studio's animated films. See Sergai Eisenstein, *Eisenstein on Disney* (London: Methuen, 1988).
72 Richard J. Leskosky, 'Two-State Animation: The Thaumatrope and Its Spin-Offs'. *Animation Journal* 2, no. 1 (1993): 22.
73 Derek Greenacre, *Magic Lanterns* (London: Shire Publications, 1999), 26.
74 Thompson, Kristin, 'Implications of the Cel Animation Technique'. In *The Cinematic Apparatus*, eds. Teresa de Lauretis and Stephen Heath (London: The Macmillan Press, 1980), 113.
75 Charles Solomon, *The History of Animation: Enchanted Drawings (Revised Edition)* (New York: Wings Books, 1994), 237.
76 Lamarre, *The Anime Machine*, xxix.
77 Lamarre, *The Anime Machine*, 124.
78 Catherine Winder and Zahra Dowlatabadi, *Producing Animation* (Boston: Focal Press, 2001), 240.
79 S. Chatman, 'What Novels Can Do That Films Can't (and Vice Versa)'. In *On Narrative*, ed. W. Mitchell (Chicago: University of Chicago Press, 1981), 118.
80 Of course, this distinction is less firm than it once was, particularly when one considers the intensive postproduction processes of digital cinema which often emulate many of animation's production processes.
81 Beckerman, *Animation*, 189.
82 Brigitta Hosea, 'Drawing Animation'. *Animation: An Interdisciplinary Journal* 5, no. 3 (2010): 363.
83 This technique of 'light animation' was developed by the creative team TOCHKA (Nagata Takeshi and Monno Kazue), who coined the term PiKA PiKA and first showcased the technique in Japan in 2005.
84 Similar equivalences of time are found in other exposure-time processes (1/25, 1/100, and so on).
85 Gilles Deleuze, *Cinema 2: The Time-Image* (Minneapolis: University of Minnesota Press, 1989), 35.

86 Deleuze, *Cinema* 2, 37.
87 George Griffin, 'Take the B Train: Reconstructing the Proto-Cinematic Apparatus'. In *Pervasive Animation*, ed. Suzanne Buchan (London: Routledge, 2013), 289.
88 McLaren, *Computer Animation*, 97.
89 Emmet, *The Passage of Nature*, 29.
90 Tom Gunning, 'The Cinema of Attraction[S]: Early Film, Its Spectator and the Avant-Garde'. In *Film and Theory: An Anthology*, eds. Robert Stam and Toby Miller (Oxford: Blackwell, 2000), 163.
91 Henri Bergson, *Time and Free Will: An Essay on the Immediate Data of Consciousness* (New York: Dover Publications, 2001), 101.
92 Bergson, *Creative Evolution*, 176.
93 Bergson, *Time and Free Will*, 105.
94 Emmet, *The Passage of Nature*, 2.
95 Deleuze, *Cinema* 2, 35.
96 Keith Broadfoot and Rex Butler, 'The Illusion of Illusion'. In *The Illusion of Life*, ed. Alan Cholodenko (Sydney: Power Publications, 1991), 269.
97 Henri Bergson, *Matter and Memory* (New York: Zone Books, 1988).
98 Deleuze, *Cinema* 2, 226.
99 There are of course exceptions to this approach. In some cases the vocal performance will be added in after the visual animation process is completed. For example, Popeye cartoons in the 1930s were often animated first, and then voices would be later dubbed in. Furthermore, a significant amount of contemporary animation might first be animated to the voice actor's dialogue and then will be subsequently dubbed with foreign language actors for overseas distribution.
100 Furniss, *Art in Motion*, 86.
101 Arthur W. Ord-Hume, *Clockwork Music* (London: George Allen and Unwin, 1973), 63.
102 James H. Bierman, 'Disney's "America Sings"'. *The Drama Review* 20, no. 2 (1976): 69.
103 Michel Chion, *Audio-Vision: Sound on Screen* (New York: Columbia University Press, 1994), 40.
104 Rescher, *Process Philosophical Deliberations*, 3.
105 Bordwell and Thompson, *Film Art an Introduction*, 276.
106 For example, see Furniss, *Art in Motion*, Wells, *Understanding Animation*.
107 Furniss, *Art in Motion*, 5.
108 Wells, *Understanding Animation*.
109 Michael Cowan, *Walter Ruttmann and the Cinema of Multiplicity: Avant-Garde – Advertising – Modernity* (Amsterdam, The Netherlands: Amsterdam University Press, 2014), 48.
110 Solomon, *The History of Animation*, 216.
111 William Moritz, Some Observations on Non-objective and Non-linear Animation'. In *Storytelling in Animation: The Art of the Animated Image* Volume 2. Ed. John Canemaker (Los Angeles: American Film Institute (1988), 21.
112 Charles Solomon, 'Animation: Notes on a Definition'. In *The Art of the Animated Image*, ed. Charles Solomon (Los Angeles: The American Film Institute, 1987), 10.

113 Frank Thomas and Ollie Johnston, *Disney Animation: The Illusion of Life* (New York: Abbeville Press, 1981), 47–69.
114 Rescher, *Process Philosophical Deliberations*, 49.
115 Whitehead, *Concept of Nature*, 168.
116 Deleuze and Guattari, *A Thousand Plateaus*, 306.
117 Andrew R. Johnston, 'Signatures of Motion: Len Lye's Scratch Films and the Energy of the Line'. In *Animating Film Theory*, ed. Karen Beckman (Durham and London: Duke University Press, 2014), 167.
118 Wells, *Understanding Animation*, 34.
119 Nicholas Rescher, *Imagining Irreality: A Study of Unrealized Possibility* (Chicago: Open Court Publishing, 2003), 75.
120 Rescher, *Process Philosophical Deliberations*, 9.
121 Whitehead, *Concept of Nature*.
122 W. J. T. Mitchell, *Picture Theory: Essays on Verbal and Visual Representation* (Chicago: University of Chicago Press, 1994), 38.
123 Deleuze, *Difference & Repetition*, 19.
124 Suzanne Buchan, 'The Animated Fulcrum'. In *Animated Painting*, ed. Betti-Sue Hertz (San Diego, CA: San Diego Museum of Art, 2007), 30.
125 Gerald Findler, *Lightning Cartoons: How to Make Funny Sketches in Five Minutes* (London: W. Foulsham, 1938), 48–59.
126 Tom Gunning, '"Now You See It, Now You Don't": The Temporality of the Cinema of Attractions'. *Velvet Light Trap*, Fall, no. 32 (1993): 3.
127 Donald Crafton, *Before Mickey: The Animated Film 1898–1928* (Cambridge: MIT Press, 1982), 11.
128 Scott Bukatman, 'Comics and the Critique of Chronophotography, or "He Never Knew When It Was Coming!"'. *Animation: An Interdisciplinary Journal* 1, no. 1 (2006): 99.
129 Registering is a process by which the animator can ensure that all of the drawings line up with each other. By holding the drawings in place with pegs, and by working over a light table, the animator is able to see the previous several drawings and keep the correct placement and consistent design of the drawings.
130 Lord and Sibley, *Creating 3d Animation*, 53.
131 Wes Anderson, cited in Michael Specter, *The Making of Fantastic Mr. Fox* (New York: Rizzoli International Publications, 2009), 45.
132 Suzanne Buchan, 'The Animated Spectator: Watching the Quay Brothers' "Worlds"'. In *Animated Worlds*, ed. Suzanne Buchan (London: John Libbey Publishing, 2006), 30.
133 Martha Sigall, *Living Life Inside the Lines: Tales from the Golden Age of Animation* (Jackson: University Press of Mississippi, 2005), 19.
134 'Disney recalls video over "nude image"'. Saturday, 9 January 1999. BBC News, news.bbc.co.uk/2/hi/entertainment/251532.stm, accessed: 1 November 2015.
135 Shamus Culhane, *Animation from Script to Screen* (New York: St. Martin's Griffin, 1988), 221.
136 134 Laura Mulvey, *Death at 24x a Second: Stillness and the Moving Image* (London: Reaktion Books Ltd., 2006), 22.
137 Frierson, *Clay Animation*, 21.

138 Klein, 'Animation and Animorphs', 22.
139 Klein, 'Animation and Animorphs', 24.
140 Alan F. Meades, *Understanding Counterplay in Video Games* (Florence: Taylor and Francis, 2015), 6.

Chapter 2

1 Nicolas Dulac and Andre Gaudreault, 'Circularity and Repetition at the Heart of the Attraction'. In *The Cinema of Attractions Reloaded*, ed. Wanda Strauven (Amsterdam, The Netherlands: Amsterdam University Press, 2006), 229.
2 Dulac and Gaudreault, 'Circularity and Repetition', 232.
3 Etienne-Jules Marey, *Movement* (New York: D. Appleton and Company, 1895), 311.
4 It should be noted that some of these devices utilized photographic imagery – particularly the work of Eadweard Muybridge.
5 Tony White, *From Pencils to Pixels: Classical Techniques for Digital Animators* (Burlington, MA: Focal Press, 2006), 223.
6 E. G. Lutz, *Animated Cartoons: How They Are Made, Their Origin and Development* (New York: Charles Scribner's Sons, 1920), 58.
7 Lutz, *Animated Cartoons*, 159–66.
8 Lutz, *Animated Cartoons*, 168.
9 David L. Nathan and Donald Crafton, 'The Making and Re-Making of Winsor Mccay's Gertie (1914)'. *Animation: An Interdisciplinary Journal* 8, no. 1 (2013): 40.
10 Roy P. Madsen, *Animated Film: Concepts, Methods, Uses* (New York: Interland Publishing Inc., 1969), 122.
11 Eli L. Levitan, *Handbook of Animation Techniques* (New York: Van Nostrand Reinhold Company, 1979), 53.
12 William Christian, *An Interpretation of Whitehead's Metaphysics* (Westport, CT: Greenwood Press, 1959), 139.
13 Richard Hanley, 'No End in Sight: Causal Loops in Philosophy, Physics and Fiction'. *Synthese* 141, no. 1 (2004): 123–52.
14 Manuel DeLanda, *Intensive Science & Virtual Philosophy* (New York: Continuum, 2002), 84.
15 Bergson, *Creative Evolution*, 230, 231.
16 Tyler Volk, *Metapatterns: Across Space, Time and Mind* (New York: Columbia University Press, 1995), 229.
17 Volk, *Metapatterns*, 230.
18 Volk, *Metapatterns*, 235.
19 Volk, *Metapatterns*, 234.
20 Lutz, *Animated Cartoons*, 233.
21 Lutz, *Animated Cartoons*, 236, 237.
22 Alfred North Whitehead, *The Function of Reason* (Boston: Beacon Press, 1958), 21.
23 White, *From Pencils to Pixels*, 242.

24 Salt, *Movements in Animation*, 55.
25 Roger Noake, *Animation: A Guide to Animated Film Techniques* (London: MacDonald Orbis, 1988), 109.
26 White, *From Pencils to Pixels*, 379.
27 Jules Engel, *Los Angeles Art Community: Group Portrait, Jules Engel* (Lawrence Weschler and Milton Zolotow, Interviewers), (Los Angeles: The Regents of the University of California, 1985), 110.
28 Furniss, *Art in Motion*, 150.
29 In order to make *Tango* (the Academy-awarded film for the category of animated short film, 1980), Rybczynski followed a frame-by-frame process in which he 'had to draw and paint about 16,000 cell mattes, and make several hundred thousand exposures on an optical printer'. Zbig Rybczynski, 'Looking to the Future – Imagining the Truth'. In *Cinema & Architecture: Melies, Mallet-Stevens, Multimedia*, eds. FranCois Penz and Maureen Thomas (London: British Film Institute, 1997), 183.
30 Whitehead, *The Function of Reason*, 22.
31 Whitehead, *The Function of Reason*, 22.
32 Miguel Sicart, *Beyond Choices: The Design of Ethical Gameplay* (Cambridge, MA: MIT Press, 2013), 38, 39.
33 Jason Eppink, 'A Brief History of the Gif (So Far)'. *Journal of Visual Culture* 13, no. 3 (2014): 303.
34 Suzanne Buchan, *The Quay Brothers: Into a Metaphysical Playroom* (Minneapolis: University of Minnesota Press, 2011), 87.
35 Joe Fordham, 'Formula for a Universe'. *Cinefex* no. 114 (2008): 36.
36 Rescher, *Process Philosophical Deliberations*, 49.
37 Thomas and Johnston, *Disney Animation*, 42.
38 Marc Steinberg, 'Immobile Sections and Trans-Series Movement: Astroboy and Emergence of Anime'. *Animation: An Interdisciplinary Journal* 1, no. 2 (2006): 199.

Chapter 3

1 Alan Baddeley, *Working Memory, Thought and Action* (Oxford: Oxford University Press, 2007), 1.
2 Jackie Andrade, 'An Introduction to Working Memory'. In *Working Memory in Perspective*, ed. Jackie Andrade (Hove: Psychology, 2001), 3.
3 Baddeley, *Working Memory*, 13.
4 Susan E. Gathercole, 'The Nature and Uses of Working Memory'. In *Theoretical Aspects of Memory*, eds. Peter Morris and Michael Gruneberg (London: Routledge, 1994), 50.
5 Baddeley, *Working Memory*.
6 Rescher, *Process Philosophical Deliberations*, 77.
7 G. A. Miller, 'The Magical Number Seven, Plus or Minus Two: Some Limits on Our Capacity for Processing Information'. *Psychological Review*, 63, no. 2 (1956): 81–97. Also see L. R. Peterson and J. M. Peterson. 'Short-Term Retention of Individual Verbal Items'. *Journal of Experimental Psychology*

58, no. 3 (1959): 193–98, J. Sweller, J. J. G. van Merrienboer and Fred Paas. 'Cognitive Architecture and Instructional Design'. *Educational Psychology Review* 10, no. 3 (1998): 251–96, Fred Paas, A. Renkl and J. Sweller. 'Cognitive Load Theory and Instructional Design: Recent Developments'. *Educational Psychologist*, 38, no. 1 (2003): 1–4.

8 Dana Ballard, 'Animate Vision'. *Artificial Intelligence* 48, no. 1 (1991): 58.

9 Torben Grodal, *Moving Pictures: A New Theory of Film Genres, Feelings, and Cognition* (Oxford: Clarendon Press, 1997), 1.

10 David Bordwell, 'Film, Emotion and Genre'. In *Philosophy of Film and Motion Pictures: An Anthology*, eds. Noel Carroll and Jinhee Choi (Oxford: Blackwell Publishing, 2006), 223.

11 Arthur P. Shimamura, 'Psychocinematics: Issues and Directions'. In *Psychocinematics: Exploring Cognition at the Movies*, ed. Arthur P. Shimamura (Oxford: Oxford University Press, 2013), 3.

12 Wolfgang Schnotz and Richard Lowe, 'A Unified View of Learning from Animated and Static Graphics'. In *Learning with Animation: Research Implications for Design*, eds. Richard Lowe and Wolfgang Schnotz (Cambridge: Cambridge University Press, 2008), 309.

13 Ballard, 'Animate Vision', 58.

14 Mary Hegarty, 'Mental Animation: Inferring Motion from Static Displays of Mechanical Systems'. *Journal of Experimental Psychology: Learning, Memory and Cognition* 18, no. 5 (1992): 1084.

15 Ballard, 'Animate Vision', 58.

16 Andy Clark, *Being There: Putting Brain, Body, and World Together Again* (Cambridge, MA: MIT Press, 1997), 28.

17 Clark, *Being There*, 29.

18 Joseph D. Anderson, *The Reality of Illusion: An Ecological Approach to Cognitive Film Theory* (Carbondale: Southern Illinois University Press, 1996), 93.

19 D. MacKay, 'Ways of Looking at Perception'. In *Models for the Perception of Speech and Visual Form*, ed. W. Wathen-Dunn (Cambridge, MA: MIT Press, 1967).

20 Clark, *Being There*, 30.

21 Laura U. Marks, *Touch: Sensuous Theory and Multisensory Media* (Minneapolis: University of Minnesota Press, 2002), 3.

22 Thomas Andrillon et al., 'Single-Neuron Activity and Eye Movements during Human Rem Sleep and Awake Vision'. *Nature Communications* 6, August (2015): 2.

23 Deleuze, *Difference & Repetition*, 76.

24 Schnotz and Lowe, 'A Unified View of Learning', 320.

25 Schnotz and Lowe, 'A Unified View of Learning', 318, 319.

26 Robert H. Logie, *Visuo-Spatial Working Memory* (Hove: Lawrence Erlbaum Associates, 1995), 71.

27 Schnotz and Lowe, 'A Unified View of Learning', 314, 315.

28 Julie Bauer Morrison et al., 'Animation: Can It Facilitate?'. *International Journal of Human-Computer Studies*, 57, no. 4 (2002): 247–62.

29 Susan R. Goldman, 'Animating the Issues for Research on Animation'. In *Learning with Animation*, eds. Richard Lowe and Wolfgang Schnotz (Cambridge: Cambridge University Press, 2008), 360.

30 Logie, *Visuo-Spatial Working Memory*, 2.
31 Bergson, *Creative Evolution*, 272.
32 Bergson, *Matter and Memory.*
33 Samuel Alexander, *Space Time and Deity, Volume 1* (London: Macmillan, 1920), 321.
34 Semir Zeki, *Inner Vision: An Exploration of Art and the Brain* (Oxford: Oxford University Press, 1999), 66.
35 Logie, *Visuo-Spatial Working Memory*, 2.
36 Stephen M. Kosslyn, *Image and Brain: The Resolution of the Imagery Debate* (Cambridge, MA: A Bradford Book, MIT Press, 1994), 350.
37 Kosslyn, *Image and Brain*, 353.
38 Vittorio Gallese, 'Intentional Attunement: The Mirror Neuron System and Its Role in Interpersonal Relations', 2005. http://www.interdisciplines.org/mirror/papers/1, accessed 2 December 2012.
39 Patrick Power, 'Character Animation and the Embodied Mindbrain'. *Animation: An Interdisciplinary Journal* 3, no. 1 (2008): 33.
40 Most animators will act out the actions of what they want their character to do before they animate it. In this way, they will get a fuller sense of what that movement is, what it looks like and what it 'feels' like. However, in a unique reversal of this approach, the animators working on *The Peanuts Movie* (Steve Martino 2015) were told specifically *not* to act out the actions of their characters. Rather than aiming for realism, the director wanted the animators to remain true to the essence of Charles Schulz's original drawing style. This often involved placing and moving the characters from one impossible pose to another.
41 Deleuze, *Cinema 1*, 58.
42 Whitehead, *Concept of Nature*, 105.
43 Martha Langford, 'Introduction'. In *Image & Imagination* (Montreal: McGill-Queen's University Press, 2005), 4.
44 Cholodenko, 'Still Photography?', 5.
45 Schnotz and Lowe, 'A Unified View of Learning', 309.
46 Joyce E. Farrell and Roger N. Shepard, 'Shape, Orientation, and Apparent Rotational Motion'. In *Mental Images and Their Transformations*, eds. Roger N. Shepard and Lynn A. Cooper (Cambridge, MA: MIT Press, 1981/1986), 287.
47 Teresa Mendes Flores, 'Stereoscopy, Film and Time-Image. An Improbable Encounter: Paz Dos Reis and Chris Marker's Photographic Films'. In *Photography and Cinema: 50 Years of Chris Marker's La Jetee*, eds. Margarida Medeiros et al. (Newcastle upon Tyne: Cambridge Scholars Publishing, 2015), 57.
48 Flores, 'Stereoscopy, Film and Time-Image', 63.
49 Schirato and Webb, *Reading the Visual*, 193.
50 Deleuze, *Cinema 2*, 37.
51 Sobchack, 'At the Still Point of the Turning World', 136.
52 Kosslyn, *Image and Brain*, 353.
53 Wells, *Understanding Animation*, 69.
54 Frierson, *Clay Animation*, 23.
55 Kosslyn, *Image and Brain*, 351.

56 Angela Ndalianis, 'Special Effects, Morphing Magic, and the 1990s Cinema of Attractions'. In *Meta-Morphing: Visual Transformation and the Culture of Quick-Change*, ed. Vivian Sobchack (Minneapolis: University of Minnesota Press, 2000), 264.
57 Alfred North Whitehead, *Modes of Thought* (New York: The Free Press, 1968), 89.
58 Frierson, *Clay Animation*, 23.
59 Whitehead, *Process and Reality*, 16.
60 Noam Chomsky, *Syntactic Structures* (New York: Moulton and Co., 1957).
61 John T. E. Richardson, *Mental Imagery and Human Memory* (New York: St. Martin's Press, 1980), 71.
62 Gillian Cohen, *The Psychology of Cognition* (New York: Academic Press, 1977).
63 Alan Baddeley and G. Hitcham, 'Working Memory'. In *Recent Advances in Learning and Motivation*, ed. G. A. Bower (New York: Henry Holt, 1974).
64 John T. E. Richardson, *Imagery* (Hove: Psychology Press Ltd., 1999), 2.
65 Kosslyn, *Image and Brain.*
66 Shepard Roger and Cooper Lynn, *Mental Images and Their Transformations.* Cambridge, MA: MIT Press 1982, Ballard, 'Animate Vision', Alan Baddeley, 'Working Memory and Conscious Awareness'. In *Theories of Memory*, eds. A. F. Collins Susan E. Gathercole, Martin A. Conway and Peter Morris (Hillsdale, NJ: Erlbaum Associates, 1993), Alan Baddeley and Andrade Jackie, 'Working Memory and Consciousness: An Empirical Approach'. In *Theories of Memory Volume 2*, eds. Martin A. Conway, Susan E. Gathercole and Cesare Cornoldi (Hove: Psychology Press Ltd., 1998), Baddeley, *Working Memory* (2007); Kosslyn, *Image and Brain* (1994); Stephen M. Kosslyn et al., *The Case for Mental Imagery* (Oxford: Oxford University Press, 2006), 137; Logie, *Visuo-Spatial Working Memory*; Andy Clark, *Being There*; and Richardson, *Imagery* are just a few of the key cognitive psychologists who have concentrated their efforts on cognitive imagery.
67 Kosslyn, *Image and Brain*, 292.
68 Kosslyn, *Image and Brain*, 286.
69 Kosslyn, *Image and Brain*, 310.
70 Kosslyn, *Image and Brain*, 310.
71 Deleuze, *Difference & Repetition*, 82.
72 Roger N. Shepard and Lynne A. Cooper were two of the more prominent researchers in this area.
73 Jacqueline Metzler and Roger N. Shepard, 'Transformational Studies of the Internal Representation of Three-Dimensional Objects'. In *Mental Images and Their Transformations*, eds. Roger N. Shepard and Lynn A. Cooper (Cambridge: MIT Press, 1982).
74 Baddeley, *Working Memory*, 69.
75 Kosslyn, *Image and Brain*, 353.
76 Kosslyn, *Image and Brain*, 292.
77 Wells, *Understanding Animation*, 80.
78 Kosslyn, *Image and Brain*, 292.
79 Kosslyn, *Image and Brain*, 310.
80 Baddeley, *Working Memory.*

81 Rescher, *Process Philosophical Deliberations*, 2–5.
82 Deleuze, *Cinema 2*, 20.
83 Clark, *Being There*, 29.
84 Cornoldi et al., 'Memory and Imagery: A Visual Trace Is Not a Mental Image'. In *Theories of Memory Volume II*, eds. Martin A. Conway et al. (Hove: Psychology Press, 1998), 107.
85 There remains some debate as to in what order our visual perceptions interact with different conceptual areas of the brain, though some have asserted that the visual perception information first interacts with information available in our working memory, which in turn interacts with our long-term memory. Robert Logie, however, has suggested that our visual perceptions *first* interact directly with our long-term memory and *then* engage with our working memory. (Logie, *Visuo-Spatial Working Memory*, 126–28.) In either case, our working memory and our long-term memory serve to augment, amplify and even modify our visual perception information.
86 Kosslyn, *Image and Brain*, 53.
87 Kosslyn, *Image and Brain*, 76.
88 Clark, *Being There*, 28.
89 Clark, *Being There*, 29.
90 Zeki, *Inner Vision*, 66.
91 Clark, *Being There*, 149.
92 Kosslyn et al., *The Case for Mental Imagery*, 137.
93 Kosslyn, *Image and Brain*, 308.
94 Kosslyn, *Image and Brain*, 286.
95 R. A. Finke, *Creative Imagery: Discoveries and Inventions in Visualization* (Hillsdale, NJ: Erlbaum, 1990), 73.
96 Kosslyn, *Image and Brain*, 287.
97 Zeki, *Inner Vision*, 66.
98 Cited in Richardson, *Imagery*, 156.
99 Kosslyn, *Image and Brain*, 370.
100 Cornoldi et al., 'Memory and Imagery', 107.
101 Draaisma, *Why Life Speeds up as You Get Older*, 56.
102 Metzler and Shepard, 'Transformational Studies', 35–37.
103 Peter E. Morris and Michael Gruneberg, *Theoretical Aspects of Memory*, 2nd ed. (London: Routledge, 1994).
104 Hegarty, 'Mental Animation', 1084.
105 Bergson, *Matter and Memory*, 81.
106 Logie, *Visuo-Spatial Working Memory*, 126–28.
107 Bergson, *Matter and Memory*, 148.
108 Rescher, *Process Philosophy*, 22.
109 Bergson, *Time and Free Will*, 101.
110 Kosslyn, *Image and Brain*, 309.
111 Noel Carroll, *The Philosophy of Motion Pictures* (Oxford: Blackwell Publishing, 2008), 149.
112 Manuel de Vega et al. 'The Interface between Language and Visuo-Spatial Representations'. In *Imagery, Language and Visuo-Spatial Thinking*, eds. Michel Denis et al. (Philadelphia, PA: Psychology Press, 2001), 123.
113 Whitehead, *Modes of Thought*, 32.

114 U. Neisser and N. Kerr, 'Changing Conceptions of Imagery'. In *The Function and Nature of Imagery*, ed. P. W. Sheehan (New York: Academic Press, 1972).
115 Wells, *Understanding Animation*, 122.
116 Andrew Crisell, *Understanding Radio*, 2nd ed. (London and New York: Routledge, 1994), 146.
117 Crisell, *Understanding Radio*, 144.
118 Crisell, *Understanding Radio*, 160.
119 Crisell, *Understanding Radio*, 160.
120 Crisell, *Understanding Radio*, 48.
121 Crisell, *Understanding Radio*, 48.
122 Crisell, *Understanding Radio*, 47.
123 Solomon, *The History of Animation*, 216.
124 Baddeley, 'Working Memory and Conscious Awareness'.
125 Olu Taiwo, 'The Dance of the Return Beat: Performing the Animate Universe'. In *The Handbook of Contemporary Animism*, ed. Graham Harvey (Durham: Acumen, 2013), 491.
126 Schnotz and Lowe, 'A Unified View of Learning', 325, 326.
127 Deleuze, *Difference & Repetition*, 70.
128 Bjorn B. de Koning et al., 'Attention Cueing as a Means to Enhance Learning from an Animation'. *Applied Cognitive Psychology* 21, no. 6 (2007): 735.
129 Mary Hegarty et al. 'The Roles of Mental Animations and External Animations in Understanding Mechanical Systems'. *Cognition and Instruction* 2, no. 4 (2003): 328.
130 Sarah Kriz and Mary Hegarty, 'Top-down and Bottom-up Influences on Learning from Animations'. *International Journal of Human-Computer Studies* 65, no. 11 (2007): 911–30.
131 de Koning et al., 'Attention Cueing', 736.

Chapter 4

1 Rescher, *Imagining Irreality*, 76.
2 McCloud, *Understanding Comics*, 29.
3 Jenkins, *Special Affects*, 118.
4 Bergson, *Matter and Memory*.
5 Deleuze, *Cinema 2*.
6 Bergson, *Matter and Memory*, 82.
7 Bergson, *Matter and Memory*, 81.
8 However, this is not entirely true, as some interpolation of movement occurred during the translation process.
9 Raymond A. Mar et al., 'Detecting Agency from the Biological Motion of Veridical versus Animated Agents'. *SCAN* 2, no. 3 (2007): 204.
10 Mar et al., 'Detecting Agency from the Biological Motion', 204.
11 Buchan, *The Quay Brothers*, 117.
12 Keith Oatley, 'How Cues on the Screen Prompt Emotions in the Mind'. In *Psychocinematics: Exploring Cognition at the Movies*, ed. Arthur P. Shimamura (London: Oxford University Press, 2013), 272.

13 Oatley, 'How Cues on the Screen Prompt Emotions', 271.
14 Oatley, 'How Cues on the Screen Prompt Emotions', 272.
15 Naoyuki Osaka et al., 'Effect of Intentional Bias on Agency Attribution of Animated Motion: An Event-Related fMRI Study'. *PLOS ONE* 7, no. 11 (2012): 2.
16 Osaka et al., 'Effect of Intentional Bias on Agency Attribution', 5.
17 Osaka et al., 'Effect of Intentional Bias on Agency Attribution', 6.
18 Crafton, *Shadow of a Mouse*, 23.
19 Crafton, *Shadow of a Mouse*, 36.
20 Crafton, *Shadow of a Mouse*, 52.
21 Torben Grodal and Mette Kramer, 'Film, Neuroaesthetics, and Empathy'. In *An Introduction to Neuroaesthetics: The Neuroscientific Approach to Aesthetic Experience, Artistic Creativity, and Arts Appreciation*, ed. Jon O. Lauring (Copenhagen: Museum Tusculanum Press, 2014), 272, 273.
22 Grodal and Kramer, 'Film, Neuroaesthetics, and Empathy', 273.
23 Grodal and Kramer, 'Film, Neuroaesthetics, and Empathy', 275.
24 I also experienced this effect during multiple cinematic viewings of *The Good Dinosaur.* On each occasion I was surrounded by viewers (both young and old) who had been overcome with emotion, and who were sobbing irrepressibly.
25 Piotr Winkielman, Kent C. Berridge and Julia L. Wilbarger. 'Unconscious Affective Reactions to Masked Happy versus Angry Faces Influence Consumption Behavior and Judgments of Value'. *Personality and Social Psychology Bulletin* 31, no. 1 (2005): 122.
26 Grodal and Kramer, 'Film, Neuroaesthetics, and Empathy', 278.
27 Grodal and Kramer, 'Film, Neuroaesthetics, and Empathy', 284.
28 First made famous in the feature film *Avatar* (James Cameron 2009), and further improved in such films as *Dawn of the Planet of the Apes* (Matt Reeves, 2014).
29 Gaut, *A Philosophy of Cinematic Art*, 139–41.
30 Wells, *Understanding Animation*, 90.
31 Buchan, *The Quay Brothers*, 96.
32 Buchan, *The Quay Brothers*, 87.
33 Anderson, *The Making of Fantastic Mr. Fox*, 31.
34 Anderson, *The Making of Fantastic Mr. Fox*, 164.
35 Anderson, *The Making of Fantastic Mr. Fox*, 31.
36 Buchan, *The Quay Brothers*, 91.
37 Masahiro Mori, 'The Uncanny Valley'. *IEEE Robotics & Automation Magazine* 19, no. 2 (2012): 98–100.
38 Saint John Walker, 'A Quick Walk through Uncanny Valley'. In *Modes of Spectating*, eds. Alison Oddey and Christine White (Bristol: Intellect, 2009), 32.
39 Thierry Chaminade et al., 'Anthropomorphism Influences Perception of Computer-Animated Characters'. *SCAN* 2, no. 3 (2007): 206–16.
40 Chaminade et al., 'Anthropomorphism Influences Perception', 207.
41 Walker, 'A Quick Walk through Uncanny Valley', 34.
42 Lisa Purse, *Digital Imaging in Popular Cinema* (Edinburgh: Edinburgh University Press, 2013), 61.

43 Jérémie Noyer, 'Madame Tutli-Putli versus The Crazy Locomotive'. http://animatedviews.com/2008/madame-tutli-putli-vs-the-crazy-locomotive/, accessed 10 December 2015.
44 Paul Wells, *Scriptwriting*, Basics Animation (Switzerland: AVA Publishing, 2007), 27.
45 See Max E. Butterfield, Sarah E. Hill and Charles G. Lord. 'Mangy Mutt or Furry Friend? Anthropomorphism Promotes Animal Welfare'. *Journal of Experimental Social Psychology* 48, no. 4 (2012): 957–60; Kim-Pong Tam, Sau-Lai Lee and Melody Manchi Chao. 'Saving Mr. Nature: Anthropomorphism Enhances Connectedness to and Protectiveness toward Nature'. *Journal of Experimental Social Psychology* 49, 3 (2013): 514–21.
46 Paul Wells, *The Animated Bestiary: Animals, Cartoons, and Culture* (London: Rutgers University Press, 2009), 105.
47 Wells, *The Animated Bestiary*, 105.
48 Wells, *Scriptwriting*, 27.
49 Wells, *The Animated Bestiary*.
50 Wells, *The Animated Bestiary*, 149.
51 Jenkins, *Special Affects*, 137.
52 Gilles Deleuze and Felix Guattari, *What Is Philosophy?* (New York: Columbia University Press, 1994), 109.
53 Deleuze and Guattari, *A Thousand Plateaus*, 258.
54 For more on the specific subject of anthropomorphic cacti, see Dan Torre, *Cactus* (London: Reaktion Books, 2017), 98–127.
55 For some further reading, see Jan Simons and Jesper Juul.
56 Sicart, *Beyond Choices*, 34.
57 Sicart, *Beyond Choices*, 45.
58 Jesper Juul, 'Perspective'. In *Debugging Game History, A Critical Lexicon*, eds. Henry Lowood and Raiford Guins (Cambridge, MA: MIT Press, 2016), 351.
59 Dennis Deninger, *Sports on Television: The How and Why behind What You See* (New York: Routledge, 2012), 1.
60 Jan Simons, 'Narrative, Games, and Theory'. *Game Studies: The International Journal of Computer Game Research* 7, no. 1 (August 2007). http://gamestudies.org/0701/articles/simons, accessed 5 September 2014.
61 Meades, *Understanding Counterplay in Video Games*, 10. However, the concept of 'counterplay' is not limited to simply manipulating the standard control mechanisms of a game and can also involve much more drastic manipulations, for example, modifying the game's computer code.

Chapter 5

1 John Hubley and Zachary Schwartz, 'Animation Learns a New Language'. *Hollywood Quarterly* 1, no. 4 (1946): 360.
2 Paul Ward, 'Animated Interactions: Animation Aesthetics and the World of the 'Interactive' Documentary'. In *Animated 'Worlds'*, ed. Suzanne Buchan (London: John Libbey, 2006), 114.

3 Lutz, *Animated Cartoons*, 256.
4 Marey, *Movement*, 312.
5 Annabelle Honess Roe, *Animated Documentary* (New York: Palgrave Macmillan, 2013), 171.
6 Roe, *Animated Documentary*, 4.
7 Robert Stam et al., *New Vocabularies in Film Semiotics: Structuralism, Post-Structuralism, and Beyond* (London: Routledge, 1992), 5. This system has been widely adapted to film studies. See Peter Wollen, *Signs and Meaning in the Cinema* (1972); Robert Stam et al., *New Vocabularies in Film Semiotics: Structuralism, Post-structuralism and Beyond* (1992); and Laura Mulvey's, *Death at 24x per Second* (2006). It is also well entrenched in the area of documentary studies. See John Corner's, *The Art of Record: A Critical Introduction to Documentary* (Manchester: Manchester University Press, 1996); Philip Rosen, *Change Mummified: Cinema, Historicity, Theory* (Minneapolis: University of Minnesota Press, 2001); and Michael Renov's, *The Subject of Documentary* (2004).
8 Charles Sanders Peirce, *Collected Papers of Charles Sanders Peirce, Volume 3: Exact Logic* (Cambridge: Harvard University Press, 1933), 211.
9 Peirce, *Collected Papers, Volume 3*, 211.
10 Peirce, *Collected Papers, Volume 3*, 249.
11 Robert Stam et al., *New Vocabularies in Film Semiotics*, 6.
12 Mary Ann Doane, 'The Indexical and the Concept of Medium Specificity'. *Differences: A Journal of Feminist Cultural Studies* 18, no. 1 (2007): 136.
13 Doane, 'The Indexical and the Concept of Medium Specificity', 144.
14 Doane, 'The Indexical and the Concept of Medium Specificity', 144.
15 Doane, *The Emergence of Cinematic Time*, 92.
16 In her discussion of medium specificity, Doane, 'The Indexical and the Concept of Medium Specificity' almost exclusively considers the photochemical nature of the film image – disregarding the photo-magnetic nature of analogue video, and ignoring all conceptions of the auditory index.
17 Richard J. Leskosky, 'The Illusion of Reality and the Reality of Illusion in Animated Film'. In *Semiotics 1988*, eds. Terry Prewitt, John Deely and Karen Haworth (New York: University Press of America, 1989), 461.
18 Leskosky, 'The Illusion of Reality', 463.
19 Scott Curtis, 'Early Warner Bros. Cartoons'. In *Sound Theory Sound Practice*, ed. Rick Altman (London: Routledge, 1992), 202.
20 Curtis, 'Early Warner Bros. Cartoons', 202.
21 Crisell, *Understanding Radio*, 2nd ed. (London and New York: Routledge, 1994), 146.
22 Michael Renov, "Animation: Documentary's Imaginary Signifier." Unpublished paper delivered at University of Westminster, 9 December 2004, Unpublished paper emailed to Torre by Renov on 3 May 2005.
23 Roe, *Animated Documentary*, 2.
24 Stephen Prince, 'True Lies: Perceptual Realism, Digital Images, and Film Theory'. *Film Quarterly* 49, no. 3 (1996): 36.
25 Prince, 'True Lies', 37.
26 An 'inclusive disjunction' can be thought of as an overlapping concept containing the many opposing, yet similar qualities of opposing perceptions.

Mullarkey, in fact, sums up Deleuze's overall philosophical approach as an *inclusive disjunction* 'between and/or'. See Mullarkey, *Post-Continental Philosophy*, 13.

27 Peter Hughes, 'From Modernity to Multimedia: The Documentary Project in Contemporary Australia'. In *The Media's Australia*, ed. Hilary Ericksen (Melbourne: The Australian Centre, University of Melbourne, 1996), 81.
28 Nicholas Rescher, *Metaphysics: The Key Issues from a Realistic Perspective* (Amherst, MA: Prometheus Books, 2006b), 21.
29 Rescher, *Metaphysics*, 27.
30 Rescher, *Metaphysics*, 49.
31 Bill Nichols, *Representing Reality: Issues and Concepts in Documentary* (Bloomington: Indiana University Press, 1991), 109.
32 Michael Renov, *Theorizing Documentary* (New York: Routledge, 1993), 26.
33 Keith Beattie, *Documentary Screens: Nonfiction Film and Television* (New York: Palgrave, 2004), 13.
34 Rosen, *Change Mummified*, 259.
35 Nichols, *Representing Reality*, 33.
36 Deleuze, *Cinema 2*, 79.
37 John Grierson, *Grierson on Documentary* (London: Collins, 1946), 80.
38 Grierson, *Grierson on Documentary*, 82.
39 Paul Ward, *Documentary: The Margins of Reality* (London: Wallflower, 2005), 77.
40 Michael Renov, *The Subject of Documentary*, ed. Michael Renov. Vol. 16, Visible Evidence (Minneapolis: University of Minnesota Press, 2004), 21.
41 Bill Nichols, *Representing Reality: Issues and Concepts in Documentary* (Bloomington: Indiana University Press, 1991), 125.
42 Rosen, *Change Mummified*, 232.
43 Whitehead, *Process and Reality*, 168.
44 Whitehead, *Process and Reality*, 168.
45 Rosen, *Change Mummified*, 263.
46 Nichols, *Representing Reality*, 149.
47 Paul Ward, 'Animated Interactions', 120.
48 Wells, *Understanding Animation*.
49 Wells and Hardstaff, *Re-Imagining Animation*, 100.
50 Rosen, *Change Mummified*.
51 However, as the JFK footage has since been so clearly contextualized and widely disseminated over the decades, most viewers should have little trouble understanding it.
52 James M. Moran, 'A Bone of Contention: Documenting the Prehistoric Subject'. In *Collecting Visible Evidence*, eds. Jane M. Gaines and Michael Renov (Minneapolis: University of Minnesota Press, 1999), 270.
53 Mark J. P. Wolf, 'Subjunctive Documentary: Computer Imaging and Simulation'. In *Collecting Visible Evidence*, eds. Jane M. Gaines and Michael Renov (Minneapolis: University of Minnesota Press, 1999), 274.
54 Rescher, *Imagining Irreality*, 265.
55 Rescher, *Imagining Irreality*, 261.
56 Rescher, *Imagining Irreality*, 262.
57 Schnotz and Lowe, 'A Unified View of Learning', 316.

58 Jose van Dijck, 'Picturizing Science: The Science Documentary as Multimedia Spectacle'. *International Journal of Cultural Studies* 9, no. 1 (2006): 14.
59 Brian Winston, *Lies, Damn Lies and Documentaries* (London: BFI Publishing, 2000), 137.
60 van Dijck, 'Picturizing Science', 10.
61 Beattie, *Documentary Screens*, 213.
62 Whitehead, *Process and* Reality, 147.
63 Rescher, *Process Metaphysics*, 29.
64 Steven Johnson, *Emergence: The Connected Lives of Ants, Brains, Cities, and Software* (New York: Scribner, 2001).
65 J. R. Hunter and M. Cox, *Forensic Archaeology: Advances in Theory and Practice* (London: Routledge, 2005).
66 Wolf, 'Subjunctive Documentary', 280.
67 Prince, 'True Lies', 33.
68 Whitehead, *Process and Reality*, 147.
69 Doane, *The Emergence of Cinematic Time*, 92.
70 Renov, 'Animation: Documentary's Imaginary Signifier', 1.
71 Of course, each category could conceivably be further subdivided (or segmented in terms of other conventions); however, these particular categories are capable and most effective in demonstrating the divisible nature of the index.
72 Wolf, 'Subjunctive Documentary', 274.
73 Stella Bruzzi, *New Documentary: A Critical Introduction* (London: Routledge, 2000), 33.
74 Wolf, 'Subjunctive Documentary', 280.
75 Crisell, *Understanding Radio*, 146.
76 See Bruzzi, *New Documentary*; Corner, *The Art of Record.*
77 Bruzzi, *New Documentary*, 40.
78 Ward, *Documentary*, 99.
79 Renov, 'Animation: Documentary's Imaginary Signifier'.
80 Bruzzi, *New Documentary*, 47.
81 Kevin Macdonald and Mark Cousins, *Imagining Reality: The Faber Book of Documentary* (London: Faber and Faber Limited, 1996), 31.
82 Wells, *Understanding Animation*, 76.
83 Emmet, *The Passage of Nature*, 11.
84 Doane, *The Emergence of Cinematic Time*, 22.
85 Paul Willemen, 'Reflections on Digital Imagery: Of Mice and Men'. In *Screen Media: Cinema/Art/Narrative*, eds. Martin Rieser and Andrea Zapp (London: British Film Institute, 2002), 15.
86 Doane, *The Emergence of Cinematic Time*, 94.
87 Rescher, *Process Philosophical Deliberations*, 108.

Chapter 6

1 Lambert Wiesing, *Artificial Presence: Philosophical Studies in Image Theory* (Stanford, CA: Stanford University Press, 2010), 101.
2 Wolf, 'Subjunctive Documentary', 287.

3 Rescher, *Imagining Irreality*, 72.
4 Rescher, *Process Philosophical Deliberations*, 49.
5 Rescher, *Process Philosophical Deliberations*, 49.
6 Hanspeter Pfister et al., 'Visualization in Connectomics'. In *Scientific Visualization Uncertainty, Multifield, Biomedical, and Scalable Visualization*, eds. Charles D. Hansen et al. (Berlin: Springer, 2014), 222.
7 A. Vilanova et al., 'Visual Exploration of Simulated and Measured Blood Flow'. In *Scientific Visualization Uncertainty, Multifield, Biomedical, and Scalable Visualization*, eds. Charles D. Hansen et al. (Berlin: Springer, 2014), 305.
8 Patric Ljung et al., 'Full Body Virtual Autopsies Using a State-of-the-Art Volume Rendering Pipeline'. *IEEE Transactions on Visualization and Computer Graphics* 12, no. 5 (2006): 869.
9 Oliver Grau, *Virtual Art: From Illusion to Immersion* (Cambridge: MIT Press, 2003), 15.
10 'The Game Artists' Guide to Vr'. *3D World*, no. 203 (2016): 41–49.
11 'The World's First 3d Model of an Entire Nation', *Position: The Australasian Magazine of Surveying, Mapping & Geo-Information*, no. 81 (2016): 10.
12 Michael Leyton, *Shape as Memory: A Geometric Theory of Architecture* (Basel, Switzerland: Birkhauser, 2006).
13 Monica L. P. Robbers, 'Blinded by Science: The Social Construction of Reality in Forensic Television Shows and Its Effect on Criminal Jury Trials'. *Criminal Justice Policy Review* 19, no. 1 (2008): 84–102.
14 Robbers, 'Blinded by Science', 88.
15 Lye, *Figures of Motion*, 39.
16 Bergson, *Creative Evolution*, 272.
17 Hunter and Cox, *Forensic Archaeology*.
18 Deleuze, *Difference & Repetition*, 55–56.
19 Mark Klett, 'Three Methods of Presenting Repeat Photographs'. In *Repeat Photography: Methods and Applications in the Natural Sciences*, eds. Robert H. Webb et al. (Washington, DC: Island Press, 2010), 32.
20 George E. Gruell, 'Forward'. In *Repeat Photography: Methods and Applications in the Natural Sciences*, eds. Robert H. Webb et al. (Washington, DC: Island Press, 2010), xix.
21 Klett, 'Three Methods of Presenting Repeat Photographs', 34.
22 Deleuze, *Difference & Repetition*, 51.
23 Flores, 'Stereoscopy, Film and Time-Image', 63.
24 Williams, *The Animator's Survival Kit*, 221.
25 Williams, *The Animator's Survival Kit*, 226.
26 Williams, *The Animator's Survival Kit*, 230.
27 Leyton, *Shape as Memory*, 54.
28 Deleuze, *Difference & Repetition*, 19.
29 Leyton, *Shape as Memory*, 17.
30 Michael Leyton, *The Structure of Paintings* (New York: Springer Wien, 2006), 7.
31 Rescher, *Imagining Irreality*, 7.
32 Rescher, *Imagining Irreality*, 7.
33 Nicholas Rescher, *Induction: An Essay on the Justification of Inductive Reasoning* (Oxford: Basil Blackwell Publisher, 1980), 7.

34 Carl N. Stephan et al., 'Methods of Facial Approximation and Skull-Face Superimposition, with Special Consideration of Method Development in Australia'. In *Forensic Approaches to Death, Disaster and Abuse*, ed. Marc Oxenham (Sydney: Australian Academic Press, 2008), 133.
35 Charles Sanders Peirce, *Collected Papers of Charles Sanders Peirce, Volume 2* (Cambridge: Harvard University Press, 1932), 375.
36 Rescher, *Induction*, 7.
37 Rescher, *Induction*, 7.
38 Nicholas Rescher, *Cognitive Pragmatism: The Theory of Knowledge in Pragmatic Perspective* (Pittsburgh, PA: University of Pittsburgh Press, 2001), 230.
39 Rescher, *Process Philosophical Deliberations*, 52.
40 Wolf, 'Subjunctive Documentary'.

Chapter 7

1 William Malpas, *The Art of Andy Goldsworthy, Complete Works Special Edition* (Kent, MI: Crescent Moon, 2004), 38.
2 Buchan, *The Quay Brothers*, 84.
3 John 'Hobart' Hughes, interview with author (Sydney 2005).
4 Darcy Prendergast, email correspondence with author (2011).
5 Andy Goldsworthy, *Stone* (New York: Harry N. Abrams, 1994), 95.
6 Barry Purves, *Stop Motion (Basics Animation 04)* (Switzerland: AVA, 2010), 56.
7 A re-working by Dan Torre of Purves above quotation.
8 Tim Edensor, *Industrial Ruins: Space, Aesthetics and Materiality* (Oxford: Berg, 2005), 87.
9 Edensor, *Industrial Ruins*, 90.
10 Darcy Prendergast, email correspondence with author (2011).
11 Rescher, *Imagining Irreality*, 75.
12 Rescher, *Imagining Irreality*, 71.
13 George Griffin has used the term 'concrete animation' in his discussions of flipbooks and other physical forms of animation.
14 Wells, *Understanding Animation*, 98.
15 Whitehead, *Modes of Thought*, 124.
16 Lamarre, *The Anime Machine*, 124.
17 Whitehead, *Process and Reality*, 67.
18 Gilles Deleuze, *The Fold* (Minneapolis: University of Minnesota Press, 1992), *passim*.
19 Greg Lynn, *Animate Form* (New York: Princeton Architectural Press, 1999), 8; cf. Paul A. Harris, 'To See with the Mind and Think through the Eye: Deleuze, Folding Architecture, and Simon Rodia's Watts Towers'. In *Deleuze and Space*, eds. Ian Buchanan and Gregg Lambert (Edinburgh: Edinburgh University Press, 2005) for more on Deleuze's concept of the fold and its application to architecture.
20 Bruce H. Robinson, Kim R. Reisenbichler, James C. Hunt and Steven H. D. Haddock, 'Light Production by the Arm Tips of the Deep-Sea Cephalopod Vampyroteuthis Infernalis'. *Biological Bulletin*, no. 205 (2003): 102–109.

21 Crafton, *Shadow of a Mouse*, 191.
22 Crafton, *Shadow of a Mouse*, 183.
23 Crafton, *Shadow of a Mouse*, 190.
24 Pranav A. Bhounsule and Katsu Yamane, 'Iterative Learning Control for High-Fidelity Tracking of Fast Motions on Entertainment Humanoid Robots', *13th IEEE-RAS International Conference on Humanoid Robots (Humanoids)* (Piscataway, NJ: IEEE Press, 2013), 443.
25 See A.J.N. van Breemen. 'Animation Engine for Believable Interactive User-Interface Robots' in *Proceedings of 2004 IEEE/RSJ International Conference on Intelligent Robots and Systems*, 28 September–2 October 2004, Sendal, Japan; M. Saerbeck and C. Bartneck, 'Perception of Affect Elicited by Robot Motion'. In *HRI 10 – Proceedings of the 5th ACM/IEEE International Conference on Human-robot Interaction* (Piscataway, NJ: IEEE Press, 2010); Tiago Ribeiro, and Ana Paiva, 'The Illusion of Robotic Life: Principles and Practices of Animation for Robots'. *Paper presented at the Human Robot Interaction* (Boston, MA, 2012); Fatemeh Maleki and Zeinab Farhoudi, 'Making Humanoid Robots More Acceptable Based on the Study of Robot Characters in Animation'. *International Journal of Robotics and Automation* 4, no. 1 (2015): 70.
26 Ribeiro and Paiva, 'The Illusion of Robotic Life', 383.
27 Ribeiro and Paiva, 'The Illusion of Robotic Life', 384.
28 Maleki and Farhoudi, 'Making Humanoid Robots More Acceptable Based on the Study of Robot Characters in Animation', 70.
29 Sandro Hauri et al., 'Multi-Robot Formation Control Via a Real-Time Drawing Interface'. In *Field and Service Robotics, Springer Tracts in Advanced Robotics 92*, eds. K. Yoshida and S. Tadokoro (Berlin: Springer-Verlag, 2014).
30 J. Storrs Hall, *Nanofuture: What's Next for Nanotechnology* (New York: Prometheus Books, 2005), 189.

BIBLIOGRAPHY

Alexander, Samuel. *Space Time and Deity, Volume 1*. London: Macmillan, 1920.
Anderson, Joseph D. *The Reality of Illusion: An Ecological Approach to Cognitive Film Theory*. Carbondale: Southern Illinois University Press, 1996.
Andrade, Jackie. 'An Introduction to Working Memory'. In *Working Memory in Perspective*, edited by Jackie Andrade. Hove: Psychology, 2001.
Andrillon, Thomas, Yuval Nir, Chiara Cirelli, Giulio Tononi, and Itzhak Fried. 'Single-Neuron Activity and Eye Movements during Human Rem Sleep and Awake Vision'. *Nature Communications* 6 (August 2015).
ASIFA. 'Disney Recalls over 3 Million Videos'. *Newsletter of the San Francisco International Film Association* (February 1999).
Baddeley, Alan. 'Working Memory and Conscious Awareness'. In *Theories of Memory*, edited by A. F. Collins, Susan E. Gathercole, Martin A. Conway and Peter Morris. Hillsdale, NJ: Erlbaum Associates, 1993.
Baddeley, Alan. *Working Memory, Thought and Action*. Oxford: Oxford University Press, 2007.
Baddeley, Alan, and Jackie Andrade. 'Working Memory and Consciousness: An Empirical Approach'. In *Theories of Memory Volume 2*, edited by Martin A. Conway Susan E. Gathercole and Cesare Cornoldi. Hove: Psychology Press, Ltd., 1998.
Baddeley, Alan, and G. Hitcham. 'Working Memory'. In *Recent Advances in Learning and Motivation*, edited by G. A. Bower. New York: Henry Holt, 1974.
Ballard, Dana. 'Animate Vision'. *Artificial Intelligence* 48, no. 1 (1991): 57–86.
Beattie, Keith. *Documentary Screens: Nonfiction Film and Television*. New York: Palgrave, 2004.
Beckerman, Howard. *Animation: The Whole Story*. New York: Allworth Press, 2003.
Benezra, N. 'William Kentridge: Drawings for Projection'. In *William Kentridge*, edited by M. Sittenfeld. New York: Harry N. Abrams, 2001.
Bergson, Henri. *Creative Evolution*. New York: Henry Holt, 1911.
Bergson, Henri. *Time and Free Will: An Essay on the Immediate Data of Consciousness*. New York: Dover Publications, 1913/2001.
Bergson, Henri. *Matter and Memory*. New York: Zone Books, 1988.
Bhounsule, Pranav A., and Katsu Yamane. 'Iterative Learning Control for High-Fidelity Tracking of Fast Motions on Entertainment Humanoid Robots'. *Paper Presented at the 13th IEEE-RAS International Conference on Humanoid Robots (Humanoids)*. Piscataway, NJ: IEEE Press, 2013.
Bierman, James H. 'Disney's "America Sings"'. *The Drama Review* 20, no. 2 (1976): 63–72.

Bordwell, David. 'Film, Emotion and Genre'. In *Philosophy of Film and Motion Pictures: An Anthology*, edited by Noel Carroll and Jinhee Choi. Oxford: Blackwell Publishing, 2006.

Bordwell, David, and Kristin Thompson. *Film Art an Introduction (Eighth Edition)*. New York: McGraw Hill, 2008.

Braun, Marta. *Picturing Time: The Work of Etienne-Jules Marey (1830–1904)*. Chicago: The University of Chicago Press, 1992.

Broadfoot, Keith, and Rex Butler. 'The Illusion of Illusion'. In *The Illusion of Life*, edited by Alan Cholodenko. Sydney: Power Publications, 1991.

Brophy, Philip. *100 Anime*, Bfi Screen Guides. London: BFI Publishing, 2005.

Bruzzi, Stella. *New Documentary: A Critical Introduction*. London: Routledge, 2000.

Buchan, Suzanne. 'The Animated Spectator: Watching the Quay Brothers' "Worlds"'. In *Animated Worlds*, edited by Suzanne Buchan. London: John Libbey Publishing, 2006.

Buchan, Suzanne. 'The Animated Fulcrum'. In *Animated Painting*, edited by Betti-Sue Hertz. San Diego, CA: San Diego Museum of Art, 2007.

Buchan, Suzanne. *The Quay Brothers: Into a Metaphysical Playroom*. Minneapolis: University of Minnesota Press, 2011.

Bukatman, Scott. 'Comics and the Critique of Chronophotography, or "He Never Knew When It Was Coming!"'. *Animation: An Interdisciplinary Journal* 1, no. 1 (2006): 83–103.

Butterfield, Max E., Sarah E. Hill, and Charles G. Lord. 'Mangy Mutt or Furry Friend? Anthropomorphism Promotes Animal Welfare'. *Journal of Experimental Social Psychology* 48, no. 4 (2012): 957–60.

Bynum, Caroline Walker. *Metamorphosis and Identity*. New York: Zone Books, 2001.

Carroll, Noel. *The Philosophy of Motion Pictures*. Oxford: Blackwell Publishing, 2008.

Chaminade, Thierry, Jessica Hodgins, and Mitsuo Kawato. 'Anthropomorphism Influences Perception of Computer-Animated Characters'. *SCAN* 2, no. 3 (2007): 206–16.

Chatman, S. 'What Novels Can Do that Films Can't (and Vice Versa)'. In *On Narrative*, edited by W. Mitchell. Chicago: University of Chicago Press, 1981.

Chion, Michel. *Audio-Vision: Sound on Screen*. Translated by Claudia Gorbman. New York: Columbia University Press, 1994.

Cholodenko, Alan, ed. *The Illusion of Life: Essays on Animation*. Sydney: Power Publications, 1991.

Cholodenko, Alan. 'Still Photography?'. *Afterimage* 32, no. 5 (2005): 5–7.

Cholodenko, Alan. 'Introduction'. In *The Illusion of Life II*, edited by Alan Cholodenko. Sydney: Power Publications, 2007.

Chomsky, Noam. *Syntactic Structures*. New York: Moulton and Co., 1957.

Chow, Kenny. 'The Spiritualfunctional Loop: Animation Redefined in the Digital Age'. *Animation: An Interdisciplinary Journal* 4, no. 1 (2009): 77–89.

Christian, William. *An Interpretation of Whitehead's Metaphysics*. Westport, CT: Greenwood Press, 1959.

Clark, Andy. *Being There: Putting Brain, Body, and World Together Again*. Cambridge, MA: MIT Press, 1997.

Clark, Tim. 'A Whiteheadian Chaosmos? Process Philosophy from a Deleuzean Perspective'. In *Process and Difference: Between Cosmological and Poststructuralist Postmodernisms*, edited by Catherine Keller and Anne Daniell. New York: State University of New York Press, 2002.

Cohen, Gillian. *The Psychology of Cognition*. New York: Academic Press, 1977.

Corner, John. *The Art of Record: A Critical Introduction to Documentary*. Manchester: Manchester University Press, 1996.

Cornoldi, Cesare, Rossana De Beni, Fiorella Giusberti, and Manfredo Massironi. 'Memory and Imagery: A Visual Trace Is Not a Mental Image'. In *Theories of Memory Volume II*, edited by Martin A. Conway, Susan E. Gathercole and Cesare Cornoldi. Hove: Psychology Press, 1998.

Cowan, Michael. *Walter Ruttmann and the Cinema of Multiplicity: Avant-Garde – Advertising – Modernity*. Amsterdam: Amsterdam University Press, 2014.

Crafton, Donald. *Before Mickey: The Animated Film 1898–1928*. Cambridge, MA: MIT Press, 1982.

Crafton, Donald. *Shadow of a Mouse: Performance, Belief, and World-Making in Animation*. Berkeley: University of California Press, 2013.

Crisell, Andrew. *Understanding Radio*, 2nd ed. London and New York: Routledge, 1994.

Culhane, Shamus. *Animation from Script to Screen*. New York: St. Martin's Griffin, 1988.

Curtis, Scott. 'Early Warner Bros. Cartoons'. In *Sound Theory Sound Practice*, edited by Rick Altman. London: Routledge, 1992.

Daniell, Anne. 'Figuring Subjectivity for Grounded Transformations: A Critical Comparison of Rosi Braidotti's and John Cobb's Figurations'. In *Process and Difference: Between Cosmological and Poststructuralist Postmodernisms*, edited by Catherine Keller and Anne Daniell. Albany: State University of New York Press, 2002.

de Koning, Bjorn B., Huib K. Tabbers, Remy M. J. P. Rikers, and Fred Paas. 'Attention Cueing as a Means to Enhance Learning from an Animation'. *Applied Cognitive Psychology* 21, no. 6 (2007): 731–46.

DeLanda, Manuel. *Intensive Science & Virtual Philosophy*. New York: Continuum, 2002.

Deleuze, Gilles. *The Fold*. New York: The Free Press, 1978.

Deleuze, Gilles. *Cinema 1: The Movement-Image*. Translated by Hugh Tomlinson and Barbara Habberjam. Minneapolis: University of Minnesota Press, 1986.

Deleuze, Gilles. *Cinema 2: The Time-Image*. Translated by Hugh Tomlinson and Robert Galeta. Minneapolis: University of Minnesota Press, 1989.

Deleuze, Gilles. *Bergsonism*. Translated by Hugh Tomlinson and Barbara Habberjam. New York: Zone Books, 1991.

Deleuze, Gilles. *Difference & Repetition*. Translated by Paul Patton. New York: Columbia University Press, 1994.

Deleuze, Gilles and Felix Guattari. *A Thousand Plateaus: Capitalism and Schizophrenia*. Translated by Brian Massumi. Minneapolis: University of Minnesota Press, 1987.

Deleuze, Gilles, and Felix Guattari. *What Is Philosophy?* Translated by H. Tomlinson and G. Burchell. New York: Columbia University Press, 1994.

Deninger, Dennis. *Sports on Television: The How and Why behind What You See.* New York: Routledge, 2012.
de Vega, Manuel, Marguerite Cocude, Michel Denis, Maria Jose Rodrigo, and Hubert D. Zimmer. 'The Interface between Language and Visuo-Spatial Representations'. In *Imagery, Language and Visuo-Spatial Thinking*, edited by Michel Denis, Cesare Cornoldo, Manuel De Vega and Johannes EngelKamp. Philadelphia, PA: Psychology Press, 2001.
Dewey, John. *Democracy and Education.* New York: Macmillan, 1916/1961.
Dewey, John. *Experience and Nature.* New York: Dover Publications, 1958.
Dijck, Jose van. 'Picturizing Science: The Science Documentary as Multimedia Spectacle'. *International Journal of Cultural Studies* 9, no. 1 (2006): 5–24.
Doane, Mary Ann. *The Emergence of Cinematic Time: Modernity, Contingency, the Archive.* Cambridge: Harvard University Press, 2002.
Doane, Mary Ann. 'The Indexical and the Concept of Medium Specificity'. *Differences: A Journal of Feminist Cultural Studies* 18, no. 1 (2007): 128–52.
Draaisma, Douwe. *Why Life Speeds Up as You Get Older: How Memory Shapes Our Past.* Cambridge: Cambridge University Press, 2004.
Dulac, Nicolas, and Andre Gaudreault. 'Circularity and Repetition at the Heart of the Attraction'. In *The Cinema of Attractions Reloaded*, edited by Wanda Strauven. Amsterdam: Amsterdam University Press, 2006.
Edensor, Tim. *Industrial Ruins: Space, Aesthetics and Materiality.* Oxford: Berg, 2005.
Eisenstein, Sergai. *Eisenstein Volume 2: Towards a Theory of Montage.* Translated by Michael Glenny. Edited by Michael Glenny and Richard Taylor. London: BFI Publishing, 1938/1991.
Emmet, Dorothy. *The Passage of Nature.* London: Macmillan, 1992.
Engel, Jules. *Los Angeles Art Community: Group Portrait, Jules Engel.* Edited by L. Weschler, M. Zolotow and Interviewers. Los Angeles: The Regents of the University of California, 1985a.
Engel, Jules. *Los Angeles Art Community: Group Portrait, Jules Engel (Lawrence Weschler and Milton Zolotow, Interviewers).* Los Angeles: The Regents of the University of California, 1985b.
Eppink, Jason. 'A Brief History of the Gif (So Far)'. *Journal of Visual Culture* 13, no. 3 (2014): 298–306.
Farrell, Joyce E., and Roger N. Shepard. 'Shape, Orientation, and Apparent Rotational Motion'. In *Mental Images and Their Transformations*, edited by Roger N. Shepard and Lynn A. Cooper. Cambridge, MA: MIT Press, 1981/1986.
Findler, Gerald. *Lightning Cartoons: How to Make Funny Sketches in Five Minutes.* London: W. Foulsham, 1938.
Finke, R. A. *Creative Imagery: Discoveries and Inventions in Visualization.* Hillsdale, NJ: Erlbaum, 1990.
Flores, Teresa Mendes. 'Stereoscopy, Film and Time-Image. An Improbable Encounter: Paz Dos Reis and Chris Marker's Photographic Films'. In *Photography and Cinema: 50 Years of Chris Marker's La Jetee*, edited by Margarida Medeiros, Teresa Mendes Flores and Joana Cunha Leal. Newcastle upon Tyne: Cambridge Scholars Publishing, 2015.
Fordham, Joe. 'Formula for a Universe'. *Cinefex*, no. 114 (2008): 34–53.
Frierson, Michael. *Clay Animation.* New York: Twayne Publishers, 1994.

Fua, Pascal, Ralf Plaenkers, WonSook Lee, and Tom Molet. 'Body Cloning and Body Motion Capture'. In *Handbook of Virtual Humans*, edited by N. Magnenat-Thalmann and D. Thalmann. London: John Wiley & Sons, 2004.

Furniss, Maureen. *Art in Motion: Animation Aesthetics*. London: John Libbey, 1998.

Gallasch, Keith. 'Re-Animating Australian History'. *RealTime Arts* no. 74 (2006): 21.

Gallese, Vittorio. 'Intentional Attunement: The Mirror Neuron System and Its Role in Interpersonal Relations'. http://www.interdisciplines.org/mirror/papers/1, accessed 2 December 2012.

Gambrell, A. 'In Visible Hands: The Work of Stop Motion'. *Animation Practice, Process & Production* 1, no. 1 (2011): 107–29.

'The Game Artists' Guide to VR'. *3D World*, no. 203 (2016): 41–49.

Gathercole, Susan E. 'The Nature and Uses of Working Memory'. In *Theoretical Aspects of Memory*, edited by Peter Morris and Michael Gruneberg. London: Routledge, 1994.

Gaut, Berys. *A Philosophy of Cinematic Art*. Cambridge: Cambridge University Press, 2010.

Goldman, Susan R. 'Animating the Issues for Research on Animation'. In *Learning with Animation*, edited by Richard Lowe and Wolfgang Schnotz. Cambridge: Cambridge University Press, 2008.

Goldsworthy, Andy. *Stone*. New York: Harry N. Abrams, 1994.

Grau, Oliver. *Virtual Art: From Illusion to Immersion*. Cambridge: MIT Press, 2003.

Greenacre, Derek. *Magic Lanterns*. London: Shire Publications, 1999.

Grierson, John. *Grierson on Documentary*. Edited by Forsyth Hardy. London: Collins, 1946.

Griffin, George. 'Take the B Train: Reconstructing the Proto-Cinematic Apparatus'. In *Pervasive Animation*, edited by Suzanne Buchan. London: Routledge, 2013.

Grodal, Torben. *Moving Pictures: A New Theory of Film Genres, Feelings, and Cognition*. Oxford: Clarendon Press, 1997.

Grodal, Torben, and Mette Kramer. 'Film, Neuroaesthetics, and Empathy'. In *An Introduction to Neuroaesthetics: The Neuroscientific Approach to Aesthetic Experience, Artistic Creativity, and Arts Appreciation*, edited by Jon O. Lauring. Copenhagen: Museum Tusculanum Press, 2014.

Gruell, George E. 'Forward'. In *Repeat Photography: Methods and Applications in the Natural Sciences*, edited by Robert H. Webb, Diane E. Boyer and Raymond M. Turner. Washington, DC: Island Press, 2010.

Gunning, Tom. 'The Cinema of Attraction[S]: Early Film, Its Spectator and the Avant-Garde'. In *Film and Theory: An Anthology*, edited by Robert Stam and Toby Miller, 229–35. Oxford: Blackwell, 1986/2000.

Gunning, Tom. '"Now You See It, Now You Don't": The Temporality of the Cinema of Attractions'. *Velvet Light Trap* Fall, no. 32 (1993): 3.

Gunning, Tom. 'Animating the Instant: The Secret Symmetry between Animation and Photography'. In *Animating Film Theory*, edited by Karen Beckman. Durham and London: Duke University Press, 2014.

Halas, John. *Computer Animation*. New York: Hastings House, 1974.

Hall, J. Storrs. *Nanofuture: What's Next for Nanotechnology*. New York: Prometheus Books, 2005.

Hanley, Richard. 'No End in Sight: Causal Loops in Philosophy, Physics and Fiction'. *Synthese* 141, no. 1 (2004): 123–52.

Harris, Paul A. 'To See with the Mind and Think through the Eye: Deleuze, Folding Architecture, and Simon Rodia's Watts Towers'. In *Deleuze and Space*, edited by Ian Buchanan and Gregg Lambert. Edinburgh: Edinburgh University Press, 2005.

Hauri, Sandro, Javier Alonso-Mora, Andreas Breitenmoser, Roland Siegwart, and Paul Beardsley. 'Multi-Robot Formation Control via a Real-Time Drawing Interface'. In *Field and Service Robotics, Springer Tracts in Advanced Robotics* 92, edited by K. Yoshida and S. Tadokoro. Berlin: Springer-Verlag, 2014.

Hegarty, Mary. 'Mental Animation: Inferring Motion from Static Displays of Mechanical Systems'. *Journal of Experimental Psychology: Learning, Memory and Cognition* 18, no. 5 (1992): 1084–102.

Hegarty, Mary, Sarah Kriz, and Christina Cate. 'The Roles of Mental Animations and External Animations in Understanding Mechanical Systems'. *Cognition and Instruction* 2, no. 4 (2003): 325–60.

Hosea, Brigitta. 'Drawing Animation'. *Animation: An Interdisciplinary Journal* 5, no. 3 (2010): 353–67.

Hubley, John, and Zachary Schwartz. 'Animation Learns a New Language'. *Hollywood Quarterly* 1, no. 4 (1946): 360–63.

Hughes, John. 'Hobart', Interview, 2005.

Hughes, Peter. 'From Modernity to Multimedia: The Documentary Project in Contemporary Australia'. In *The Media's Australia*, edited by Hilary Ericksen. Melbourne: The Australian Centre, University of Melbourne, 1996.

Hunter, J. R., and M. Cox. *Forensic Archaeology: Advances in Theory and Practice*. London: Routledge, 2005.

Jenkins, Eric S. *Special Affects: Cinema, Animation and the Translation of Consumer Care*. Edinburgh: Edinburgh University Press, 2014.

Johnson, Steven. *Emergence: The Connected Lives of Ants, Brains, Cities, and Software*. New York: Scribner, 2001.

Johnston, Andrew R. 'Signatures of Motion: Len Lye's Scratch Films and the Energy of the Line'. In *Animating Film Theory*, edited by Karen Beckman. Durham and London: Duke University Press, 2014.

Juul, Jesper. 'Perspective'. In *Debugging Game History, A Critical Lexicon*, edited by Henry Lowood and Raiford Guins. Cambridge, MA: MIT Press, 2016.

Keller, Catherine. 'Process and Chaosmos: The Whiteheadian Fold in the Discourse of Difference'. In *Process and Difference: Between Cosmological and Poststructuralist Postmodernisms*, edited by Catherine Keller and Anne Daniell. New York: State University of New York Press, 2002.

Kitagawa, Midori, and Brian Windsor. *Mocap for Artists: Workflow and Techniques for Motion Capture*. Oxford: Focal Press, 2008.

Klein, Norman. 'Animation and Animorphs'. In *Meta-Morphing: Visual Transformation and the Culture of Quick-Change*, edited by Vivian Sobchack. Minneapolis: University of Minnesota Press, 2000.

Klett, Mark. 'Three Methods of Presenting Repeat Photographs'. In *Repeat Photography: Methods and Applications in the Natural Sciences*, edited by Robert H. Webb, Diane E. Boyer and Raymond M. Turner. Washington, DC: Island Press, 2010.

Kosslyn, Stephen M. *Image and Brain: The Resolution of the Imagery Debate*. Cambridge, MA: A Bradford Book, MIT Press, 1994.

Kosslyn, Stephen M., William L. Thompson, and Giorgio Ganis. *The Case for Mental Imagery*. Oxford: Oxford University Press, 2006.

Kriz, Sarah, and Mary Hegarty. 'Top-Down and Bottom-Up Influences on Learning from Animations'. *International Journal of Human-Computer Studies* 65, no. 11 (2007): 911–30.

Lamarre, Thomas. *The Anime Machine: A Media Theory of Animation*. Minneapolis: University of Minnesota Press, 2009.

Lamarre, Thomas. 'Coming to Life: Cartoon Animals and Natural Philosophy'. In *Animating Film Theory*, edited by Karen Beckman. Durham and London: Duke University Press, 2014.

Lamarre, Thomas. 'From Animation to Anime: Drawing Movements and Moving Drawings'. *Japan Forum* 14, no. 2 (2002): 329–67.

Langford, Martha. 'Introduction'. In *Image & Imagination*. Montreal: McGill-Queen's University Press, 2005.

Layton, R. *Australian Rock Art: A New Synthesis*. Cambridge: Cambridge University Press, 1992.

Leskosky, Richard J. 'The Illusion of Reality and the Reality of Illusion in Animated Film'. In *Semiotics 1988*, edited by Terry Prewitt, John Deely and Karen Haworth. New York: University Press of America, 1989.

Leskosky, Richard J. 'Two-State Animation: The Thaumatrope and Its Spin-Offs'. *Animation Journal* 2, no. 1 (1993): 20–34.

Leslie, Esther. 'Animation's Petrified Unrest'. In *Pervasive Animation*, edited by Suzanne Buchan. London: Routledge, 2013.

Levitan, Eli L. *Handbook of Animation Techniques*. New York: Van Nostrand Reinhold Company, 1979.

Leyton, Michael. *The Structure of Paintings*. New York: Springer Wien, 2006a.

Leyton, Michael. *Shape as Memory: A Geometric Theory of Architecture*. Basel, Switzerland: Birkhauser, 2006b.

Ljung, Patric, Calle Winskog, Anders Persson, Claes Lundström, and Anders Ynnerman. 'Full Body Virtual Autopsies Using a State-of-the-Art Volume Rendering Pipeline'. *IEEE Transactions on Visualization and Computer Graphics* 12, no. 5 (2006).

Logie, Robert H. *Visuo-Spatial Working Memory*. Hove: Lawrence Erlbaum Associates, 1995.

Lord, Peter, and Brian Sibley. *Creating 3D Animation: The Arardman Book of 3D Animation*. London: Harry N. Abrams, 2004.

Lutz, E. G. *Animated Cartoons: How They Are Made, Their Origin and Development*. New York: Charles Scribner's Sons, 1920.

Lye, Len. *Figures of Motion: Len Lye/Selected Writings*. Auckland: Auckland University Press, 1984.

Lynn, Greg. 'Introduction'. In *Animate Form*, edited by Greg Lynn. New York: Princeton Architectural Press, 1999.

Lynn, Greg, ed. *Animate Form*. New York: Princeton Architectural Press, 1999.

Macdonald, Kevin, and Mark Cousins. *Imagining Reality: The Faber Book of Documentary*. London: Faber and Faber Limited, 1996.

MacKay, D. 'Ways of Looking at Perception'. In *Models for the Perception of Speech and Visual Form*, edited by W. Wathen-Dunn. Cambridge, MA: MIT Press, 1967.

Madsen, Roy P. *Animated Film: Concepts, Methods, Uses*. New York: Interland Publishing Inc., 1969.

Maleki, Fatemeh, and Zeinab Farhoudi. 'Making Humanoid Robots More Acceptable Based on the Study of Robot Characters in Animation'. *International Journal of Robotics and Automation* 4, no. 1 (2015): 63–72.

Malpas, William. *The Art of Andy Goldsworthy, Complete Works Special Edition*. Kent: Crescent Moon, 2004.

Mar, Raymond A., William M. Kelley, Todd F. Heatherton, and C. Neil Macrae. 'Detecting Agency from the Biological Motion of Veridical vs. Animated Agents'. *SCAN* 2, no. 3 (2007): 199–205.

Marey, Etienne-Jules *Movement*. New York: D. Appleton and Company, 1895.

Marks, Laura U. *Touch: Sensuous Theory and Multisensory Media*. Minneapolis: University of Minnesota Press, 2002.

Massumi, Brian. *Semblance and Event: Activist Philosophy and the Occurrent Arts*. Boston: MIT Press, 2011.

McCloud, Scott. *Understanding Comics: The Invisible Art*. New York: HarperCollins, 1994.

Meades, Alan F. *Understanding Counterplay in Video Games*. Florence: Taylor and Francis, 2015.

Metzler, Jacqueline, and Roger N. Shepard. 'Transformational Studies of the Internal Representation of Three-Dimensional Objects'. In *Mental Images and Their Transformations*, edited by Roger N. Shepard and Lynn A. Cooper. Cambridge: MIT Press, 1974/1982.

Miller, G. A. 'The Magical Number Seven, Plus or Minus Two: Some Limits on Our Capacity for Processing Information'. *Psychological Review*, 63, no. 2 (1956): 81–97.

Mitchell, W. J. T. *Picture Theory: Essays on Verbal and Visual Representation*. Chicago: University of Chicago Press, 1994.

Moran, James M. 'A Bone of Contention: Documenting the Prehistoric Subject'. In *Collecting Visible Evidence*, edited by Jane M. Gaines and Michael Renov, 255–73. Minneapolis: University of Minnesota Press, 1999.

Mori, Masahiro. 'The Uncanny Valley'. *IEEE Robotics & Automation Magazine* 19, no. 2 (1970/2012): 98–100.

Moritz, William. 'Some Observations on Non-objective and Non-linear Animation'. In *Storytelling in Animation: The Art of the Animated Image*, edited by John Canemaker. Vol. 2. Los Angeles: American Film Institute, 1988, 21.

Morris, Peter E., and Michael Gruneberg, eds. *Theoretical Aspects of Memory*, 2nd ed. London: Routledge, 1994.

Morrison, Julie Bauer, Barbara Tversky, and Mireille Betrancourt. 'Animation: Can It Facilitate?' *International Journal of Human-Computer Studies* 57, no. 4 (2002): 247–62.

Mullarkey, John. *Post-Continental Philosophy*. London: Continuum, 2006.

Mulvey, Laura. *Death at 24x a Second: Stillness and the Moving Image*. London: Reaktion Books Ltd., 2006.

Nathan, David L., and Donald Crafton. 'The Making and Re-Making of Winsor Mccay's Gertie (1914)'. *Animation: An Interdisciplinary Journal* 8, no. 1 (2013): 23–46.

Ndalianis, Angela. 'Special Effects, Morphing Magic, and the 1990s Cinema of Attractions'. In *Meta-Morphing: Visual Transformation and the Culture of Quick-Change*, edited by Vivian Sobchack. Minneapolis: University of Minnesota Press, 2000.

Neisser, U. and N. Kerr. 'Changing Conceptions of Imagery'. In *The Function and Nature of Imagery*, edited by P.W. Sheehan. New York: Academic Press, 1972.

Nichols, Bill. *Representing Reality: Issues and Concepts in Documentary*. Bloomington: Indiana University Press, 1991.

Noake, Roger. *Animation: A Guide to Animated Film Techniques*. London: MacDonald Orbis, 1988.

Noyer, Jérémie. 'Madame Tutli-Putli vs. The Crazy Locomotive'. http://animatedviews.com/2008/madame-tutli-putli-vs-the-crazy-locomotive/, accessed 10 December 2015.

Oatley, Keith. 'How Cues on the Screen Prompt Emotions in the Mind'. In *Psychocinematics: Exploring Cognition at the Movies*, edited by Arthur P. Shimamura. London: Oxford University Press, 2013.

Ord-Hume, Arthur W. *Clockwork Music*. London: George Allen and Unwin, 1973.

Osaka, Naoyuki, Takashi Ikeda, and Mariko Osaka. 'Effect of Intentional Bias on Agency Attribution of Animated Motion: An Event-Related fMRI Study'. *PLOS ONE* 7, no. 11 (2012): 2.

Paas, Fred, A. Renkl, and J. Sweller. 'Cognitive Load Theory and Instructional Design: Recent Developments'. *Educational Psychologist* 38, no. 1 (2003): 1–4.

Packel, Edward. *Animating Calculus*. New York: Springer-Verlag Telos, 1996.

Peirce, Charles Sanders. *Collected Papers of Charles Sanders Peirce, Volume 2*. Edited by Charles Hartshorne and Paul Weiss. Cambridge: Harvard University Press, 1932.

Peirce, Charles Sanders. *Collected Papers of Charles Sanders Peirce, Volume 3: Exact Logic*. Edited by Charles Hartshorne and Paul Weiss. Cambridge: Harvard University Press, 1933.

Peterson, L. R., and J. M. Peterson. 'Short-Term Retention of Individual Verbal Items'. *Journal of Experimental Psychology* 58, no. 3 (1959): 193–98.

Pfister, Hanspeter, Verena Kaynig, Charl P. Botha, Stefan Bruckner, Vincent J. Dercksen, Hans-Christian Hege, and Jos B. T. M. Roerdink. 'Visualization in Connectomics'. In *Scientific Visualization Uncertainty, Multifield, Biomedical, and Scalable Visualization*, edited by Charles D. Hansen, Min Chen Christopher, R. Johnson, Arie E. Kaufman and Hans Hagen. Berlin: Springer, 2014.

Power, Patrick. 'Character Animation and the Embodied Mindbrain'. *Animation: An Interdisciplinary Journal* 3, no. 1 (2008): 25–48.

Prendergast, Darcy. Email correspondence with author (19 September 2011).

Prince, Stephen. 'True Lies: Perceptual Realism, Digital Images, and Film Theory'. *Film Quarterly* 49, no. 3 (1996): 27–37.

Purse, Lisa. *Digital Imaging in Popular Cinema*. Edinburgh: Edinburgh University Press, 2013.

Purves, Barry. *Stop Motion (Basics Animation 04)*. Switzerland: AVA, 2010.

Renov, Michael, ed. *Theorizing Documentary*. New York: Routledge, 1993.

Renov, Michael, ed. *The Subject of Documentary*. Edited by Michael Renov. Vol. 16, Visible Evidence. Minneapolis: University of Minnesota Press, 2004a.

Renov, Michael. 'Animation: Documentary's Imaginary Signifier'. Unpublished paper delivered at University of Westminster, 9 December 2004b, Unpublished paper emailed to Torre by Renov on 3 May 2005.

Rescher, Nicholas. *Induction: An Essay on the Justification of Inductive Reasoning*. Oxford: Basil Blackwell Publisher, 1980.

Rescher, Nicholas. *Process Metaphysics*. New York: State University of New York Press, 1996.

Rescher, Nicholas. 'On Situating Process Philosophy'. *Process Studies* 28, no. 1/2 (1999): 37–42.

Rescher, Nicholas. *Process Philosophy*. Pittsburgh, PA: University of Pittsburgh Press, 2000.

Rescher, Nicholas. *Cognitive Pragmatism: The Theory of Knowledge in Pragmatic Perspective*. Pittsburgh, PA: University of Pittsburgh Press, 2001.

Rescher, Nicholas. *Imagining Irreality: A Study of Unrealized Possibility*. Chicago: Open Court Publishing, 2003.

Rescher, Nicholas. *Process Philosophical Deliberations*. Frankfurt: Ontos Verlag, 2006a.

Rescher, Nicholas. *Metaphysics: The Key Issues from a Realistic Perspective*. Amherst, NY: Prometheus Books, 2006b.

Ribeiro, Tiago, and Ana Paiva. 'The Illusion of Robotic Life: Principles and Practices of Animation for Robots'. *Paper Presented at the Human Robot Interaction*, Boston, MA, 2012.

Richardson, John T. E. *Mental Imagery and Human Memory*. New York: St. Martin's Press, 1980.

Richardson, John T. E. *Imagery*. Hove: Psychology Press Ltd., 1999.

Robbers, Monica L. P. 'Blinded by Science: The Social Construction of Reality in Forensic Television Shows and Its Effect on Criminal Jury Trials'. *Criminal Justice Policy Review* 19, no. 1 (2008): 84–102.

Robinson, Bruce H., Kim R. Reisenbichler, James C. Hunt, and Steven H. D. Haddock. 'Light Production by the Arm Tips of the Deep-Sea Cephalopod Vampyroteuthis Infernalis'. *Biological Bulletin*, no. 205 (2003): 102–9.

Roe, Annabelle Honess. *Animated Documentary*. New York: Palgrave Macmillan, 2013.

Rosen, Philip. *Change Mummified: Cinema, Historicity, Theory*. Minneapolis: University of Minnesota Press, 2001.

Ruddell, Caroline. 'From the "Cinematic" to the "Anime-Ic": Issues of Movement in Anime'. *Animation: An Interdisciplinary Journal* 3, no. 2 (2008): 113–28.

Rybczynski, Zbig. 'Looking to the Future – Imagining the Truth'. In *Cinema & Architecture: Melies, Mallet-Stevens, Multimedia*, edited by Francois Penz and Maureen Thomas. London: British Film Institute, 1997.

Saerbeck, M., and C. Bartneck. 'Perception of Affect Elicited by Robot Motion'. In *HRI 10 – Proceedings of the 5th ACM/IEEE International Conference on Human-Robot Interaction*, Piscataway, NJ: IEEE Press, 2010.

Salt, Brian. *Movements in Animation: Volume 1*. Oxford: Pergamon Press, 1976.

Schirato, Tony, and Jen Webb. *Reading the Visual*. Sydney: Allen and Unwin, 2004.

Schmitz, Jerry. *The Art and Making of Blue Sky Studios the Peanuts Movie by Schulz*. London: Titan Books, 2015.

Schnotz, Wolfgang, and Richard Lowe. 'A Unified View of Learning from Animated and Static Graphics'. In *Learning with Animation: Research Implications for Design*, edited by Richard Lowe and Wolfgang Schnotz. Cambridge: Cambridge University Press, 2008.

Scott, Bukatman. *The Poetics of Slumberland – Animated Spirits and the Animating Spirit*. Berkeley and Los Angeles: University of California Press, 2012.

Seiter, Ellen. *Sold Separately: Parents & Children in Consumer Culture*. New Brunswick: Rutgers University Press, 1993.

Shepard, Roger, and Lynn Cooper. *Mental Images and Their Transformations*. Cambridge, MA: MIT Press, 1982.

Shimamura, Arthur P. 'Psychocinematics: Issues and Directions'. In *Psychocinematics: Exploring Cognition at the Movies*, edited by Arthur P. Shimamura. Oxford: Oxford University Press, 2013.

Sicart, Miguel. *Beyond Choices: The Design of Ethical Gameplay*. Cambridge, MA: MIT Press, 2013.

Sigall, Martha. *Living Life Inside the Lines: Tales from the Golden Age of Animation*. Jackson: University Press of Mississippi, 2005.

Simons, Jan. 'Narrative, Games, and Theory'. *Game Studies: The International Journal of Computer Game Research* 7, no. 1 (2007): http://gamestudies .org/0701/articles/simons, accessed 5 September 2014.

Singer, Gregory. 'Dream Is Destiny: Waking Life'. *Animation World Magazine*. www.awn.com/animationworld/dream-destiny-waking-life, accessed 1 June 2015 (2001).

Snyder, Tom, and A. Lyman. 'USA Patent No. 6252604'. U.S., 2001.

Sobchack, Vivian. 'At the Still Point of the Turning World'. In *Meta-Morphing: Visual Transformation and the Culture of Quick-Change*, edited by Vivian Sobchack. Minneapolis: University of Minnesota Press, 2000.

Solomon, Charles. 'Animation: Notes on a Definition'. In *The Art of the Animated Image*, edited by Charles Solomon. Los Angeles: The American Film Institute, 1987.

Solomon, Charles. *The History of Animation: Enchanted Drawings (Revised Edition)*. New York: Wings Books, 1994.

Specter, Michael. *The Making of Fantastic Mr. Fox*. New York: Rizzoli International Publications, 2009.

Stam, Robert, Robert Burgoyne, and Sandy Flitterman-Lewis. *New Vocabularies in Film Semiotics: Structuralism, Post-Structuralism, and Beyond*. London: Routledge, 1992.

Steinberg, Marc. 'Immobile Sections and Trans-Series Movement: Astroboy and Emergence of Anime'. *Animation: An Interdisciplinary Journal* 1, no. 2 (2006): 190–206.

Stephan, Carl N., Ronn G. Taylor, and Jane A. Taylor. 'Methods of Facial Approximation and Skull-Face Superimposition, with Special Consideration of Method Development in Australia'. In *Forensic Approaches to Death, Disaster and Abuse*, edited by Marc Oxenham. Sydney: Australian Academic Press, 2008.

Sweller, J., J. J. G. van Merrienboer, and Fred Paas. 'Cognitive Architecture and Instructional Design'. *Educational Psychology Review* 10, no. 3 (1998): 251–96.

Taiwo, Olu. 'The Dance of the Return Beat: Performing the Animate Universe'. In *The Handbook of Contemporary Animism*, edited by Graham Harvey. Durham: Acumen, 2013.

Tam, Kim-Pong, Sau-Lai Lee, and Melody Manchi Chao. 'Saving Mr. Nature: Anthropomorphism Enhances Connectedness to and Protectiveness toward Nature'. *Journal of Experimental Social Psychology* 49, no. 3 (2013): 514–21.

Tarbell, Harlan. *Chalk Talk Stunts*. Chicago: TS Denison & Company, 1926.

Thomas, Frank, and Ollie Johnston. *Disney Animation: The Illusion of Life*. New York: Abbeville Press, 1981.

Thompson, Kristin. 'Implications of the Cel Animation Technique'. In *The Cinematic Apparatus*, edited by Teresa de Lauretis and Stephen Heath. London: The Macmillan Press, 1980.

Torre, Dan. 'Cognitive Animation Theory: A Process-Based Reading of Animation and Human Cognition'. *Animation: An Interdisciplinary Journal* 9, no. 1 (2014): 47–64.

Torre, Dan. 'Boiling Lines and Lightning Sketches: Process and the Animated Drawing'. *Animation: An Interdisciplinary Journal* 10, no. 2 (2015): 141–53.

Torre, Dan. 'The Metamorphosis of Place: Projection-Mapped Animation'. In *Animated Landscapes: History, Form and Function*, edited by Chris Pallant. New York: Bloomsbury Academic, 2015.

Torre, Dan. *Cactus* (Botanical). London: Reaktion Books, 2017.

van Breeman, A. 'Bringing Robots to Life: Applying Principles of Animation to Robotics'. *CHI'04 WS on Shaping Human-Robot Interaction*, 2003.

van Breemen, A.J.N. 'Animation Engine for Believable Interactive User-Interface Robots'. In *Proceedings of 2004 IEEE/RSJ International Conference on Intelligent Robots and Systems*, Sendal, Japan, 28 September–2 October 2004.

Vilanova, A., Bernhard Preim, Roy van Pelt, Rocco Gasteiger, Mathias Neugebauer, and Thomas Wischgoll. 'Visual Exploration of Simulated and Measured Blood Flow'. In *Scientific Visualization Uncertainty, Multifield, Biomedical, and Scalable Visualization*, edited by Charles D. Hansen, Min Chen Christopher, R. Johnson, Arie E. Kaufman and Hans Hagen. Berlin: Springer, 2014.

Volk, Tyler. *Metapatterns: Across Space, Time and Mind*. New York: Columbia University Press, 1995.

Walker, Saint John. 'A Quick Walk through Uncanny Valley'. In *Modes of Spectating*, edited by Alison Oddey and Christine White. Bristol: Intellect, 2009.

Ward, Paul. '"Rotoshop" in Context: Computer Rotoscoping and Animation Aesthetics'. *Animation Journal* 12 (2004): 32–52.

Ward, Paul. *Documentary: The Margins of Reality*. London: Wallflower, 2005.

Ward, Paul. 'Animated Interactions: Animation Aesthetics and the World of the "Interactive" Documentary'. In *Animated 'Worlds'*, edited by Suzanne Buchan. London: John Libbey, 2006.

Wells, Paul. *Understanding Animation*. London: Routledge, 1998.

Wells, Paul. *Animation and America*. Edinburgh: Edinburgh University Press, 2002b.

Wells, Paul. *Scriptwriting, Basics Animation*. Switzerland: AVA Publishing, 2007.

Wells, Paul. *The Animated Bestiary: Animals, Cartoons, and Culture*. London: Rutgers University Press, 2009.

Wells, Paul, and Johnny Hardstaff. *Re-Imagining Animation: Contemporary Moving Image Cultures*. Switzerland: AVA Academia, 2008.

Whitaker, Harold, and John Halas. *Timing for Animation*. New York: Focal Press, 1981.

White, Tony. *From Pencils to Pixels: Classical Techniques for Digital Animators*. Burlington, MA: Focal Press, 2006.

Whitehead, Alfred North. *Concept of Nature*. Cambridge: Cambridge University Press, 1920/1978.

Whitehead, Alfred North. *Process and Reality (Corrected Edition)*. New York: The Free Press, 1929/1978.

Whitehead, Alfred North. *Adventures of Ideas*. New York: The Free Press, 1933/1967.

Whitehead, Alfred North. *Modes of Thought*. 1966 Free Press Paperback edition. New York: MacMillan Publishing, 1938/1968.

Whitehead, Alfred North. *The Function of Reason*. Boston: Beacon Press, 1958.

Wiesing, Lambert. *Artificial Presence: Philosophical Studies in Image Theory*. Stanford, CA: Stanford University Press, 2010.

Willemen, Paul. 'Reflections on Digital Imagery: Of Mice and Men'. In *Screen Media: Cinema/Art/Narrative*, edited by Martin Rieser and Andrea Zapp. London: British Film Institute, 2002.

Williams, Richard. *The Animator's Survival Kit: A Manual of Methods, Principles and Formulas*. London: Faber and Faber, 2001.

Winder, Catherine, and Zahra Dowlatabadi. *Producing Animation*. Boston: Focal Press, 2001.

Winkielman, Piotr, Kent C. Berridge, and Julia L. Wilbarger. 'Unconscious Affective Reactions to Masked Happy versus Angry Faces Influence Consumption Behavior and Judgments of Value'. *Personality and Social Psychology Bulletin* 31, no. 1 (2005): 121–35.

Winston, Brian. *Lies, Damn Lies and Documentaries*. London: BFI Publishing, 2000.

Wolf, Mark J. P. 'Subjunctive Documentary: Computer Imaging and Simulation'. In *Collecting Visible Evidence*, edited by Jane M. Gaines and Michael Renov. Minneapolis: University of Minnesota Press, 1999.

Wollen, Peter. *Signs and Meaning in the Cinema*. Bloomington: Indiana University Press, 1972.

'The World's First 3D Model of an Entire Nation'. *Position: The Australasian Magazine of Surveying, Mapping & Geo-Information*, no. 81 (2016).

Zeki, Semir. *Inner Vision: An Exploration of Art and the Brain*. Oxford: Oxford University Press, 1999.

ANIMATION/ FILMOGRAPHY/ OTHER MEDIA

25 Ways to Quit Smoking (Bill Plympton 1989) [Film].
555 Kubrik. Germany, 2009 [Live Projection].
600th Anniversary of the Prague Clock Tower. Czech Republic, 2010 [Live Projection].
800th Anniversary of Santiago de Compostela Cathedral. Spain, 2012 [Live Projection].
A Scanner Darkly (Richard Linklater 2006) [Film].
A Very Nice Honeymoon (Simmonds Brothers 2006) [Film].
AANAATT (Max Hattler 2008) [Film].
Abductees (Paul Vester 1995) [Film].
Accident (Jules Engel 1973) [Film].
The Adventures of Ichabod and Mr. Toad (Jack Kinney, Clyde Geronimi, James Algar 1949) [Film].
The Adventures of Tintin (Steven Spielberg 2011) [Film].
Against the Grain (Jonathan Chong 2012) [Film].
Allegretto (Oskar Fischinger 1936) [Film].
The Amazing Spider-Man (Marc Webb 2012) [Film].
An American Family (Craig Gilbert 1973) [Film].
Astro Boy (Tezuka Osamu 1963–1966) [Animated Series].
The Automatic Moving Company (Romeo Bossetti 1910) [Film].
Automatic Writing (William Kentridge 2003) [Film].
Avatar (James Cameron 2009) [Film].
Babe (Chris Noonan 1995) [Film].
Bambi (David Hand 1942) [Film].
Beauty and the Beast (Gary Trousdale and Kirk Wise 1991) [Film].
Bears on Stairs (DBLG 2014) [Film].
Big Bang Big Boom (Blu 2010) [Film].
Big Hero 6 (Don Hall and Chris Williams 2014) [Film].
Bottle (Kirsten Lepore 2011) [Film].
Cars (John Lasseter 2006) [Film].
Chase Me (Gilles-Alexandre Deschaud 2015) [Film].
Chicago 10 (Brett Morgen 2007) [Film].
Chicken Run (Nick Park, Peter Lord 2000) [Film].

The Chronicles of Narnia: The Lion, the Witch and the Wardrobe (Andrew Adamson 2006) [Film].
Citizen Kane (Wells 1941) [Film].
Clutch Cargo (Haas 1959–1960) [Film].
Colour Box (Len Lye 1935) [Film].
Colour Flight (Len Lye 1938) [Film].
The Corpse Bride (Tim Burton and Mike Johnson 2005) [Film].
Das Rad (Chris Stenner, Arvid Uibel and Heidi Wittinger 2001) [Film].
Dawn of the Planet of the Apes (Matt Reeves 2014) [Film].
Deadpool (Tim Miller 2016) [Film].
Dots (Norman McLaren 1940) [Film].
The Dowager's Idyll (Joan Gratz 2001) [Film].
Dr Katz: Professional Therapist (1995–2000) [Series].
Dug's Special Mission Dog (Ronnie del Carmen 2009) [Film].
Dumbland (David Lynch 2000) [Series].
Earth Shiver (John 'Hobart' Hughes 2006) [Film].
Eatliz (Yuval Nathan and Merav Nathan 2010) [Film].
Epic (Chris Wedge 2013) [Film].
Fantastic Mr Fox (Wes Anderson 2009) [Film].
Feet of Song (Erica Russell 1988) [Film].
Felix in Exile (William Kentridge 1994) [Film].
Final Fantasy: The Spirits Within (Hironobu Sakaguchi 2001) [Film].
Finding Nemo (Andrew Stanton and Lee Unkrich 2003) [Film].
The First Thing I Remember (Tamara Meem 2005) [Film].
Flowers and Trees (Burt Gillett 1932) [Film].
Frozen (Chris Buck and Jennifer Lee 2013) [Film].
Funny Little Bunnies (Wilfred Jackson 1934) [Film].
Furniture Poetry (Paul Bush 1999) [Film].
Gerald McBoing Boing (1951) [Film].
Gertie the Dinosaur (Winsor McCay 1914) [Film].
Going Equipped (Aardman 1989) [Film].
The Good Dinosaur (Peter Sohn 2015) [Film].
Grand Theft Auto V (RockStar Games 2013) [Video Game].
Grasshopper (Bob Sabiston 2003) [Film].
Grave of the Fireflies (Takahata 1988) [Film].
Guardians of the Galaxy (James Gunn 2014) [Film].
Gumbasia (Art Clokey 1955) [Film].
Hard Boiled (Dan Torre 2015) [Film].
Harry Potter and the Chamber of Secrets (Chris Columbus 2002) [Film].
Harry Potter and the Prisoner of Azkaban (Alfonso Cuaron 2004) [Film].
Herr Meets Hare (Freleng 1945) [Film].
His Mother's Voice (Dennis Tupicoff 1996) [Film].
Hoppity Goes to Town (Fleischer 1941) [Film].
How to Kiss (Bill Plympton 1989) [Film].
How to Train Your Dragon (Dean DeBlois, Chris Sanders 2010) [Film].
The Hulk (Ang Lee 2003) [Film].
Hunger (Peter Foldes 1974) [Film].
I Married a Strange Person (Bill Plympton 1998) [Film].

I Met the Walrus (Josh Raskin 2007) [Film].
Ident (Aardman 1989) [Film].
Insert Coin (Rymdreglage 2010) [Film].
Inside Out (Peter Docter 2015) [Film].
It's Like That (Southern Ladies' Animation Group 2003) [Film].
Jasper and the Haunted House (George Pal 1942) [Film].
Jean Cocteau (Jacques Barsac 1996) [Film].
The Jungle Book (Wolfgang Reitherman 1967) [Film].
Jurassic Park (Steven Spielberg 1993) [Film].
The Kid Stays in the Picture (Brett Morgen 2002) [Film].
King of the Hill (1997–2010) [Animated Television Series].
Land (Eric Leiser 2012) [Film].
The Life and Mind of Mark DeFriest (Gabriel London 2014) [Film].
Little Big Planet 3 (Media Molecule 2014) [Video Game].
The Lord of the Rings (Peter Jackson 2001–2003) [Film].
Love & Theft (Andreas Hykade 2010) [Film].
Lucky (Darcy Prendergast's 2009) [Film].
Madame Tutli-Putli (Chris Lavis, Maciek Szczerbowski 2007) [Film].
The Many Adventures of Winnie the Pooh (Wolfgang Reitherman, John Lounsbery 1977) [Film].
Mapping Projection of Christ the Redeemer. Brazil, 2010 [Live Projection].
The Meadow (Jules Engel 1994) [Film].
Mobius (Benjamin Ducroz 2011) [Film].
Model Starship (Max Hattler 2012) [Film].
Modern Love series (The New York Times 2013–) [Film].
Mr. Magoo (UPA 1949–1959) [Film].
Mr. Nobody Holme – He Buys a Jitney (1916) [Film].
My Mothers Coat (Marie-Margaux Tsakiri-Scanatovits 2010) [Film].
My Pet Dinosaurs (Mark Everest 2007) [Film].
Neighbours (Norman McLaren 1952) [Film].
Nothing Like the First Time (Jonas Odell 2005) [Film].
The Old Mill (Wilfred Jackson 1937) [Film].
One Hundred and One Dalmations (Wolfgang Reitherman, Hamilton Luske, Clyde Geronomi 1961) [Film].
One of Those Days (Bill Plympton 1988) [Film].
ParaNorman (Chris Butler, Sam Fell 2012) [Film].
The Peanuts Movie (Steve Martino 2015) [Film].
Pen Giant (Florian Giefer, Peter Göltenboth 2010) [Film].
Perspective Lyrique: An Interactive Architectural Mapping. France, 2010 [Live Projection].
Phoenix Baptist Hospital [Animated advertisement].
Pinocchio (Luske & Sharpsteen 1940) [Film].
The Plague Dogs (Martin Rosen 1982) [Film].
The Polar Express (Robert Zemeckis 2004) [Film].
Plants vs. Zombies: Garden Warfare (PopCap Games 2014) [Video Game].
Poor Us: An Animated History of Poverty (Ben Lewis 2012) [Film].
Presto (Doug Sweetland 2008) [Film].
Princess Mononoke (Hayao Miyazaki 2001) [Film].

Prometheus's Garden (Bruce Bickford 1988) [Film].
Rabbit Rabbit (Greaves 1995) [Film].
Ratatouille (Brad Bird and Jan Pinkava 2007) [Film].
Red Hot Riding Hood (Tex Avery 1943) [Film].
The Rescuers (Wolfgang Reitherman, John Lounsbury 1977) [Film].
The Revenge of the Cameraman (Ladislas Starewich 1911) [Film].
Revolver (Jonas Odell 1993) [Film].
Rhythmus 21 (Hans Richter 1921) [Film].
The Ricky Gervais Show (Craig Kellman, Dan Fraga 2010–2012) [Animated Series].
Rippled (Darcy Prendergast 2011) [Film].
Robin Hood (Wolfgang Reitherman 1973) [Film].
Ryan (Chris Landreth 2004) [Film].
Safe House (Lee Whitmore 2006) [Film].
Shift (Max Hattler 2012) [Film].
Sin City (Robert Rodriguez, Frank Miller 2005) [Film].
The Sinking of the Lusitania (Winsor McCay 1918) [Film].
Sisyphus (Marcell Jankovics 1974) [Film].
The Skeleton Dance (Walt Disney 1929) [Film].
Snack and Drink (Bob Sabiston 1999) [Film].
Snow White and the Seven Dwarfs (David Hand 1937) [Film].
Sony Bravia Television advertisement (Frank Budgen 2009) [Film].
Speed Racer (Andy Wachowski, Lana Wachowski 2008) [Film].
Spider-Man (Sam Raimi 2002) [Film].
Star Wars: The Empire Strikes Back (George Lucas 1980) [Film].
The Stitches Speak (Nina Sabnani 2010) [Film].
The Street (Caroline Leaf 1976) [Film].
Street of Crocodiles (Quay Brothers 1986) [Film].
Swinging the Lambeth Walk (Len Lye 1939) [Film].
The Sword in the Stone (Wolfgang Reitherman 1963) [Film].
Tango (Zbigniew Rybczynski 1980) [Film].
The Tell-Tale Heart (Ted Parmelee 1953) [Film].
Terminator 2 (Rymdreglage 2011) [Film].
The Three Caballeros (Norman Ferguson 1944) [Film].
Toy Story (John Lasseter 1995) [Film].
Triangle (Erica Russell 1994) [Film].
Tussilago (Jonas Odell 2010) [Film].
Twister (Jan De Bont 1996) [Film].
Two Sisters (Caroline Leaf 1990) [Film].
Two Space (Larry Cuba 1977) [Film].
Ty the Tasmanian Tiger (John Aitchison) [3D zoetrope].
UP (Pete Docter and Bob Peterson 2009) [Film].
Utopia Parkway (Joanna Priestley 1997) [Film].
Vital Voices, Hawa Abdi (Aaron Kisner 2013) [Film].
Waking Life (Richard Linklater 2001) [Film].
Walking with Dinosaurs (Tim Haines and Jasper James 1999) [Film].
Wallace and Gromit: A Grand Day Out (1989) [Film].
Waltz with Bashir (Ari Folman 2008) [Film].

When the Day Breaks (Wendy Tilby and Amanda Forbis 1999) [Film].
Who Framed Roger Rabbit (Robert Zemeckis, Richard Williams 1988) [Film].
The Wind Calls Your Name (John 'Hobart' Hughes 2004) [Film].
The Wrong Trainers (Kez Margrie 2007) [Film].
X-Men: Days of Future Past (Bryan Singer 2014) [Film].
Your Face (Bill Plympton 1987) [Film].
Zombie Pace (Rymdreglage 2014) [Film].

INDEX

Note: Locators in bold indicate figures and locators followed by n denotes note number.